Shaping History

Shaping History

The Role of Newspapers in Hawai'i

Helen Geracimos Chapin

University of Hawai'i Press
Honolulu

01 00 99 98 97 96   5 4 3 2 1

Library of Congress Cataloging-in-Publication Data
Chapin, Helen Geracimos.
    Shaping history : the role of newspapers in Hawai'i /
Helen Geracimos Chapin.
        p.   cm.
    Includes bibliographical references and index.
    ISBN 0–8248–1718–4
        1. Journalism—Hawaii—History.   2. Hawaii—History.
I. Title.
PN4897.H33C48   1996
079' .969—dc20   95–43101
                                                             CIP

University of Hawai'i Press books
are printed on acid-free paper and meet
the guidelines for permanence and durability
of the Council on Library Resources

Design by Cameron Poulter

For Hank,
Georganne, Julia, Chip,
and Nick

Contents

Contents

Acknowledgments

I want to express my great appreciation for the invaluable help I've received from so many in pursuing the story of how the newspapers of Hawai'i have affected Hawaiian history.

Among those lending cheerful and competent assistance have been Hawai'i's librarians, from both the public and private sectors: Joan Hori, Nancy Morris, Karen Peacock, and Chieko Tachihata of the Hawaiian and Pacific Collections, Hamilton Library, University of Hawai'i at Mānoa; Frances Jackson, formerly in charge of the War Records Depository, University of Hawai'i at Mānoa; Stephen Simpson, head, and Vicki Dworkin and the reference staff of the Meader Library, Hawaii Pacific University; Lela Goodell, formerly with Hawaiian Mission Children's Society; and Barbara Dunn and Maryellen Hennessy of the Hawaiian Historical Society. Barbara Dunn and rare book expert David Forbes, both also very knowledgeable about Hawaiian history, helped to track down little known and sometimes elusive periodicals. Others who have provided substantial assistance include: Mary Ann Akau, Jolyn Tamura, and Richard Thompson of the Hawai'i State Archives; Ruth Itamura, formerly with the State Archives; Cynthia Timberlake, former librarian at the Bernice Pauahi Bishop Museum; and present and former librarians at the Hawaiian Sugar Planters' Association: Jean Debagh, Harriet K. Iwai, Ann Marsteller, Deborah Sato, and Susan Campbell. It was a special pleasure to be allowed to read the old papers in their original form, on newsprint, a pleasure likely to be denied to future historians because so many papers, once they are microfilmed, are now discarded.

I also want to thank leaders of two organizations—the Hawaiian Historical Society and Hawaii Pacific University—who have been most supportive. Members of the editorial board of *The Hawaiian Journal of History*, sponsored by the society, were especially helpful in reviewing sections of the manuscript and offering valuable suggestions: Lela Goodell, Alison Kay, Nancy Morris, Eleanor Nordyke, Philip "Fritz" Rehbock, and Bob Schmitt. From Hawaii Pacific

University, Chatt G. Wright and L. Jim Hochberg Sr. have both generously given institutional and personal support and encouragement.

Others who were generous with time and information include the almost 100 interviewees, many of whom were and are professional journalists with daily deadlines to meet. Additionally helpful were Paul Kahn, very knowledgeable about the Hawaiian newspapers, and Hawaiian scholar Edith McKinzie. An unexpected stroke of good fortune was to be part of an informal history writers group, whose members responded to the manuscript in progress: Teresa Bill, Laurel Cox-Forsythe, Connie Fournier, Arlen Gill, Linda Peterson, and especially Jane Silverman.

Several people deserve special acknowledgment. Agnes Conrad, retired Hawai'i State Archivist, extended professional assistance as well as friendship and a critical reading of the entire manuscript. Photographer Bill Langer, who had to work with old, often damaged material, was important in drawing the project together visually. Iris Wiley, executive editor of the University of Hawai'i Press, provided steady encouragement and invaluable insights. I want to thank, too, the person most supportive of the project from its first days through to completion—my husband and chief editor, Hank Chapin.

I am indebted as well to several sources. These include Mary Kawena Pukui and Samuel H. Elbert, *Hawaiian Dictionary* (1986), and Mary Kawena Pukui, Samuel H. Elbert, and Esther T. Mookini, *Place Names of Hawaii* (1974), for spelling and usage in the Hawaiian language, such as the use of the *'okina* (') and the *kahakō* or macron to indicate pronunciation and meaning. (It should be noted that direct quotations from the newspapers, in English, Hawaiian, and other languages, follow their original spelling, except that the titles of major newspapers have been abbreviated.) I am grateful, too, for two particularly reliable sources for circulation figures and other data relating to the papers: the *State of Hawaii Data Book,* compiled yearly since 1967 by the indefatigable Bob Schmitt, and the national annual, the *Ayer Directory of Publications.* Having acknowledged such good friends, colleagues, and sources, I must add that I alone am responsible for any errors in fact or interpretation.

Finally, I must acknowledge and thank all the dedicated and hard working newspapermen and newspaperwomen, from the past to the present, from those in the back shops to the front offices, who have been involved in the saga of the newspapers in Hawai'i. Their characters and personalities were and are incredibly varied—from the wicked to the virtuous, from the rash and impulsive to the painstakingly careful, from the foolish and cowardly to the wise and the brave. All have immeasurably enriched the history that is recounted here.

Introduction

There are many histories of Hawai'i. But there are no assessments of the role that newspapers have played in that turbulent and contested history. Yet newspapers have not just recorded events since their inception in 1834, they have been active agents in shaping Hawaiian history. By newspapers, I mean publications with titles and mastheads, without covers, appearing serially and regularly on newsprint. The size and content vary, but newspapers are recognizable by their format and topical subject matter.

To understand the role of newspapers, one should consider them within their own historical context. They are a relatively recent development in our lives. In prehistoric times, we gained information from each other through signs and the spoken word. About 3,500 years ago, the written word became a source of knowledge. But only since the fourteenth century in Europe and the invention of movable print by the machinery of a "press," have literate societies come to rely upon print as a chief means of communication. And only since the sixteen hundreds, as a direct outgrowth of the industrial revolution, has the newspaper become a major source of information (Smith 1979).

A remarkably mobile medium, newspapers spread from England to America in the seventeenth century. Adapted by printers in the colonies, and continuing in the new United States, that model entered Hawai'i with the American Protestant missionaries from New England, who installed a printing press in a thatch-roofed house at Honolulu, O'ahu, in 1822. In 1834, they produced the first newspaper at Lahaina, Maui. The American-style newspaper immediately took hold in the Kingdom, to coincide with and abet the rise of American domination of the Hawaiian Islands.

An assessment of them is all the more necessary because newspapers held an information monopoly from their inception to the last quarter of this century. Their sheer number is astonishing. Even though many holdings cannot be found, making an exact count impossible, there is evidence of more than 1,000 separately titled

papers appearing in time frames from daily to monthly in at least
nine different languages. Newspapers remained the primary communications medium until 1976 and the introduction of live television news by satellite. After 1976, the newspapers began to diminish
in influence. Today they are a secondary source of information; but
in their heyday, the newspapers of Hawai'i formed one of the most
diversified, vigorous, and influential presses in the world. They
acted upon a unique history that unfolded in the world's most isolated archipelago, a history that spanned an independent country, a
republic, a territory, and a state.

The role of these American-style papers is complicated by what
has been defined as an inherent doubleness (Hynds 1980). This dual
role emerged in the colonies with James and Benjamin Franklin's
New England Courant (1721–1727) when the colonial government
attempted through licensing to control what was printed. The
Franklins refused to accept such limitations for two reasons: it was
their duty to inform the public, and they needed to make a living.
The first cause, of providing information, was so important that
the framers of the U.S. Constitution guaranteed freedom of speech
and the press in the First Amendment. This guarantee is grounded
in the belief that a democratic society depends upon the participation of informed citizens. The second cause, less lofty in principle
but important nonetheless, is that newspapers are a business. This
is yoked to the Protestant ethic in which profit is viewed as a
reward for the deserving, not just in heaven, but on earth. In
Hawai'i, both causes have undergirded and shaped the function of
newspapers.

Categories of Newspapers

The significance of newspapers to Hawaiian history is partly attributable to their operating within certain boundaries. Although they
have been enormously diverse, they have all fitted into just four categories: establishment, opposition, official, and independent. These
groupings are flexible, for newspapers sometimes shift or overlap
categories as their roles change in the context of their times (Chapin
1984).

Establishment papers make up the first and by far the most
numerous type. Also called the mainstream or commercial press,
establishment papers exemplify the controlling interests of a town
or city, region or country, and need not represent the majority of
people. Rather, establishment papers, such as large city dailies and

community suburban papers, are part of a power structure that formulates the policies and practices to which everyone is expected to adhere.

The American Protestant Mission introduced an establishment press to Hawai'i (Day and Loomis 1973). Mission editors in the Hawaiian and English languages promoted American culture and values. Almost immediately after their arrival, members of the tiny group from New England became advisors to the Hawaiian monarchy. As the English language gained dominance through the century, so, too, did establishment papers in English gain even greater power. By the end of the century, an alliance of missionary descendants and haole (Caucasian) American business interests, operating as an oligarchy, backed by the American military, and aided and abetted by the oligarchy's newspapers, overthrew the queen and the Hawaiian government representing the majority population.

The oligarchy's press, Republican in politics and capitalist and expansionist in conviction, dominated into the 1950s. In 1954, when a Democratic coalition overthrew the Republican oligarchy, power spread into a multiethnic establishment. An ardent Americanism remains, however, now linked to the promotion of Hawai'i as a Pacific leader. Coinciding with and abetting this are formerly home-owned papers that are now controlled by huge absentee corporations with global economic agendas. If it is a truism that the powerful write history, so, too, do they publish papers. Over two centuries, the establishment press has exercised the dominant influence upon the history of Hawai'i.

Opposition is the second category of newspapers. A paradoxical quality of the American press is that it fosters dissent, as it did during the American Revolution with Tom Paine's *Crisis* papers in 1776. An opposition or alternative press has been a major force in Hawai'i over two centuries, beginning in the 1830s when Americans outside of the mission set up their own business-oriented journals. After midcentury, Native Hawaiians and their sympathizers, speaking for the indigenous culture, created a Hawaiian nationalist press that challenged and resisted American political and economic domination. Taking a leaf from the pages of American Revolutionary journalists, this press articulated the arguments for autonomy and sovereignty. Ahead of their time by a hundred years, the opposition was defeated at the end of the nineteenth century, illustrating how most opposition papers eventually are absorbed or driven out by a better financed and united establishment press. But their arguments resurfaced in the late 1960s, to force discussion of sovereignty into the mainstream press and successfully modify the latter's opinion.

Other opposition newspapers include ethnic language and labor periodicals. Ethnic papers—Chinese, Portuguese, and Japanese before 1900 and Filipino, Korean, African American, Jewish, Vietnamese, Hispanic, and Samoan after 1900—in themselves present a wonderful paradox. An American establishment usually considers these to be in opposition simply because they appear in languages other than English or represent ethnic cultures. Their dual function, however, is peculiarly American: fostering assimilation into the new society while helping to preserve ethnic identity (Heuvel 1991). Labor papers have also played an important and paradoxical role by fighting for American ideals of social and economic justice for an underclass to bring them into the mainstream. Since the 1960s, an alternative press has produced underground and counterculture papers that have challenged and changed conventional American values. Alternative papers are integral to Hawaiian history.

Official papers make up the third category. These are sponsored by governments, whether the system is a monarchy, republic, territory, state, city, or federal. In the nineteenth century, Hawaiian kings sponsored newspapers to maintain their country's autonomy. In the twentieth century, government-sponsored papers issued from city hall and military bases continue to advance official views.

Independent papers, not allied to any special interest, compose the fourth and smallest category. Almost all newspapers trumpet their own independence, but in actuality editors and publishers seldom take positions contrary to those of their paymasters. Truly "independent" means no organizational affiliation that, in turn, means few financial backers and advertisers. Independent papers live short lives, except infrequently, like *Ka Leo o Hawaii* (1922–), the University of Hawai'i student paper that is supported by student fees and protected by an independently appointed Board of Publications which hires the staff and then leaves them alone.

There are interesting hybrids. Prison papers, an American phenomenon dating from the early 1800s and beginning in Hawai'i in the 1930s, have been produced within the establishment by those opposed to it. During World War II, an omnipresent military government enforced an all-encompassing censorship over all four categories of the islands' papers; so in effect there was a single, powerful official press.

To summarize, over the years a majority of the newspapers in Hawai'i, regardless of category, have been competitive business enterprises. They thus have filled the time-honored role of American newspapers: to publish the news, to interpret it and thereby influence public opinion, and to succeed financially (Salmon 1923).

Criticism of the Press

The dual nature of papers—that they are a public service, yet a business—has led to demands upon the press and expectations of it that have impacted the kind of influence newspapers wield. Those who produce newspapers usually consider press freedom to be absolutely essential. In the nineteenth century, both religious and secular journalists imported the Jeffersonian ideal of a free press and pressured the Hawaiian monarchy to similarly protect newspapers. The Kingdom's Constitution of 1852 guaranteed freedom of speech. An establishment press, protective of itself, however, sometimes betrays the cause of press freedom. In the 1890s, Native Hawaiians, who had fervently adopted the Jeffersonian belief, learned a bitter lesson—the oligarchy's press claimed freedom for itself but strenuously denied it to others. Besides distorting coverage or failing to report important events, this power elite brought the economic force of libel suits down upon the Hawaiian nationalist papers to silence them. Libel suits are still used to stifle dissent. As A. J. Liebling, a journalist and pungent critic of the press has said, freedom of the press is guaranteed only to those who own one (Liebling 1961).

Another group has demands and expectations—the public that buys or is affected by the papers. Although there was public distrust of the press in the last century—a distrust of journalism that violated privacy, destroyed reputations, and emphasized sex and violence in its drive for profit (does all this sound familiar?)—in recent years, nationally and locally, media bashing has increased (Fishman 1980; Shaw 1984; Isaacs 1986). Public unhappiness led in 1969 to the creation of the Honolulu Community Media Council to mediate disagreements between the public and the press. Media bashing may be self-serving or genuine. Those who engage in self-serving media bashing try to deflect close scrutiny of their own actions; when they say they want a "fair" press, they usually mean a positive one toward themselves. But criticism may be genuinely levied by a public that feels that the press makes too many mistakes and has too few regrets over these. The public resents, too, what it perceives as its manipulation through "managed news" (Cater 1959; Tuchman

1978; Compaine 1982; Bennett 1983; Willis 1991). Today, few love the newspapers.

A Newspaper Technology

Another factor that must be considered in any assessment of the role of the press in acting upon history is technology (Mott 1950; Dunnet 1988). One view is that technology is not revolutionary or cataclysmic but a gradual progress, a response to social relations (Winston 1986). Hawai'i, however, defies that interpretation.

A newer technology spectacularly disrupts and abrades an older one and drives it into niches and even oblivion. Before the outside world's invasion of the Islands in the 1770s, Hawai'i was an oral, memory-based culture with a nature-based religion and a barter economy dependent upon food yields from the ocean and land. Contact with the West ushered in printing and literacy, private property, competition, Christianity, money, and a market economy. Communications expert Harold Innis has said that print itself is the great colonizer and empire builder. Further, the "bias of communication" is that a technology changes our habits and modifies the structure and functions of the society we live in (Innis 1951, 1972).

Print combined with newspapers washed over the isolated Hawaiian Islands, forever modifying the ancient rhythms of life. In the 1830s, 1840s, and 1850s, the adventurous American roving printer brought printing presses with him to try his luck at producing four-, six-, and eight-page papers. News and advertising gathering was a personal, leisurely effort for weeklies and monthlies. Woodcut engravings reproduced by lithography accompanied columns of print. The editor or printer, often the same person, set type by hand and manually operated the wood and iron contraption that in an hour cranked out 100 pages, which were then distributed by foot or horseback or by interisland ships to locations where buyers picked them up.

By midcentury, first a steam driven cylinder press, then the web-perfecting press, which printed both sides of sheets of paper from a continuous unwinding reel, increased the numbers of pages and sped up production (Mott 1950). A half dozen or more people were needed to turn out a newspaper. Within three decades, workers in this labor-intensive industry organized the International Typographers Union in 1884, the first trade labor union in Hawai'i and a harbinger of future labor-management conflict. In the 1890s, typewriters, telephones, and electric cylinder presses sped up the response to the breaking news and deadlines. The Linotype set hot lead type mechanically, and editions of 20,000 copies of ten- to sixteen-page papers could be printed in two hours. Newspaper production was now an industry employing a large work force divided into departments: business, including advertising and circulation; editorial; and production. A publisher oversaw the entire operation. The newspaper became a vehicle of the streets, with newsboys hawking papers in cities and towns.

In 1898, the news of annexation to the United States filled the front pages—and took seven days by steamship to arrive. Illustrating Marshall McLuhan's point in *The Gutenberg Galaxy* (1962) and *Understanding Media* (1964) that technology is as revolutionary as political events, it was the Pacific cable five years later, in 1903, that physically linked Hawai'i to the mainland United States and annihilated distance. Electronic circuitry instantly cut through ocean barriers, and international wire services closed the gap between Hawai'i and the rest of the world. The numbers of newspapers substantially increased on the major islands.

Another transported American invention, mass advertising, was made possible by a newspaper technology. By the 1900s, advertisements filled 60 percent of a newspaper's space and provided the bulk of its revenue. From 1913 on, the Audit Bureau of Circulation compiled accurate figures so that businesses could contract for advertising space based on actual, not on fictitious or merely hopeful, estimates. Since World War II, immense amounts of advertising have created the 100-page-plus editions. Papers appear today that are void of editorial content and are given away (Brandsberg 1969). Is the *Shopper* or the *Penny Saver* the truly "free" newspaper?

A more recent contrivance is linked to advertising and marketing and has a direct influence on the public. A joint operating agreement reached in 1962 by Honolulu's two major dailies has allowed them to centralize business and production services through the Hawaii Newspaper Agency. "Marketing strategies" yield a product whose content is 70 percent advertising to 30 percent editorial; that is, news, features, cartoons, letters, and everything else besides ads. The product is marketed and zoned for delivery by van or air (Thorn and Pfiel 1987). So central is advertising that a noted historian of journalism, Ernest C. Hynds, states that a primary goal of newspapers today is to foster development of the nation's economy through advertising (Hynds 1975, 1980; Udell 1978).

Another revolutionary invention is the camera. Linked to newspapers, photojournalism is the branch of photography that uses the camera to record and report events as they happen (Fulton 1988). Photojournalism was introduced in the Islands by the *Advertiser* in 1900 and eliminated the laborious lithograph method that depended on an artist's rendition. Social analyst Susan Sontag assesses photography's influence on us as so enormous that it has replaced our looking at things directly and has become the way we "see" (Sontag 1973). Photography has had another impact. Since the 1960s, increased use of photo-offset, a relatively inexpensive process that creates pages by indirect image transfer, has enabled the smallest to the largest enterprise to produce a newspaper more cheaply and quickly.

The time it takes for an older technology to be overtaken by a newer one has rapidly narrowed. In the 1970s, the computer and "cold type" virtually killed the old hot lead technology: "Look Closely—You Won't See it Again" (*Adv.*, July 30, 1973). Reporters produce copy at video display terminals (VDTs), and editors send this to the presses that turn out 100,000 copies of 40-, 50-, or 100-page editions in two to three hours. Wire press and syndicated material enter directly into the computer. At the center of the plant's operation is the central processing unit (CPU).

May 9, 1976, is a crucial date. That is when the news was first beamed to Hawai'i by satellites 22,300 miles above the equator. Communication within the envelope of global space is pushed to outer space. A global information network encompasses Hawai'i. The papers receive 1,000 words a minute of stock market lists or sports box scores. A full page including headlines and pictures transmitted by satellite can be set in six minutes (Emery 1975).

The Future?

Will there be a newspaper in the future? If there is, what will it be like? Those who produce papers assiduously target the young in hopes that Jessica and Johnny, Lani and Kimo will grow up buying the papers. Many papers have moved toward easier reading: shorter headlines and sentences, larger type, more white space and color. Their emphasis is on entertaining the reader. But the young prefer the experience of television.

Instant information has led to a decline in household penetration by the papers. Today, 97 percent of the Islands' households have television, yet newspaper circulation remains at 1970s and 1980s levels, reaching roughly 20 percent of the Islands' households. The precarious existence of newspapers is widely acknowledged.

The afternoon paper in particular is an endangered species, not only unable to directly compete with the evening broadcast news, but no longer able in many traffic-choked cities to be home delivered (Benjaminson 1984). The family- or individually-owned newspaper is almost an artifact of the past. At the end of World War II, 80 percent of daily newspapers were independently owned. By the 1990s, 80 percent were owned by corporate chains. Presently, national and international media groups control more than 70 percent of daily circulation in the United States, and daily papers directly compete with one another in fewer than 5 percent of U.S. cities.

There is another competitor for the public's interest and money besides radio and television, the "international electronic superhighway." Gannett, a major player in Hawai'i, sees itself as a total information company rather than just a newspaper corporation. It is actively fighting the telephone industry's involvement in the electronic information business. Other newspaper companies are pouring development dollars into multimedia presentation formats and the "electronic newspaper." Multinational companies may eventually control the communications systems of the entire world (Shawcross 1992). Centralized "news management" and control of information by huge corporate media companies with direct lines into government may make the old questions of "press freedom," not to mention democracy itself, seem quaint and antiquated (Bagdikian 1990).

Newspapers today are produced by a fraction of their formerly large work forces. Gone are the days of the grime of printer's ink, the smoke of charred mats and hot metal, and the clacking and clamor of the print shop. The old Linotype is a museum piece—literally so in the Honolulu News Building on Kapi'olani Boulevard. The new technology is quiet and clean, like the laser system in place at the *Maui News*, the most technologically advanced of the Islands' newspapers.

Soon to be gone, according to photographer Terry Luke, are the darkroom, film, and prints (Luke 1993). The photojournalist once carried the Speed Graphic and his equipment on his shoulders, then adopted a more handy, lighter 35-millimeter camera. Electronic cameras now send images directly from the scene of the event to the newsroom and the production department and onto the press. Digital imaging systems make manipulations so easy that one cannot tell if the "photo" is a composite, heightening the public's suspicion of the newspaper product.

The electronic age is restructuring the patterns of our personal

lives and social interdependence (McLuhan 1962, 1964; Smith
1980b). History professor and journalist Dan Boylan points out that
leisurely reading of the morning paper at breakfast is almost an
action of the past (Boylan 1992). Conversations no longer begin with,
"Did you see in the paper?" Jeanne Fujikawa, who works at city hall,
describes how she and her husband at the end of their work day,
between picking up the children from school, juggling their after-
school activities, and shopping for dinner, barely have time to catch
the evening television news (Fujikawa 1992). In fact, there are journalists who themselves admit to no longer reading the entire paper
but only their own stories.

There is another more positive vision, however, that views
Hawai'i as a center of information and information processing—a
sort of electronic Pan-Pacific dream. Electronic circuitry gives us the
"breaking news" or what is happening. Newspapers, still the source
of hometown news and advertisements, document in detail what
has happened. The customer may call up the paper for global or local
information in print and on the computer screen.

Jim Dooley, Hawai'i's highly respected and best known investigative reporter since the mid-1970s, uses "computer assisted reporting" to glean research on computer tape and views Hawai'i as "a
journalism laboratory." "The stories can't run away," Dooley states
(Dooley 1993). The newspaper is still the memory of the community. That memory keeping is still alive to report the details of Saturday's football game, complaints about government officials and
the city transit system, births, and obituaries—the last, in veteran
newsman Charles Frankel's words, capsule histories of Hawai'i's
people (Frankel 1993).

I would like to suggest another influence. In 1976, the year that
Hawai'i is projected into the information space age, newspapers
chronicle the older, oral Hawaiian culture. Even as the satellite
evening news flashes the event before us, the papers record for history
the stunning achievement of *Hōkūle'a*, the Polynesian voyaging
canoe that has navigated, without instruments, over the open ocean
between Hawai'i and Tahiti, as Hawaiians had a thousand years earlier. The newspapers thus continue to document the stubborn persistence of "Idols of the Tribe"—our identification with our origins since
we first evolved as humans: our body types, names, kinship, place,
language, history, religion, and nation (Isaacs 1975). One recalls that
print itself, even as it is used in computers, bears ethnic identification: Roman, Gothic, Egyptian, Arabic, Venetian, Dutch, Italic.

The Shape of This Study

My goal has been to chart how Hawaiʻi's newspapers have helped shape major historic events in the Islands from their introduction by American missionaries to contemporary times and how the newspapers have largely been in the service of and promoted American ideals and practices. The selections here are just that—selections of events in which newspapers played a significant or a typical role. There are, of course, many others. Nor is there an absolute way to separate or quantify a paper's effect from the variety of other influences with which it exists (Strentz 1989). "News" implies immediacy. Influence, however, may be subtle, indirect, cumulative, even unintended.

Nevertheless, there are only so many kinds of stories that newspapers print: human interest, exposés or moral disorder, hero stories, "gee-whiz" or surprises, role reversals (Stephens 1988). I have chosen from among these a range of topics about which the public repeatedly shows a strong interest: land and development; education and schools; churches and religion; money, business, and labor; crime and the law; family and health; government and politics; race, class, and gender; sports and entertainment; war and censorship. I have also looked at placement, which is almost as important as content. Did coverage appear on the front page above the fold in the most eye-catching place in the upper right-hand corner? Or was the story or photo assigned to an inside page? What did the "cutlines" or captions for the photos say? Just as critical, why were there no reports or only distorted coverage of an important event?

I believe that even though we exist in a global community, it is premature to write off newspapers. As *Advertiser* executive Ann Harpham states, there will always be a need for a local paper (Harpham 1992). And the newspapers are the only retail service delivered daily door to door. Our parochial desire for information is as deep as ever. What movies are playing? What's on sale this week in the stores? What government agency is being investigated for wrongdoing? Who's ahead in the mayor's race? Is the milk that our children drink contaminated? New papers still surface, such as gay-lesbian journals, as well as three papers on the island of Molokaʻi alone in the 1990s. Some are even successful, like the nicely named establishment *Downtown Planet* (1979–), the alternative African American *Mahogony* (1988–) and *Honolulu Weekly* (1991–), and the specialist *Sports Hawaii* (1994). The newspaper remains the first rough draft of history.

PART I

"To Exhibit Truth in an Attractive Form": An Establishment Press Arrives—1834–1850

1. *Ka Lama:*
"The Light" Is Brought to Hawai'i

The first American Protestant missionaries to arrive in the Sandwich Islands, as Hawai'i was known in 1820, brought a printing press from Boston on their 18,000-mile trip around Cape Horn. Hawai'i's first press was a manually operated Ramage flatbed that utilized hand-set type, much like the one on which James and Benjamin Franklin printed their newspaper in colonial Boston. As in the American colonies in the seventeenth and eighteenth centuries, a print technology in Hawai'i in the nineteenth century became a revolutionary force for change. And as Harold Innis has demonstrated in *Empire and Communications* (1972), it is print that has enabled imperialism to spread its power across continents and oceans. The imposition of print upon the Hawaiian Islands coincided with the rise of America as an imperialist Pacific power. American-style newspapers were a major contributor to this expansion.

The overriding intent of the missionaries and their sponsor, the American Board of Commissioners for Foreign Missions (ABCFM), was to bring enlightenment to those they considered benighted—a Christian enlightenment imbued with American values. They intended to achieve their goals through "preaching, teaching, and printing" (Kuykendall 1938). By 1822, the mission equipment was producing educational, commercial, religious, and government materials at the rate of 100 single sheets an hour.

Printing was introduced to Hawai'i by New Yorker Elisha Loomis just four decades after the event that opened the remote Pacific islands to the outside world—the arrival of the British explorer Captain James Cook in 1778—and just a year after the death in 1819 of the great king Kamehameha I who had united the separate chiefdoms into a nation. Print technology when introduced into oral cultures either overwhelms them or drives them into pockets of resistance. In Hawai'i, an oral, memory-based traditional culture, a culture that had thrived in isolation and in balance with nature for more than a thousand years, was rapidly displaced by codified laws, constitutions, and newspapers.

15

After gaining fluency in Hawaiian, the New Englanders set up a periodical press, in the words of Hiram Bingham, "to exhibit truth in an attractive form" and to supply the Native Hawaiians with "useful knowledge in the arts and sciences, history, morals, and religion" (Bingham 1847). When Honolulu missionaries received a new press, they shipped the old Ramage in 1831 to Lahaina Luna School on Maui, the Kingdom's first high school (Day and Loomis 1973). In 1834, Lahaina Luna opened the first newspaper building west of the Rocky Mountains. There, a former Kentucky compositer and pressman, the Reverend Lorrin Andrews, who had joined the mission in Boston, taught his male Hawaiian students how to gather information, write it up, and print it. His model was the religious newspaper, well developed in the eastern United States by the early 1800s (Mott 1950). Printing was entirely in Hawaiian since by 1826 the missionaries had converted the spoken language to the written. Native Hawaiians quickly and eagerly adopted literacy and the printed page.

The Calvinists named their first newspaper *Ka Lama Hawaii* (The light or The Hawaiian luminary) (1834) and quickly followed it with *Ke Kumu* (The teacher) (1834–1839). They thus inaugurated an establishment press—establishment in that even though the papers spoke for just a handful of people and not for the vast majority of the native population, in just a few years they had come to exert a dominant influence on the Islands.

What were these papers like? The Reverend Andrews and his students printed 200 copies of each issue of *Ka Lama* and distributed them free. In half-sheet quartos, approximately nine by eleven inches in size, the papers delivered new and exciting information and an air of immediacy about the world thousands of miles away. *Ka Lama* also introduced the illustrated periodical, another fascinating novelty, by reproducing prints made from wood blocks on a lithograph press. Dr. Alonzo Chapin, a physician posted to the mission, hand carved forty four-footed beasts like the lion, camel, zebra, buffalo, and reindeer, all of which except for the dog and horse were unknown to the Hawaiians (Mookini 1985). Explanatory text spoke to the "superiority" of American culture, the Christian religion, and the Protestant work ethic. *Ka Lama* presented the concept of the miscellany, still the essence of a newspaper. Accounts relate how, upon receiving their copies, students would immediately sit down to read them through. By such "truth in an attractive form" were Hawaiian readers indoctrinated into the new culture.

With a popular royalist system in place, the mission editors took

Ka Lama, on May 16, 1834, introduced the newspaper to Hawai'i, the communication medium that became the primary source of information for 150 years. *Ka Lama* helped to impose American values on the isolated Island archipelago. (Hawaiian Mission Children's Society)

the offensive in guiding the monarchy toward an American constitutional government. Lead articles in *Ka Lama* and *Ke Kumu* discussed the rights and responsibilities of Native Hawaiian leaders in Western terms, along with the desirability of an American-style government, and promoted the Declaration of Rights in 1839 and a Constitution in 1840. Just a few sample titles of the dozen or so mission-sponsored papers that followed *Ka Lama* and *Ke Kumu* in the next few decades demonstrate their proselytizing nature: *Ka Elele Hawaii* (The Hawaiian messenger) (1845–1855); *Ka Nonanona* (The ant) (1841–1845), after that diligent insect and in contrast to the capricious grasshopper; *Missionari Hawaii* (1856–1857) (Mookini 1974). These appeared monthly, semimonthly, or weekly, achieving circulations of 1,000 to 1,500 per issue, attesting to the spreading influence of their main themes of "Americanism" and Christian "morality."

Significantly, American editors moved into official positions in the Hawaiian government, reinforcing the Protestant group's almost immediate rise to power and influence. *Ka Lama*'s Andrews left his editor's post and became a justice of the Kingdom's Superior Court in 1847. E. O. Hall, a secular printer, became director of the government press in 1849. The Reverend Richard Armstrong edited several mission-sponsored papers, sometimes behind the scenes, even after his appointment as minister of Public Instruction for the Kingdom's newly created education department in 1848.

Paradoxically, the New Englanders imported other American values, including the ideals of freedom of conscience and speech. Literacy empowers people to think and speak for themselves. Both *Ka Lama*'s Andrews and *Ke Kumu* editor, the Reverend Reuben Tinker, a former Massachusetts newsman, were products of a revolutionary America that produced a Constitution with a first amendment that guaranteed freedom of speech and the press. These newsmen/missionaries objected to the mission's acceptance of funds from slave-holding states, particularly Tinker who provoked within the mission a free speech controversy. Tinker thought the ABCFM exercised a despotic censorship over everything written for publication and resigned in protest from *Ke Kumu* in 1838, from the mission soon after, and returned to the United States in 1840 (Mookini 1974).

Missionary Bingham responded to the unexpected success and prosperity of the Hawaiian mission by lamenting that "the world creeps in" (Bingham 1847). *Ka Lama* not only enabled the world to creep in but hastened the speed by which America established itself in Hawai'i.

2. The Solemn Responsibility of Dissent

After two Hawaiian language newspapers representing American Protestant missionaries' beliefs appeared in 1834, an expanding mercantile community demanded a voice of its own. Although the small, independent country was an arena for large contending foreign powers—England, France, Russia, the United States—America by the 1830s had achieved a dominant position.

American businessmen were as firmly convinced as their missionary brethren of the desirability of Hawai'i having an American-style government and a periodical press. They added to this another cause—the promotion of capitalist values and practices, like world trade from abroad and commerce at home. In 1836, within two years of the appearance of an establishment Hawaiian language press, the first commercial and English language newspaper sprung to life.

The *Sandwich Island Gazette and Journal of Commerce* (1836–1839) was backed by merchants Stephen Reynolds and Henry A. Peirce. Its editor, Stephen MacIntosh, was a twenty-four-year-old adventurous newspaperman from Boston who was the forerunner of the "strolling printer," a type later made famous by Mark Twain, an 1866 visitor to the Sandwich Islands. When MacIntosh and a partner, Nelson Hall, tried to set up a print shop in an old building where Hall lived, on the grounds of the Catholic mission, the Protestants prevailed upon Kamehameha III to ban the proposed paper (Hoyt 1954). The influential Reynolds brought pressure to bear on behalf of the merchants, and the king relented.

MacIntosh was a newspaper pioneer who paved the way for a mainstream press in which religious and economic principles would become reconciled. He presented the popular model of an American newspaper with intertwined functions of informing the public, exercising freedom of opinion, and making a profit. In his opening issue of July 30, 1836, the young journalist stated that the *Sandwich Island Gazette* was a business enterprise that would promote commerce, navigation, and agriculture and would publish "items of news, amusement, and utility." Unlike the two mission-supported papers, it carried advertising—the "good news" of a paper, in contrast to the "bad news" that is the news itself. The *Sandwich Island Gazette* introduced American secular newspaper crusading. Unlike his missionary counterpart, the Reverend Tinker, who fought the suppression of free speech behind the scenes, MacIntosh brought the principle of a free press into public focus: "We expect to obtain liberty of the press," the editor asserted. Dissent was his "solemn responsibility."

Whom did this first English language newspaper expect to influence? By today's standards there were few readers. Foreign residents in Hawai'i numbered about 500. At its height the paper had about 100 listed subscribers. By all reports, however, it was immediately popular and widely read, copies passing from hand to hand and island to island, even reaching the United States and England.

Its four pages contained foreign and local news, vital statistics, ship departures and arrivals, passenger lists, and a crime column. MacIntosh advocated sidewalks, improved roads, shipping schedules, and a cemetery. Writing most of the paper himself, the editor sought relief by adopting an American journalism practice of reprinting fillers from other journals. He printed sentimental verse, fiction that might run serially over several weeks, and essays on such topics as the profitability of cultivating the Indian opium trade, the first mention in the Hawai'i press of the drug that was to gather great publicity to itself later in the century.

The paper appeared every Saturday, the major trading day. Hawai'i in these years had both a barter and a money economy, and one could trade a bullock, hides, or other goods for a subscription costing six dollars yearly. Advertising, resembling that of contemporary classifieds, enhanced by woodcut illustrations, accounted for one-fourth of the paper's space. Laboriously hand set, these ads sometimes ran for months, long past the dates paid for by advertisers. They demonstrated the growing port of Honolulu's needs and interests: auctioneer's services, ship carpenters and sailmakers, saddles and bridles, pearls, dry goods, fresh produce, and remedies against rats and roaches. MacIntosh supplemented a precarious living, as many printer-editors of his day did, by engaging in retail trade and job printing. The print shop also served as a clearinghouse for mail. But MacIntosh's heart was in the editorial side of the paper.

His was the first paper to discuss the decline of the Hawaiian population. While members of the mission also expressed concern, the difference was that MacIntosh came to blame the missionaries, whom he accused of using the Islanders as beasts of burden to carry huge rocks through the public streets. He was in favor of building the church (Kawaiaha'o Church, a coral structure completed in 1842 and today a center for Native Hawaiian Christian worship), but in "the true spirit of Christianity." The missionaries were probably not aware of their "relentless cruelty," and he asked that horses and oxen be used in place of "the harassed natives" (Feb. 3, Aug. 25, 1838). This and other unpopular positions—for example, tolerance toward liquor consumption because "public houses" were necessary to cities and port communities—assured him of the mission's enmity.

It was on behalf of "liberty of conscience" that MacIntosh waged his most successful crusade. The missionary-government alliance was determined to prevent Roman Catholicism from getting a foothold. Rumors flew through the tiny foreign settlement that Mr. and Mrs. MacIntosh were "Papists" (they were Unitarians). Protestant preachers thundered against the evils of Papism. Catholic priests from Europe had first arrived in July 1827 and were expelled twice in the next few years (Kuykendall 1938). In 1837, when Catholic missionaries were again threatened with deportation, there was a newspaper to support them. "A barbarous act of persecution," MacIntosh cried, and invited letters to the editor on the subject: "Justice to the oppressed! Truth to the mistaken! Free discussion to the candid! And fair play to every member of the human family. . . . The Sandwich Island Gazette advocates the dearest of all liberty, the most natural of all privileges, the Liberty of Conscience" (Apr. 15, 1837).

Kamehameha III, stung into replying, declared in a June 24 letter to the paper that he had every right to his actions. MacIntosh repeated his demands. The king was pressured, too, by other events. In 1839, Hawaiian sovereignty was threatened by the actions of a presumptuous French naval officer and armed French marines. Captain C. P. T. Laplace, commander of the frigate *L'Artemise,* forced an unequal treaty upon Hawai'i not only for religious toleration for Roman Catholics but for specific trade privileges for the French (Kuykendall 1938). The king in 1839 proclaimed a Declaration of Rights and an Edict of Toleration.

The *Sandwich Island Gazette and Journal of Commerce* had a short life. With a market of only a scattered foreign community, the paper could not succeed economically and folded in 1839. Debt-ridden, MacIntosh left Hawai'i with his wife and children but continued his newspaper career in St. Louis and New Orleans until he died of ill health at the age of twenty-seven. MacIntosh made history in his brief life.

His press equipment had another life. The Roman Catholic Mission in 1841 bought this equipment and set up its own print shop. Father L. D. Maigret eventually received a new press—he had complained to his European superiors, "The Protestants have excellent presses of the new kind, while we have only a bad one, the characters of which do not work" (Yzendorn 1927)—to produce the first Catholic paper, *He Mau Hana I Hanaia* (Works done) (1852–1859) (Mookini 1974). Thus began the tradition of Catholic publications, which has continued to the present.

MacIntosh's secular crusade for freedom of the press linked to commerce was the parent of a multitude of offspring. American merchants and traders supported new ventures and in 1839 backed the *Sandwich Island Mirror and Commercial Gazette* (1839–1841), a monthly printed by R. J. Howard. The idealistic slogan beneath its title stated, "In truth's bold cause, to honor each fearless heart." But true to its capitalist basis, the *Mirror's* prospectus stated that it would "serve the interests of commerce and agriculture" (Aug. 15, 1839).

3. The *Polynesian:* In the Service of America and the Kingdom

The *Polynesian* (1840–1841, 1844–1864), generally regarded as the most famous of the Islands' papers in the nineteenth century, entered history as the enterprise of a young Bostonian, James Jackson Jarves. From June 1840 to December 1841, in its first series, it was supported by Jarves' friends from the mission, as well as by advertisements and subscriptions from members of the business community. The *Polynesian* thereby demonstrated the closing gap between religious and secular American interests.

As was true for other commercial journalistic enterprises of the day, Jarves had a difficult time keeping the paper afloat financially, and he shut it down for two-and-a-half years and tried other enterprises. He revived it in 1844, and the second series, running from May 1844 to February 1864, achieved financial stability by becoming the official voice of the Hawaiian government (Hunter 1953). (It returned to being privately owned in 1861 until its end in 1864.) But even though it was sponsored by Kamehameha III and Kamehameha IV, the English language weekly during its most influential period served as an outpost of America in commerce, science, government, and culture.

The restless and adventurous Jarves first arrived in the Islands in 1837 at the age of nineteen, left, and returned again in 1839 with a wife, Elizabeth, to began the newspaper (Steegmuller 1951). It should be noted that Elizabeth Jarves ran the *Polynesian* during her husband's several absences to other islands and to the United States, making her unofficially the first woman editor in the Pacific, a fact overlooked by James Jarves and history.

American Allegiance

Jarves' role in several events in 1840 illustrates an important function of the press—what the editor chooses to emphasize helps to set the immediate agenda and influences what history will deem important. The paper thoroughly and enthusiastically reported the visit of the Wilkes U.S. Exploring Expedition and the creation of an Ameri-

23

can-style constitution. It threw its considerable weight behind naming the Islands with the designation by which they have become
permanently known. But it gave little space to a hanging, a Western-
type of execution that demonstrated almost as well as the constitution the imposition of foreign—that is, American—law upon
Hawai'i.

From their earliest presence in Hawai'i, the United States used
naval power to broaden its influence in the Pacific. While Europe
was embroiled in the Napoleonic Wars, America had a clear field for
expansion. The vast majority of ships entering Hawai'i from the
1820s on were American trading or military vessels, but there were
no newspapers to greet them.

In 1840, the *Polynesian* eagerly anticipated the arrival of an
American naval-scientific venture. Commanded by Lieutenant
Charles Wilkes, the Wilkes U.S. Exploring Expedition (1838–1842)
was an almost four-year global voyage from the East Coast to the
Antarctic and Asia that engaged in surveying, mapping, and other
endeavors (Kuykendall 1938; Joesting 1972). This was a stunning
example of technology combined with Manifest Destiny, the God-
given right, according to the United States, of its expansion over the
continent and overseas. The *Polynesian* anxiously informed readers: "The arrival of the squadron . . . in our port may be daily looked
for" (June 20, 1840). A delay for repairs in Sydney, Australia, caused
the ships to finally arrive on September 30, the *Polynesian* enthusiastically greeting the expedition in its October 3 edition. "We are
glad" to have these "valued friends," Jarves stated. "Our best
wishes attend them, and may their visit be one of unmingled satisfaction" (Oct. 3, 1840). The expedition sounded Honolulu Harbor,
measured the height of Mauna Loa, and surveyed the Pearl River,
whose harbor the United States would have exclusive rights to
enter after 1887.

The *Polynesian* introduced what would become standard fare in
society pages after 1900—write-ups of the entertainment of military
officers by the host community. It rhapsodically described a party
given by Hannah Holmes, the Hawaiian daughter of an American
businessman. Some 200 guests, including the governor of O'ahu and
60 expedition officers, enjoyed Miss Holmes' hospitality, which
included her living room decorated with the flags of many nations,
a sumptuous buffet, and the ascension of a hot air balloon on the
lawn (Dec. 5, 1840).

In the same edition that welcomed the Wilkes expedition, Jarves reported on the murder trial of two men. There were no newspapers to record the first American-style executions, two hangings in 1826 and 1828. In 1840, however, the trial that would lead to the hanging of two prominent men consumed public interest for weeks. Chief Kamanawa II, grandfather of two future monarchs, David Kalākaua and Lydia Makaeha Lili'uokalani, had divorced, but the law stated that he could not remarry while his former wife lived. Kamanawa II and an accomplice, Lonopuakau, poisoned her. Jarves editorialized approvingly on the trial, presided over by Governor Kekuanaoa, and the findings of the jury composed of twelve "intelligent Hawaiians" (Oct. 3, 1840).

Having rather fully reported on the crime, Jarves gave only a few scant lines to the actual hanging on October 20: "The murderers Kamanawa and Lonopuakau expiated their crime on the scaffold on Tuesday last, at the Fort in the presence of a large concourse of people" (Oct. 24, 1840). Had the news value of the event played itself out? Not likely—10,000 spectators witnessed the execution. The answer may lie in Jarves' statement in the *Polynesian*'s opening issue. Its first principle, the Bostonian said, was "Pro bono publico"—for the public good. The paper's columns were open to all opinions, just so they were of "an elevated character, avoiding scurrility . . . or any thing tending to excite without improving the community" (June 6, 1840). "Excite without improving" is a fitting epitaph to the event.

In the very same edition that welcomed the expedition and reported the murder trial, Jarves raised the question of "Hawaii, Versus Sandwich Islands." The latter term, British in origin, was used extensively. In this instance, the editor responded to the feelings of Native Hawaiians who disliked "Sandwich Islands"—he was not always so sensitive—for these feelings happened to coincide with the interests of foreign Americans: "We give preference to Hawaii for the group, Hawaiians for its inhabitants, and its derivative adjective, for these reasons. The natives have ever used 'Hawaii nei' as applicable to the Islands collectively, and consequently style themselves Hawaiians" (Oct. 3, 1840). By 1840, "Hawaii" and "Hawaiian Islands" took precedence.

The Hawaiian Government Asks to Be Heard

The *Polynesian* in its first series was a commercial venture aimed at the 600 foreign residents in Honolulu. Advertisements were plentiful, from Ladd & Company, Hawai'i's first (in 1835) permanent sugar plantation, to those offering hundreds of imported items for sale, from boots, silk umbrellas, and shovels, to dresses and window glass. But Jarves still was only able to keep his newspaper going for nineteen months. To Jarves' good fortune, Kamehameha III decided that he had to explain his policies directly to the foreign community. What better way than to adopt a proven method of communication?—the newspaper.

As early as 1841, the *Polynesian* had anticipated its coming role—a traditional role for official American journals from the American Revolution to the present is to publish the laws—when Jarves printed Hawai'i's first constitution, of 1840, in its entirety (Feb. 6, 1841). In May 1844, the king acquired the *Polynesian* to be published "by authority." Two months later, in July, the Kingdom hired Jarves as editor. This was well ahead of the Organic Acts, formulated between 1845 and 1847, that associated the government legally with the printing and newspaper business. It is interesting that the physical size of the *Polynesian* grew, from four columns and eleven by sixteen inches in size in its private enterprise years to a larger, more expensive format of five columns and twenty-four by seventeen inches in its years as a government organ. Given a five-year contract and a rent-free house, Jarves was now assured of a livelihood.

The second Organic Act specifically set up a Bureau of the Government Press and a newspaper. Provisions were made for printing government laws and notices in both Hawaiian and English and for distributing the newspaper throughout the Islands. In the United States, licensing was common practice, having been applied in colonial times as a control measure over papers. In the second Organic Act, the government instituted a licensing system from which noncommercial journals, such as those sponsored by the mission, and official papers were exempted. Publishing without a license otherwise carried penalties of $500 and up to six months imprisonment (Lydecker 1918).

These provisions, as well as newly defined libel laws, were clearly aimed at the secular English language press that the monarchy believed attacked it unfairly. Libel laws give a government or dominating interests a powerful weapon against dissenting voices. Periodicals were permitted "open and full discussion," but "publishers were responsible in personal damages to any private party agrieved, for libellous matter, or false and injurious charges." Nothing disrespectful was to be printed toward the king and royal premier. Furthermore, the government would not "suffer articles of a nature offensive or disparaging to other friendly powers . . . of communications of a libellous or indecent nature" (Lydecker 1918).

Jarves used the editorial, in its heyday in the nineteenth-century United States, to influence public opinion (Salmon 1923; Mott 1950). Editorials, often disguised as "news" articles or as "letters," which might be written by the editor himself or friends, were usually strongly opinionated and often vituperative. Jarves stated that the Hawaiian government now had the means of publishing "so that the world can judge for itself its capability to conduct its relations with foreign interests." But although he promised that nothing slanderous or disrespectful would be printed against other nations "so long as the Government, or its members, are treated with like courtesy" (*Poly.*, June 13, 1845), Jarves' condescending ethnocentrism infected his journalism. His contemporaries shared his views, but Jarves' opinions carried extra weight in that he had a public platform. It is still distressing to read the opinions of the man some historians have labeled as the "government's champion."

What were some of these views? Hawaiians, Jarves believed, were inferior and unable to compete with whites, who were their racial superiors. Polynesian culture had little value. Hawaiian speech was "rude and uncultivated, destitute of literature" and not worth preserving. Hawaiians had "only a few misty traditions, oral records of the sensualities and contests of the barbarous chiefs, the rites of an inhuman religion." In a classic example of blaming the victims, Jarves declared the Hawaiians at fault for beginning to die off after Captain Cook's arrival (June 19, Aug. 2, Oct. 4, 1845).

In contrast to all of this, Jarves held up Western culture as the epitome of humankind's efforts to become civilized and declared that the *Polynesian*, boosting the trinity of Western values of Christianity, agriculture, and commerce, would help Hawaiians attain civilization: "Christian civilization with all its error is vastly preferable to semi-savage stupidity" (Aug. 2, 1845).

"Semisavage" is an unconsciously revealing term. Native Hawaiians called Jarves "*po'o kanaka* (skull man)." Jarves gathered native skulls from sand dunes around O'ahu, remnants of the victims of ancient battles and more recent imported diseases, and with semisavage stupidity of his own sent the grisly bundles to his father in New England.

Jarves effectively performed the job for which he had been hired, to serve as a voice for the king in his efforts to bring Hawai'i into modern life, and he was well rewarded for his services. When Jarves left the Islands in 1849, it was as a special envoy of the Hawaiian government to the United States, Great Britain, and France. In the tradition of many newspapermen, he later pursued a career as an author and novelist.

4. The English Flag and the English Language

In the 1840s, the Reverend Richard Armstrong and his newspapers illustrate the press' ability to focus public attention and shape public attitudes. Armstrong arrived from New England with the fifth company of missionaries in 1832. With a wife and ten children to support, he turned to various enterprises such as sugar cultivation. But Armstrong loved literacy and education best. He began the Atheneum, the forerunner of a public library, and in 1848 he withdrew from the mission to become the Kingdom's first minister of Public Instruction. As a way to advance literacy and Christian-American morality, he also turned to another educating medium, newspapers.

Among the journals that he edited through the years, several were particularly effective: *Ka Nonanona* (The ant) (1841–1845), a semimonthly in Hawaiian and English; *Ka Elele Hawaii* (The Hawaiian messenger) (1845–1855), in Hawaiian; and with his son Samuel, *Ka Hae Hawaii* (The Hawaiian flag) (1856–1861) (Mookini 1974). Each shifted categories as the times required, from establishment to opposition and back again, but maintained their influence.

In the 1840s, acrimonious relations were the norm between British and American residents. British power was on the wane in the North Pacific, and a quarrelsome English trader serving as British consul in Hawai'i meant to reverse that tide. In 1841, Richard Charlton conspired to add the Hawaiian archipelago to the British Empire, and while doing so, instigated the first press scandal in the Islands.

Charlton objected in 1841 to a series of editorials in the *Polynesian* that criticized British residents who had complained that the governor was drafting their servants for road work. Charlton, no friend to free speech, along with a companion, accosted *Polynesian* editor Jarves and attempted to horsewhip him. They were found guilty and each fined six dollars, the maximum fine (Steegmuller 1951). Jarves was luckier than some of his fellow journalists. This was an era in the United States of violent attacks upon editors, as in 1837 in Alton, Illinois, where a mob burned the presses of abolitionist editor Elijah Lovejoy and murdered him. Jarves escaped with a few bruises.

Complaints by Charlton and other British residents against Hawaiian authorities found their way to the British Foreign Office in London. In 1843, Rear Admiral Richard Thomas, commander of the British Squadron in the Pacific, sent Lieutenant Paulet and the frigate *Carysfort* to Honolulu to protect British interests. The *Carysfort* arrived in Honolulu on February 10, 1843, and Paulet issued a series of ultimatums, culminating in his demand for the cession of the Hawaiian Islands to Great Britain. Kamehameha III was forced to yield (Kuykendall 1938).

Armstrong's *Ka Nonanona*, the only newspaper in print, opened its columns to those opposed to an English naval officer's usurpation of Hawaiian (and American) rights. Sponsored by the Protestant mission and speaking on behalf of the Hawaiian government, this paper became an effective voice of protest from February 25 to July 26, 1843, when the British flag flew over Hawai'i. *Ka Nonanona* printed several letters against the naval officer and his rule. One, addressed to the British government by Kamehameha III and his premier, read in part: "All good men will sympathize with us in our present state of distress; and now we Protest in the face of all men, against all such proceedings both towards ourselves and foreigners, subjects of other Governments, on the part of Rt. Hon. Lord George Paulet" (July 25, 1843). Another, in the same edition, this one from the American naval officer Laurence Kearney, commander in chief of the U.S. naval force in the East Indies, also strongly objected to Paulet's piratical action.

The timing of the king's and Kearney's letters couldn't have been better. The British government, which had joined France in recognizing Hawaiian independence (the United States had already formally recognized the Hawaiian Kingdom), repudiated Paulet's actions. Admiral Thomas, arriving in Honolulu on July 26, ordered the British flag lowered on July 31 and the Hawaiian flag restored to sovereignty.

Armstrong's major cause over the years, however, was to promote education. It was his vision that every Hawaiian child should become literate. Fluent in Hawaiian himself, he at first vigorously advocated in his papers that Hawaiian be taught in the schools. Other American editors opposed him and ran editorials that argued that change was inevitable. James Jackson Jarves urged the mission schools to teach the students in English (*Poly.*, July 5, 19, Aug. 2,

1845); and C. E. Hitchcock added that "foreigners"—that is, Americans—wanted English to be taught in the public schools (May 20, 1848).

By 1850, on the five principal islands, there were more than 15,000 children, out of a total population of 84,000, enrolled in the schools that Armstrong oversaw. Now almost a certainty that English would become the language of Hawaiians, Armstrong shifted his position. His editorial name in *Ka Elele* was Limaikaika, meaning a strong hand or arm, and his journalistic evangelical arm indeed had force. His revised view was that the mastery of English was essential to Native Hawaiians if they were to be able to cope with their present and future worlds. Many Hawaiians of his own day agreed with him.

Armstrong with his son Samuel Armstrong edited *Ka Hae Hawaii* (The Hawaiian flag), the organ of the Department of Public Instruction (Mookini 1974). They formed the first, but by no means the last, father-son publishing team in the Islands. Charging only one dollar per year for a subscription, *Ka Hae*'s primary purpose was to encourage reading among Native Hawaiians.

Within a short time, the legislature of 1853–1854 provided money for the support of English schools for Hawaiians. This action would lead inexorably to English becoming the compulsory language of instruction in the public schools in 1896 and the closing of Hawaiian public schools in 1900.

Educator Benjamin Wist has called Armstrong "the father of American education in Hawaii" (Wist 1940). Others have been less kind. In the 1980s, linguist Dr. Richard R. Day and Hawaiian scholar Larry Kimura have labeled replacement of the Hawaiian language by the English language in the schools in the nineteenth century as "linguistic genocide" (Day 1985; Kimura 1985).

In one of those paradoxes of history, Armstrong's newspapers assisted in determining that the English were unsuccessful in taking over the Islands, but that the English language would be victorious beyond all expectations.

5. God Gives Way to Mammon: The Mahele of 1848

In the ancient Hawaiian land tenure system, land was highly valued as the source of subsistence but held no monetary exchange value. No one "owned" the land. The Mahele of 1848 was the instrument that changed that by dividing the land among the king, the chiefs, and the people. (A further division separated land assigned to the king and his family from "crown" lands.) An act of 1850 extended the right to aliens to acquire fee simple land titles (Fuchs 1961; Kame'eleihiwa 1992). All the newspapers, secular and religious, advanced this concept of Western property that forever—and for Native Hawaiians, tragically—altered the social system of Hawai'i. Their basic argument was that all "civilizations" had property rights specified by law.

There were a number of factors contributing to this land revolution. The belief among Christians that one received one's rewards in heaven was giving way to the Protestant ethic—that God rewards the most deserving on earth with wealth. Economic conditions and demographics further conspired against the Hawaiians. Whaling had begun its decline (its peak year was 1846), sending fears of a depression through the mercantile community. Furthermore, because of the continued rapid decline of the native population from imported diseases, many haole (Caucasians) were convinced that the Hawaiians were doomed to extinction and that land redistribution was therefore essential.

From the very first issue in 1840 of the *Polynesian,* the most important newspaper of the period, land was a leading topic of discussion. The "progress" of the Kingdom was hindered, editor Jarves argued, because people lacked permanent land titles that were essential to attract investment capital. The whole system of land tenure must be "remodelled and placed upon a basis at once equitable and liberal. This of itself will give a stimulus to the domestic industry of the kingdom" (Oct. 12, 1844). Through 1845 and 1846, Jarves argued that land ownership not only would bring prosperity, but would actually "preserve" the native population by providing them with an "incentive." Jarves urged the chiefs and king to give land to the people, just as they had given religious and civil rights in the earlier Declaration of Rights in 1839, and in the Constitution of 1840 (Oct. 25, 1845).

Kamehameha III, the great king at midcentury, initially was opposed to the conversion. How did this change of policy happen then? During his reign (1825–1854), the king witnessed the most radical upheavels and experienced personal tragedy. The missionaries forbade him marrying the girl he loved, his sister Nahi'ena'ena, and when she and their child died, the Calvinists cited this as proof of God's punishment. He had a wild youth, but seeing the destructiveness of alcohol, he took up the cause of temperance, forbidding liquor in his domain and trying himself to abstain. Although married to Kalama in Christian services, he later repudiated the religion (Joesting 1972). Through great inner strength he preserved his own personality and that of his people by bringing back the ancient games and hula after the mission attempted to force these into oblivion.

Aggressive foreign intervention that shook the country's independence caused the most radical upheaval. The king had to satisfy ever more demanding outside interests while trying to serve his own people. In 1845, Native Hawaiians petitioned their king and legislature to not yield to the pressures of foreigners, including those in the government, to change the land system:

> Oh, Your Majesty, our king, oh Kauikeaouli, show love towards us, and free your people from this difficulty that is coming upon us, if so many foreigners enter into this kingdom! . . . Foreigners come with their property in dollars; they are prepared to buy the land; but we have no property, a people unprepared as we. . . . If you assent quickly, oh Chiefs, to the buying of land by foreigners, it will soon lead to our being reduced to servitude! The dwelling of many foreigners in this kingdom will tend to increase . . . though not to increase our prosperity. (*Poly.*, Aug. 9, 1845)

Ka Elele Hawaii, under the editorship of the Reverend Richard Armstrong, who believed in the principle of a free press, published the petitions in Hawaiian. The *Polynesian* translated these into English to mock them for being "illogical."

The king attempted to explain to his people that he needed foreign advisors until Hawaiians could be trained to deal with the larger world and that a land conversion was necessary for Hawai'i to take its place among the world's nations. Among the more powerful men who advanced the king's positions in the newspapers were Robert Crichton Wyllie and Gerrit Parmelee Judd. Wyllie, from Scotland, arrived in Hawai'i in 1844 and joined the king's cabinet in 1845 as minister of Foreign Affairs (a position he held until his death in 1865) (Kuykendall 1938, 1953). In a series of articles in the *Friend*, Wyllie staked out what was now the government position, to convert the system to land ownership, particularly in agriculture, to "awaken the energies of the people" (July 1, Oct. 9, 1844). Judd, a medical, nonordained missionary, who arrived in 1828, held the key position of minister of Finance from 1842 to 1854 and was instrumental in setting up the Board of Commissioners to Quiet Land Titles in December 1845. He regularly planted unsigned articles in the papers in support of the king.

The five-member Land Commission or Land Board, as it was also called, was dominated by Americans and heard claims and made awards between 1845 to 1854 (Kuykendall 1938; Joesting 1972). The Reverend William Richards helped to write the Constitution of 1840 establishing a constitutional monarchy. Attorney John Ricord arrived in Hawai'i in February 1844, to be immediately appointed attorney general of the Kingdom, and, with William L. Lee, another American lawyer, drafted the Organic Acts of 1845–1847 that provided statute laws for the Kingdom.

There were three Hawaiian members of the original commission, and they, too, supported the king's aims: James Young Kanehoa, the son of Kamehameha I's niece and the king's famous adviser, the English seaman John Young; John Papa Ii, a Kona chief's son who was in the House of Nobles, on the Privy Council, and associate justice of the Superior Court; and Z. Kaauwai.

The legislature capitulated to the pressures of the Land Commission, the mercantile community, the newspapers, and the king. The king signed the Mahele into law on January 27, 1848. The *Polynesian* crowed: the older land tenure system, "fraught with evil" and a "relic of a darker age," had been a great obstacle to the people's "advancement" and prevented people from making permanent improvement on the lands they occupied (Sept. 16, 1848). Later, abandoning its previous argument that the Mahele would "preserve" the Hawaiian people, the paper predicted that by 1930 fewer than 100 "Natives" would survive (Jan. 26, 1850). Caucasians attached the adjective "Great" to the Mahele; and coinciding with the laws that created modern "real estate," advertisements appeared in the newspapers for the buying and selling of land.

As to what the Mahele truly meant to Hawaiians, this emerged in *Ka Elele Hawaii*, the only Hawaiian language paper in print in 1850. Editor Armstrong's sympathies lay with the new land laws— he, himself, was to make land investments. Lee, who had arrived in 1846 and enjoyed a meteoric rise to the position of chief justice of the Kingdom, prepared the program to permit commoners to claim *kuleana* (small pieces of property) lands. He outlined in *Elele* how Hawaiians could apply for these within a certain time period or lose their claims. Lee baldly told the Islanders that "two courses" were open to them: "Either to secure your lands, work them and be happy, or to sit still, sell them and then die. Which do you choose?" (trans., *Poly.*, Feb. 15, 1850).

As to the king, in whose reign the Mahele occurred, his character was assessed by a kinder, gentler American, the Reverend Samuel Chenery Damon, in his paper, the *Friend* (1843–1954). Damon wrote the king's obituary upon his death at the age of forty-one in December 1854, and it is how history has remembered the monarch: "Much of the good which has been accomplished, much of the evil which has been prevented, and many of the happy changes which have taken place, were doubtless brought about through the soundness of his judgment and the mildness of his character. The late sovereign of the Hawaiian people was gifted by the God of nature with many of those traits which qualify a person to be a good ruler, in trying scenes and peaceful times" (XII 1855).

But more needs to be said about the *Friend*, for it so well illustrates how even the best intentions may turn out to have a different effect than the one intended. Damon began the paper in 1843 and continued as its illustrious editor until 1885. (It ran to 1954.) The paper's formal title was the *Temperance Advocate, and Seamen's Friend*, its primary interests prominently displayed in the motto, "Devoted to Temperance, Marine and General Intelligence." A Protestant minister from New England but not a member of the mission, Damon was chaplain for the Seamen's Bethel and Sailor's Home, an alternative living situation for mariners in the brawling port town of Honolulu (Cooper 1992). Unlike the editors of the commercial papers, Damon would not accept advertisements for liquor. Readers came to simply call Damon's paper, noted for its fairness and balance, by a fitting sobriquet, "the *Friend*."

One of Damon's primary intentions, that his newspaper would contribute to Hawai'i's history, has been well met. The *Friend* is consulted to this day as a rich repository of whaling information. Damon also published the first women's liberation newspaper west

Samuel Damon's the *Friend* was an important nineteenth century newspaper because of its comprehensive information on the whaling industry.

of the Mississippi River. In essence, Damon advanced a feminist agenda that promoted temperance, social purity, and women's suffrage (Hobson 1987). Damon printed and distributed the *Folio* as an insert in the *Friend* in November 1855. Two women, who at the time remained anonymous, were the *Folio*'s actual editors: Julia Damon, Samuel Damon's wife, and Catharine Whitney, wife of

On November 16, 1855, the progressive Damon printed and distributed the *Folio,* the first feminist newspaper west of the Rocky Mountains. (Hawaiian Historical Society)

Henry Whitney, who eight months later would begin the *Pacific Commercial Advertiser* (Chapin and Forbes 1985). The two young women had brought advanced ideas on feminism with them from the American East Coast. The *Folio*'s prospectus repeated the language of the 1848 Seneca Falls (New York) declaration of the "Rights of Women" and added: "Now, then, the hour has come when your name can be made immortal by becoming the defender, supporter, aye, creator of Women's Rights in Hawaii!" The writers wittily called upon Pele, the Hawaiian goddess of fire, "to avenge the indignities inflicted on—women!" (*Folio,* Dec. 1855).

Although it promised future editions, only a single issue appeared. No reasons were given. Perhaps the little newspaper overstepped the traditional bounds of a "woman's place" in the tiny Calvinist community in the middle of the Pacific. Nevertheless, the *Folio* is the great-grandmother of twentieth-century feminist periodicals in the Islands.

An unintended effect resulted from Damon's involvement in another event that actually preceded the Mahele and would seem not allied to it. The discovery of gold in California, Hawai'i's nearest neighbor, on January 24, 1848, reinforced the allurement of exploiting the land for profit. The *Friend* was among those papers that helped to spread "gold fever," or the rush for buried property.

The *Polynesian,* under "Prospects of California," on June 17 carried the first information of the discovery. The new editor, Charles E. Hitchcock, soon reported that "an exceedingly rich gold mine had been discovered in the Sacramento Valley" and added that people were deserting their occupations and rushing "en masse to the mines to make their fortunes" (June 24, 1848). Hitchcock described "gold fever" as "a restless sensation—an excited state of the system—a wild expression of the eye . . . [and] a desire to obtain implements for digging and washing gold" and "a rush for the 'first boat' " for California (July 15, 1848).

Hitchcock himself succumbed, abandoning the paper to seek his fortune in the gold fields, as did his successor, E. O. Hall, and most of the editors of the English language papers that in the next year or two only erratically met publishing deadlines. Damon joined the throng. Suspending the *Friend* for the summer of 1849, Damon drafted a series of articles on Oregon and California that appeared in later editions and persuasively described the benefits to be found there.

All this, but especially the Mahele, presaged Hawai'i's future. Later generations of Damons would own a major bank and one of Hawai'i's largest landholding estates. Hawai'i's newspapers to this day, with a few exceptions, actively promote the development of land and acquisition of property.

PART II

"Fiery Polemic Contests" for the Public's Support— 1850–1887

6. The *Honolulu Times* Welcomes the City of Honolulu

In midcentury, an American editor of an English language journal provided the sole newspaper opposition to the rising tide of American control of Hawai'i. Americans had already risen to positions of power and influence in the government of Kamehameha III, and by 1850, both locally and abroad, there was speculation about the possibility of the United States annexing Hawai'i.

Newspapers like the *Sandwich Island Gazette* and *Sandwich Island Mirror* had expressed strong sentiments against the influence of the Protestant mission, but they themselves preached and practiced American dominance of the Islands. Proprietor Henry L. Sheldon of the *Honolulu Times* (1849–1851) also opposed the missionary establishment. But Sheldon went considerably further. The four-column, four-page *Honolulu Times* was the first newspaper to question the efficacy of American power.

A printer from Rhode Island, Sheldon had attempted to ply his trade in San Francisco during the gold rush. Hawai'i beckoned this latest bohemian adventurer, and he set up shop on dusty Printers' Row—today's Merchant Street in downtown Honolulu (Sheldon n.d., 1877). Sheldon was also the first American journalist to marry a Native Hawaiian woman, thus forming a Hawaiian family whose sons would be among the printers and journalists who would challenge the oligarchy's conspiracy for annexation in the late nineteenth century.

Yet there is a poignancy of Sheldon's position. He inadvertently advanced the very situation he deplored—the Americanization of Hawai'i. As an American Caucasian involved in a capitalist newspaper enterprise and as an enthusiastic booster of a rapidly growing Honolulu, Sheldon himself was an agent of change. That he internalized such a fundamental ambiguity likely contributed to the difficulties of his later life.

Sheldon in 1849 found his voice in challenging the new laws, particularly the Mahele that permitted foreigners to buy land outright.

Mid-nineteenth century editors set up their print shops on dusty Printers'
Row, or present-day Merchant Street. (Hawai'i State Archives)

Sheldon declared the laws detrimental to the Hawaiian people, and
he laid the blame upon the king's Caucasian advisers for the new
land laws and for effecting closer ties to the United States. When two
future kings and their American chaperone went abroad during
1849–1850, the *Polynesian,* the Hawaiian government's official
paper, provided effusive coverage (Sept. 15, 1849; Sept. 14, 1850). The
travelers were Alexander Liholiho, heir apparent to the throne, his
brother and successor Lot Kamehameha, and Dr. Gerritt P. Judd,
their chaperone, who had left the mission in 1842 to become the
king's deputy minister and minister of Finance.

The *Honolulu Times* strenuously objected to the entire enterprise. Judd's appointment for the occasion as "Special Commissioner
and Plenipotentiary Extraordinaire" was "a poor choice," according
to Sheldon, for Judd was "ill-equipped, narrow, and not wise in the
ways of the world." Sheldon raised the issue of American racism,
warning the princes that they would meet with "some mortification
in the U.S., especially if their color should be made the subject of
criticism." The contrast with Great Britain, the editor added, would

draw the princes closer to that country—in his opinion, however, "a good thing" (Feb. 13, Apr. 3 1850).

The *Polynesian* by contrast never alluded to any difficulties but approvingly reported on their extensive tour of the United States, Great Britain, and France and happily noted an important result: the Treaty of Friendship, Commerce, and Navigation made with the United States. Sheldon's predictions were later borne out by Alexander Liholiho's journal, in which he described the confining and irksome actions of Dr. Judd and of the prejudice that he and his brother encountered in America in contrast to being kindly treated in England (Liholiho 1967). The princes, later Kamehameha IV and V respectively, were indeed to be known as pro-British.

Sheldon employed his considerable wit in his attacks on American missionary influence. He "hadn't a word to say against" some religious leaders, he wrote, such as "the venerable Thurston, the literary Damon, or the disinterested Father Maigret"—in other words, yoking Protestant ministers Asa Thurston and Samuel Damon to their religious rival, the Roman Catholic bishop. Sheldon more seriously objected to "the detestable machinations of the missionary clique, who had succeeded in getting the Government under their own hands" (*Hono. Times,* Feb. 27, 1850). The Calvinists should have instituted sanitation and medical treatment, he asserted, before attempting to Christianize the Hawaiians.

Sheldon never directly criticized the king, nor did the other English language papers at this time. When he attacked the *Polynesian* and the men around the king, Sheldon insisted that he wished to protect the monarch from "bigots" who would make "the Mosaic Code the Law of the Land" and would "unite Church and State." Sheldon compared the "Missionary Caste, . . . a thoroughly selfish faction," to the Indian caste system in its accumulation of special privileges and functions. He favored industry and prosperity but despised what he identified as greed on the part of some of the king's influential Caucasian advisers. Was the Reverend Richard Armstrong, head of the Department of Education, enriching himself on land deals, Sheldon asked? Why had the Reverend Jonathan Green involved himself in a pre–Mahele experiment to sell land at Makawao on Maui? Why was E. O. Hall, formerly the assistant secular agent for the mission, given the position of chief of the Treasury Bureau? (*Hono. Times,* Mar. 6, 13, Apr. 3, 1850).

The *Polynesian,* in the meantime, under the editorship of the same E. O. Hall whom Sheldon had attacked, accused Sheldon of lying and deceitfulness. Sheldon and his supporters were simply a jealous "clique of discontented men" (*Hono. Times*, Feb. 27, 1850).

It was true that Sheldon was discontented. He wanted "good government" based on "American government principles and practices." Here, too, Sheldon contributed to the Americanization of Hawai'i. The American custom of voting had been introduced earlier in the century, and Sheldon objected to a new law that attempted to restrict the franchise. In the *Honolulu Times*, he accused the king's "foreign advisors" of bad faith because voting was now tied to property, and he demanded that the people be given full rights in electing their representatives (Aug. 21, 1850). Sheldon's criticism had an effect: the vote was expanded the next year to all males twenty-one years and older.

Sheldon also attacked the legislature for discussing public issues in private sessions. He was thus the first journalist, but by no means the last, to call attention to the undemocratic practice of the people's representatives legislating behind "closed doors" (July 10, 1850).

In yet another area, Sheldon's sincerely held beliefs ironically served to draw Hawai'i closer to the United States—the promotion of Honolulu to city status. The English language press for a number of years had raised this issue, and in 1848 the *Sandwich Island News* requested that the town be incorporated as a city (June 8, 1848), for Honolulu's population was approaching 11,000 (out of a total island-wide of 70,000), making it the Islands' main population center. The papers also lobbied for an allied function, an official postal system. Earlier in the century, newspapers began to arrive irregularly through the mails from overseas. After editors set up print shops, mail bags were dumped on their floors, and people rummaged through them for their letters and packages. The Hawai'i-U.S. Treaty of December 1849 provided for the official exchange of mails, and the Hawaiian government inaugurated a post office department in 1850 (Kuykendall 1953), an action praised by the *Honolulu Times* as well as by the *Polynesian*. In 1850, Honolulu was officially designated a city and declared the capital of the Kingdom (Johnson 1977, 1991). The *Honolulu Times* reported favorably on various city events, such as the formation that year of a chamber of commerce, an American group dedicated to business, and the organization in 1851 of the Honolulu Fire Department.

Sheldon's career as the proprietor of the *Honolulu Times* was noteworthy for advancing another American cause, freedom of speech and the press. Charles De Varigny, a Frenchman whose activities included editing a California paper and serving as a government official in Hawai'i, characterized this period as one of "complete freedom of expression" to wage "fiery polemic contests" for the public's opinion (Varigny 1968). In 1852, a year after the paper's closing, free speech was guaranteed in the Constitution of 1852: "All men may freely speak, write and publish their sentiments on all subjects, being responsible for the abuse of that right; and no law shall be passed to restrain or abridge the liberty of speech, or of the press" (Kuykendall 1938).

In the meantime, the *Polynesian* had become the principle vehicle for publishing all enacted laws, printing these in Hawaiian and English. Laws in the older, traditional Hawaiian society had been orally communicated but were widely understood. In a literate society undergoing rapid change, laws and the penalties for breaking them must be stated and reinforced by the written word (Black 1976). The *Polynesian* on July 13, 1850, and in subsequent issues, printed the new Criminal Code. Within this code was the definition of libel—the malicious publication of material that directly tends to injure the fame, reputation, or good name of another person. Penalties were provided for second and first degree libel, ranging from one month to six months at hard labor and fines of $15 to $500 (Lydecker 1918). Libel was to have far-reaching implications for the press, including an impact on Sheldon's sons.

Other "criminal" laws affected Sheldon himself and reveal the strains that his conflicting roles must have caused him. Sheldon apparently embezzled funds while employed as a government land agent and was convicted and jailed. Upon his reentry into the community, Sheldon again took up newspapering, but on behalf of the establishment that he had formerly deplored. He worked for the *Advertiser* and the *Daily Bulletin* until his death in 1883. In his memoirs, Sheldon pointed to his career with the *Honolulu Times* as the high point of his life (Sheldon n.d.).

7. The Chinese Arrive

All the newspapers in print in 1852—three commercial or government-sponsored journals in English, and four mission-sponsored in Hawaiian—uniformly favored recruiting labor from abroad for the sugar fields of Hawai'i. The midcentury climate of heated debate did not extend to criticism of the law of June 21, 1850, "an Act for the Government of Masters and Servants." Previously, the *Polynesian* had approved the founding of the Royal Hawaiian Agricultural Society by Caucasian planters (the body that would formulate immigration and labor policies until the end of the monarchy). The uniform opinion across establishment, opposition, and official newspaper lines was that the decline of the Native Hawaiian population meant that there was a need for foreign labor to build up the labor pool. Arguments arose only over what races should be recruited.

The *Polynesian* heartily welcomed the Islands' first contract laborers, who arrived in Honolulu on January 3, 1852. The paper's rhetoric set the tone for all future recruitment, whereby economic necessity was justified by the good it would do the laborers. The *Polynesian* announced the "Arrival of Coolies" on the British bark *Thetis*:

> to this port a few days since from Amoy, China, with a cargo of Coolies most of whom were contracted for by planters and others. . . .
>
> The subject of cheap labor is one which has for a considerable period engaged the attention of the planters here as an indispensible requisite to successful competition with Manila and China, in the production of sugar and coffee. The scarcity of native laborers . . . induced those engaged in agriculture to make the experiment of introducing from overflowing China a class of laborers which . . . would combine good service with economy. . . .
>
> We sincerely hope that their introduction here may prove, not only serviceable to the islands, but also to themselves; and

that they have exchanged want and oppression for a comfortable home and the protection of a government and people actuated by Christian principles. (Jan. 10, 1852)

The *Polynesian* and other papers enjoyed the fruits of the venture by selling advertising, such as: "Arrived Jan. 3 Furniture and Silk goods ex Thetis from China for Sale by A. P. Everett" (Jan. 31, 1852).

The arguments that soon surfaced over what races should be recruited were an indication of the shabby treatment of Asian labor at the hands of the planters (Char and Char 1975; Takaki 1983). Recruiters' early enthusiasm for the Fukien Chinese quickly turned to contempt, and workers, initially willing participants, became disillusioned. The *Friend* in May 1856, in an article by the Reverend William Speer on "The Chinese in the Sandwich Islands," suggested bringing in natives from the provinces of Kwantung or Canton because they would be better liked than the "Fukien coolies." Stories in other newspapers complained about the exclusive male character of the migration and blamed the Chinese for "causing problems" and for "ingratitude" when they abandoned their low-paying contracts for better jobs.

But it was not planter dissatisfaction that temporarily halted labor recruitment. This was accomplished by a depression in sugar prices and the American Civil War. Recruitment was renewed at the war's end in 1865. That year, the *Hawaiian Gazette* (1865–1918) became the official government voice (until 1873, when it would revert to private hands). The *Gazette*, supporting recruitment efforts, welcomed two shiploads of Cantonese by printing a Cantonese-English vocabulary (Nov. 25, 1865) for use by the "Coolies' " employers, a vocabulary that strikingly reflects the attitudes of the day:

Be still.	He struck me.
Stand up.	This is good for nothing.
Who are you?	I have a sore finger.
I am sick.	Don't be afraid.
Wash your hands.	This is hard work.
Don't be lazy.	These two look alike.
The rice is all gone.	Light the lamps.
You can't catch me.	He is an impudent fellow.

8. A Prophet Without Profit: Fornander Topples Judd

By midcentury, journalism exerted another kind of influence when a newspaper brought down a government leader—the first instance of its kind in Hawai'i. The outbreak of smallpox in 1853 was the catalyst for Abraham Fornander's concentrated attack upon the government minister, Dr. Gerrit Parmele Judd. Fornander had previously hurled verbal missiles at the physician, but he now launched a full frontal attack, accusing Judd of single-handedly making the epidemic worse by incompetence, negligence, and false dealings. Fornander's four-page, tabloid-size *Weekly Argus* was in print for less than two years, from January 1851 to September 1853, but it had a powerful impact.

Earlier, Fornander gained practice in crusading journalism when he wrote a series of letters for Henry Sheldon's *Honolulu Times* attacking American missionary influence upon the Hawaiian government. Signifying their importance, they appeared under the designation of "Alpha," the first letter of the Greek alphabet. After the *Honolulu Times* folded, Fornander began his own periodical. With the most slender resources, he and a partner, the American Mathew K. Smith, secured quarters for the *Weekly Argus* on Printers' Row. Fornander again applied a Greek appelation—Argus was the ancient mythological all-seeing God—and upon Smith's return to California, took over the paper early in 1852.

Fornander and Judd—what were they like? How is it that such different men, holding such antithetical beliefs in religion, politics, and culture, adopted the newspaper for their battlefield? In fact, in temperament the two were considerably alike.

Fornander was from Sweden and university educated (Davis 1979). Sweden had passed a law in 1776 allowing its citizens the right of free publication (Smith 1979), so Fornander held positive views on a free press. The son of a clergyman, Fornander was a Deist and a Freemason who believed in the perfectability of human behavior and society. He found his way to the Islands as a harpooner on a whaler, was naturalized, and married Alanakapu Kauapinao, daughter of the

48

governor of Moloka'i. Dedicated to the well-being of the Hawaiian people, he became fluent in the Hawaiian language and promoted a Royal Hawaiian Museum to preserve artifacts and relics. He advocated public education and government hospitals supported by taxes, and he later served as a judge. Fornander explained in the *Honolulu Times*, "I am a naturalized citizen— . . . I have a native wife and family, and . . . thus the native interest is my interest, in contra distinction [sic] from the monopoly interest" (Dec. 13, 1849). Admirers saw Fornander as one of those very few foreigners who genuinely understood and respected Hawaiian culture (Davis 1979). He was much beloved by family and friends. His detractors called him an atheist, an infidel, and a mischief maker. He was tough, stubborn, combative, and opinionated, and thrived on advocacy journalism.

Judd, from New York and equally well educated, arrived in the Islands in 1828 with his young wife Laura to serve as a lay preacher and physician and surgeon for the ABCFM. He, too, gained fluency in the Hawaiian language (Judd 1960). His Calvinism meant that he believed in the perfectability of man only after death. Judd's need to support a family of nine children and an unswerving conviction that Protestant Americanism was best for the Hawaiian people led him to leave the mission for a career in government. Appointed president of the Treasury Board of the Kingdom in 1842, he became the king's most powerful minister. Judd was drawn to journalism and wrote many articles in support of the goverment (Gregg 1982), some under his signature, others anonymously that he planted in *Ka Elele Hawaii* and the *Polynesian*. His missionary-journalistic zeal involved him in a press scandal in 1848. The *Sandwich Island News* had printed a satirical series that scorned Judd. Judd, with less confidence in free speech than Fornander, allegedly bribed the printer, James Peacock, with $300 to produce the original manuscript so as to ascertain the author. *Sandwich Island News* editor E. A. Rockwell sued Judd in police court for receiving stolen property, but Judd, a member of the king's cabinet, was not subject to arrest and thereby escaped trial (Sheldon n.d.). Judd's admirers praised him as "Hawai'i's friend" who set up the Kingdom's first system of financial accounting and held the Kingdom together (Judd 1960). His detractors, who called him "King Judd," claimed he was power hungry and a mischief maker (Varigny 1968; Joesting 1972). Stubborn, combative, and opinionated, Judd, too, thrived on public controversy.

Under Fornander, the *Weekly Argus* stated its position as "to provide an opposition voice to the government-subsidized Polynesian"

(Jan. 28, 1852). The journal's bedrock causes were that it was against the government selling lands to former missionaries, against legally enforced teetotalism, and especially against the participation of clergy in government—a "self-perpetuating oligarchy." The arguments converged in 1853 during the smallpox epidemic.

Smallpox was not new to the Islands. In 1837, the *Sandwich Island Gazette* warned: "There is a rumor that Small Pox has made its appearance in Honolulu. . . . Extreme caution and watchfullness [sic] will be the only safeguard against its destructiveness" (Apr. 15, 1837). "Caution and watchfullness" were not enough to stay the disastrous epidemic, carried to the Islands on an American ship from California, that struck the Hawaiian population on February 10, 1853. Although a vaccine existed, inoculation was sporadic and voluntary, and the vaccine sometimes lost its potency in the long ocean voyage from the eastern United States around the Horn. In 1853, Fornander's paper called for stricter measures and bitterly quoted from the *Yonkers* (N.Y.) *Herald:* "Manifest Destiny. It is clear from the whole history of the Anglo Saxon race, that its mission is to extirpate all other races with which it may come in contact. Its genius is not more excursive than its touch is fatal. . . . It is an ogre among the races" (Mar. 9, 1853).

In April, two months into the epidemic, nineteen-year-old Alexander Liholiho ascended to the throne as Kamehameha IV. The new king chose Judd to lead a Royal Commission of Public Health. The resources of the commission and the Kingdom were clearly inadequate for the disaster—in a population of 84,000, there were approximately 11,000 cases and 6,000 deaths (Greer 1969c). Representing the government's position, the *Polynesian*, under editor Edwin O. Hall, attempted to downplay the epidemic by filling the paper's columns with information on whaling, shipping, free trade, and temperance. Hall published little on the epidemic even as it raged out of control, never mentioning the unburied bodies lying in houses or on the streets or rooted out of shallow graves and eaten by dogs and hogs. When Hall did infrequently report on the catastrophe, he insisted that the government's ministers were doing all humanly possible to alleviate it. He called the *Weekly Argus* a "sewer of filth" and attempted to explain away the tragic decrease of the Hawaiian race claiming, for example, that estimates of a 300,000 population by Captain James Cook were "far too high," lapsing from his usual clear prose into doublespeak: "The decrease of the population of the islands, contemporaneously with the introduction of christianity and civilization is certainly a result greatly to be regreted [*sic*]. It is one, however, by no means attributable to the former, but in spite of it, nor to the latter, necessarily; but unfortunately so connected with it" (*Poly.*, July 3, 1853).

On his part, Fornander castigated Judd and the Protestant missionaries for preaching that national calamities were a "divine judgment" on Hawaiians. When former missionary Richard Armstrong, head of public education and an influential government leader, blamed the disaster upon the "ignorance and stupidity" and "careless health habits" of the Hawaiians and asked the king to order June 14 as a day "of humiliation, fasting and prayer, that the Almighty may remove from among us the Smallpox," Fornander angrily retorted that these views only confirmed a fatalism to which Hawaiians were prone. Smallpox, he insisted, had a natural cause, not a supernatural one (June 23, 1853).

It was Judd, however, whom Fornander blamed for bearing the most responsibility for the epidemic. Calling him "the White King," the editor accused Judd of taking bribes from ships' captains who wanted to avoid quarantine. Avoiding direct criticism of the king, the *Weekly Argus* argued that the proceedings of the legislature and the cabinet had lost the public's confidence and urged Kamehameha IV to dismiss his ministers.

The "infidel," as Hall called Fornander, contracted the disease himself, and the *Weekly Argus* was not published for five weeks while the editor was incapacitated. He recovered, returned to the print shop, and resumed his cause, strengthened by a petition signed by a "Committee of Thirteen" from a frightened business community. The king asked for resignations from Judd, Armstrong, and two other government leaders and reappointed all except Judd. The young king, sensitive to the situation, took over as health commissioner himself (Kuykendall 1938). Judd returned to his medical practice.

Fornander celebrated his victory editorially in October 1853 and renamed his newspaper the *New Era and Weekly Argus* (1853–1855). The paper's reputation spread, reaching abroad to the United States and England. Once victory was achieved, however, Fornander had fewer causes (Davis 1979). Too, the prosperous mercantile houses, some with connections to the mission, refused to advertise with him, in effect boycotting the paper. The advertisements he was able to procure were mostly from small merchants, boarding houses, carpenters, a "barber and perfumer," an artist, and play houses. Fornander had trouble collecting what little money was owed him, and the *Argus* folded.

Fornander returned to newspapering in 1861, buying out the *Polynesian* in that year and operating it briefly by government subsidy under Kamehameha IV. The government shifted its support, from the *Polynesian* to the *Hawaiian Gazette,* and the *Polynesian* folded in 1864. Fornander continued to write, if with less vituperation, producing the *Sandwich Island Monthly,* a literary and historical magazine, and a three-volume *Account of the Polynesian Race.*

9. The *Advertiser* Enters History

July 2, 1856, witnessed the birth of the *Pacific Commercial Advertiser,* the journal that for a century and a half has been a forceful presence in reporting and shaping the news. Henry M. Whitney, the entrepreneurial son of members of the first company of New England missionaries, created the four-page weekly and accurately predicted that it was "destined . . . to exert more than an ephemeral influence on the industrial and social condition of our community and nation" (*Adv.,* July 2, 1856).

The *Advertiser,* as it has been called from that day to this, became a daily in 1882 and the *Honolulu Advertiser* in 1921. Except from 1870 to 1888, it remained until 1992 in the hands of descendants of American Protestant missionaries. Whitney also began the *Daily Bulletin* in 1882, the forerunner of the *Honolulu Star-Bulletin.* He is thus the parent of Honolulu's two major dailies.

Whitney, to whom newspapering was more than just a business, declared emotionally in the opening edition: "Thank Heaven, the day at length has dawned when the Hawaiian nation can boast a free press, untrammelled by government patronage or party pledges, unbiased by ministerial frowns or favors" (July 2, 1856). Whitney, celebrating the Fourth of July, claimed his paper would be truly independent and free. He welcomed the formation of an "American Club."

Whitney's expression was sincere but inaccurate. The *Advertiser,* from Whitney's day to this, on each occasion of the newspaper's anniversary, claims that Whitney introduced a free press to the Islands. It overlooks the obvious, that the *Sandwich Island Gazette* pioneered that achievement in 1836. What Whitney meant was that his newspaper, unlike its contemporary, the *Polynesian,* was "free" of government control—the *Polynesian* was subsidized from 1844 to 1861.

Henry Whitney's real accomplishment is twofold. One, he produced the Islands' first successful, commercial, English language newspaper, which, except for one lapse, represented those who were

53

to determine Hawai'i's future. Two, he produced the longest-running and most successful Hawaiian language journal, *Ka Nupepa Kuokoa* (The independent newspaper) (1861–1927).

Whitney's emotional outburst stemmed from a mixture of concerns. From a missionary family who did not enrich themselves, Whitney was always acutely aware of having to make a living. It galled him that the *Polynesian,* by printing all public announcements, siphoned off potential revenue. Too, non-Americans occasionally edited the *Polynesian.* But through all the contradictions of his complicated personality, including his evolution from a young idealist to an old conservative, the single unifying thread in him was a total belief in American culture and values. Or as he boasted in his reminiscences, the *Advertiser* "was independent in politics always, but an ardent advocate of annexation to the United States" (*Adv.,* July 2, 1900).

Whitney's fervent pro-Americanism was typical of American papers in the United States during his time. The *Advertiser* in the nineteenth century, however, was ostensibly a foreign language paper. Among foreign language journals, it was (and is) common for the leaders to feel strongly patriotic to their native countries (Park 1922; Tebbel 1963). Their descendants, however, even though they may have a nostalgia for their parents' country of birth, usually identify with the new land. Not so Whitney and his fellow journalists of missionary descent. Although they were born in Hawai'i, fluent in Hawaiian, and, like Whitney, called Kamehameha IV "our Sovereign," they identified with their parents' "home," the United States. The *Advertiser* was an evangelical cheerleader, "a trumpet of jubilee" (Altschull 1990), the phrase an apt description of journalistic jingoism that arose out of geographic insularity in remote places like the American West and Hawai'i. A remarkable number of American papers, in fact, have been born on the Fourth of July.

Whitney's success with periodicals was itself part of his Americanism. Mission children in the mission's early years were sent "home" to America for schooling to ensure that they would not succumb to Hawaiian ways. Sent to New York in his youth, Whitney subsequently took up farming, then the printing trade, eventually working in New York City for the *New York Commercial Advertiser* (1831–1889) (Dutton 1955). Whitney used this paper as his model for the *Pacific Commercial Advertiser.*

Whitney returned to the Islands with an American wife in 1849 to work first in the Polynesian office as a printer for the Hawaiian government, then as postmaster after 1850. Using a crude set of forms, the clever printer combined his offices and produced the one-, five-, and thirteen-cent stamps, today known as the "Missionaries" and among the rarest stamps in the world (Dutton 1955).

In 1856, Whitney set up his new enterprise in a small frame building on Printers' Row, where he also operated a stationery store and bookshop. Even before its debut, the prospect of a new journal aroused considerable interest in the foreign community. In 1855, David L. Gregg, U.S. commissioner to the Hawaiian Kingdom, recorded in his diary that word was abroad of the paper's imminent appearance (Gregg 1982). The prospective editor was only awaiting the arrival of a new press from Boston. Impatient with the delay, Whitney bought the mission's old equipment for $1,300 that he was to repay in printed matter (*Encyclopedia of Hawai'i* 1980).

Whitney produced the *Advertiser* on a Washington handpress with a capacity of 600 copies per hour. Circulation was about 1,000 weekly, swelling to 1,500 during the whaling season. At the end of the first three weeks, the newspaper claimed 494 subscribers, including 75 Native Hawaiians. A subscription cost six dollars for a year. Within the year, Whitney employed a staff of six and printed on a new Adams Power Press that could produce several thousand pages per hour.

Whitney's first issue stated that he was responding to the "necessity for a reliable domestic Newspaper, devoted to inter-island Commerce, Agriculture and the whaling interests in the Pacific." The *Advertiser*'s title or "flag" featured a woodcut of Honolulu Harbor filled with ships. Whitney's formula was surefire—to present lots of local news, such as the marriage of Kamehameha IV, foreign events like U.S. elections, items on town recreation, verse and short fiction, and letters to the editor, and to solicit many advertisements, from small shops and services to large wholesalers and sugar planters.

In the second issue, Whitney proudly recounted the history of Independence Day celebrations in the Islands. In 1814, with three American ships in the harbor, Kamehameha I, "the warm friend of the foreigner," offered a "liberal feast" to all. "It was a grand day," said Whitney without irony, in spite of "the hand of a seaman blown off in the discharge of a canon" [*sic*] salute (July 10, 1856). At the beginning of the American Civil War, Whitney asked rhetorically, "But why celebrate the Fourth of July upon foreign soil?" He answered that "our country" is in danger at present (July 11, 1861).

Wishing to expand his outreach, Whitney first printed the fourth page of the *Advertiser* in Hawaiian and entitled it *Ka Hoku Loa o Hawaii* (The morning star of Hawaii). In 1861, Whitney developed this into its own four-page paper, *Ka Nupepa Kuokoa.*

Exhibiting Whitney's youthful independence, articles in early editions of the *Advertiser* and *Kuokoa,* for example, expressed religious tolerance, even favoring the establishment of the Episcopal Church. Nor did Whitney become involved in the frequent newspaper quarrels between the Protestant and Catholic missions. But when Whitney attacked the profits of the planter-business-missionary alliance, it was a different story. Whitney, a committed abolitionist, waged a two-year campaign, from 1868 to 1870, against the contract labor system that imported Asians for work in the sugar industry and which Whitney called "slavery." Whitney and *Kuokoa* coeditor, the Reverend Luther H. Gulick, a missionary son and missionary himself, reported abuses of the workers and asked for the abolition of "the coolie system" and repeal of certain sections of the Masters and Servants Act (Hawaiian Ethnological Notes n.d.).

Whitney deeply believed in the Jeffersonian ideal of an agricultural nation. He wanted to recreate in Hawai'i an American countryside populated with Hawaiians remodeled into farmers. He reprinted articles from periodicals abroad on sheep grazing and cotton growing and proposed dividing sugar lands into 100-and 200-acre plots so that farmers could cooperatively mill their produce, thereby preventing the good lands from being absorbed by a few "bloated monopolists."

"Slavery"? "Bloated monopolists"? With statements like these, the young editor threatened those who had spawned and supported him. Maui planters brought him to heel in August 1870 by stopping the flow of blood to the newspaper's lifeline—advertising. Within one month, Whitney, financially and emotionally drained, sold out to printers James H. Black and William Auld. Financed by the planters, Black and Auld immediately reversed the editorial line, and advertisements quickly returned to the *Advertiser's* pages. Whitney always denied that he had sold the newspaper under duress. He returned to the orthodox fold, however, later editing the *Hawaiian Gazette* and the *Planters' Monthly,* a magazine, and remained in the fold until his death in 1904.

Interestingly, Whitney was able to maintain leadership of *Kuokoa* even when he lost the *Advertiser.* Perhaps the establishment found *Kuokoa* less threatening. Its significance should not be underestimated, however. Whitney hired capable Hawaiian editors, such as Joseph Kawainui, S. K. Mahoe, and J. M. Poepoe, who published what turned out to be materials of the greatest importance to Hawaiian history (Hawaiian Ethnological Notes n.d.). In *Kuokoa* are geneologies, tales of gods and goddesses, vivid descriptions of Hawaiian birds, bird catching and fishing practices, instructions on canoe building, summaries of medical practices, accounts of travel through the Islands, and how to speak the Hawaiian language correctly. In its pages, too, first appeared the writings of John Papa Ii and Samuel M. Kamakau, which were later gathered together respectively as *Fragments of Hawaiian History* (1959) and *The Ruling Chiefs of Hawaii* (1961).

Attesting to the paper's popularity among Native Hawaiians, who otherwise largely rejected the establishment press, *Kuokoa* achieved a circulation of 5,000 in the nineteenth century, far beyond that of the *Advertiser*. *Kuokoa* was enhanced with lithographic illustrations and was the first to use color in local newspapers, an engraving of "Our Hawaiian Flag" in red and blue in the New Year edition of January 1, 1862. Rising above its narrow mission to "improve" the Hawaiians, *Kuokoa* has made a lasting contribution as a rich source of Hawaiian history, thus serving to preserve what Whitney both loved and hated.

Love and hate—love for the Islands and the Hawaiian language; contempt for Hawaiians. A few examples of Whitney's basic ethnocentrism should suffice, as in his editorials on the inferiority of Hawaiians and the evil of the hula. Whitney wrote:

> The intellectual and physical improvement of the native race . . . shall be sought for by any true philanthropist residing here. Though inferior in every respect to their European or American brethren, they are not to be . . . wholly despised. . . . They are destined to be laborers in developing the capital of the country. . . . In proportion as they come in contact with the foreigner, and acquire correct habits, skill and industry, in that proportion do they rise in our estimation, and command a higher reward for their services. (*Adv.*, Mar. 5, 1857)

In his periodic tirades against the "pagan" hula and its "ruinous influence," he fumed:

> The fairest girls . . . in their wild demented state . . . appeared before the spectators. . . . The dance consisted of gestures and posturings indicative of licentious acts, accompanied with music and often with the most vulgar and unchaste songs which the tongue is capable of uttering. . . .

Not only are they demoralizing in their tendency to excite in the spectators the vilest licentiousness, but they have another equally debasing influence, in creating indolence. (*Adv.*, Apr. 21, 1859)

Yet there is another paradox. At the same time that he deplored Hawaiian culture, Whitney, in many articles in the *Advertiser* and the *Hawaiian Gazette*, praised the Islands' uniqueness. His *Hawaiian Guide Book for Travelers* (1875) was the first book on tourism, leading historian Ralph Kuykendall to declare that "Whitney may rightly be counted on as one of the important promoters of the Hawaiian tourist industry" (Kuykendall 1967). Whitney thus made another permanent mark on the Islands' future.

10. A Hawaiian Nationalist Press Is Born

The birth of a vernacular Hawaiian language press in 1861 received scant mention beyond Samuel Damon, editor of the *Friend,* commenting upon Hawaiians' "attachment to newspapers" (*Friend,* Jan. 1, 1862). Yet it was a most significant event. In the early years, control of Hawaiian language publications rested with Protestant missionaries, their descendants, or the Hawaiian government. None spoke directly for Native Hawaiians. It was a remarkable achievement that within three short decades of acquiring literacy and a newspaper technology Native Hawaiians set up and controlled their own press.

The origin of a Hawaiian nationalist press—for such it was from its first day—is a striking illustration of literacy joined to a newspaper technology conferring empowerment. Those involved gain a sense of participating in history. Nationalist newspapers were to lead the fight for Hawaiian independence in the 1880s and 1890s. That they lost the battle against overwhelming odds in no way detracts from their singular achievement. A vivid example of a people's resiliency, it was this press that laid the foundation for the arguments for Hawaiian sovereignty that would reemerge in the late twentieth century. As Esther K. Mookini has said in her pioneering work on Hawaiian newspapers, "[they] were not only reflections of politics and culture in its many dimensions; but primary instruments of movements and individuals, and influences on events, trends and attitudes. Hawaiian newspapers are . . . indispensable sources for every aspect of our history. In their early, pioneering achievements, they also constitute an important chapter in the history of American and Pacific journalism" (Mookini 1974).

Chief David Kalākaua sponsored *Ka Hoku o ka Pakipika* (The star of the Pacific) (1861–1863), the first Hawaiian language paper produced solely by Native Hawaiians. The future king, known affectionately to his people as "editor king," was the first of many educated leaders to support journals. Editors of *Ka Hoku* included J. K. Kaunamano and G. W. Mila. Another paper that Kalākaua spon-

A vigorous Hawaiian nationalist press emerged in the 1860s, within just three decades of the introduction of a newspaper technology to the Islands. It quickly gained and held the largest circulation and the majority of readers until the century's end. (Hawaiian Historical Society)

sored was the daily *Ka Manawa* (The times) (1870), which appeared just four years after the first English language daily, the *Daily Hawaiian Herald* (1866). (Kalākaua also backed a literary journal, *Ka Hoku o ke Kai*, in 1883.)

The Hawaiian nationalist press displayed a rich diversity in points of view (Johnson 1976; Hawaiian Ethnological Notes n.d.). But they were united in sharing several basic themes that were markedly different from those of establishment papers: one, a conviction that Hawaiians knew what was best for themselves; two, an awareness that the decline of the native population was a serious matter; three, an insistence that Hawai'i remain an independent nation; four, a deep respect for the monarchy; and five, a great love for their land.

From their first days, these papers expressed self-confidence, reminding readers that the haole did not know what was best for Hawaiians. Editor S. K. Kaolanui, for example, angry at the *Advertiser* and *Kuokoa* for their continuous promotion of American institutions and culture, accused owner Whitney of being "rich and well-situated" and the "limited" voice of haole businessmen. Editors were unafraid of printing criticism against themselves, as when Kaolanui, in *Ka Hoku o ka Pakipika* (Nov. 11, 1861; July 3, 1862) ran a letter from "a haole missionary descendant" requesting that the paper stop printing "pagan chants" and substitute "civilized hymns" (trans., Hawaiian Ethnological Notes n.d.).

A recurring, more somber theme was that of the decline of the native population, as in this melancholy passage by one J. H. Kanepuu of Maunalua (near Koko Head), again in *Ka Hoku o ka Pakipika* (May 1, 1862):

Ke Emi Ana o na Kanaka
(The Decrease of the Population)

In the year 1852 and a little later the population of these places were seen to be large, Niu, Kuli'ou'ou I, Kuli'ou'ou II, Koko, Keawāwa, Haha'i-one and . . . Maunalua. There were over three hundred and ten, but in the month of April, 1862, only a hundred and forty are found on these lands. . . . One third of these children are not old enough for school and almost half of the remainder just wander away with their parents for several weeks and then return. So it goes.

    Half of . . . the adults are aged ones. Many have died and many have moved away. . . . Some haven't any place to plant sweet

potatoes in mounds on these lands and the places are also over-
run by animals. Many of those who remain just wander about
seeking a means of livelihood else-where. (trans., Hawaiian Ethnological Notes n.d.)

But the newspapers also exhibited views that were less pessimistic.
Many Hawaiian papers, as is true of newspapers everywhere that are
agents of empowerment, were optimistically entitled, such as *Ke Au
Okoa* (The new era) (1865–1873). *Ke Au Okoa* was edited by the
many-faceted and energetic John Makini Kapena, a relative of
Kalākaua's, who served as governor of Maui, in the House of Nobles,
as minister of Finance, and as minister of Foreign Affairs. Kapena in
1874 accompanied the king to Washington, D.C., to gain a reciprocity treaty with the United States. He traveled, too, to Japan in 1882
in the interest of immigration and to accompany three Hawaiian
youths who were to study there (Quigg 1988).

Ke Au Okoa set several patterns that would be followed by
Hawaiian language papers into the twentieth century. It reported on
local events as well as items of interest from abroad, such as the
death of Abraham Lincoln. It ran tables of dates important to Hawaiian history. It featured travel literature, like "Traveling About Molokai" and a "Visit to Niihau."

These newspapers also achieved a standard of quality illustrative
of literary talent that has always drawn writers into journalism (Ben
Franklin, Mark Twain, Ernest Hemingway). *Ke Au Akoa* printed
sketches by Samuel M. Kamakau, who was a government official
under Kamehameha III, and by David Malo, whose articles would
later be gathered together as *Ka Moolelo Hawaii, Hawaiian Antiq-
uities* (1903). More importantly, the newspapers encouraged the continuance of the Hawaiian language and kept alive the Hawaiian
culture.

11. "A New Era Has Dawned": Sugar Is King

Even as a nationalist press advocating Hawaiian independence was gaining in numbers and readers, an opposite force was propelling Hawai'i toward loss of its independence. The role of establishment papers as agents in gaining a consensus for public and private sector policies that would yoke Hawai'i to America is clearly evident in the period that led up to a reciprocity treaty being signed between the two countries. Signed in 1875 and implemented in 1876, the treaty allowed for the mutual admittance of products duty free. It included rice and other commodities, but sugar was the primary product. Planters were now assured of their profits for at least seven years, with the likelihood of extensions (Kuykendall 1953). In essence, the newspapers promoted government support of private enterprise through a combination of public-private protectionist capitalism, a system that would become permanently embedded in the economics of the Islands.

Prior to 1875, Hawaiian newspapers expressed a wide range of opinions on reciprocity. Those run by the establishment, like *Kuokoa*, promoted the treaty. Those outside the establishment mostly opposed it. The latter feared precisely what American residents desired—that the pact would tie Hawai'i so closely to America that annexation would be inevitable. Hawaiian kings, representing a skeptical native public, had varying degrees of reservations, for they saw the dangers of entanglement with their powerful neighbor. But they came to hope that the treaty and a prosperous Hawai'i could be a bulwark against annexation. In the 1870s, Hawaiian language papers loyally supported David Kalākaua, especially during his campaign for the throne, when he himself shifted from opposing to backing the treaty.

All the English language journals favored reciprocity, and they only raised questions on how to achieve a treaty. For example: should land concessions be offered to the United States as an inducement; what races were to be recruited for labor; if reciprocity failed, should annexation then be sought.

From their earliest days, all the English language papers preached the importance of sugar to Hawai'i's economy. In 1837, the *Sandwich Island Gazette* began the practice of running sugar export statistics. In 1848, after the United States acquired California from Mexico and a reciprocity treaty was first proposed, the *Polynesian* was its chief proponent. The *Polynesian* and the *Hawaiian Gazette* introduced another practice that has continued to aid and abet the industry. Free laudatory features or "puffs," such as articles on the importance of digging artesian wells to provide water for expanding cane field acreage, were positioned next to advertisements paid for by the industry.

Underlying the urgency to gain a protected industry was the recurrence of boom and bust cycles. The 1851 depression caused the *Polynesian* to urge: "If . . . our present treaty with the United States could be so modified as to admit our sugars into California and Oregon free, as our coffee now is, an equivalent could be made by allowing their lumber, flour and salmon to be introduced to these islands free. Such a concession would operate favorably upon . . . the commerce and business generally of all concerned" (Jan. 17, 1852). In rhetoric to become familiar, the paper lamented the absence of reciprocity: "We groan under burdens. . . . Our hands are tied, while theirs [the Pacific states] are free. . . . We can make sugar of the very best quality, but we want a market for it, unencumbered by a burdensome duty of 30 per cent" (Jan. 31, 1852).

In the next decade, sugar exports increased during the American Civil War, then disastrously fell at the war's end. The *Hawaiian Gazette*, adopted as the official paper by Kamehameha V's government, picked up the reciprocity refrain. Under the editorship of an American dentist, John Mott-Smith, who had arrived in Honolulu via the California gold fields and then joined the government, the *Gazette* pleaded for action, joining the business and planter community and the king in pressuring the Native Hawaiian legislature: "The Legislature [now] impressed with the necessity of encouraging agriculture, has resolved to come forward in aid of private enterprise. Both his Excellency the Minister of Finance [Charles De Varigny] and his Honor Judge [George M.] Robertson expressed their belief that the Government will cooperate with the Society in any desirable object connected with agricultural improvements" (May 27, 1865).

The *Gazette* further contributed to the climate of favorable opinion by printing import and export statistics of all products to and from America and figures on sugar consumption worldwide—or, as it put it, sugar consumed by even "the smallest civilized European consumers" (Apr. 15, 1868). Citing sugar tonnage figures, the *Gazette* added that "beyond a doubt, a new era has dawned" in which sugar is the mainstay "of our Islands" (June 17, 1865).

The intensity of newspaper campaigns mirrored the goal's elusiveness. Three of the four requisites for full development of Hawaiian agriculture had been met by 1865 — land, labor, and capital. Land was made available by the Mahele of 1848. Labor needs were provided by the Masters and Servants Act of 1852, the organization of the Bureau of Immigration in 1864, and the union of the Planters' Society (formed in 1864) with the Royal Hawaiian Agricultural Society in 1865. The fourth, however, a duty free market, had yet to be gained (Kuykendall 1953). The treaty had powerful foes abroad: mainly, Southern congressmen protective of their agricultural interests and fearful of the racial composition of the Islands; and California sugar refiners who didn't want competition. California papers, especially the *Alta California* (1849–1863?) and the *San Francisco Chronicle* (1869–) fought the treaty.

Increasing the fervor of its arguments, the English language press promoted the travel of successive government emissaries to Washington, D.C. The *Advertiser* urged one emissary, (Civil War) General Edward M. McCook, U.S. minister to Hawai'i, to present to America the fundamental and overriding reason for a treaty: "American influence has always been, and must ever continue to be, the paramount influence here, by the simple force of circumstances and natural causes" (*Adv.*, Jan. 16, 1867).

Some editors allowed themselves to believe that reciprocity would enable Hawai'i to remain independent. So argued Samuel Damon in the pages of the *Friend*. Writing for the *Gazette*, Mott-Smith stated that reciprocity would be "a true Hawaiian policy ... most advantageous to all, both Hawaiian and foreign, whose homes are upon this soil" (*Gaz.*, Jan. 22, 1868).

As the campaign gained momentum in the early 1870s, another editor, W. L. Green, first advanced the suggestion that Pearl Harbor be leased to the United States for fifty years (*Adv.*, Feb. 8, 1873). But this proposal faced mounting resistance from Hawaiians who opposed any land cessions, and Green, with his eye on office, backed off. Kalākaua as king rewarded Green by appointing him minister of Foreign Affairs.

In 1874, yet another event connected to reciprocity—American-style elections—involved the newspapers as agents of change. Lunalilo had died without naming an heir. For the first time, an American-style election was held for the throne. The contest between David Kalākaua and Dowager Queen Emma employed typical American tactics, including lavish dissemination of printed bulletins and posters that urged the public to support one side or the other. These bulletins adopted inflammatory tactics that were only surpassed by huge political rallies complete with torchlight parades. The *Advertiser,* under planter-supported editors Black and Auld—they had replaced Henry Whitney when he had defied planter interests and either quit the paper or was forced out—backed David Kalākaua. On the dowager queen's behalf, Whitney printed and distributed a bulletin in Hawaiian that supported her candidacy. Copies were defaced, very likely by employees of Black and Auld who scratched over the print with such statements as, "We do not wish to see the petticoat putting on britches." Kalākaua was elected, and riots broke out. Order was finally restored by 200 American marines and British sailors deployed from ships in Honolulu Harbor, and the victorious *Advertiser* expressed how very grateful it was for their intercession.

In the meantime, Kalākaua, turned for additional support to the bilingual *Nuhou* (News) (1873–1874). *Nuhou* was run by Walter Murray Gibson whose task was to not just campaign for Kalākaua but to address those Hawaiian language papers opposed to reciprocity, like *Ke Au Okoa.* Edited by John M. Kapena, *Ke Au Okoa* had argued that the treaty would "not be for the mass of the people but for a few" (trans., *Adv.,* Mar. 24, 1868).

Nuhou revealed the inherent contradictions in its and Kalākaua's position. *Nuhou's* slogan was "Hawaii for the Hawaiians." Editor Kipikona (Gibson) claimed that the paper advanced "the well being and prosperity of the country." It vigorously opposed ceding any land to any country and fiercely defended Hawaiian sovereignty. Yet the nature of that sovereignty had already changed, from an inherited chiefdom to one by election, and reciprocity, rather than guaranteeing autonomy, would make Hawai'i more dependent than ever on the United States. *Nuhou,* only in print for fourteen months, was quite effective. With a circulation of four to five thousand, it was double the size of any other Hawaiian language periodical.

Gibson absorbed the financially strapped *Ke Au Okoa,* merging it with *Nuhou,* and John D. Kapena abandoned his opposition to reciprocity and joined the king's party when Kalākaua traveled to Washington, D.C. in 1874 in pursuit of the treaty. They sailed on U.S. naval vessels as guests of the American government, an act with lit-

The Hawaiian language paper, *Nupepa Kuokoa*, displaying the Hawaiian flag in this edition of January 7, 1871, nevertheless represented establishment opinion and successfully campaigned for a reciprocity treaty with the United States. (Hawai'i State Archives)

eral and symbolic implications. The English language press heaped praise upon the king and his successful journey.

In 1876, less than a year after the treaty went into effect, the *Hawaiian Gazette* proclaimed that sugar was king (June 17, 1877). A future newspaper editor expressed doubts still held by many Hawaiians—but in private. Joseph Kahooluhi Nawahī, a legislator from the Puna District, who would work on several nationalist newspapers and publish *Ke Aloha Aina* (The patriot) (1895–1920), wrote in his private papers, "The treaty of reciprocity becoming law for the land will be the first of annexation, . . . and the kingdom, its flag, its independence, and, its people will become naught. . . . will be lost" (Sheldon 1988).

For reciprocity did not ultimately satisfy American interests. Land cessions would follow, as in the granting to America in 1887 of exclusive coaling rights at Pearl Harbor, and in ceding to the United States an entire country in 1898.

12. The Politics of Health

In reporting the scourges that struck the Hawaiian people, newspapers chose sides according to whether they functioned as cultural imperialists or cultural relativists (Lim-Chong 1978). It should be no surprise that the American-dominated establishment press usually fell into the cultural imperialist camp. When they talked about diseases, they explained them as moral failings or as sins of the flesh. This view they especially applied to venereal diseases because the primary method of transmitting them was through sexual contact. Cultural relativists, by contrast, viewed disease as physical in origin and therefore treatable.

Prior to the arrival of Captain James Cook and his men in 1778, Native Hawaiians had lived in isolation for a thousand years. They brilliantly adapted medicine, of ancient origin with its roots in survival, to their environment. Hawaiians were among the healthiest people in the world. From 1778 on, the native population, without immunities to disease, was almost destroyed by the "gifts of civilization"—Dr. O. A. Bushnell's ironic phrase for the alien germs that entered Hawai'i from Europe, America, and Asia (Bushnell 1993). Hawaiian medicine's healing power diminished with the repeated onslaught of diseases and by being banned by the Protestant missionary-controlled government after midcentury. As to Western medicine, it was a crude affair at best: doctors prescribed morphine for pain, calomel and Epsom salts for internal disorders, wine as a tonic, and bloodletting for anything "serious."

Before newspapers, private hospitals had been set up for various nationalities beginning in 1833. After its inception, the *Sandwich Island Gazette* recommended local boards of health, which were authorized in 1839. In 1849, the *Polynesian* proposed that the government finance hospitals. The smallpox epidemic of 1853 and the continued decline of the population further demonstrated the desperate inadequacy of health services.

Kamehameha IV's address to the 1855 legislature declared, "The decrease of our population ... is a subject, in comparison with which all others sink into insignificance" (Kuykendall 1953). Venereal diseases were likely the single greatest cause of death in that these struck at the core of regeneration: sterility or death for adults, and sick or stillborn babies. There were no effective cures for gonorrhea and syphilis. The king took steps for the government to set up hospitals, with Queen Emma joining the king in this endeavor, and to regulate prostitution. Between 1855 to 1860, the king's two proposals were an Act to Institute Hospitals for the Sick Poor, signed into law on May 15, 1855, but not implemented until 1859, and the Act to Mitigate Evils and Disease Arising from Prostitution, passed by the legislature in 1860.

The first act was only implemented after direct appeals by the king and queen, who personally raised money in the community and donated their own funds. The king appointed a five-member board that included only one minister of the gospel, Samuel C. Damon, who sometimes took positions independent of the Protestant mission and, in the pages of his newspaper, the *Friend*, supported a government hospital. In the meantime, before the hospital was built, Director William Hillebrand, a practical German physician, began to treat adult female patients at a temporary dispensary, thus opening the way for the treatment of prostitutes (Greer 1969a).

Two newspapers defined the conflict. The *Advertiser* spoke for those who argued that the measures were immoral, expensive, and unnecessary. The *Polynesian* spoke for those who viewed the proposals as humane and essential to the well-being of the entire community. *Advertiser* editor Henry M. Whitney strongly, even rabidly, opposed any health measures connected to prostitution. Calvinists held a basic, cruel assumption that the biblical "wages of sin are death." The Islanders, paying the price for their "immorality," were doomed to disappear. Conversely, the *Polynesian* under the editorship of Charles Gordon Hopkins, an enlightened Englishman (he served as editor from 1848 to 1849 and again from 1856 to 1860), advanced the government position of favoring the acts.

In response to the first act to organize hospitals, the *Advertiser* repeatedly warned against unnecessary governmental expenses. When the government purchased permanent acreage "mauka on Beretania" and "running partly up Punchbowl" for a proposed two-story hospital building, Whitney expressed concern for the area's "property values," recommending that the land be "fenced in" and "a good structure erected" so that the value of the property in the vicinity be "enhanced" (Feb. 2, 1860). There was only a small, grudging notice of ground-breaking ceremonies presided over by the king. And Whitney printed without comment the year-end report by the hospital's board of trustees in which they expressed "a high degree of satisfaction" with the success of the Institution" (June 27, 1860).

The Act to Mitigate Evils and Disease Arising from Prostitution involved a system of registering, examining, and treating the women. Hopkins and the *Polynesian* spoke for passage of the act on the basis that the foundation of every state is in its population and that the state must assist the public in protecting themselves and must "build up or repair the social fences" (*Poly.*, Aug. 4, 1860). An Anglican (Episcopalian), Hopkins advised those against the measure that they would do well to practice Christian charity.

In rebuttal, the *Advertiser* argued that the government should not come between "Scripture and the people." Whitney printed a series of unsigned letters opposed to the act. The following is typical: "A Hospital for the poor dying natives! This looks well in print, and [may] be of use; and, were it not to come in close proximity with several other things, bearing a different aspect, I would pronounce it benevolent. . . . [but] I would respectfully inquire: Is there not some cheaper and more effectual way to meet the necessities of the people than those now before the Legislature?" (Feb. 10, 1859). Whitney's own editorials vacillated between attacking "the rank hypocrisy of the measure" and hoping to find it "inoperative" (Aug. 23, 1860).

The act was passed, and the *Polynesian* hailed it as "a blessing to humanity" (Aug. 25, 1860), whereby the *Advertiser* printed another anonymous letter, this one directly attacking Hopkins: "The Editor of the Government Prostitution Organ, intoxicated with his success in lobbying through . . . [the] bill . . . in patronizing lust and insuring a class for whom he seems to have a particular affection, against the natural consequences of their favorite amusements, fairly bursts with exultation while overflowing with bitterness against all who have had the manliness to oppose this act." To this writer, "The Act to Mitigate," instead of "driving the guilty perpetrators of such shameless deeds into the dark . . . it organizes them into a sisterhood . . . and at the public expense employs a state physician to shield them from the natural and terrible penalty for the infraction of a Divine Law" (Aug. 30, 1860).

To her great credit, Queen Emma ignored the establishment papers and bequeathed the bulk of her estate to the hospital (today, the Queen's Medical Center in Honolulu). Hopkins, who later served as secretary to the queen, declared that the causes he was most proud of supporting in his life were his newspaper battles for hospitals and for regulating prostitution (*Poly.*, Oct. 6, 1860).

The politics of health by no means died in 1860; the debate on prostitution continues into this century (Hobson 1987; Klaidman 1991; Ziporyn 1988). Among the cultural imperialists who are primarily concerned with what is good for business a new argument arose. For example, in 1907 and 1908 the *Advertiser* raised the old moralistic arguments and urged Board of Health president Lucius E. Pinkham (later a territorial governor) to close down the Iwilei district where the brothels were concentrated. The Board of Health controlled the brothels through periodic examinations and health certification of the women. The *Evening Bulletin* demurred, replying that business would suffer if the U.S. fleet were not accommodated: "A little more of this alleged morality business and Honolulu's visions of the glories of the Fleet will go glimmering" (Apr. 8, 1908). Regulation continued.

Times have changed—somewhat. During World War II, the major dailies closed ranks behind "what's good for business." When higher military echelons expressed alarm at the sight of hundreds of men in military uniform lined up in broad daylight outside the brothels on River and Hotel Streets, awaiting their turn, the *Advertiser* and the *Star-Bulletin* both feared that Hawai'i would be deprived of income if the armed forces followed through on their threat to move Pacific headquarters westward if there wasn't a cleanup. Both papers editorialized for the closing of Honolulu's "active houses of prostitution" (*Star-Bull.*, Sept. 21, 1944). The houses were shut down, and the prostitutes dispersed into Honolulu's residential neighborhoods (O'Hara 1944) and later onto the streets of Waikīkī. Venereal disease, unchecked by any system of medical inspection and indiscriminately attacking all ethnic groups, has been on the increase ever since.

PART III

Nationalists versus the Oligarchy: An Uneven Battle—1887–1899

13. A Pan-Pacific Dream

Previous to the reign of King Kalākaua, and regardless of their categories, if newspapers opposed a king or his policies, they were careful to confine their criticism to cabinet members, advisers, or legislators. They never attacked the king himself.

From 1880 on, the concept of a Pan-Pacific confederacy formed the ideological background for projects undertaken during Kalākaua's reign and became the focus of the establishment's wrath. The English language editors, except for the king's ally, Walter Murray Gibson, and two or three moderate newsmen, aimed their invective and ridicule at the government in general and Kalākaua personally. Their rhetoric, emboldened as the king became more vulnerable, culminated in curbing his authority by the imposition upon him of the Bayonet Constitution of 1887. This act was the harbinger, within the space of six short years, of the overthrow of the entire Hawaiian monarchical system. The rhetoric of these newspapers so influenced history's assessment of Kalākaua—Gavan Daws' successful *Shoal of Time* (1968) refers to these years as "the Empire of the Calabash," a phrase taken from the hostile *Hawaiian Gazette*—that until recently Kalākaua was accorded little respect or recognition for his significant contributions.

Earlier, when establishment newsmen spoke of a confederacy with Hawai'i as the leader and protector of Pacific island nations, the idea was accorded some respect. Australian journalist Charles St. Julian (1818–1872) first articulated the idea, and the *Polynesian* reprinted it in June 1855. St. Julian, in fact, was in the employ of Kamehameha III's government, from 1853 to 1872, as a political and commercial agent to those islands "of the Pacific not under the protection or sovereignty of any European government" (Kuykendall 1967).

In 1877, Henry L. Sheldon, formerly an oppositionist newsman, had joined the establishment *Advertiser* and repeated the concept: "Already the Maoris of New Zealand have allowed the British to get a definite footing. . . . Their independence is now lost for ever. . . . On

75

the neighborly continents of North and South America and Asia, the colored races have not advanced under the whites either socially or religiously, like the people of the Hawaiian Islands. The conclusion is, that the Polynesians ought to strive to maintain what suits them best—their national independence . . . [and] adopt a common flag" (*Adv.*, Nov. 17, 1877).

By 1880, the vision and supporting events lost the rising oligarchy's sympathy, these events including: an Italian adventurer's presence, a coinage controversy, an opium scandal, and the voyage of the *Kaimiloa* to Samoa. Too, the vision collided with American aspirations for Hawai'i. In essence, the dream was a century ahead of its time. In the 1960s, when Governor John Burns advanced the concept of a "Pacific Century," mainstream papers would wholeheartedly adopt it. In the 1880s, establishment papers fastened upon it to sink the dream, Gibson, and the king.

Controversy first focused upon a globe-trotting adventurer, Celso Caesar Moreno, and led to a public relations disaster for the king. Moreno, from Italy, had met the king in 1874 in Washington, D.C., when Kalākaua traveled there in search of a reciprocity treaty (Kuykendall 1967). Moreno's own dreams of empire included laying an ocean cable between Asia and America and making Honolulu the opium processing center for the Pacific. Arriving in Hawai'i in 1879, Moreno, only months after his arrival in 1880, became Hawaiian minister of Foreign Affairs. The appointment enraged establishment journals that labeled him a "pretentious stranger," a "fraud," and the king's "evil" adviser (*Adv.*, June 12, 1880). The *Hawaiian Gazette* fumed, "Our Government is at present like the house built on the sand, it has no foundation" (Sept. 15, 1880). An embarrassed king cleverly got rid of his friend by having him accompany young Hawaiian scholars who were to study in Europe. But the damage was done—henceforth, the papers would directly attack the king.

The next major controversy directly involved a newspaper and newspaperman. The dream of empire had fully taken hold in Walter Murray Gibson, who believed that he was of noble English birth (Daws 1980). He pursued his destiny around the globe, turning up in Salt Lake City, where he affiliated with the Church of the Latter Day Saints, then in Hawai'i, in 1861, where he founded the Mormon community at Pālāwai on Lāna'i. Seeking a larger arena for his talents, Gibson moved to O'ahu where he gained the confidence of the king and rapidly rose to a position of influence.

Gibson proved his loyalty when he published *Nuhou* (The news)

(1873–1874), as a campaign paper for Kalākaua's successful bid for the throne. In August 1880, Gibson took over the principal English language daily, the *Advertiser*, to give the king a friendly voice. But indicative of the precarious nature of the enterprise, Gibson bought the *Advertiser* on borrowed money. He struck an agreement with minister of the Interior John E. Bush, by which the government advanced $15,000 and Gibson agreed to do public printing to work off the loan. Claus Spreckles, sugar and shipping magnate, banker, and the largest foreign investor in the Islands, probably put up the additional $10,000 of the total $15,000 purchase price (Kuykendall 1967; Gibson 1973). Spreckles was a businessman first, whose loyalty was to the profit margin. By contrast, the idealistic Gibson viewed his papers as instruments to advance the health and well-being of the native population and to support the king.

At this point, along with the sharp increase in hostility to the monarchy, there was a sharp increase in the numbers of papers, almost doubling. These provided a widening public arena for the controversies (Chapin 1984). The English language journals reached far fewer readers than the Hawaiian language papers. No English language paper could claim more than 1,500 to 2,000 circulation, except for the *Advertiser* when Gibson ran it, while a Hawaiian nationalistic press had papers reaching from 4,000 to 7,000 each. But in actuality, those run by the planter-missionary-business alliance, regardless of fewer readers, were gathering the power to enforce their will. Power only appeared to be in the hands of Walter Murray Gibson, who with five newspapers seemed to be a kind of local press lord (Seldes 1938).

The establishment lineup was formidable. It furnishes an excellent example of the way a power structure meshes its political, economic, and social interests with journalism. In English, there was the *Daily Bulletin, Daily Hawaiian, Daily Herald, Daily Honolulu Press, Hawaiian Gazette,* and *Saturday Press;* in Hawaiian, *Kuokoa,* which remained establishment after the *Advertiser* split off from it. The *Gazette* had been the official government paper and now was ostensibly "independent." Taking turns running it were businessman William R. Castle, a missionary descendant and briefly attorney general for Kalākaua in 1876; Alfred S. Hartwell, a former judge and attorney general; attorney Sanford Ballard Dole, future president of the Republic of Hawai'i and the first governor of the Territory; and the Reverend Charles McEwen Hyde, a missionary.

In 1881, the king enjoyed a brief respite from attack when he concluded a successful trip abroad in search of immigrant labor for the sugar fields. This respite ended when Gibson, increasingly unpopular as he became increasingly influential with the king and his newspapers reached a widening Native Hawaiian audience, picked up St. Julian's thesis and published his own series on the "Primacy of the Family of Polynesian States" in the *Advertiser* and *Ka Elele Poakolu* (The Wednesday express) (1880–1881). The "policy of this kingdom," Gibson stated, should be to assist and preserve the independence of other nations "of the same race as Hawaiian" (*Adv.*, Nov. 19, 1881). When Gibson became premier in 1882, establishment papers stepped up their attack. New phases of the dream, in 1882 and 1883, involving a new palace and a coronation, were like red flags before the establishment bull journals. The king and Gibson intended these to enhance the status of king and country and to raise the people's morale and pride. But the *Gazette* condemned spending $100,000 on the palace and $30,000 on the coronation as a "racket" and a "folly." Kalākaua's sponsorship of ancient Hawaiian hula and chanting were not just wasteful, but fostered "witchcraft" and "kahuna lore" (*Gaz.*, Sept. 6, 1882).

The *Daily Bulletin* (1882–1895) at first temporized. But when the anti-Kalākaua activist G. Carson Kenyon assumed the editorship in 1882, it called the Pan-Pacific vision a dangerous, crackpot idea, "a Napoleonic Dream of Acquisition" that "has been dreamt before; but clear headed, unpoetic, matter-of-fact men have smiled incredulously at its recital" (Nov. 16, 1882). Attorney Lorrin A. Thurston was among those who wrote editorials for the *Bulletin*—Thurston was a missionary descendant who was soon to become central to plotting the overthrow and leading the annexationist cause. The *Bulletin* advised the king and government to confine Hawai'i's attention to herself.

As to the establishment's principal Hawaiian voice, it should be noted that *Kuokoa* employed eminent Hawaiian Christian journalists who agreed with the Americans. Editors Joseph Kawainui and Samuel Kaaikaula disapproved of the lavish events of state and addressed "the Hawaiian People": "Some will come to learn what is being done, whether it will make rulers more sacred and will elevate their prestige. Others will come to see the event for themselves, to see the sweat of their brows, the earning with which they have paid taxes, being lavishly wasted and thrown away in gainless pleasure. What a waste of your earnings, O people" (trans., Jan. 27, 1883).

To *Kuokoa*, Gibson was a demagogue, a "worthless good-for-nothing," a "devil," and a "renegade haole" who spoke in "the black tongue of hypocrisy." The paper asked Hawaiians to ignore the festivities because "respectable" people would not participate (Feb. 3, 17, 1883).

But it was a newcomer to the journalism scene who through four newspapers helped to sink the ship of state. Thomas G. Thrum became enamored with printer's ink at the age of twelve when he visited the *Weekly Argus* print shop run by Abraham Fornander. Fornander likely influenced the young Thrum occupationally (Davis 1979). Both shipped out as youths on whalers and became outstanding publishers. In 1875, Thrum founded *Thrum's Annual*, a handbook and statistical and descriptive record of the Islands for the next fifty-eight years. Thrum was otherwise untouched by Fornander's enlightened views.

Thrum began the *Saturday Press* (1880–1885) with the backing of a group of merchants who moved their advertisements to the new journal (Damon 1957; Kuykendall 1967). The Thrum paper prospered, not from circulation, but from advertising dollars. The boycott of Gibson's *Advertiser* left to that paper only advertisements by blacksmiths, repairmen, photographers, poi makers, and horse traders—in other words, those outside the looming power structure. "I trust that Gibson will be starved out before long," Sanford Dole wrote to his brother (Damon 1957).

Thrum believed he had the weapon to dethrone Gibson, the pamphlet (Allen 1933). The political pamphlet is an old journalistic device that thrives in periods of acrimony and dissent, as during the American Revolution when Thomas Paine incited Yankee fervor against the British. Thrum wrote and printed *The Shepherd Saint of Lanai* that was aimed at influencing the elections of 1882 and at testing the government's strength. Printed first in installments (*Sat. Press*, Dec. 10, 1881–Jan. 21, 1882), it was then separately issued by the thousands. But the audience to whom the pamphlet was directed ignored it. Why? In one of his few publishing errors, Thrum failed to have it translated into Hawaiian. Gibson carried the election by 1,153 out of 1,451 total votes cast. Nevertheless, the sarcastic sobriquet of "Shepherd Saint" was permanently attached to him.

Thrum turned his venom upon the king himself. The coronation was a "childish display," a "disgrace." In the *Saturday Press*, he invoked the "outrage" of the "long suffering of the business community," ominously alluded to the French Revolution, and asked,

"And what of the king who dishonors his state and station? . . . "
(June 30, 1883).

To Thrum goes the dubious honor of giving newspaper voice to
accusing those opposed to the power elite of fomenting "an antago-
nism of races" between haole and Hawaiians. Thrum had asked earlier, "Who is a Hawaiian?" His answer was that people like himself
and Lorrin Thurston were Hawaiian "by birth, . . . [or] by education,
sympathies, early association, and subsequent career" (*Sat. Press,*
Oct. 9, 1880). Fair enough. Yet Thrum, who was born in Australia
(his great-grandfather had sailed with Captain Cook), would or could
not recognize that within his own definition Gibson had as good a
claim to being "a Hawaiian" as he did. He would not credit Gibson
for sincerity in his repeated assertions that he believed that all of
Hawai'i's people should participate in its life and government.

Thrum and the oligarchy had an additional cause for concern.
Gibson's papers, which were printed in two languages, did not
always report events the same way. This was true of other nineteenth-century papers in which the English and Hawaiian sections
of a journal generally reported much of the same material but sometimes with differences in nuances and tone (Johnson 1984). For
example, Gibson's *Advertiser,* in English, defended the king's Pan-
Pacific aspirations and scolded the king's attackers for their "poor
taste" and "discourteous criticism" (*Adv.,* Jan. 22, 1881). *Elele Poakolu* in Hawaiian, however, labeled its detractors as "traitors" and
"rebels."

A coinage controversy escalated the verbal assaults. Dreams of
empire require money if they are to be realized. The king also needed
money to run his country. In 1883, the government issued coins
bearing the king's countenance, and in 1884 Kalākaua backed a
Coinage Act, which attempted to institute a national coinage and to
regulate the money supply (Adler 1966; Andrade 1977). The king was
swimming against the tide. Missionaries had not only printed the
first newspaper but engraved and printed the first paper money at
Lahaina Luna in 1843 (Schmitt and Ronck, 1995). By the 1880s, for
all practical purposes, Hawai'i's monetary system had become an
extension of America's.

Kalākaua was accused of personal vanity and of allowing a
scheme that mostly benefited Claus Spreckles who printed the
money. Thrum again attacked, lashing out at "The Coinage
Scheme" and "The Coinage Muddle" (*Sat. Press,* June 2, 9, 1883). "In
the name of outraged and swindled community we ask, how long the

present policy in the matter of currency is to be persisted in by the Government and submitted to by the people?" (*Daily Hono. Press,* Nov. 5, 1885).

Licensing opium was the next issue to incense the establishment and was added to the growing list of Kalākaua's "blunders" and "moral failings." Every legislature and king from midcentury on faced the dilemma of whether to license and regularize the opium trade or restrict and prohibit it. The illegal trade fostered rampant criminality—many reports of robbery, assault, and murder were hidden opium cases (Lim-Chong 1978). In 1887, when it appeared that the need for money had led people close to the king, the king himself sold the same opium license twice; the *Hawaiian Gazette* kept the "scandal" before the public for weeks.

The king's enemies were further outraged by another issue connected to the Pan-Pacific dream. The government had purchased a British steamer, refitting and renaming it *Kaimiloa* (far seeker). John E. Bush, appointed commissioner to different island groups and himself a newspaperman, sailed on the *Kaimiloa* to Apia, Samoa, on a goodwill tour in July 1887. The *Kaimiloa*, Bush, and the kingdom found themselves embroiled in an incident involving the British, Germans, and, most importantly, the United States (Kuykendall 1967).

Gibson's *Advertiser* and most Hawaiian language papers defended the venture. The popular *Ko Hawaii Pae Aina* (The archipelago) (1878–1891), led by brothers Joseph and Benjamin Kawainui, had earlier attacked the coronation as wasteful. *Ko Hawaii* now attempted to make amends and asked that the king and his ideas be accorded respect. Ignoring all reason, the *Daily Bulletin* accused *Ko Hawaii Pae Aina* of being "anti-haole" and labeled the Samoan episode as "political lunacy" (*Daily-Bull.,* Mar. 19, 1887).

In late May 1887, the *Daily Bulletin* ran a series entitled "The People's Position and Demands." It practically ordered the king to adopt the British model of reigning and not ruling, reminding him that he was "not king by right of inheritance, but by vote of the Legislature, secured by the white man's management. . . . The people of the country, who represent its agriculture, its commerce, its industries, its enterprise, its progress, and its wealth, who pay the bulk of the taxes of the support of the government, are the people who put the king on the throne. . . . They intended that he should be the country's first gentleman and at the same time the servant of the people" (*Daily Bull.,* May 23, 1887). The *Hawaiian Gazette* fulmi-

nated about "the empire of the calabash." Almost on the eve of news
of the dismissal of the king's cabinet—that is, the imposition of the
Bayonet Constitution—the *Gazette* charged: "The Government of
the country is rotten. . . . From King downward, the Government
positions are chiefly held by men who are notoriously corrupt and
debauched" (June 27, 28, 1887).

In early July, the *Daily Bulletin* and the *Gazette* covered a "mass
rally" staged by the Hawaiian League and the Honolulu Rifles. The
Hawaiian League was a predominantly haole group that met in
secret beginning in early 1887. Among its newsmen/conspirators
were Alatau T. Atkinson, an Englishman; W. R. Castle; Sanford Dole;
and Lorrin Thurston. The Honolulu Rifles was a quasi-military
group that had supported the king but now turned against him (Loomis 1976). The rally was ostensibly attended by "2,000 angry citizens." But then, as now, newspapers inflated numbers of attendees
at events they supported and deflated numbers at those they didn't.
The *Gazette* declared, "A New Constitution and a New Government Demanded." The *Friend*, in the hands of the arrogant Sereno
Bishop, a son of missionaries, joined the pack. The Reverend Bishop
was as different from the *Friend*'s founder, the Reverend Samuel C.
Damon—who had praised the coronation as "eminently historical"
(*Friend*, Mar. 1883)—as a narrow alley from a boulevard. Bishop
gushed over the brief reign of temperance—stores and saloons were
closed for the afternoon—and "the immense attendance, chiefly of
white men," and "a testimony to those accustomed to popular
assemblies in England and America." Bishop added, "How the taw-
dry show of coronations and jubilees pales below the stately majesty's [sic] of the righteous will!" (July 1887). Only the *Daily Herald*
(1886–1887), edited by Daniel Logan who was among the milder of
the king's critics, reported on a true mass rally, if an unsuccessful
one, in July of Hawaiians, Chinese, and some Japanese, protesting
the Bayonet Constitution and the exclusion of Hawaiians and
Asians from voting.

Kalākaua's humiliation and defeat swiftly followed. The *Gazette*
jubilantly reported the king's capitulation on July 6. The new constitution of July 7 was printed by the *PCA* under new hands on July 8.
Written by three or four men, it replaced that of 1864 that had protected the prerogatives of the Crown. Lorrin Thurston, as minister
of the Interior, was virtually in control of the cabinet. The papers
lavished praise on every method the new government used to ensure
control, such as the reinstatement of property qualifications for vot-

ing. The king until his death four years later was a figurehead, a ceremonial sovereign, betrayed by the same power alliance that had
helped to elect him to the throne.

The oligarchy's papers crowed over the downfall of Walter Murray Gibson, the "turncoat haole" they so despised, and his and his
son-in-law Fred Hayselden's removal by the Honolulu Rifles to the
docks on July 12, and their exile to California. Gibson died soon
after. The papers duly noted his body's return to the Islands in February 1888 but downplayed funeral services attended by thousands
of Native Hawaiians.

In 1887, speaking for a confident oligarchy, the *Gazette* stated
that a "blurred page" of Hawaiian history "has been turned over. We
have now a clean leaf to write on" (July 12, 1887). *Gazette* editor Alatau Atkinson resigned, secure in his knowledge that he had helped
to shape events that diminished the monarchy and led Hawai'i
closer to the United States.

The dream of a Hawaiian empire ended, and the dream of a giant
American empire permanently imposing itself upon the little country was to soon become a reality.

14.   Robert Wilcox,
"the Napoleon of Printers' Lane"

Caucasian political activists who were also journalists toppled the king from power through the Bayonet Constitution of 1887. Native Hawaiian political activists/newsmen also fought on two fronts, on the battlefield and on the printed page, to restore power to Native Hawaiians. Of these, Robert W. Wilcox was the most outstanding.

Wilcox became an ignominious symbol of defeat in part because his causes lost, in part because of his own complicated personality and mixed motives. Histories of Hawai'i have labeled him a "loser" and a "turncoat" and his followers "a raggle taggle of part-Hawaiians and a few down-at-heel foreigners" (Daws 1968). Another way of assessing Wilcox, however, is as a genuine symbol of resistance (McGregor-Alegado 1979). Like other heroes, he was all too flawed, but he was consistently brave in his primary cause—to restore power to the Hawaiian people. Between 1889 and his death in 1903, Wilcox edited and published three bilingual newspapers, wrote for several more, and in the process cast a lasting influence upon modern Hawaiian history.

After the imposition of the Bayonet Constitution of 1887, which cemented the oligarchy's power, the establishment press abruptly repositioned itself from being a severe critic of the government to becoming its staunchest supporter. This press turned from threatening Kalākaua, who no longer had any real power, to attacking a new scapegoat—the opposition press and Robert Wilcox. The *Hawaiian Gazette* informed the nationalist papers that they had no right to urge the Islanders to make demands for changing the Bayonet Constitution of 1887. In an editorial on "Christian Civilization," it accused *Ka Nupepa Elele* (The newspaper messenger) (1885–1892) and *Ka Oiaio* (The truth) (1889–1896) of "falsehoods and irritating statements" about the new government leaders and added a veiled threat: "We have simply this to say to the conductors of these journals that there is a point beyond which it is not safe to proceed, and it will be wise to heed this advice." *Gazette* editor Henry Whitney warned that peace must be preserved and any attempts "to instigate

popular insurrections" would be stopped "if necessary, by force"
(Apr. 6, 1889).

Wilcox's Rebellions

The first Wilcox rebellion, on July 30, 1889, thrust him onto the
front pages of establishment papers. Hereafter, when not demoted to
just "Bob"—he was almost never referred to as Robert or even Wilcox—he was labeled a "traitor" and the "devil."

The rebellion's objective was the replacement of the 1887 Bayonet Constitution by one similar to that of 1864 that had broadened
the rights of the king. The rebels were made up of a loose association
of Hawaiians, Europeans, and several Chinese. They briefly succeeded in occupying the palace grounds and nearby government
buildings. In the ensuing battle, government forces killed seven
insurgents and wounded a dozen more. The rebellion was quickly
quashed, with order reinforced by a detachment of armed men from
the USS *Adams* (Kuykendall 1967).

Who was Wilcox? Historian and newspaper bibliographer Nancy
Morris has observed in her introduction to his biography that the
scrappy part-Hawaiian was a complicated mixture of American,
Hawaiian, and Italian cultural values, values sometimes in conflict
with each other, who was nonetheless dedicated to the Hawaiian
people (Nakanaele 1981). Robert William Kalanihiapo (royal first
born) Wilcox, born in 1855 on Maui, was the son of a sea captain
from Rhode Island and a mother descended from the brother of
Maui's King Kaulahea. His classmates and teachers in Wailuku
included descendants from the missionary Thurston family. He
himself became a teacher and legislator. One of several promising
young Hawaiians whom the king sent abroad for further education,
Wilcox graduated in 1885 in the top half of his class from the Royal
Military Academy at Turin, Italy, and served as a subaltern lieutenant of artillery. The "reform" government in July 1887 recalled him,
and he arrived home with an Italian bride (who shortly thereafter
returned to Italy) and involved himself in political intrigue and journalism (Sobrero 1991). As a result of the 1889 rebellion, in which he
led his men in red garibaldi shirts like those worn by the great Italian
revolutionist, Wilcox, six feet tall and with burning dark eyes and
Roman nose, became to admiring fellow Hawaiians "the Iron Duke"
and "the Hawaiian Garibaldi." As a result of his newspaper career,
he became "the Napoleon of Printers' Lane"; that is, Printers' Row.

The rebellion caused tremendous excitement in oligarchy papers.

Earlier in 1889, the *Gazette* and the *Advertiser* had joined together under the same roof to share a printing plant and a business manager, Henry Whitney. Although both papers claimed editorial independence, in fact, almost identical heads and stories appeared of the "Great Riot!" or "Insurrection!" and the "Attempt to Overturn the Government by Bob Wilcox and 150 Natives" (*Adv.*, July 31, 1889; *Gaz.*, Aug. 6, 1889). Calling the events of July 29 and 30 "treason"— only rebellions that win escape that charge—and a "silly and hopeless revolt," both papers expounded: "It is the first time, in the history of civilized Hawaii, that Riot and Rebellion have shaken their gory locks at constitutional reform, and arranged to destroy the Government and the peace of our hitherto peaceful isles. It is the first time that Treason has drawn its sword and spilled the blood of Hawaiians" (*Adv.*, *Gaz.*, July 31, 1889). The newspapers demanded "a traitors doom" for the "rebel rioters." Prompt death by hanging without delay would serve as a deterrent to further uprisings.

On a lighter note, the *Daily Bulletin* missed its printing deadline "owing to our mechanical staff partaking of the common excitement on Tuesday" (July 30, 1889). Its report was somewhat more temperate; the *Bulletin* acknowledged what the other papers denied, that there had been "several turbulent incidents within living memory" and that all had not been peaceful in the Islands over the years. The *Bulletin* even suggested that it may not have been "necessary" or "wise" for the Reform League's actions in 1887, for change might have been obtained "within a reasonable period by peaceful agitation." Abandoning this modest attempt at independent thought, the *Bulletin* concurred with other establishment papers that Wilcox and his crew were "traitorous, outrageously foolish and enormously criminal" (Aug. 1, 1889).

The government brought Wilcox to trial, along with another journalist, Ho Fon. (A third man, the Belgian Albert Loomens, was fined and released.) Ho Fun, a young Chinese reporter and part owner of the Chinese News Company, was tried by a "foreign"—that is, haole—jury, and found guilty of conspiracy for allegedly serving as a go-between for the nationalists and sympathetic Chinese merchants (McGregor-Alegado 1979). He was eventually fined and released.

Wilcox was tried by a Native-Hawaiian jury. This double system of separate Caucasian and Hawaiian juries was an outgrowth of earlier consular courts that were devised to shield foreigners from Hawaiian justice. Wilcox and Ho Fon were not the first of the Islands' newsmen to be brought to trial—the 1880s saw a host of

Foreshadowing the 1960s, the two major establishment dailies—in 1894, the *Advertiser* and the *Hawaiian Gazette*—entered into a joint operating agreement, sharing production costs but claiming "editorial independence." (Hawai'i State Archives)

libel suits against editors and publishers. But they were the first to be accused of treason. A jury of his peers refused to convict Wilcox of conspiracy. During his imprisonments, in 1889 and 1895, his fellow Hawaiians flocked to visit him in jail.

Neither the failed uprising nor the trial discouraged him. He and his chief ally, John E. Bush, to become the theoretician of Hawaiian

nationalism, and other oppositionist newsmen attacked those who
blamed the Hawaiians for fighting back. *Ka Nupepa Elele*, under
haole newsmen Arthur Johnstone and Daniel Lyons, exhorted the
people to save the nation of their ancestors and pledged itself "to
support His Majesty King Kalakaua, in all his constitutional rights,
against all parties...and the Hawaiian people against making
Hawaii a republic for the convenience of the clique who now run
Hawaiian affairs" (July 27, 1889; trans., *Gaz.*, Aug. 13, 1889). In *Ka
Leo o ka Lahui*, Bush demanded answers: "Who are the murderers?
Who shot these native Hawaiians to death? Who gave the authority
and by what right can a number of whites seize guns and shoot the
natives?...Whose hands are stained?" (trans., *Gaz.*, Oct. 15, 1889).

The question arises, why did establishment papers translate and
print these defiant challenges? The answer is that they intended to
demonstrate how untrustworthy the dissident newsmen were in
contrast to those who accepted haole rule, and they also meant to
stoke the fires of haole fear and apprehension. The oligarchy's journals resurrected Thomas Thrum's earlier accusations against the
Gibson papers, hurling charges of "race prejudice" against Wilcox
and Bush. It refused to acknowledge what was obvious, that there
were few, if any, total racial divisions in the nationalist papers
between Caucasians and Hawaiians.

It is likely that Wilcox himself aggravated his enemies' fears. He
was deliberately controversial and, besides that, charismatic—in the
parlance of today, a newsmaker. He was the subject of countless articles, features, and cartoons. His first paper, the bilingual *Liberal*
(1892–1893), besides supporting his candidacy for the legislature in
1892, advocated "responsible" government "sanctioned by the people" and asked to put the question of the Pearl Harbor cession into
the hands of a commission. And Wilcox sometimes hurt his own
cause. Both Wilcox and Bush, for example, attacked the queen as a
woman incapable of leading the people. At another point, they recommended annexation by the United States if it would bring equality and dignity to Hawaiians. Oligarchy papers made much of
Wilcox's inconsistencies.

After the overthrow of the monarchy in 1893, Wilcox laid aside
his criticism of the queen and in 1895 led the fight to restore her to
the throne. Wilcox knew he had little chance of success, but he
fought bravely at Diamond Head and led the retreat action. Calling
his cause "the poi flag," establishment papers daily predicted his
imminent capture. Wilcox and a few comrades held out for two

weeks against hundreds of government soldiers. Half starved and with Wilcox convinced he would be shot on sight, they came down from Nu'uanu Valley to surrender.

Once again Wilcox faced the hangman's noose. The *Advertiser* and *Gazette* goaded the "military tribunal," set up by the Provisional Government, to execute the rebels. The "tribunal" sentenced Wilcox and five "ringleaders" to death. The president of the Republic of Hawai'i, Sanford B. Dole, with an eye to appearing reasonable to Washington, D.C., where annexation was under consideration, commuted the sentences to imprisonment and hard labor. By the year's end, the Dole government released the men.

Wilcox agreed as a condition of his release that he would "not go against" the government. He remained a thorn in its side, however, accusing government leaders, for example, in the pages of his *Ke Aloha Aina Oiaio* (The only aloha aina) (1896–1897), of mistreating Hawaiians.

Home Rule

After formal annexation, Wilcox waged perhaps his finest battle. With restored voting rights, Hawaiians in 1900 elected him, the head of the Home Rule party, to the U.S. Congress as the Territory's first delegate. He was joined by his second wife, Theresa Wilcox, in copublishing the bilingual *Home Rula Repubalika* (1901–1902). The Wilcoxes gained national attention in newspapers from California to Washington, D.C., and Home Rule became the newest threat to the power elite (Bennion 1990). Resorting to the same tired rhetoric, the *Gazette* called Home Rule a "counterfeit cause" to which "no haoles need apply." The *Gazette* then showed its own color by declaring, "If color is to rule any subdivision of American territory that color will be white" (Apr. 20, 1900.) Establishment papers literally portrayed Wilcox as the devil incarnate. In one cartoon he had horns and held a pitchfork (*Gaz.*, Oct. 16, 1900). In the *Independent*, he was a *kahuna* (priest, sorcerer) with evil magical powers (Jan. 4, 1901). In yet another, he was "Mephisto Bob" luring voters with false promises. Repeating a favorite accusation, that Hawaiians needed to be guided by their wiser, white fathers, the *Advertiser* patronizingly called Home Rulers "sulking children" (April 19, May 7, 1901).

Home Rula Repubalika was indeed a threat. It advocated educational qualifications as the basis for voting rights—the oligarchy favored property rights. It drew the distinction between the "mis-

Robert Wilcox, in his Italian officer's uniform, and the regal Theresa Wilcox were a dynamic husband and wife publishing team of several Hawaiian nationalist papers through the 1890s. After annexation, their *Home Rula Repubalika* supported Wilcox as the Territory's first delegate to the U.S. Congress. (Hawai'i State Archives.)

My... Year in Washington

By Mrs. ROBERT W. WILCOX.

PRINCESS THERESA OWANA KAOHELELANI.

sionary boys"—those "rich haole kamaainas who preached Christianity and laid up treasures not only in heaven"—and their own supportive haole friends who had less money and position (Nov. 2, 1901).

Cleverly, the oligarchy put an end to Wilcox rebellions by engineering a split in the Hawaiian vote. They co-opted Hawaiian leaders, such as William C. Achi, a newspaperman who had been loyal to the queen, and Prince Jonah Kūhiō Kalaniana'ole. When Kūhiō defeated Wilcox in 1902 for the congressional seat, the *Advertiser* crowed, "Prince Kuhio Makes Clean Sweep...and Is Delegate Elect." A cartoon showed Kūhiō with the wings of an angel, casting Wilcox into the shade (Nov. 5, 1902).

The Wilcoxes continued their newspaper until Wilcox fell ill during the 1903 elections while campaigning for Home Rule. He died at the age of forty-eight. Although Home Rule party President Charles K. Notley supported two more papers (Mookini 1974), the cause went into decline.

Now safely dead, Wilcox was granted lengthy obituaries by establishment journals that finally acknowledged his talents. The *Gazette* wrote, "Aside from his politics Mr. Wilcox had many warm friends. The natives have a great aloha for the dead leader" (Oct. 27, 1903). To *Advertiser* editor Walter G. Smith, Wilcox "was a man stronger in the elements of leadership than all but one of his native kings." Smith stated, "We may condemn the nature of that influence as we please; but the fact remains that it made history and gave Wilcox rank as a tribune of his people" (*Adv.*, Oct. 25, 1903).

Today, Wilcox, warrior, newsman, and politician, is given credit for helping to lay the foundation of the arguments of the modern Hawaiian rights movement. A downtown city park was dedicated to him in 1989.

15. Revolution and the Suppression of Freedom of Speech

The overthrow of the monarchy in 1893 to bring about the annexation of Hawai'i by the United States was in essence an act of revolution. Journalists who were political activists chose up sides. Those who plotted the overthrow of the queen formed the Provisional Government and Republic of Hawai'i until annexation could be secured. In effect, they led a combined establishment-official press, for they controlled the government and the economics of Hawai'i. Those dedicated to preserving Hawai'i as an independent country formed the opposition. It was they who led a Hawaiian nationalist press that challenged the annexationists.

Population figures are revealing. Out of a total of 90,000 people, Hawaiians and part-Hawaiians numbered 40,600, or 45 percent of the population (1890 census figures). Another 39 percent were comprised of Asians (32 percent) and "other Caucasians" like the Greeks, Italians, and Jews (7 percent) who were not Portuguese (Nordyke 1989). Thus the establishment-official press spoke for no more than 5 or 6 percent of the population. But as Linda Peterson states in her study of power and the media, when two groups are in conflict, regardless of size, the more powerful will prevail (Peterson 1992).

This minority press led by political activists included: in English, the *Advertiser, Hawaiian Gazette, Daily Bulletin,* and *Hawaiian Star.* The *Advertiser,* with the largest circulation, had a press run of about 1,300. In Hawaiian, there were several church-related bulletins and *Kuokoa. Kuokoa* once enjoyed a circulation of perhaps 5,000 but had lost readers who no longer were willing to overlook its pro-Americanism, or as John Sheldon, editor of the nationalist *Holomua,* expressed it, *Kuokoa* had to be "given away free" to Islanders who used it to start morning cooking fires (*Holomua,* Mar. 10, 1893).

Opposition papers represented the vast majority of people and readers—or roughly 85 percent of the population. Their leaders, both men and women, Native Hawaiian and Caucasian, were outside the power structure. The newspapers of choice for this large group doubled in number during the Kalākaua years and reached a high point between 1891 and 1896, to include at least two dozen in the Hawaiian language or in Hawaiian and English and two printed solely in English (Chapin 1984). The important ones were, in Hawaiian, *Ka Leo o ka Lahui* (The voice of the nation) (1889–1896) with a circulation of 4,000 and, in Hawaiian and English, *Hawaii Holomua* (Hawaii progress) and *Hawaii Daily Holomua* (1891–1895) with a circulation of 5,000. Another paper, the *Independent* (1895–1900), in English, had a circulation of about 3,000.

This combined large number fueled the oligarchy's fear that the opposition might actually prevail. In addition, opposition journalists completely accepted and practiced the American credo of a free press. The nationalists so alarmed the oligarchy that it enacted special libel laws to jail the leaders and suppress the papers.

In addition, oligarchy members poured money into their papers. In these years they purchased new press machines costing $40,000 to $50,000 each and Linotype machines costing $4,500 each. The Linotype itself enabled a paper to mechanically set and redistribute type at five times the speed of the compositor who set type by hand (Smith 1979), a process Hawaiian nationalist papers still used into the early 1900s. Caucasian printers and pressmen earned twenty-five dollars weekly, which was considered good pay. By contrast, their counterparts on the Hawaiian language papers averaged eighteen to twenty dollars weekly (*Star-Bull.*, Mar. 22, 1961).

Another indicator of economic disparity is the ratio of advertising, the lifeblood of a commercial paper. The *Advertiser* enjoyed a ratio of 60 percent advertising to 40 percent editorial content, carrying large advertisements by the sugar factors, banks, shipping companies, and retail outlets. *Ka Leo o ka Lahui* and *Holomua*, by contrast, had a lopsided ratio of 30 percent advertising to 70 percent editorial content. Their customers, royalist in sympathy, were, for the most part, Chinese and Hawaiian attorneys and the "lesser haole" tradesmen—Lawrence Fuchs' ironic term for, among others, Jewish dry goods store owners, Greek hotel and cafe proprietors, and Irish blacksmiths (Fuchs 1961). When the *Advertiser*'s Henry Castle applied the word "impecunious" to the queen's supporters, John Bush of *Holomua* bitterly replied: "We are willing to admit that the great majority of the loyal people are not wallowing in untold wealth, such as we suppose the Castle family possess; nor do they perhaps enjoy such unlimited credit as some of the great missionary firms can command . . . nor are they perhaps able to paper the walls of their rooms with gilt edged sugar-stock" (Feb. 7, 1893).

Today it seems to have never been in doubt that the unified money and power of the oligarchy and its press would control events and forge the Islands' future. But from 1893 to 1895 the outcome was not obvious. The oligarchy's press dedicated itself to justifying its actions in the Islands and projecting a favorable image abroad to the United States to influence public opinion there.

The Overthrow of Queen Lili'uokalani

A brief survey of the events of the overthrow may be useful in plac-ing the newspapers in context. Lydia Kamaka'eha Pākī had suc-ceeded her brother, David Kalākaua, to the throne after his death in San Francisco on January 20, 1891. She began her reign even as the ill effects of the McKinley Tariff Act, wiping out the favorable differ-ential for Hawaiian sugar, were being felt (Kuykendall 1967).

Upon her ascension to the throne, the oligarchy's papers were as condescending to her as they had been to her brother and as filled with warnings: "Long Live the Queen!" the *Advertiser* proclaimed, (Feb. 3, 1891), adding two days later:

HER MAJESTY QUEEN LILIUOKALANI ascends the throne of Hawaii with every presumption of a long, peaceable and happy reign . . . To reign, and not to govern, has been accepted as the definition of the duty of a modern Constitutional Sover-eign. . . . So, too, if Her Majesty has seen much to admire and to endeavor to imitate, she has seen much in the last few years which may be well considered as a warning to be remembered, an example to be shunned. . . .

May Her Majesty . . . reign happily, and each successive anniversary of her succession to the throne be celebrated by a united, thriving, progressive nation, loyal to her person and her throne. (Feb. 5, 1891)

A woman of strong character, the queen not only faced up to a deep-ening economic depression but was determined to restore power to the monarchy that had been lost in the Bayonet Constitution of 1887 (Liliuokalani 1898). When she proposed such measures as raising money through a lottery and licensing opium, and having her cabi-net ministers serving at her pleasure (the power elite packed her cab-inet), all measures anathema to the establishment, conspirators met in secret in 1892 to plot a coup d'état. They sought support in Wash-ington, D.C., and from the U.S. minister to Hawai'i John L. Stevens (Fuchs 1961; Kent 1983).

The *Advertiser* shrilly denounced the "consummate folly" of the lottery proposal as an evil that cast "a terrible shadow over Hawaii" and her cabinet appointments as "an affront to the commercial interests of the whole country." Her attempt to promulgate a new constitution, the paper warned, was a course "which must hasten the downfall of the Hawaiian Monarchy" (Jan. 12, 14, 1893).

On Saturday night, January 14, 1893, a "Committee of Public Safety" met at Lorrin A. Thurston's home; its seven members included four active on newspapers: Sanford Ballard Dole, W. O. Smith, W. R. Castle, and Thurston. On Sunday, the committee met again to plan for a "mass meeting" to be held the next day. On Monday, January 16, Minister Stevens ordered Captain Wiltse, commander of the USS *Boston,* to land troops to "assist in preserving public order" (Kuykendall 1967; Loomis 1976). On Tuesday, January 17, the committee proclaimed the dissolution of the monarchy. The *Advertiser* said the Committee of Public Safety represented "The Will of the People" and the "mass meeting"—attended by some 1,200 persons—was "one of the most unanimous as well as one of the most enthusiastic expressions of popular sentiment which has ever come from the foreign community of this city." It added that the determination to resist the aggression of the queen was "universal" and that "temporizing measures would be of no avail" (Jan. 17, 1893). The paper downplayed a competing and peaceable meeting on the same day at Palace Square, this one attracting 5,000 or more Hawaiians and their sympathizers. With American troops in occupation and able to read the writing on the wall and in the oligarchy's newspapers, the queen yielded under protest. The monarchy came to an end.

Usurpers universally rest their claims to legitimacy by stating that civil disorder threatens the populace and that they, the self-selected saviors, represent public interest in keeping order. Interestingly, the usurpers at first hung the word "revolutionary" upon the queen under the headline, "The Revolution": "Her Majesty Queen Liliuokalani without authority or color of law, attempted to overthrow the Constitution of the Hawaiian Kingdom." The action of the queen "was illegal and revolutionary." Her supporters were "agitators," "anarchists," "lawbreakers," and "rebels" (*Adv.,* Jan. 16, 1893). The *Advertiser* rushed to legitimize the usurpers: "The Citizens Convene and Form a Committee of Public Safety." A "Provisional Government" would operate "until terms of union with the United States of America" have been agreed upon: "Tuesday, the

Sanford Ballard Dole and Lorrin Andrews Thurston were political activists and newspapermen. Shown here in Dole's office in the early 1890s, they helped to engineer the overthrow of the monarchy in 1893 and influenced American public opinion to bring about annexation in 1898. (Hawai'i State Archives)

17th day of January 1893, will go down to history. . . . The people . . . have asserted the prerogative inherent in every people to determine the form of their own government, and have done away with the monarchy" (*Adv.,* Jan. 18, 1893).

The oligarchy soon woke up to the American connotations that linked "revolution" to republicanism and salvation, and "revolution," first a dirty word, soon became a clean word. Earlier, Stevens, himself a former newsman, in a Memorial Day speech had spoken of monarchies as "a vile curse" of the "monarch-cursed and enslaved nations of Europe" (*Adv.,* May 31, 1892). In 1894, the *Advertiser*'s Lorrin Thurston produced *Memoirs of the Hawaiian Revolution,* copies of which were sold at the *Advertiser-Gazette* office.

In 1894, the oligarchy formalized the creation of a "Republic" to coincide with that famous revolution, the Fourth of July. The *Advertiser,* giddy with delight, gushed, "A more glorious sun could not have risen over the Republic of Hawaii than that of yesterday" (July

5, 1894). The *Hawaiian Star* (1893–1912)—the *Star* was founded on March 18, 1893, as the official voice of the Provisional Government by American businessman J. Atherton; its name symbolized the star of annexation—took the opportunity to warn Hawaiians to abandon the idea of bringing back a form of monarchy, which would be a "retrogression" and "Their Last Political Absurdity" (July 2, 5, 1894). The usurpers now owned the word "revolution."

Suppression of the Nationalists

Rumors flew through Honolulu from 1893 into the beginning of 1895 about another possible rebellion (Loomis 1976). Thoroughly understanding that a united front enables a minority to prevail, editor W. N. Armstrong, one of the "missionary boys" (Thurston's phrase), called for "unity of thought and action" in which "good journalism should become a powerful agency." To Armstrong, potential rebels were "yelling savages" flying "the black flag, and skull and bones of monarchy" (*Adv.*, Jan. 2, 1895). Oligarchy leaders labored to have their views prevail, lobbying in Washington, D.C., and writing articles that appeared in newspapers from California to New York. They subscribed to American clipping services so that they would be up-to-date on American public opinion and able to respond quickly to it.

Unconvinced of the legality of the overthrow, President Grover Cleveland sent U.S. commissioner James H. Blount to assess the Hawaiian situation. Blount's report confirmed that the sentiment of the majority of people was for the queen and against the Provisional Government and annexation (Loomis 1976). This was amply demonstrated by nationalist journalists, such as John Sheldon, John Bush, F. J. Testa, and Joseph Nawahī, who continuously refuted the annexationist arguments. For example, when reporting on the queen's protests and appeals to the American government to restore her to the throne, nationalists used the words "usurpation" and "illegality." They threw American ideals back in the oligarchy's face by repeating that the best government was founded on principles of liberty and equality. John Bush, in particular, kept this point before the public in *Ka Leo o ka Lahui*, having as early as 1891 attacked the oligarchy's "sycophantic" and "Hireling Press" for its lack of independent expression. Bush firmly believed that "a sound and just opposition to a government is a help to it and should be counted [on] without fear" (Jan. 9, 1891).

John Sheldon in the pages of *Holomua* disputed the Provisional

Government's claim that the whole foreign population had sprung to arms against the queen. If a ballot were taken, he said, less than one-half of the foreigners and hardly any Britishers would support this government. Of a so-called pro-annexation poll, many signatures were those of convicts harassed into signing (Jan. 26, 1893). *Holomua* ran closely reasoned explanations about land inheritance under kings and chiefs and warned readers to beware of deliberate distortions of language (Feb. 2, Apr. 24, May 13, 1893).

Something should be said here about language and its role in the resistance. As a matter of principle, Bush and Nawahī in 1892 had almost ceased to carry English columns in their papers. News items from abroad were translated into Hawaiian. This action may be interpreted in more than one way. The newsmen were making a statement that linked the English language to imperialism—or, in the words of linguistic analyst Richard R. Day, Hawaiian was already the "language of inequality" (Day 1985), English having replaced it in the 1870s as the original language on government documents (Kimura 1983).

There is another way, however, to view the Hawaiian editors' position. They had an eye to history. Those who produced newspapers were educated men and women. The men attended Lahaina Luna School or the Kamehameha School for Boys; the women learned on the job with editor husbands. Additionally, they found the communal organization of a newspaper congenial. With its workforce roots in medieval guilds, print had long been conducive to family or clan working arrangements. By 1890, Hawaiian papers employed fathers and sons, husbands and wives, and cohorts. Henry Sheldon, of the old *Honolulu Times*, contributed several sons to Hawaiian journalism, including editor John G. M. Sheldon and printer Laurence Sheldon of *Hawaii Holomua*. J. M. Poepoe, who edited a record-setting eight papers between 1888 and 1912, was a lawyer, teacher, Hawaiian scholar, and legislator, who had two editor sons. Robert and Theresa Wilcox and Joseph and Emma Nawahī formed outstanding husband-wife teams. Emma Nawahī continued the immensely popular *Ke Aloha Aina* (The Hawaiian patriot) (1895–1920) after her husband's death in 1896 until 1910.

These newspapers have provided us with primary documents that to this day are a vital source for those who want to study the language, thinking, and culture of the Hawaiian people. A survey of their titles confirms their breadth: *Ka Makaainana* (The commoner) (1887–1902), *Ka Leo o ka Lahui* (The voice of the nation), *Ka Oiaio*

Newsboys on street corners were the chief distributors of newspapers until well into the 1950s. At the turn of the century, carriers gathered to have their photograph taken outside the office and print shop of *Ke Aloha Aina* (The Hawaiian patriot), among the most popular and successful of all Hawaiian language papers. (Hawai'i State Archives)

(the truth), *Hawaii Holomua* (Hawaii progress), *Ka Leialii o Hawaii* (The crown of Hawaii) (1892), *Ka Malamalama* (The light of knowledge) (1892), *Nupepa Aloha Aina* (Patriot newspaper) (1894–1895), *Ke Aloha Aina* (The Hawaiian patriot), and the *Independent*. A striking example of a primary document is the queen's eloquent protest to the overthrow, which was only printed in the nationalist papers, in Hawaiian and English: "I, LILIUOKALANI, by the Grace of God and under the Constitution of the Hawaiian Kingdom, Queen, do hereby solemnly protest against any and all acts done against myself and the Constitutional Government of the Hawaiian Kingdom by certain persons claiming to have established a Provisional Government. . . . I yield to the superior [force] of the United States of America" (*Holomua*, Jan. 18, 1893). The oligarchy refused to carry the protest in any of the papers it controlled.

As to the Caucasians who supported Hawaiian nationalism—the "turncoats," as the establishment-official papers called them—they remained defiant. Among the most outspoken were Daniel Lyons and Edmund Norrie. Lyons, from Nevada, was recruited by Walter Murray Gibson in the early 1880s to lead *Ka Nupepa Elele*, then he launched his own paper, the *Daily Hawaiian* (1884–1885). It was not a business success, and he subsequently wrote critiques of the oligarchy for other papers. Lyons career was sadly cut short by the loss of his three children and his wife to diptheria and his own death at the Kalihi Insane Asylum in 1895 (Hunter 1953).

The belligerent and colorful Edmund Norrie, more of a survivor, was an émigré from Denmark who married into the prominent Richardson family of Maui. Norrie edited *Hawaii Progress Holomua*, the English language version of *Hawaii Holomua*, and was proprietor of the *Independent*. Norrie took on everyone. He won one battle against Dr. J. S. McGrew, editorial chief of the *Hawaiian Star* and president of the Annexation Club, who "reported" that Norrie had been struck with a spittoon in a saloon brawl. A teetotaler, Norrie sued McGrew for libel. The *Star* apologized, McGrew left the paper, and the libel case was discharged (*Daily Bull.*, May 31, 1893). Norrie attacked the *Friend*, edited by the Reverend Sereno Bishop, calling it "the Enemy" because of its "usual lying and black-guarding style." The oligarchy was "an American Mafia" of "knavish pirates in a plot to steal a nation and compel America to receive stolen goods." As to the *Hawaiian Star*'s leaders, they were a "conceited missionary minority." And the paper?—"A more dastardly, disgraceful and cowardly journal has probably never been published in any community" (*Holomua*, Oct. 4, Dec. 8, 1893; Jan. 2, 1894). Throughout the Republic's years, Norrie kept up his defense for civil rights and his running attack on annexationists: they were selling out the Islanders; they hired "government spies" to spy upon royalist newsmen; the planters' association was a "gigantic tyranny"; the government was a "Bogus Hawaiian Republic."

Although Norrie was effective in worrying the oligarchy, he unfortunately illustrates another dynamic. The establishment-official press leaders hung together. Any criticisms they may have had of each other were in private. Not so the opposition. As early as 1892, Bush ran a series on "The Transient Nature of the Hawaiian Monarchy" in *Ka Leo o ka Lahui*, in which he predicted a movement toward democratic—that is, nonmonarchical, institutions (Feb. 15, 19, 22, 1892). The cantankerous Norrie called Bush a "political charlatan" and "a Braying Ass" (*Holomua*, Apr. 13, June 19, 1894).

The opposition press demonstrates still another significant dynamic. Print is a double-edged sword. It encourages independent thinking, as it did in Bush and Norrie, but it also fosters centralized government, censorship, and libel laws to kill dissent (Forer 1987). That is what happened between 1893 and 1895.

The Provisional Government, in the words of James Blount reporting back to President Cleveland, took aim at "crushing out all opposing opinions by forceful methods" (Kuykendall 1967). John Sheldon, for example, was arrested for publishing a contemptuous article against the government in response to Lorrin Thurston's statement that if the native regime were reinstated, foreigners would have to leave Hawai'i. "He lies! and he knows it," charged Sheldon, pointing out that four generations of Thurstons had lived peaceably in the Islands (*Holomua*, Feb. 15, 1893).

Freedom of speech was drastically curbed. Each constitution since 1851 had guaranteed freedom of speech: "no law shall be passed to restrain or abridge the liberty of speech or of the press." Article 3 of the Republic's Constitution of 1894, however, altered the definition of libel. As Hawaiian newspaper scholar Rubellite Johnson states, the new constitution included the most restrictive statement on freedom of speech in more than fifty years (Johnson 1976). All men could speak, write, and publish their sentiments, except—and this was a large exception—that "no person shall advocate, by writing, printing or speaking, the restoration or establishment of a monarchial form of government in the Hawaiian Islands." In addition, the Republic "may enact such laws as may be necessary, to restrain and prevent publication or public utterance of indecent or seditious language" (Lydecker 1918).

Under charges of "indecent or seditious language" and "conspiracy," the government filed suits against a dozen Hawaiian and Caucasian newsmen. All lost their cases in the oligarchy-controlled courts. Bush, Nawahī, and E. C. Crick were picked up at Bush's plant and charged with "conspiracy." They were refused bail, then jailed, fined, and released. Bush was incensed, for, as he repeatedly stated, his criticisms were entirely public and therefore could hardly be considered conspiratorial.

In another case, G. Carson Kenyon, editor of the English page of the *Daily Hawaiian Holomua*, was charged with criminal libel for reproducing an editorial from the *Akron* (Ohio) *Indicator* that criticized U.S. Minister Stevens. In yet another, when Edmund Norrie stated that "Mr. Dole was president of Hawaii through treason, fraud and might," this was declared "seditious libel," and the editor was fined $100 and costs. After Norrie reprinted the entire charge, he was fined an additional ten dollars for contempt of court (*Holomua*, Dec. 6, 1894).

On January 6, 1895, the oligarchy's worst fears were borne out when rebellion did indeed materialize in an attempt to restore the queen to her throne. The oligarchy's papers hastened to assign to it the word "counterrevolution" to indicate its "illegality." The rebellion was crushed within days. Newsmen targeted with arrest included Bush, Crick, Daniel Logan, Nawahī, Norrie, Thomas Tamaki Spencer, W. J. Kapi, J. K. Kaunamano, Kenyon, and F. J. Testa —Testa worked for Norrie and also published the popular daily, *Ka Makaainana*. Bush and Norrie tied for the record of total number of arrests of five each between 1893 and 1895. In 1895, their newspapers stopped printing while they were jailed, an action that brought happiness to a new establishment editor, Wallace Rider Farrington, who would himself make newspaper history in the twentieth century. The imprisoned men "are enjoying a long-needed term of rest," he gloated. "The editors are passing their vacations in Oahu Prison" (*Gaz.*, Jan. 18, 1895).

Through the queen's arrest and trial in February 1895 and subsequent house arrest, oligarchy papers advocated the harshest penalties, including hard labor. They heaped abuse upon her, ridiculing her appeals for justice to U.S. presidents, Congress, and the courts. They didn't bother to pursue logic, on the one hand ordering her to accept American dominion, on the other stating that she was "resigned" to it. To the *Advertiser* and *Gazette*, she was the "Ex Queen," "Lil," and "Mrs. Dominis." It was only after annexation that the oligarchy's papers found her acceptable, assigning the respectful label "the former Queen" to her.

As to the nationalist journalists, the Republic offered exile to the Caucasian newsmen in place of jail sentences. Norrie, however, refused to leave Hawai'i, served his sentence, and left jail to return to writing slashing attacks in the *Independent*. Hawaiian newsmen left the courtroom or jailhouse to resume support of the former queen's cause, until their businesses folded. Some went on to work on small papers (no establishment papers would hire them) or to different careers. While annexation was still pending, they were liable to arrest at any time upon the charge of having been identified as opposed to the Republic.

After formal annexation, the right to free speech was once again guaranteed, now by the American Constitution. Robert and Theresa Wilcox were free to verbally challenge the oligarchy, which they did in their *Home Rula Repubalika*. But the Hawaiian nationalist press was in decline. Dailies ceased. Norrie left the *Independent* in 1900 and did odd jobs until he secured a minor city post that he kept until retirement (obituaries, *Adv., Star-Bull.,* Oct. 4, 6, 1939). Weeklies and semimonthlies continued to 1948, then disappeared.

But if this seems to be the usual melancholy tale of indigenous people caught in the path of imperialist onslaughts, it is also inspirational. The opposition papers advanced the arguments for Native Hawaiian rights that would arise again in the late twentieth century to take center stage in contemporary Hawai'i and constitute a force to be reckoned with by the present establishment.

A testimony to a people's resiliency, too, is the reemergence of nationalist periodicals in the Hawaiian renaissance. When the country lost its sovereignty, the great days of the Hawaiian nationalist press passed into history. But they made a permanent contribution to that history.

16. The Republic Burns Down Chinatown

Even as Hawai'i was being absorbed by the United States, a plague and a fire struck the Islands. Technically, however, these twin disasters occurred on the eve of annexation. Hawai'i was still an independent Republic in 1899, and it was this government that set fire to Chinatown.

Rumors of plague flew through Honolulu for days. The Chinese language press in 1899 carried the first news of the plague, in a semiweekly published by Dr. K. F. Li and the Sun Chung Kwock Bo, but there is little additional information about this paper because the great Chinatown fire of 1900 consumed the Chinese newspapers and their printing plants (*Star-Bull.*, Mar. 27, 1964).

The Chinese initiated the ethnic language press in the Islands in 1881. Their first newspaper, *T'an Shan Hsin Pao* (Hawaiian Chinese news) (1881–1883), was joined by several others so that by 1900 there were: *T'an Shan Hsin Pao Lung Chi* (Hawai'i Chinese news) (1883–1907); *Wah Hu Bo* (Chinese times) (1893–1907); and *Lai Kee Bu* (Beautiful news) (1895–1900). These papers were important sources of information to the Chinese community that represented 20 percent of the Islands' population (Glick 1980; Encyclopedia of Hawai'i 1980).

The Chinese papers, like later nineteenth-century ethnic journals produced by the Portuguese and Japanese, were led by an intellectual and professional cadre. But unlike the others, the Chinese papers were often organs of political parties or literary groups that financed them, and so were not dependent for revenue upon subscriptions and advertisements. *T'an Shan Hsin Pao* and *T'an Shan Hsin Pao Lung Chi* were voices for Dr. Sun Yat-sen (Encyclopedia of Hawai'i 1980), who attended 'Iolani School and was to become the father of the Chinese Revolution and the first president of the Chinese Republic.

T'an Shan Hsin Pao was probably originally produced on slates, then handwritten and printed by duplicator until Dr. Sun's organization could secure a press and Chinese type from Hong Kong. Thereafter the pages were painstakingly prepared by printers handpicking thousands of characters from boxes of type. These papers were very popular. Reports describe how readers gathered in large numbers outside the newspaper offices, located in storefronts on Maunakea, Smith, and Bethel streets, to see copies of the pages, posted in the windows, announcing business transactions, festivals, funeral arrangements, and other events.

The plague's presence was confirmed for the English reading public by the *Advertiser* on December 13, 1899:

> BUBONIC PLAGUE
> IT MAKES ITS APPEAR-
> ANCE IN HONOLULU
> FIVE DEATHS REPORTED

The *Advertiser* announced that the Republic's Board of Health in special session on December 12 had declared a citywide emergency and quarantine. During the next month, the public received information on the plague both through the Chinese and English language papers.

As Lani Iwamoto shows in her definitive study of the event, the scourge cut across race, class, and property lines. By the time the disease ran its course, there would be sixty-one deaths among seventy-one total cases. Of the seventy-one cases, forty-one lived within or adjacent to the "plague area," as the papers called it, but thirty did not. Of the sixty-one deaths, nine were on Maui and one on the island of Hawai'i. The majority, or thirty-three of the sixty-one victims, were Chinese, but twenty-eight were Japanese, Hawaiians, Caucasians, and a "South Sea Islander" (Iwamoto 1969).

The newspapers were agents in the Republic's response that ignored the distribution of plague cases and focused on the Chinese and the forty-acre area bounded by Queen and Kukui streets and Nu'uanu Avenue. Chinatown had a mixed population of 7,000 residents out of Honolulu's total of 40,000 and included Japanese and Hawaiians. All lived and worked in a congested area of small stores and businesses, offices, rooming houses, lean-tos, stables, chicken coops, privies, and restaurants. *Advertiser* publisher Lorrin A. Thurston served as chairman of the newly formed Citizens' Sanitary Committee, and the *Advertiser* moralized editorially on "the white man's burden" to clean up Chinatown (Jan. 9, 1900).

This was the most recent epidemic of the "black death" that had appeared in the sixth century in the Middle East, spread to Asia, and devastated Europe in the fourteenth century, killing from one-fourth to one-third of the population. Isolated cases of the disease, which spread by flea-infested rats from oceangoing ships, were reported in the Islands' newspapers from the 1830s on. In ancient and medieval times, authorities attempted to contain the plague by fire; that is, by torching the infected houses of victims, as well as the bodies of the dead. On December 30, 1899, the Board of Health chose the medieval method of fire as the "surest, most thorough, and most expeditious" way to get rid of the plague (Iwamoto 1969).

English and Chinese language papers were posted through the city to explain how Chinatown was to be divided into districts for building-to-building cleansing and fumigation. The papers carried orders to occupants of stricken structures that told them to move to detention camps on the edge of the area. The militia then prevented residents from leaving the camps and others from entering Chinatown.

Chinatown had burned to the ground once before in April 1886. That fire was not deliberately set but was inadvertently started from a Chinese cookhouse or eatery on the corner of Smith and Hotel streets. When throngs of people blocked the streets and prevented the fire company from reaching water for the hoses, a twelve-block area of thirty-seven acres was destroyed and 8,000 left homeless. Chinatown residents viewed the fire as a disaster. The *Daily Bulletin* saw it as an opportunity to create a "sweeter, healthier" town (Apr. 21, 1886); the *Advertiser* called it "an ultimate blessing" (Apr. 23, 1886).

By contrast, the fire in 1900 was deliberately set. The Board of Health drew up a plan for an area between Kaumakapili Church and Nu'uanu Avenue that had been the site of five plague deaths within a week. People were removed to detention centers, and Fire Department personnel doused surrounding buildings. On Saturday morning, January 20 at 9:00, Chief Hunt and his firemen set the fire. Firemen with water hoses stood by to prevent the spread of flames.

For the first hour everything went as planned. Then the wind rose and shifted, and blazing embers flew onto the dry roofs of the closely packed buildings. A panic-stricken populace fled as flames spread toward the wharves, enveloped fire engines, and injured several firemen. The raging fire burned thirty-eight acres and rendered 4,000 people homeless. Amazingly, there was no loss of life, but Chinatown was burned to the ground.

The response of the English language press? On one level, it functioned well. *Hawaiian Star*'s composing and press rooms on the afternoon of January 20 were without power when electric lines collapsed. The enterprising *Star* staff printed an "Extra," running off the single sheets on a hand-cranked machine.

On another level, it was déjà vu. "A Higher Power," editor Alatau T. Atkinson of the *Hawaiian Star* declared, had guided the events that in a few hours wiped away "the mass of corruption and filth" (Jan. 20, 1901). The *Advertiser* (Jan. 22, 1900) had no regrets:

THE BIG FIRE OF SATURDAY
How Chinatown Went Up in Smoke
ALMOST A CLEAN SWEEP

Chinatown's inhabitants whose homes had been burned out did not share the papers' sanguine view nor believe that their fate was inevitable. Some saw in the events decades of virulent anti-Chinese sentiment—the Chinese were the first immigrant group specifically excluded by the United States in the Exclusion Acts of 1885 and 1895, acts that set the precedent for defining immigrants by their place of origin—or as the *Advertiser* warned about the "Celestials," the "deluge whose moral effects will be as destructive to society here as was the Noachian deluge" (Jan. 4, 1879).

The newspapers, like the *Advertiser,* referred to Chinese and other non-Caucasians only by race as reported on January 9, 1900:

ADD ONE NEW
PLAGUE CASE
A CHINAMAN DIES AT
HOSPITAL

By contrast, Caucasians were given their names as reported on January 17, 1900:

SUDDENLY
DEATH CAME
MRS. BOARDMAN'S LIFE
GOES OUT
ONE HAWAIIAN ALSO DIES

To many Chinese, the fire was only the most recent instance of how their property and personal rights were disregarded. No plague-stricken structures outside of Chinatown were burned. Even after it declared the city clean on April 30, 1900, the Board of Health contin-

The great Chinatown fire of 1900 destroyed the Chinese press, but it sprang to life again after the fire, to continue as an important voice for the Chinese community. The *Hawaii Chinese Journal* of February 18, 1938, helped to raise money for war relief during the Japanese invasion of China. (University of Hawai'i Hawaiian and Pacific Collection)

ued to torch suspected dwellings, setting some forty-one fires between December 31, 1899 and August 13, 1900.

The Chinese community may have temporarily lost its primary source of communication—its newspapers—in the conflagration, but disaster soon turned into partial victory. Business owners sued for damages and recovered some money. Chinese and Japanese residents took up quarters in neighborhoods like Mō'ili'ili and McCully, thus partly breaking down segregated housing patterns. A chagrined government instituted improvements, including a new sewer system and an improved water supply (Iwamoto 1969). And new papers, including *Hsin Chung-Kuo Pao* (New China press or New China daily press) (1900–1941) and four others arose from the ashes in the following decade as Chinatown was rebuilt. Among the thirty or so papers appearing between 1881 and today, the most notable is the

Hawaii Chinese Journal, the weekly or biweekly voice for the Chinese American community from 1936 on (Ku 1993). Still printing in Chinatown is the daily, *Chung Hua Hsin Pao* (United Chinese press) (1900–), with a circulation of 4,000. Its editor, K. K. Liu, states that it is the principal source of information for émigrés from China (Liu 1993).

PART IV

"Here to Stay": A U.S. Territory— 1900–1941

17.   Annexation and the Pacific Cable

Two events at the turn of the century irretrievably yoked Hawai'i to the United States. Annexation as the political act received the most attention. But the Pacific cable, a technological breakthrough, may have had as great an impact.

Annexation

The idea of annexation first appeared in 1849 in an upstate New York newspaper and locally in the *Polynesian,* then regularly reappeared in the press through the century until annexation was accomplished. In 1898, the news that had such import for Hawai'i actually reached its shores a week after the fact. President William McKinley signed the joint resolution of Congress on July 7. The information was relayed on the Pacific mail steamship *Coptic* that arrived offshore on July 13 and flew signal flags to announce the momentous event. The *Advertiser* rushed an "Extra" onto the streets. An aging Henry Whitney, who had declared thirty years earlier, "I am an annexationist" (*Adv.,* Feb. 8, 1868), proudly signed his name to verses from "The Star-Spangled Banner" that were overprinted with the Stars and Stripes onto the banner headline, "ANNEXATION!" followed by "Here to Stay!" (*Adv.,* July 14, 1898). A month later, when Hawaiian sovereignty was transferred to the United States, *Advertiser* editor William N. Armstrong, who had harbored annexation sentiments even while a member of King Kalākaua's government, exulted, "Hawaii Becomes the First Outpost of Greater America" (Aug. 13, 1898).

The annexation "extra" was not the first. That distinction goes to the *Advertiser*'s "Boys in Blue Edition," on July 13, that in a paroxysm of patriotism greeted the first naval expedition headed for the Philippines, whose own annexation followed. What this signified was that the Spanish-American War of 1898 was as much a deciding factor as any other for annexing the strategically located Hawaiian Islands (Loomis 1979). Military activities, formerly handled in a col-

Annexation received greater attention in the *Advertiser,* on January 14, 1898, than did the installation of a Pacific cable connecting Hawai'i to the mainland, in the edition of January 2, 1903. The second event, however, may have had as strong an influence on the Americanization of the Islands' journalism. (Hawai'i State Archives)

umn, now had their own page, swelling to a section of several pages on special occasions.

The papers capitalized on annexation for their own purposes. Advertisements moved to inside pages, for example, reserving for the first pages attention-getting photos and new page makeup, such as the full-width banner headline. Growing economic prosperity resulted in enlarged classified ad sections, and real estate ads mushroomed in size and number.

Yet, interestingly, what emerged was the beginning of a long ret-

rospection, not by the Hawaiian language papers—the leading papers, *Ke Aloha Aina* and *Ka Makaainana*, for example, if without enthusiasm, accepted annexation—but by the papers of the Caucasian oligarchy that had striven so mightily to give away Hawai'i to the United States. Armstrong sounded a nostalgic note for the old days: "At noon yesterday the little drop of Hawaiian nationality merged in the vast ocean of American nationality. . . . There were present many men who had lived most pleasantly and happily under the Hawaiian flag and who regretted deeply not that Annexation had come about, for they rejoiced in this, but that they saw a Flag of a People lowered. It was solemn, it was sad, it was a remembrance that will dwell with a man forever" (*Adv.*, Aug. 13, 1898).

But not too nostalgic. In 1900, on the occasion of the formal handing over by the Republic of the reins of government to the new Territory, Alatau T. Atkinson, former *Hawaiian Gazette* editor who headed up the first U.S. census of Hawai'i, composed "An Admission Day Song" (*Adv.*, June 14, 1900). On the opening day of the new century, the *Advertiser* put out the first of what was to be its yearly "progress" editions: "The New Year Brings the Twentieth Century and an Insurance of Great Things for Hawaii Nei" (Jan. 1, 1901).

Among those "great things" was a proliferation of newspapers themselves. Edwin S. Gill introduced the first daily newspaper with a Sunday edition, the *Honolulu Republican* (1900–1903). The papers spread to the other islands. In anticipation of annexation, Hilo already had gained two papers, the *Hilo Tribune-Herald* in 1895 and the *Hawaii Herald* in 1896. The *Maui News* began publication in 1900 and the Kaua'i *Garden Island* in 1902.

The Pacific Cable

After formal annexation in 1900, the Islands in many ways were as ocean isolated as ever. But this was short-lived. Within three years, the Pacific cable made a domestic pond of the vast ocean. On January 1, 1903, at 8:15 A.M., the cable, carrying telegraphic messages, annihilated geographic space and chronological time, yoking Hawai'i within seconds to the continental United States and the rest of the world. The cable, an electronic technology, was second in technological significance only to the introduction of printing itself in 1822.

Stemming from the invention (in 1844) of the telegraph, for the first time in human life messages traveled faster than the messenger. Information was detached from any solid commodity and space inconsequential (McLuhan 1964).

Unlike annexation, the cable was never controversial. Through the nineteenth century, papers across all categories were intrigued by its prospects. *Kuokoa* dedicated a *mele* (chant), "He Mele No Ka Nupepa Kuokoa," to it:

> Here in the Independent Newspaper
> The prying crowbar of wisdom
> The iron cable of the Hawaiian Kingdom
> Lying across the Pacific Ocean . . .
>
> (Oct. 24, 1861)

A part of King Kalākaua's Pan-Pacific dream, expressed in the pages of *Nuhou*, was to link the Islands to Asia and to America by cable. In the establishment *Hawaiian Gazette*, editor Henry Whitney observed, "A cable connecting us with the outside world will make a complete revolution of the business methods in this community" (Sept. 10, 1889). Nationalist newsmen Robert Wilcox and John Bush promoted a cable in the early 1890s, as did Queen Lili'uokalani. By 1900, countries and continents of the world were linked by electrical communications, but not to Hawai'i. Nor were the Islands linked to each other until radio wireless achieved that on November 12, 1900.

On New Year's in 1903, the first message, telegraphed from Secretary of Hawai'i Henry E. Cooper to President Theodore Roosevelt in Washington, D.C., underscored the new proximity of Hawai'i to the United States. "We all believe that the removal of the disadvantage of isolation will prove a strong factor in the upbuilding of a patriotic and progressive American commonwealth in these Islands" (*Adv.*, Jan. 2, 1903).

Newspapers made much of "Cable Day," a territorial holiday. The *Advertiser* ran a special cable edition and printed Bandmaster Henry Berger's composition for the occasion, the "Pacific Cable March" (Jan 3, 1903). The *Hawaiian Star* headlined that Associated Press wire service messages could now be relayed: "First Regular News Service Dispatches Sent to the Hawaiian Islands. Marks a New Era" (Jan. 3, 1903). Wire service dramatically increased the amount of incoming news, and events occurring only hours earlier in Madrid and Berlin, Caracas and New York, Tangier, and San Francisco, shortly appeared locally.

The cable was the primary conduit for newspapers until newer technologies were put into operation: the radio in the 1920s and 1930s and television in the 1950s. Service was discontinued in November 1951 and the cable abandoned. Today, it lies forgotten on the bottom of the Pacific, symbolically and literally washed over, as the news reaches Hawai'i by satellites positioned in the skies 23,300 miles above it.

18. The 1909 Strike and the Japanese Language Press

With annexation having formalized Hawai'i's position as an American outpost and cementing the oligarchy's control, it would seem that labor-management conflicts in the new Territory inevitably would be decided in favor of all-powerful management. In a conflict in 1909, victory appeared to go to the planter oligarchy and its press. But it is a paradox of "Americanism" that it can be racist and colonialist, while harboring democratic ideals. Ultimately Yasutaro Soga, the newspaper leader of this first major strike in Hawai'i, was to be the real winner of the struggle for basic human and economic rights. In the words of newspaper scholar Shigehiko Shiramizu, Soga became one of the "two great men in the Japanese community" (Shiramizu 1986). The other is Frederick Kinzaburo Makino, whose exceptional career with *Hawaii Hochi* would span the 1910s through the 1950s. Soga was the first combined editor and labor leader of any of the Islands' papers. Soga and his *Nippu Jiji* defined the issues, accurately recorded the events, and were the forerunners of the 1950s movement to cast off the oligarchy's yoke and democratize Hawai'i.

Establishment papers prior to 1909 downplayed or ignored labor disputes. No paper recorded the first plantation strike at Kōloa on Kaua'i in 1841 when Hawaiian workers disputed how they were paid—twelve-and-a-half cents per day in scrip redeemable only at the company store. The strike was quickly settled in favor of management (Beechert 1985). This dynamic of sporadic labor unrest, quick settlement, and lack of interest by the papers continued through the century.

After 1900, "labor actions" increased dramatically—a total of thirty-nine on plantations and another twenty-five allied strikes in longshore and urban organizations between June 1900 and the end of 1905. A powerful establishment press was in place on the four major islands to present only one side of the events to the public: the *Hilo Tribune Herald*, the *Maui News*, and the *Garden Island* on Kaua'i, plus a host on O'ahu. When Japanese laborers struck at Kīhei, on

Maui, in May 1900, the *Maui News*, which carried the slogan on its masthead, "A Republican Newspaper," set the tone that would echo through the decades: "The masses of Japanese on the plantations do not favor the strike" but are forced "by a few bold and unscrupulous leaders." This was an "insurrection" to which "no concessions should be made. Force must be met with force" (*Maui News*, May 5, July 7, 1900). *Advertiser* editor Walter Smith in Honolulu sounded another recurring chord: "The plantation coolie is the lowest type of the Japanese race," and added that "this should be a white man's country" (*Adv.*, July 26, 1904).

The 1906 Waipahu strike received greater attention because of the plantation's proximity to Honolulu. But the response was the same—a denial of grievances, a charge of ingratitude, and an assignment of blame for a "conspiracy" to "outside agitators" (*Adv.*, Jan. 17–23, 1906).

By 1909, a Japanese language press was securely in place to meet the needs of the Japanese community (Sakamaki 1928). These papers were conceived in opposition, which is not unusual for ethnic or foreign language journals (Kessler 1984). The exception was the Portuguese papers, initiated in 1885, that supported the oligarchy, thus reflecting the role the Portuguese were recruited for—as buffers between the dark-skinned laborers and the Caucasian oligarchy (Knowlton 1960). The Hawaiian language papers were (and are) an indigenous, not a foreign language press.

The first Japanese newspaper of record outside of Japan, *Nippon Shuho* (1892), was conceived in opposition by its originator, Bunichiro Onome, an ex-immigration inspector, to expose ineptness and corruption in the Japanese section of the Immigration Bureau (Sakamaki 1928). Onome's position embarrassed the bureau, and private contractors brought in laborers from 1894 to 1898. The second paper, *Hawaii Shinpo* (1894–1926), under the name *Kazan* and in 1895 the first to become a daily, also questioned the status quo, although it later modified its editorial views. The third, Soga's *Nippu Jiji* (1895–1985), would become the organ that would lead the 1909 strike.

By 1900, there were 61,000 Japanese in a total population of 154,000. There were fifty-two plantations and forty-six mills employing 35,500 workers (Beechert 1985; Nordyke 1989). By 1908, Japanese, mostly males, made up the majority of workers and were, except for the Filipinos, the lowest paid. Their large numbers so alarmed the power structure, which, of course, had recruited them, that the *Advertiser* editorialized, "Japanese Are Taking Possession of

Hawaii": "Once the Jap seemed a very tractable, satisfactory element in the land, fairly hardworking, peaceable creature, willing to
labor a day long at a rate of $14 a month. . . . But he has increased in
numbers at an astounding rate. . . . Already the Jap nearly owns
Hawaii" (Nov. 15, 1905). This heavy immigration led to a "Gentlemen's Agreement" between the United States and Japan in 1908,
binding the Japanese government to not issue passports to laborers
(Takaki 1983). An unforeseen outcome was that the attention of the
Japanese turned from their old to their new home and focused their
papers on topics of assimilation.

By 1909, the Islands' Japanese language press was among the
most advanced foreign language press in the United States where
there were approximately 800 ethnic papers in print (Emery and
Emery 1992). In Hawai'i alone there were an astonishing thirty periodicals in Chinese, Portuguese, Japanese, Korean, and several Filipino languages, or approximately 30 percent of the 100 or so total
publications in print. In the words of labor historian Ed Beechert,
"Hawaii supported a foreign language press unparalleled among agricultural economies based upon immigrant labor" (Beechert 1985).
Besides those on O'ahu, newspapers on the neighbor islands from
1897 to 1909 included: on the Big Island, papers in Kona, Pāhala, and
'O'ōkala, and in Hilo at least two more; on Maui, two papers in
Wailuku; and on Kaua'i, two papers in Līhu'e.

Of the Japanese papers, there are few records of the numbers of
copies printed. But we know of their successful outreach (Okahata
1971). The papers were passed from reader to reader, plantation
camp to plantation camp, and island to island. They were published
as dailies, weeklies, biweeklies, and monthlies. Printed in Japanese
or in Japanese and English, they reached immigrants who not just
read Japanese but were quickly learning Hawaiian and English, as
evidenced by the appropriately titled *Aloha* (1893). Perhaps 70 percent of all Japanese in the Islands were literate, a very high rate for
immigrants (Beechert 1985). Most Japanese did not read the establishment papers, except for the *Garden Island* in its early years
because it was started by a Japanese resident, Sometaro Sheba.

One cannot overestimate the importance of the Japanese language papers and their multiple roles. They looked back to the
homeland as a source of pride (Satsuma 1989), over the years fully
reporting Japanese military adventures. They informed readers of
local topical matters and acculturated them into the new land by
explaining practices and customs.

Their editorial views were by no means uniform, however. An ethnic press is almost always divided according to class and political interests: from politically conservative and counseling caution, to moderate and fence straddling, to the more radical that seek improved conditions for its people in the new land. Their titles reflect how they viewed themselves. In Honolulu, there was the conservative *Hinode Shinbun* (Rising sun) (1896–1897). On the Big Island, Dr. Harvey Saburo Hayashi's *Kona Hankyo* (Kona echo) (1897–1951) was a moderate bilingual country weekly and a family enterprise. Also on the Big Island was the pro-labor *Jiyu Shinbun* (Hawaii freedom) (1904–1908). To the establishment, however, the Japanese papers all seemed the same. As Professor Shunzo Sakamaki in his comprehensive study wryly observed, all those "unintelligible ideographs" obviously made them candidates for anti-Americanism and "harboring sinister plots and motives" (Sakamaki 1928).

The story of *Nippu Jiji* reflects the development and influence of the Japanese language press. *Nippu Jiji* was founded in 1895 as *Yamato*, became *Yamato Shinbun* in 1896, then *Hawaii Shinbun*, then *Nippu Jiji* in 1906. It would become the *Hawaii Times* in 1942 and remain in print until 1985. "*Yamato*" is an old and poetic name for Nippon or Japan. "*Shinbun*" and its variations simply mean newspaper. "*Nippu*" is combined from two written characters, translating cleverly into "Japan and Hawai'i." In "*Jiji*," the first character signifies time, and the second an account or current events (Sakamaki 1928).

Nippu Jiji was poised for the 1909 strike. In 1908, one Gunkichi Shimada traveled through Hawai'i to gather information for a book. Editor Hazo Tsurushima of *Hawaii Nichi Nichi Shinbun* (Hawaii daily newspaper) (1901–1914), printed Shimada's material that made the point that "prices had recently increased more than 20 per cent, but that the wage of the Japanese laborer, if he worked 26 days a month, did not exceed $18.00, and this made it difficult for him to gain a livelihood" (Aug. 25, 1908, trans. *Pacific Citizen*, Dec. 23, 1960).

Within four months, four men, all journalists, organized the Higher Wages Association. Two worked for *Nippu Jiji*, editor Yasutaro Soga and reporter Yokichi Tasaka. The third, future *Hochi* publisher Frederick Makino, operated a drugstore. The fourth, Motoyuki Negoro, an excellent researcher and writer, was a graduate of the University of California law school. An alien, Negoro was unable to practice law in Hawai'i and so clerked in the law office of former

Advertiser editor Alatau Atkinson. Tasaka and Negoro were probably the first investigative reporters in the Islands (Brislin 1995).

Yasutaro Soga spoke for the leadership in January of 1909, presenting a series by Negoro in *Nippu Jiji* that in effect called for the Hawaiian Sugar Planters' Association (HSPA) to increase pay, standardize pay rates as opposed to pay by ethnicity or race, provide a ten-hour working day, and improve housing conditions and camp sanitation. The HSPA had fixed wages and instituted a passbook system that prohibited Asian laborers from moving their employment from one plantation to another. Under the title "The Higher Wages Question," Negoro stated, "We regret that wages in Hawaii are disproportionately low in comparison with the large profits." Food and clothing costs were escalating and workers had "pig sty" living conditions. The thrust of the Japanese position was that plantations had to be made into decent communities. Negoro asked the Japanese government to intercede for the laborers, for "its subjects are not born to be slaves to the capitalists of Hawaii" (trans., *Pacific Citizen*, Feb. 9–Mar. 16, 1960). Atkinson fired Negoro. *Nippu Jiji's* circulation soared. On Maui, a struggling *Maui Hochi* under Yokoichi Tasaka reprinted the charges and dramatically increased subscriptions from twenty-five or thirty to hundreds.

Soga's rise as a journalist and labor leader is inspirational. Soga was born near Tokyo in 1873 and studied law at the English Law Institute. Following his arrival in Hawai'i in 1896, he worked as a salesman and store manager for Japanese stores on O'ahu and Moloka'i and often served as an interpreter between management and labor. Of the middle class, Soga nevertheless came to identify with the contract laborers' deprivations. He first took over *Hawaii Shinpo* in 1899, next acquired *Yamato Shinbun* in 1906, and changed its name to *Nippu Jiji*. He issued ten-page editions and filled job printing orders out of a wooden building on Nu'uanu Avenue near Beretania Street. Soga, in the tradition of the printer-editor, could perform all the tasks from the back shop to the front office. He and his associates hand set type from thousands of Japanse kana and kanji characters on a large rack.

Publicly, the oligarchy's papers and the HSPA at first refused to even admit to the existence of the Higher Wages Association. In May, 7,000 workers walked off of O'ahu plantations. The papers responded with a vengeance. None would print the workers' case. Their editorial line, spilling over into the news columns, was that laborers who did not accept management's policies and practices were dangerous "agitators": "High Wage Conspirators Stir Up a Strike at Aiea Plantation." Events were described to fit the editorial position: "Impossible Demand Made on Manager Andrew Adams of Kahuku" (*Adv.*, May 19, 21, 1909).

There may have been Caucasians in the community who initially sympathized with the workers. But the dailies were their main source of information, and it would have been difficult for them to ignore the steady abuse these heaped upon Soga, association leaders, and the "Jap strikers" who were likened to "animals" and "thugs." Adept at disinformation, the *Advertiser* alleged that Japanese were purchasing revolvers and that financial help was coming from Japan (June 16, 1909). It refused to print the association's firm and repeated denials.

In fact, association leaders in speeches and articles warned the striking men against violence. Workers generally behaved with decorum, but sporadic unruliness broke out as the strike dragged on. This was translated by the *Evening Bulletin* and *Advertiser* as "rioting" by "mobs." After the planters hired replacement workers at higher wages—$1.50 per day plus transportation—strikers at Waimānalo Plantation surrounded the automobiles of Sheriff William "Billy" Jarrett and deputies who were attempting to arrest strikers who had allegedly beaten up a worker. Jarrett's experience was reported as: "Sheriff Jarrett Relates Thrilling Encounter With Strikers at Waimanalo" (*Evening Bull.*, July. 12, 1909). Jarrett had actually kept his head through the fracas, called for reinforcements on the plantation office phone, and calmly brought the arrested men into Honolulu without injury to anyone.

The vulnerability of the ethnic press—chronic money problems and internal division—was all too apparent to management. When *Nippu Jiji*'s strike issue of May 9, 1910, reported that the Japanese and Chinese had joined forces, the oligarchy pressured the Chinese consul to prevail upon the Chinese to return to work. Management imported Filipinos and Puerto Ricans to replace the strikers. And in 1909, the planters installed an effective new practice, recruiting spies from the ranks of the Japanese editors (Beechert 1985). The principle spies were Sometaro Sheba, formerly of the *Garden Island* and now publisher of *Kauai Shinpo*, and Hazo Tsurushima of *Hawaii Nichi Nichi Shinbun*. Even though they agreed that workers should be paid more money, both opposed the strike, counseled patience, warned against "reckless action," and urged workers to meet with planter representatives (which they had tried to do).

Planters or their business allies paid Sheba and Tsurushima $100 per month to inform upon association leaders and to sow confusion among the workers. Planters engineered a Bank of Hawaii "loan" of $5,000 to Sheba who was struggling to keep *Kauai Shinpo* alive (*Pacific Citizen*, Dec. 23, 1960).

Sheba's and Tsurushima's defection should be placed in context. Sheba, from the samurai class, had been an interpreter and language teacher to missionaries in Kobe. He came to Hawai'i at the age of twenty-one in 1891 and worked for eleven years in C. H. Bishop stores on Kaua'i. Among the few Japanese Christians there, he seems to have gravitated toward the haole power structure. Sheba apparently cultivated Tsurushima who suffered ill health and economic hardships. Years later, Tsurushima recanted his anti-Higher Wages Association actions.

Nippu Jiji did not bend. In an attempt to prevent its publication, police and sheriff's deputies, without warrants, raided the newspaper offices, carted off files and safes, and arrested reporters and pressmen. Just the printing of a story or essay urging workers to strike was considered evidence of "conspiracy." Newspaper and strike leaders were tried before an all-haole jury for "conspiracy" to "impoverish the plantations by intimidating the Japanese working for them." The *Advertiser* called Japanese onlookers outside the courtroom "a sullen mob" and sneered at habeas corpus proceedings for the "Big Four"—Soga, Negoro, Makino, and Tasaka (June 12, 1909).

A dramatic act of violence by a strike sympathizer delivered the final blow to the strike and the Higher Wages Association. Sheba testified during the trial that his life was in danger. During a recess one day as he walked down King Street, Sheba was followed by a man who once worked for Frederick Makino. Tomekichi Mori, unemployed and desperate, accosted Sheba, called him a traitor, and attacked him with a pocket knife. Mori narrowly missed his victim's throat but inflicted a gash to the scalp. Sheba, small but powerfully built, wrestled Mori to the ground and yelled for help. Sheba begged to be taken to a doctor because he was losing blood, but passersby took both men to the police. Sheba almost died from loss of blood (*Pacific Citizen*, Dec. 23, 1960). He made a full recovery, but the attack on him was all that the oligarchy papers needed to prove their case. Under the headline, "Higher Wage Thug Stabs to Kill," the *Evening Bulletin* stated: "The expected has at last happened. Sheba, the courageous Japanese editor who has stood by his guns manfully" and fought "for justice and fair play, has been laid low by the assassin" (Aug. 3, 1909). Within two days, workers returned to their jobs.

The *Advertiser* and *Evening Bulletin* treated the trial's outcome as a foregone conclusion. They praised the planters' attorney, William A. Kinney, for "brilliant" cross-examinations in which he laid Negoro "carefully on the grill" and basted him "to a deep brown on every side" (*Adv.*, Aug. 6, 1909). They accorded little respect to the dedicated defense attorney, Joseph Lightfoot, an Englishman and former minister and school teacher. The "Big Four" were each sentenced to ten months in prison and fined $300. In addition, K. Yokogawa, editor of *Maui Shinbun*, was jailed on three charges of sending obscene—that is, pro-strike—material through the mails. Lightfoot's appeals failed. Kinney opined that events would be remembered for the "criminal organization" of the Japanese. Lightfoot called this a lie and prophesied that they would be remembered with shame by the good citizens of the Territory. To reward Sheba, the *Advertiser* in its New Year's edition selected him and his *Shinpo* from among all of the Japanese papers to highlight in a full-page laudatory spread, entitled "Making of a Japanese Paper" (Jan. 2, 1910).

But the aftermath brought unexpected victories. On July 4, 1910, when Soga, Makino, and the other prisoners were released from prison, the lei-bedecked men were greeted as heroes at a large rally at 'A'ala Park. Soga immediately ran an essay in *Nippu Jiji*, "Impressions on Leaving Jail." The HSPA, three months after the strike's end, raised the wages of the Japanese laborers and abolished the system of wage differentiation based on nationality.

It is one of those fortunate ironies of history that on the occasion of his death, the *Advertiser* chose to recognize Yasutaro Soga's fifty-seven years of service, his "patience," and his role as the "father of Hawaii's Japanese newspapers" (Mar. 4, 1957). The paper thus elevated the reputation of a man it had tried to destroy.

19. Respected Residents Become the Enemy: World War I and the Germans

American patriotism escalated as the United States drifted toward war, reaching a fever pitch of anti-German hysteria during World War I in the pages of the *Advertiser, Star-Bulletin,* and *Maui News.* The *Garden Island* on Kaua'i cautioned moderation, but it was not read on O'ahu, site of most of the anti-German sentiment. There were no German language papers in the Islands to defend their community. If there had been, they would likely have suffered the same fate, that of extinction (Kessler 1984). That the Islands' papers reflected a national pattern does not lessen their culpability. They brought great harm to those whom the community had viewed for sixty-five years as exemplary residents.

Individual Germans had settled in the Islands in the early nineteenth century. After the arrival from Hamburg of Captain Heinrick Hackfeld in 1849, they became visibly influential (Kuykendall 1938). Between 1881 and 1884, German male immigrants entered various levels of employment in the sugar industry, and family members put down roots. Prominent German firms prior to World War I included H. Hackfeld & Company, F. A. Schaefer & Company, and Hoffschlaeger & Company. (Wagner-Seavey 1980). By 1910, there were approximately 905 German-born residents in the Islands, plus Hawai'i-born descendants. The majority lived on O'ahu, but a small, cohesive group lived on Kaua'i (Hormann 1931). They assisted each other, as minority groups do, by preserving customs through social clubs and benevolent societies. They organized German Lutheran churches on O'ahu and Kaua'i and a German school on Kaua'i. Groups ran notices of meetings and gatherings in the English language papers.

The establishment press, like those nationally, observed an official neutrality at the outbreak of the European war in August 1914, even on occasion expressing pro-German sentiments. From about 1910 to 1915, the *Friend,* which had lost its influence by this time, carried a "Peace Supplement," and the *Advertiser* in 1914 ran several antiwar cartoons depicting pride and greed standing behind

"Demon War." The papers ran countless breathless wire-press accounts of the European conflagrations, these only yielding the front page to local elections, a grisly crime, or volcanic activity.

Pro-German sentiment surfaced when Germans collided with the Japanese. The ships of three belligerents, Japan, Britain, and Germany, sailed the Pacific. The Territory's neutral ports were suddenly in the middle of the action, and by October 1914, eight German merchant ships were interned at the ports of Hilo and Honolulu (Wagner-Seavey, 1980). A certain pride was expressed in "Honolulu Is Haven for Warbound Ships" (*Adv.*, Sept. 23, 1914). Front page news that fall concerned the arrival and internment of the gunboat *Geier*, accompanied by a collier. Captain Karl Grasshof of the *Geier* declared that the ship had to have repairs, which permitted it under neutrality laws to remain longer than twenty-four hours. In effect, Grasshof outwitted the Japanese lying offshore waiting for the Germans' departure. The papers called the *Geier*'s sailors "clean cut young gentlemen," adding, "They have committed no wrong. By the fortune of war they are our guests" (*Adv.*, Dec. 24, 1914). Favorable reports appeared of crew members taking English classes at the YMCA and being hosted at Christmas parties at which the German consul led toasts to the kaiser. The papers publicized the German community's support of the German Red Cross Society.

By 1915, their position began to shift, the papers speculating as to what would happen to German merchant ships if a war broke out between Hawai'i and Germany, but there was still no rancor. By 1916, however, enthusiasm for Germany was on the wane. The papers promoted Liberty Loans and War Savings Stamps. Furthermore, they made the connection of America's preparations for war to an improved local economy. Sugar prices were on the rise, and there was a buildup of army and navy installations.

Paranoia and fears of conspiracy began to form. By 1917, on the eve of America's entrance into the war, the *Advertiser* and *Star-Bulletin* were unable or unwilling to tell the difference between the actions of local residents and those of the German government. Too, it came to light that the *Geier* had secretly transmitted messages to the "Fatherland." Honolulu papers attacked the Islands' Germans, such as the German-American Alliance, a local branch of a national association that encouraged citizenship and sponsored German cultural events: "There can be no divided allegiance. All who are not for the United States are against her" (*Adv.*, Feb. 9–12, 1917). Persecution on the basis of one's ancestry was legitimized by severance of

U.S. diplomatic relations with Germany on February 3 and the declaration of war on April 6.

In the meantime, newspapers also revealed that in 1915, prior to U.S. involvement, George Rodiek, manager of Hackfeld, and Heinrich Augustus Schroeder, a Hackfeld employee, were involved in a scheme to ship German arms to revolutionaries in India whom the Germans hoped would revolt against the British. Arrested in 1917 for violation of American neutrality, Rodiek and Schroeder pleaded guilty but insisted that they did not intend disloyalty to the United States. Rodiek, HSPA president and a chamber of commerce officer, had bought $3 to $4 million in Liberty Bonds with personal and business funds. Nevertheless, Rodiek was fined $10,000, and his rights as a citizen were abrogated. Schroeder was fined $1,000 (Wagner-Seavey 1980). The Honolulu dailies helped to swing public opinion against the men and expressed indignation at the "leniency" shown Rodiek. (*Star-Bull.*, Dec. 24, 1917).

The newspapers assisted in ruining several other careers for the cause of "patriotism." The case of George Roenitz was much in the news from February through October 1917. Roenitz, a civil servant who was employed as secretary to the captain of the Fourteenth Naval District well before the United States entered the war, was accused of espionage for having apparently obtained unauthorized documents and sketches. Roenitz was forced to resign and was sentenced to a $250 fine and a year at hard labor. German employees of the Queen's Hospital—all but one were U.S. citizens—were accused of having supplied food to the *Geier's* crew (*Adv.*, July, 23, 1917). Superintendent Werner Roehl defended his employees until he himself came under suspicion. The papers called for "eternal vigilance" against the "ceaseless conspiracies of the enemy" and the "faithlessness of the German word" (*Star-Bull.*, Sept. 7–13, Dec. 13, 1917).

On Maui, the *Maui News* got into the act when an anthrax epidemic hit cattle. Max Weber, a Pioneer Mill timekeeper, was accused of spreading poisonous germs (*Maui News*, July 13, 27, 1917; *Adv.*, July 29, 31, 1917). The Maui paper subsequently buried a semi-retraction on an inside page that the "mysterious bottle" found on Weber contained personal medicine (Aug. 3, 1917).

The Heuer case was the most luridly handled. The College of Hawaii (it became the University of Hawai'i in 1920) in December 1917 became a storm center in the campaign to eradicate German influence in Hawai'i (Kuykendall 1928). Just before the war's outbreak in Europe, Minna Maria Heuer joined the College to teach

German. In response to anti-German sentiment, the Board of Regents required a letter of loyalty from each faculty member. Heuer refused to sign, stating that she was by principle against any war and would never attempt to influence students with thoughts of hatred and discord. Calling her a Benedict Arnold, the *Advertiser* demanded in a front-page editorial that she be dismissed: "It is not the habit of the Advertiser to attack women, nor is it through inclination that this paper must insist that action be taken in the case of Fraulein Heuer [but]. . . . those who are not for us, are against us" (Dec. 22, 1917).

To their credit, College President Arthur Dean and *Star-Bulletin* publisher Wallace Rider Farrington, a regent, defended Heuer: "It is difficult to be loyal to humanity over nationality in times of peace; it is virtually impossible in times of war" (*Star-Bull.*, Dec. 21, 24, 1917). Heuer became resentful, however, said indiscreet things about fairness, and admitted to pro-German feelings. Farrington and Dean joined those who believed that she should resign. The *Advertiser* headlined, "Disloyal Teacher Resigns" (Dec. 27, 1917). After she resigned from the College, Heuer moved to Kaua'i and taught home economics at the Līhu'e School. Trouble followed her. When she had the janitor lower the flag at the end of the school day, the Honolulu papers accused her of disrespect to the Stars and Stripes (*Star-Bull.*, Mar. 22, 1918).

In contrast during this period, the *Garden Island* on Kaua'i tried to be evenhanded. This was the typical small-town paper, so popular in the United States in the early part of this century. The *Garden Island* was just as solidly Republican and patriotic in sentiment as the other establishment papers, but it benefited from a series of editors who were not doctrinaire. K. C. Hopper, for example, supported women's suffrage. The paper's attitude during World War I was probably attributable to personal friendships between staff members and German residents.

The *Garden Island* up to 1917 continued to cover community suppers at which guests sang old German military songs and celebrated German war victories. It deemed it front-page news when the prominent Isenberg family entertained. Paul Isenberg, married to a missionary descendant, was a principal partner in H. Hackfeld and a close friend and adviser to Hawaiian monarchs. At the same time, the *Garden Island* promoted Liberty Bonds and praised President Woodrow Wilson's increasingly belicose speeches (Vought 1994).

After America entered the war, editors Hopper and J. C. Lydgate printed lists of names of those called up by Selective Service and ran stories of young men who volunteered. But they also treated local Germans with respect, editorially extending good wishes to the Reverend Hans Isenberg, who was ailing and had "with characteristic generosity . . . specially requested . . . that the German Christmas trees festivities should be conducted as usual this year." The editors recommended showing a spirit of peace and goodwill: "Bitterness and enmity may find an inevitable place on the battlefield; in rural communities such as ours, far removed from the scenes of war, it can do no good on either side to foment strife and stir up bad feeling . . . that will continue to bear an evil harvest when the actual war is over and peace should reign again" (*Garden Isl.*, Dec. 25, 1917). Unlike mainland editors who on occasion cast a cool eye on anti-German hysteria, the *Garden Island* editors were not persecuted for pro-German sympathies.

By this time, President Woodrow Wilson had declared that America was fighting a "Holy War." The Honolulu dailies featured encampments on the grounds of 'Iolani Palace. They editorially urged the changing of street names of German origin. More damaging, they praised the organization of a "Vigilance Corps." When the water system was mistakenly thought to be contaminated, the *Advertiser* suggested that it might have been poisoned by local Germans. It editorially supported the confiscation of stock shares and the sale to "American businessmen" of H. Hackfeld & Company, which became American Factors, and the reorganization of B. F. Ehlers Company into Liberty House (*Adv.*, Jan. 12, Aug. 3, 1918).

Paranoia and commercialized patriotism sold advertisements and papers. Merchants promoted a banana campaign: "Buy Bananas by the Bunch and Beat the Boches Back to Berlin" (Kuykendall 1928). The dailies ran rave reviews of films, such as one showing at the Bijou, a downtown theater: "To Hell With the Kaiser," reviewed as "the great patriotic photo-drama . . . for which Honolulu fandom has been eagerly waiting" (*Adv.*, Nov. 1, 1918).

By the war's end in November 1918, with the handy help of the papers, the German community in Hawai'i had disappeared. The Kaua'i German school was shut down, the study of German was eliminated from public schools, and teaching German was not resumed at the University until the fall of 1927. German families anglicized their names and stopped speaking the language. Max Weber left Hawai'i, and Maria Heuer moved back to Germany.

20. Suppressing the News and Contributing to a Massacre

The establishment press' treatment of Island Germans during World War I was sensational and ugly, but the papers provided the public with necessary information about the war. This press waged another battle in the period leading up to and during the strikes of 1920 and 1924. Imprinted on the banner of "Americanization" was anti-Bolshevik and anti-Japanese rhetoric, fed by twin fears. One fear of the Islands' capitalists was that the Russian Revolution might foment Bolshevism and Socialism—thought to be one and the same —in the cane fields of Hawai'i (Weinberg 1967). The second, tied to the first, was that labor leaders would take advantage of workers' unrest and unite the Japanese and Filipinos.

Violence between labor and police sent to quell strikes was commonplace on the mainland but relatively rare in Hawai'i. Yet the planters fastened upon the Ludlow Massacre as the model to avoid. Ludlow, Colorado, in 1913, was the scene of a protracted, bitter strike in which some 9,000 miners and their families were evicted from their homes and then fired upon in their tent shelters. Forty men, women, and children were shot or burned to death, and dozens more were wounded.

The approach of the oligarchy papers was either to slant the news or suppress it entirely. Additionally, a new type of periodical was introduced to control communications—the plantation newspaper (Chapin 1989). Yet what the oligarchy most feared, they assisted in bringing about. By their tactics of slanting or suppressing information, they contributed to the desparate confusion that led to the Hanapēpē Massacre on Kaua'i in 1924.

The 1920 Strike

Even during World War I, the papers prepared for postwar conditions. They propagandized the public in Sugar and Plantation News sections by featuring plantation improvements, such as the "Old Men's Home" above Pā'ia Plantation on Maui and the new hospital at McBryde Plantation on Kaua'i, as in this story: "Plantation compa-

131

nies in Hawaii do much for the comfort and welfare of employes even after their period of usefulness has ended, when they are well, when they are ill and in some instances when they are aged" (*Adv.*, Jan. 7, 1918). They editorialized that the wartime experiences of Filipino and Japanese soldiers in the American military might have "spoiled a lot of good plantation laborers" (*Trib.-Herald,* Nov. 4, 1918; *Adv.,* Nov. 5, 1918).

In 1919, the Hawaiian Sugar Planters' Association, which controlled every phase of the Islands' main economy, instituted a Committee on Industrial Relations, patterned upon the one formed after Ludlow by mine owner John D. Rockefeller Jr. and his associates. Under "welfare capitalism"—labor historian Edward Beechert's term—the HSPA inaugurated village planning such as improved housing for workers, medical care, sanitation, and recreation (Takaki 1983; Beechert 1985)—and to herald these advances, the plantation newspaper. Industrial relations departments produced the paper. This was all considered good business to keep "contented people working in the best interests of the plantations" (Beechert 1985). The *Garden Island* on Kaua'i extended its congratulations: the interest and attention that the planters gave to problems and plans of social welfare at the recent Planters meeting is "a very significant new departure" in the Islands' history (Dec. 16, 1919).

In the 1909 strike, even though establishment papers demonstrated racist attitudes toward the Japanese, they primarily placed that strike in a local frame. In fact, Walter Smith and Wallace Rider Farrington, editors respectively of the *Advertiser* and *Evening Bulletin,* said that it was "ridiculous" to imagine that the "flag of the rising sun" was in the business of taking over the Territory or supporting the demands of strikers (*Adv.,* July 12, 1909; *Evening Bull.,* Aug. 3, 1909).

During and after the war, the cry for Americanization became shriller. The *Star-Bulletin* declared, "The red flag must not be raised in America"; the *Advertiser* demanded, "Wipe the Bolsheviki off the earth." Editorial outburts reached a hysterical pitch in comparing Island Japanese language papers to mainland German language ones that were "vipers" in the national breast (*Star-Bull.,* Jan. 7, 1919; *Adv.* Mar. 8, 11, 1919):

Things of evil crawl in the dark when the light is let in upon them, they generally shrivel up and die. . . . The war taught us that all during the years that had gone before, the German language press had been working against the interests of the United States. . . .

So here in Hawaii today, there are Japanese papers that do not actively teach anti-Americanism, but they do teach Japanism, and that amounts to the same thing. (*Adv.*, Dec. 11, 1919)

The "vicious" Japanese press, hand in glove with "pagan Japanese priests and foreign language educators," should be wiped out (*Adv.*, Dec. 13, 1919). The *Star-Bulletin* descended into inanity, promising, "That spawn of purgatory, the 'Red' agitator, will butter none of his poisoned parsnips in Hawaii" (Jan. 5, 1920).

In the meantime, the 1909 dynamic of labor leaders who were newspapermen recurred, this time among the Filipinos. Pablo Manlapit arrived in Honolulu from Luzon in 1910 to work on the Kūkaʻiau Plantation on the Big Island until dismissed in 1912 for union activities. He moved to Hilo, operated a pool hall, and began the Filipino language press in 1913, only seven years after the arrival of the first recruited laborers. Manlapit was to become a legendary figure (Alcantara and Alconel 1977; Kerkvliet 1991).

Manlapit, in the weekly *Ang Sandata* (The sword) (1913), in English and Tagalog, promoted the American ideals of justice and self-determination. He was not yet considered dangerous, the *Advertiser* stating that Manlapit was "an intelligent young Filipino, who officiates in the local courts as Filipino interpreter" (Feb. 12, 1913). Later, in Honolulu, he worked as a stevedore and studied law with Hawaiian attorney William J. Sheldon, himself a political activist and editor in the 1890s (Kerkvliet 1991). Between 1913 and 1923, despite the difficulty of printing in Tagalog, Visayan, Ilocano, and English to reach readers, some half-dozen papers appeared in Hilo, Līhuʻe, and Honolulu. Manlapit organized the Filipino Higher Wage Movement, addressed to uniting Japanese and Filipino workers. Manlapit and the editors of the four leading Japanese language newspapers—*Hawaii Shinpo, Hawaii Hochi, Hawaii Choho,* and *Nippu Jiji*—supported the dual union strike that began on January 20 because "their problem is your problem" (*Nippu Jiji*, Jan. 20, 1920).

Unity, however, faced formidable obstacles, including a storm of accusations. Even when *Kauai Shinpo* editor Sometaro Sheba, who was pro-management, wrote mildly on "The Japanese Question," the *Garden Island* restated his position as "The Japanese Problem" (Dec. 28, 1920). *Nippu Jiji*'s position, of supporting the strike to promote harmony between capital and labor, was considered dangerous.

Management drove a wedge between the Japanese and Filipinos, blaming the strike on the Japanese, an "alien race," who refused to become part of American society (Reinecke 1958). The charge was particularly illogical in that under U.S. law Japanese-born people were ineligible for American citizenship. "Shall Hawaii Be American or Alien?" asked the *Advertiser*. As to the Filipinos, they were "catspaws" being "used by wily Japanese" (Jan. 27, 1920).

On Kaua'i, the *Garden Island* at first doubted that the Filipinos or Japanese would strike: "There is too much actual cream coming to labor right now for them to forego it for something problematical in the future" (Jan 27, 1920). "Cream" seemed to mean seventy-seven cents a day in wages. It accused the strikers of a deliberate attempt "to ruin the sugar business in these Islands" built up by long years of "patient industry, intelligence and enterprise." Forgetting its own praiseworthy defense of German residents during World War I, the *Garden Island* added: "We will not stand for German domination of the industry and the Islands,—and we will not stand for Oriental domination" (Jan. 27, 1920). The Kaua'i paper intensified the attack. "It is the priest and the language school man—who are Japanese to the core, and who know no more about Americanism than a Jack rabbit knows about ping pong,—who are stirring up all this trouble—with the able assistance of the Japanese press" (Feb. 24, 1920).

Establishment papers called for the "anti-American" Japanese press not to be just "muzzled like a mad dog" but "exterminated." They abandoned their 1909 position that it was "ridiculous" to imagine the Japanese government in the business of supporting strikers and now accused Japan of "pulling strings" to "take over" the Territory. The strike was a "conspiracy on the part of unscrupulous Japanese agitators" who were "loyal only to their fatherland" (*Adv.*, Feb. 8, 19, 1920). Japanese editors, priests, and educators would deliver 25,000 Japanese laborers to "The Mikado," who in turn would direct the political destiny of the Islands (*Star-Bull.*, Feb 13, 1920). Heaping racial insult upon economic injury—low wages, poor camp conditions, insufficient medical treatment—the Honolulu dailies stated that it was the "Anglo-Saxon" who brought civilization to the Islands. It was impossible for "Asiatics" to assimilate into America, for they were inherently incapable of cooperating with other racial groups (*Star-Bull.*, Mar. 27, 1920).

The few voices of reason were lost in the clamor, such as that of Acting Governor Curtis Iaukea. Iaukea, in the absence of Governor Charles J. McCarthy—in Washington, D.C., on an unsuccessful mission to have the ban lifted against the importation of Chinese laborers, now looked upon as favorable alternatives to the dangerous Japanese and foolish Filipinos—complained that the press voice of the planters deliberately emphasized the racial issue to cloud economic issues (Fuchs 1961).

Management broke the strike by July 1, 1920. Labor failed to gain a single concession. The planters did raise pay scales a few months later, but workers' frustrations remained, for which they were blamed, as in "Filipinos Run Amuck in Lihue." This "scrap" was caused by the attempted eviction of two Filipino cane loaders, who, "while not having worked much this month, were occupying plantation houses with their families" and "became infuriated" when told to move (*Garden Isl.*, July 20, 1920).

The HSPA and the Territory brought charges against the "instigators," including Manlapit, plus Soga and nine other Japanese. They were convicted and jailed for conspiracy or libel. The newsmen, however, were released after brief prison stays. To avoid such "leniency" in the future, the oligarchy promoted the enactment of laws against "criminal syndicalism, anarchistic publications, and picketing" and a press control statute that declared any publication illegal if it attempted to restrain persons "from freely engaging in lawful business or employment"—that is, if they spoke against the sugar industry. Act S.L. 216 was signed into territorial law in 1921 (Beechert 1985).

In the meantime, the plantation newspaper came into being. Initiated in November 1919 on Kaua'i, the *Makaweli Plantation News* (1919–1924) was likely the first paper in the world supported by the sugar industry. It is the ancestor of fifty-five separate weeklies and monthlies published by sugar and pineapple industry management. These spread between 1919 and the 1970s to O'ahu, Maui, Moloka'i, Lāna'i, and Hawai'i islands (Chapin 1989). The *Makaweli* four-page monthly, in English, Filipino, and Japanese, attempted to present management in a good light and build "positive" worker attitudes. A village with a population of 3,500, of which 1,700 were on the Alexander & Baldwin payroll, Makaweli lay in the isolated and mountainous west side of Kaua'i, an area conducive to reaching people removed from other forms of communication. The paper was circulated free in mail boxes and other locations.

E. L. Damkroger, "director of Welfare Work" and assigned to the Industrial Relations Department, edited the unique tabloid. The young Damkroger—pictured in one issue as a tall, lean, smiling young man, clad in white shirt, dark tie, and jodphurs and boots—appeared to sincerely wish to appeal to his readers: "The paper will publish news items of the plantation of interest to all, and strive to be a real help." He ran articles about the feeding of children, basketball and baseball games, and Filipino workers enrolled in English lessons (*Makaweli News*, Nov. 1, 1919, Jan. 1, 1920). Damkroger also showed movies in the camps. The 1920 Manager's Report stated that these measures are "certainly having a good effect on gambling and other vices." So successful did the paper appear to be that the HSPA began the *Plantation News* in 1921, which was distributed islandwide.

The 1924 Strike

In 1924, new Japanese and Filipino language papers, although still holding a range of opinions, were less conciliatory than those in 1920. They represented a combined Filipino-Japanese workforce composed of more than 70 percent of the total labor force. *Yoen Jiho* (Hawaii star) (1921–1941), also called the *Koloa Times*, was sponsored by the Kaua'i Labor Union and was the most radical of the ethnic language papers in that it was Marxist in orientation. Editor Ichiro Izuka was joined by future labor leaders Jack Kimoto and Ginjaro Arashiro. With a hefty circulation of 1,000, *Yoen Jiho* gained inclusion in the list of "dangerous" periodicals compiled by a territorial commission on "subversive activities" (Sakamaki 1928). A more moderate weekly, *Ti Silaw* (The light) (1924–1942), the "Filipino Labor Publication of Hawaii," appeared in Honolulu as Filipino labor's main voice. *Ti Silaw* warned management of deep-rooted, bitter labor resentment but was ignored (Alcantara and Alconel 1977).

Before 1924, the *Garden Island* occasionally felt charitable toward the Filipino community. Editor Luther D. Timmons, for example, had recommended better treatment of the workers (July 25, 1916). During the 1920 strike, the paper misspelled his name but printed a speech by the Reverend N. C. Dizon, a Protestant minister who represented the Filipino National Association. Dizon reminded the planters of the patriotism of Filipinos who had fought for America during the recent war and attempted to explain the hopes and aspirations of the workers (*Garden Isl.*, May 6, 1920).

In 1924, the *Garden Island*'s response to rising tensions and labor unhappiness was to black out any labor news, except for an occasional inaccurate item. The paper demoted and denigrated Manlapit to the position of "self-styled leader of the higher wages movement" and elevated Cayetano Ligot, head of a management-front group called the Brown Brothers Society, to the position of "true leader" of the Filipinos: "The majority of the Filipinos in the Hawaiian Islands have faith in the leadership of Cayetano Ligot . . . and as long as he advises against a strike the majority of the Filipinos will be governed by his advice" (Feb. 26, Mar. 4, 1924).

Manlapit called a strike on April 1; islandwide walkouts followed on twenty-three out of forty-five plantations. The *Garden Island* ignored the strike. The Honolulu dailies buried it on inside pages and only quoted industry leaders and government officials: " 'According to complete reports, . . . there is nothing to indicate a general strike among the Filipino plantation workers on this or any of the other islands,' said [HSPA] Secretary J. K. Butler" (*Adv.*, Apr. 2, 1924). The Honolulu papers assigned to their front pages such items as Francis Brown, Hawaiian golf champion, establishing a record for the course at the San Jose, California Country Club.

Finally, the papers sensed impending disaster. New walkouts brought about dismissals of large numbers of workers and evictions of families from their homes. The HSPA rushed in fresh supplies of Ilocano laborers to replace Visayan strikers. The *Garden Island* acknowledged "a near riot" at Hanapēpē but didn't attempt to understand it (July 29, 1924). The "near riot" turned to full-scale war at the neighboring villages of Makaweli and Hanapēpē. Armed with cane knives, rocks, and clubs, strikers captured two Ilocano strike breakers and refused to release them to a sheriff's posse. The ensuing battle at Hanapēpē left sixteen laborers and four police dead.

Was there any attempt to understand Hanapēpē after the disaster and failed strike? Hardly. The *Garden Island* had a new leader, Charles Fern, the daring and colorful pilot from New York who served in the Air Corps during World War I and barnstormed on Kaua'i in 1920 (*Garden Isl.*, May 11, 1920). He joined the paper in 1922, soon becoming managing editor (and in 1929, owner of Kaua'i's principal paper). Fern ran photos from the *Advertiser* to accompany its story on the "Strike Riot" (*Garden Isl.*, Sept. 9, 1924) but mainly devoted his pages to "air news," chamber of commerce meetings, piano recitals, Polo Club activities, and birthday parties for children of managers. He addressed his editorial pen to "Support the Republican Nominees" and "Success in Advertising."

Even so, the *Garden Island* was relatively mild in comparison to the rabid Honolulu papers. These ran special bulletins from Kaua'i with blatantly false "eye-witness" accounts of Filipinos at Hanapēpē with "a revolver in each hand" or "a pistol in one hand, a knife in

the other." They called for Manlapit's head, *Star-Bulletin* editor
Riley Allen declaring:

> If the striker murderers at Hanapepe are not to be repeated else-
> where, the people of this territory must line up once and
> unmistakeably for law and order and against the criminal labor
> agitators and all their ilk.
>
>   On one side we have a great majority of liberty-loving and
> law-abiding Americans.
>
>   On the other side we have, first the labor "leaders" and their
> deluded, ignorant followers; second, their alien backers; third,
> the fringe of hangers on—the professional agitators, the "reds,"
> the I.W.W.'s—who are egging on the Filipino leaders and preach-
> ing class warfare and the destruction of American institutions.
> (*Star. Bull.*, Sept. 11, 1924)

Accusing the "professional agitators" of making "a soft living" out
of strikes, the *Star-Bulletin* advanced management's position:
"There is abundant evidence to prove that the alien nationalism
which raised its ugly head in the strike of 1920 is still at work in
Hawaii, burrowing deep and secretly, but still alive and still vicious"
(*Star-Bull.*, Sept. 11, 1924).

      In the aftermath, the federal government deported issei (Japanese
born) labor leaders to Japan. The oligarchy brought lawsuits against
the ethnic language papers and their editors. Pablo Manlapit was
among the seventy-six "rioters" brought to trial, sixty of whom were
given four-year jail sentences (Fuchs 1961). The charges against
Manlapit included perjury, criminal conspiracy, and libel, the last for
an article in *Ang Bantay* (1923), a Honolulu weekly, in which Manlapit accused the hospital operated at Waipahu by O'ahu Sugar Company of having discharged a striker's sick baby who subsequently
died. Manlapit was fined $100 and given a prison term of two to ten
years. The bar association disbarred him (Kerkvliet 1991). The
Waipahu hospital episode and others remain murky to this day
because some prosecution witnesses subsequently recanted their
testimony and because several HSPA witnesses were later returned
to the Philippines at HSPA expense. But even the territorial Parole
Board recommended parole for Manlapit without conditions. Frederick Makino led the fight in the pages of *Hawaii Hochi*, a paper with
rising influence, to release Manlapit, who was finally paroled in
1927 on the condition set by the governor that he leave the Territory
(*Adv.*, Mar. 11, 1927).

Manlapit returned twice to Hawai'i. In 1932, when he tried to reorganize Filipino workers, he was threatened with arrest by the HSPA and left for the Philippines. In 1949, he returned to see his family. To indicate how territorial officials still feared him, he was placed in the custody of the Philippine Consulate and had to agree not to address any meeting nor speak on any radio station nor attend church mass nor write in any newspaper. Manlapit died in the Philippines in 1969 (Kerkvliet 1991).

The *Makaweli Plantation News,* unsuccessful in attacking patterns of resistance, also died—with the workers and police at Hanapēpē.

21. The Three Rs—Reading, 'Riting, and Racism

The relationship of schools to newspapers dates from the early nineteenth century when American missionaries transported both from the United States to the Hawaiian Islands and connected them at Lahaina Luna School on Maui. Despite this symbiotic relationship, the Islands' papers have had a partial apathy toward education, neglecting it or failing to support its aims. Only a major issue will disturb this apathy (McKinney 1940). Race was the major issue in the 1920s when the Territory attempted to abolish the Japanese-language schools. A testimony to the power of newspapers, *Hawaii Hochi* and its great editor, Frederick Kinzaburo Makino, serving as the conscience of the entire community, led the fight against the Territory's unconstitutional actions and saved the schools.

In midcentury, newspapers mentioned education only to reflect concern about the language of instruction—would it be Hawaiian or English?—and to promote English, as did the *Polynesian*, for "the further elevation of the Hawaiian people" (Aug. 18, 1860). By 1896, during the Republic, the papers so assumed the primacy of the English language that they hardly commented upon legislation making it official that English was the language of instruction in public schools. Yet the schools were racially changing again because of labor importation practices of the sugar industry.

By 1900, there were 61,000 Japanese out of a total Island population of 154,000; and many were setting down roots in the Islands and having families (1900 census figures). And just as Protestant Americans in 1841 had founded the private English language Punahou School as an alternative to the Hawaiian language schools, so, too, did the Christian Japanese in 1893 begin the first Japanese-language schools. They, too, wanted their children to know their mother tongue and culture. The Reverend Takie Okumura, minister of the Nu'uanu Congregational Church and a founder of the schools, explained that he and other ministers did not want the children of laborers to grow up without a sound knowledge of Japanese (Wist 1940).

By the 1920s, with a rapidly expanding Asian population in the schools, a Caucasian middle class that could not afford private schools pressured the Territory to provide a public alternative for their children (Hormann 1950). Educators proposed an "English standard" model—a racial system that separated Caucasian and Hawaiian children from almost everyone else by assigning a child to a school based on testing his or her spoken English. The papers again hardly noticed, except to praise the opening of the first nonstandard high school: "McKinley Hi Starts Year As One of Best Equipped in World" (*Adv.*, Sept. 2, 1924).

Nor did the Japanese language papers, several of which functioned in the opposition category, criticize this dual system—or tri-system, if the private sector is included. Apparently most parents accepted the system, Caucasians overwhelmingly in favor of it and non-Caucasians placing emphasis on the quality of their children's education (Hughes 1993). By this time, too, the Chinese and Koreans supported language schools for their children to attend after regular school hours, which satisfied their wishes that their children correctly learn the parents' first language.

But a big change was in the offing. After World War I, between 1919 and 1923, there arose an intense campaign to Americanize the Japanese community (Weinberg 1967). The Territory hastened to implement the recommendation of a visiting Federal Survey Commission in 1920 that foreign language schools be outlawed. This was interpreted as not applying to the Korean and Chinese schools. Nor did it apply to the Hawaiian ones, which existed only informally in family settings or in churches. The Territory attempted to abolish the Japanese language schools, and this application of race to education blew apathy sky-high.

The first bill against foreign language schools was introduced in the 1919 territorial legislature but failed to be enacted. All the establishment papers, from Hilo to Līhu'e, favored the legislation, and the *Advertiser* and *Star-Bulletin* launched a full-scale campaign. They emphasized census figures of an expanding Japanese population and accused the schools of being "headquarters" for "Japanese saboteurs," that is, teachers brought in from Japan. In 1918, there were only five items in the two major Honolulu dailies on "Americanization"; in 1919, there were 275. The *Star-Bulletin* in banner headlines shouted that language schools were "ALIEN INSTITUTIONS" and a "VITAL MENACE" to Americanizing the youth of the Territory (Jan. 10, 1920). The *Friend*, a Christian periodical, approvingly quoted University of Hawai'i President Arthur L. Dean that the Japanese language schools are "so foreign to the aims of an American community that they cannot be continued" (August 1920). Establishment papers demanded action against this "deadly peril" to the foundations of American government: "The time has come when the menace presented by the foreign language schools in Hawaii must be eliminated. Americanism demands that the legislature either at the special session or in regular assembly next spring shall . . . curb them" (*Star-Bull.*, Nov. 13, 1920). In November 1920, legislation to curb the schools was passed and signed into law by Governor Charles J. McCarthy. Additional laws were enacted by subsequent legislatures.

Legally, the language schools were placed in a catch-22. The legislature decreed that the schools must be "licensed" by the Department of Public Instruction (DPI). But because they were licensed, they were denied private school status. This allowed the DPI to regulate all operations. The DPI eventually limited attendance to one hour daily after public school hours for pupils who had completed

✤ ✤ *The Language School Game* ✤ ✤

Establishment papers, from 1919 to 1927, ran dozens of anti-Japanese political cartoons in support of the Territory's efforts to close down the Japanese-language schools, as in this edition of the *Advertiser* on November 2, 1919. (Hawai'i State Archives)

the eighth grade of public school or passed the age of fourteen. The schools were banned from operating if they failed to pay a one dollar per pupil head tax, a heavy burden for the Japanese schools with an enrollment of 20,000. Nonetheless, by 1924, there were 163 language schools, including 5 Korean and 5 Chinese. Issei parents of modest means were willing to carry the costs of tuition, books, staffing, and facilities for their children.

In 1922, Frederick Makino picked up his editorial and legal cudgels and for five years never lost focus on the education and race issue. Other opposition papers including *New Freedom* (1913–1935), a weekly "devoted to progressive democracy," joined Makino, but it was the daily *Hochi* that led the cause. Pro-labor, anticapitalist or "greed," and against a "Nordic superiority complex," it could and did render impartial judgments—Makino, like *Advertiser* editor Lorrin A. Thurston, for example, opposed "dual citizenship" granted by Japan to nisei (second generation) born in Hawai'i, and both promoted tourism.

Makino, born in Yokohama of an English silk merchant father and a Japanese mother, was fluent in both languages. His life experience and education, therefore, prepared him to function in a biracial environment, appreciative of both strains within him. Makino came to Hawai'i—two brothers also emigrated—at the age of twenty-two and married Micheye Okamura of Kaua'i in 1903. He worked as a plantation bookkeeper on the Big Island and ran a drug store and law office in Honolulu, although he was not a lawyer. His actions on behalf of strikers in the 1909 strike won him a jail sentence. He began *Hawaii Hochi* in 1912 and in its early years had to operate it with cash because no one would give him credit. Believing absolutely in the equality of all races, his lifetime goal was to make the Japanese partners in a democracy (Shiramizu 1986; Brislin 1992).

How were Makino and *Hochi* perceived? One might expect the establishment papers to thoroughly dislike them, and they did. Lorrin Thurston believed that the "wild-eyed" and "rabid" *Hochi* should be suppressed (*Adv.*, Apr. 28, 1923). Too, the size of its circulation must have alarmed them. In a total territorial population of 190,000 in 1924, the *Advertiser* and *Star-Bulletin* had circulations of about 15,000 each, while the principal Japanese language dailies, *Nippu Jiji* and *Hochi*, had 10,000 each.

The Japanese language papers, including *Nippu Jiji*, however, did not all agree with Makino. Editor Yasutara Soga had bravely fought with Makino on the side of labor during the 1909 strike, but after he was prosecuted and jailed, Soga retreated. In editorials between August 1922 and January 1923, he counseled Japanese residents to be conciliatory, to act as guests in their new home, and to work toward assimilation (Shiramizu 1986; Brislin 1992). In words to be repeated for many years, either by those who agreed with Soga or by those who ridiculed him, Soga stated that although the situation was deplorable, the Japanese community should "weep into silence and drop the entire matter." He feared the Japanese were taking passage on a "ghost ship" headed for a "shipwreck" (Shiramizu 1990; Brislin 1995). *Nippu Jiji* agreed with the *Star-Bulletin* that the Japanese children should only be taught in public schools. Perhaps not so coincidentally, the printing plants of both *Nippu Jiji* and the *Star-Bulletin* held a $30,000 inventory of bilingual textbooks that had been prepared for sale to the public schools after the Japanese schools were abolished.

Undeterred, *Hochi* in 1925 introduced an English section, called the *Bee* for its sting. The *Bee* broadened *Hochi*'s outreach, especially to nisei who, like children of immigrants everywhere, preferred to use the language of their own birth land. *Bee* editor George Wright was an Ohio mining engineer who moved to Hawai'i in 1917 as a machinist for the navy and was fired in 1925 for union activities (*Hochi*, Sept. 18, 1987). Mr. and Mrs. Wright were converts to Buddhism. George Wright developed into an accomplished journalist who brought the topic of the language schools before the English-reading public. For his efforts, he was shadowed by detectives. Both sections were highly readable, with comic strips, political cartoons, and topical events ranging from the Gene Tunney–Jack Dempsey fight to the rise of Mussolini. *Hochi* adopted the tabloid form, which came into its own in the United States in the 1920s, its half-sheet format featuring big headlines and lots of photos.

Hochi was joined by eighty-seven schools in its suit to test the constitutionality of the anti-Japanese school laws. Joseph Lightfoot, who had defended the Japanese strike leaders in 1909, handled the case, a difficult and costly one. Headlines in all the papers of February 21, 1927, proclaimed the U.S. Supreme Court's decision that the law was unconstitutional. Twenty-one states with similar laws were put on notice. Lightfoot, who died in December 1927, was able to savor the victory.

Still, the matter was not dropped. Watchdog *Hochi* aired all attempts to circumvent the law, especially by the *Star-Bulletin* and

Fighting back vigorously, editor Frederick Makino and the paper he led, *Hawaii Hochi*, claimed victory when the U.S. Supreme Court, in 1927, declared the territorial laws against the language schools to be unconstitutional. *(Hawaii Hochi)*

Governor Wallace Rider Farrington, who gave voice "to sentiments that are a disgrace to one of his intelligence. . . . He digs open an old wound that has practically healed, and proceeds to slander and malign the Japanese language schools . . . [and] the young Japanese-Americans" whom he says "are taught that Japan is the government

to which they must always give allegiance" (*Hochi*, Oct. 22, 1927).
Hochi and the *Bee* labeled such efforts as "Farringtonisms."

Ahead of their time, Makino and Wright predicted a coming
political reality—the increased number of registered nisei voters
eventually leading to a "Balance of Power," and "young American
citizens of Japanese ancestry" being able to "elect any candidate
they choose" (Oct. 25, 1927).

For their part, Farrington and the *Star-Bulletin* in these years per-
fectly illustrate the intimate relationship within the establishment
of business, newspapers, and government. A newsman from Maine,
Farrington was recruited in the 1890s by Henry Northrop Castle to
be managing editor of the *Advertiser*, in which Castle had an interest. Farrington also edited the *Hawaiian Gazette*. Disagreeing with
the *Advertiser* on business matters, Farrington left the Islands but
returned in 1898 to run the *Evening Bulletin*. He led the merger of
that paper and the *Hawaiian Star*, the two becoming the *Star-Bulletin* in 1912.

Appointed by President Warren Harding and reappointed by President Calvin Coolidge, Farrington was governor of the Territory
from 1921 to 1929. Like publishers of his day, he saw no conflict
between his private business interests and his public service position—as evidenced by that $30,000 book order—and retained finan-
cial interest in the paper while governor. Upon leaving office, he
became vice president with majority control of the *Star-Bulletin*
(obituary, *Star-Bull.*, Oct. 6, 1933).

Finally, in December 1927, the newly formed Hawaii Education
Association, the public school teachers' group, extended the hand of
goodwill and invited the Japanese-language school teachers to meet
with them. Generous in victory, *Hochi* urged them to do so. When
the United Press wire service opened in Honolulu, *Hochi* and the
Bee offered to cooperate with the *Advertiser* for "rendering of the
best possible service to the public (*Hochi*, Feb. 2, 1927).

Its fight for justice by no means over, *Hochi* continued to stay
alert to other education and race issues. It helped to defeat a proposal
that would have reduced the number of Hawaiians and Asians
enrolled at the University of Hawai'i by making the ability to use
the English language "correctly and fluently" a basic requirement
for admission (*Hochi*, Feb. 9, 1931). During the depression, *Hochi*
fought any proposals to cut public school expenditures. On the tenth
anniversary of the language schools victory, under the headline,
"Freedom and Sanctity of Education Preserved," Makino retraced

the long years of the bitter struggle and recounted the "toil and suffering" of Japanese parents who, had they lost the case, could have also lost their property that they had mortgaged to pay for the litigation (Feb. 21, 1937).

Having said all this, what about the dual school system? Why did so few protest it? Educationists always believed it to be a temporary adjustment (Wist 1940). And in a fine irony of history, the system worked well. One need only point to McKinley High School and its recognized dedication to preparing students to be knowledgeable citizens, not to mention its outstanding student publication, the *Pinion*. Begun on October 14, 1920, the *Pinion*, a four-page newspaper, became the *Daily Pinion* in 1935 and has over the years won national and international honors. The two Wright sons were on the staff. After graduation, Theon and J. Sowell Wright became professional journalists, both joining the *Advertiser* and Theon going on to work for United Press.

It is another irony, but a tragic one, that an estimated 85 percent of the brave nisei soldiers serving in the 100th Infantry Battalion and 442nd Infantry Regiment during World War II attended Japanese-language schools in the 1920s and 1930s (Murphy 1955). So much for the anti-Americanism of the language schools! Returning nisei veterans, in a strong position at the war's end, helped to abolish what was an undemocratic public school system. Looking toward statehood, the mainstream dailies now editorialized for the public schools to be "In the National Pattern" (*Adv.*, Feb. 12, 1948). A unified school system was phased in during the 1950s.

The Makino legacy remains impressive: changes in immigration laws ending the degrading practice of mass weddings for picture brides and the deportation of teachers of Japanese-language schools; winning citizenship for Japanese soldiers who fought for the United States during World War I; fighting for racial solidarity of workers during the 1920s and 1930s (*Haw. Herald*, Sept. 18, 1987). Of all his battles for civil rights, however, Makino's greatest victory and the one with the longest lasting effects may have been the showdown with the territorial government over its attempts to destroy the Japanese-language schools.

More than 1,000 attended the Buddhist funeral services for Frederick Makino on February 17, 1953. The *Star-Bulletin*, having discarded its racial biases of earlier decades, placed Makino's photo and obituary on page 1 (Feb. 18, 1953).

22. "Reclaiming" Waikīkī for the "Aloha Spirit"

A newspaper may have introduced the phrase "aloha spirit" into everyday use to describe what is supposed to distinguish Hawai'i from the rest of the world. *Advertiser* publisher Lorrin P. Thurston personally wrote enthusiastic articles under gushing headlines that proclaimed the completion of the Royal Hawaiian Hotel: "If Sugar Is 'King' and Pineapple 'Queen' of Hawaii, Tourist Trade Is Surely the Hawaiian 'Prince Royal,'" and "Hotel Opening Brilliant—Aloha Spirit Hovers Over Great Palace" (*Adv.*, Feb. 1, 2, 1927). The Royal Hawaiian in 1927 was the latest and most impressive edifice aimed at tourists.

In 1837, Hawai'i's first English language newspaper, the *Sandwich Island Gazette,* ran the first paid advertisement on July 1, 1837, that boosted Waikīkī as a tourist attraction:

HOTEL AT WAITITI
Including a Bowling alley and such
other facilities for amusement and recreation . . . of gentleman who may honour us
with their visits.

In the 1860s, newspapers editorially advocated services that would ease Waikīkī traffic: the construction of a public road through the area. In the 1870s, they backed a privately owned omnibus service, and in the 1880s, tramcars. Henry Whitney extolled Waikīkī's attractions in his newspapers and authored the first tourist guide in 1875 and a second guide in 1890. Waikīkī had long had been a favorite residence and recreation center for kings and chiefs. English language papers periodically remarked upon this while praising the area's accessibility and beauty of coconut groves, white sand beaches, gentle breezes, and temperate waters. Thus the intimate relationship of advertising to editorial content grew through the nineteenth century, the one supportive of the other, and both in the service of a growth industry, tourism.

But Waikīkī was also home to Native Hawaiians on small

kuleana (property) grants and to Chinese and Japanese farmers. The interior wetlands supported a healthy agricultural system of taro and rice. Barry Nakamura, in his close analysis of the "reclamation" of Waikīkī, traces plans for the area's "improvement" beginning with laws enacted in 1896 during the Republic (Nakamura 1979). In 1906, a study by the territorial Board of Health concluded that "drainage" and "sanitation" were imperative to saving the citizens from "unsanitary swamps." After a century of proclaiming Waikīkī to be healthy and its waters therapeutic, business interests and their newspapers realized that a fortune was to be made from Waikīkī.

Mythologizing Waikīkī as unhealthy proceeded as Walter F. Dillingham, founder of Hawaiian Dredging Company in 1902, sought new projects for his dredging firm. Buyouts of land by Dillingham and other moneyed interests were abetted by the political power structure, including Walter F. Frear, married to a Dillingham and governor from 1907 to 1913, and Lucius E. Pinkham, employed by the Dillinghams and the first president of the Board of Health, then governor of the Territory from 1913 to 1918 (Nakamura 1979). The newspapers more than cooperated—Walter Dillingham was to become a major shareholder of the *Advertiser*—by editorializing that the marshes should be dug out so that a lagoon encircled by a boulevard could be built as an "attractive resort" for "aquatic pleasures." *Advertiser* editor Walter Smith added his own proposal: "It would be a good place in which to keep a flotilla of torpedo boats" (May 13, 1909).

Was there a protest? Not by the newspapers. Tenant farmers hired lawyers, but Dillingham interests bought out Bishop Estate leases of the farmers' taro and rice farms. The latter won paltry damages in the amounts of $100 and $200 but lost their tenancy.

In the clash between agriculture and urbanization, urbanization handily won (Johnson 1991). Government reports urged that wet crops be removed to "rural areas." Marshes became "swamps" demanding to be "drained"; duck ponds were "impediments" to housing. A 1918 special legislative session provided for the acquisition of the right of way for the future Ala Wai Canal, designed to keep Waikīkī dry. Successive press campaigns backed mosquito extermination drives, sewer expansions, and new streets and bridges. A 1921 act created the Waikiki Improvement Commission.

In 1924, the newspapers featured the last Hawaiian family on a *kuleana* grant as they were about to be moved from their old wooden home so that it could be razed and the canal completed. The Paias

As part of their ongoing promotion of tourism, the Honolulu dailies provided free "puffs," like this February 1, 1927, "special edition" on the opening of Waikīkī's Royal Hawaiian Hotel. (Hawai'i State Archives)

had been forced to sell their one-acre tract for $3,012 to the Territory. The *Advertiser* reported that Mrs. Paia was reluctant to leave "until the dredge was literally at their door." Not only the living, but the dead were in the way as well. Mrs. Paia's ancestors, Chief Kamualii and Kaaikuala, were buried there: "Bones of a Hawaiian Chief Reverently Exhumed for Improvement in Waikiki" (*Adv.*, Apr. 16, 1924). The Paias, dead and alive, contributed to the "aloha spirit."

The first major hotel, the Moana, had opened on March 12, 1901, to rave notices. It was, however, the opening of the Matson Navigation Company's Royal Hawaiian Hotel in 1927 that increased advertisements to multiple pages and reviews to new levels of ecstasy. The $4 million beachfront hotel stood on fifteen acres of grounds. Members of the press were guests at the grand opening. The papers printed verbatim press releases by the Hawaii Tourist Bureau. Special editions of the *Star-Bulletin* and *Advertiser*—the latter alone ran three editions of twenty-four pages each—were filled with congratulatory advertisements, promotionals, and photo essays on the housekeeping staff, chefs, porters, head bellboy, and "Intelligence Office" (security), as well as on the managers and their assistants. Nostalgia for the passing of a way of life was sentimentally bolstered by old, bucolic photos and offset by the anticipation of future profits. One article in the *Advertiser* on February 1, 1927, opined: "Truly, the new Royal Hawaiian Hotel is admirably located for a tourist resort, close to the shore which has so many historic associations with . . . the misty, legendary days of ancient Hawaii." In the same edition, real estate ads urged investors:

ROYAL HAWAIIAN HOTEL
OPENING MARKS A NEW ERA
IN WAIKIKI
Buy now and watch the value of your property advance.

An *Advertiser* editorial noted approvingly that property prices were rising spectacularly and that beach frontage that had sold for $100,000 in 1923 was selling for $350,000 in 1928.

The "Pink Palace" would continue to capture the public fancy, and Waikīkī would continue to be viewed as a money-making opportunity. In 1959, just prior to statehood and another development spurt, bolstered by hyping of the "aloha spirit," the *Star-Bulletin* described the "miracle mile" in its magazine section: "It took a far sighted Territorial Legislature to make Waikiki what it is today . . . a gold mine" (Nov. 29, 1959).

23. Getting Away With Murder: The Massie Case

Only four years after newspapers proclaimed the opening of the Royal Hawaiian Hotel as a testimony to the "aloha spirit," a different kind of event in Waikīkī captured headlines and profoundly threatened that image. The news of what was to become the most famous crime case in Hawai'i hit the Honolulu streets on a Monday morning in 1931: "Gang Assaults Young Wife Kidnapped in Automobile; Maltreated by Fiends" (*Adv.*, Sept. 14, 1931).

From the moment the major dailies broke the story, it was a trial by newspapers and an index of race relations in Hawai'i. The *Massie* case was a combination of the "moral disorder" story, which is a hallowed tradition in journalism wherein those not expected to misbehave do so, and a sensational murder, the most fascinating of all crime stories. Also, the event occurred when the country was gripped by the Great Depression and served as a diversion for the public.

The two principal Honolulu dailies, as well as the *Hilo Tribune-Herald*, did not just respond, but rushed to confer judgment and create a "crime wave" that thrust Hawai'i into the national spotlight. As a result, the Associated Press listed the Massie story—a tale of "terror in Paradise," of dark-skinned "natives" lusting after a white woman, followed by an avenging "code of honor" murder—as nationally among its ten most important news events of the year (the kidnapping-murder of the Lindbergh baby was number one) (Pratte 1976). Hawai'i's status as a Territory was threatened by a proposal that the Islands be placed under a commission form of government.

There were long-term changes, too. The criminal justice system was reorganized. And the son of *Star-Bulletin* publisher Wallace Rider Farrington, Joseph Farrington, left his post as managing editor to take up public relations work to try to improve Hawai'i's national image. In 1934, Joe Farrington entered political life, becoming Hawai'i's delegate to Congress and a chief proponent of statehood (Pratte 1976). Fallout from the *Massie* case produced another result. Resentments of ethnic groups because of the handling of the episode have so impacted other rape and murder cases that coverage of almost any rape-murder crime to this day will refer back to the earlier case.

The story is well known (Wright 1966): on a Saturday night, September 12, 1931, Thalia Massie wandered off from a party at the Ala Wai Inn, a Waikīkī "tea house," at which there was heavy drinking of bootleg liquor (prohibition was still in effect). She was found by passersby some two hours later with her face bruised, mouth bleeding, and jaw broken. When her husband reached her by phone at home, she said something "terrible has happened." She first reported to police that she was beaten by "some Hawaiian boys"; later she added that she had been abducted and forced into a car, raped, and abandoned. At first she could not identify the suspects. After repeated trips to her hospital room by police accompanied by five young men they had picked up for questioning in another case, she made a positive identification. The men, Benny Ahakuelo, Henry Chang, Horace Ida, Joseph Kahahawai, and David Takai, had attended a party in Waikīkī and afterward got into an altercation several miles away with a couple in another car. One of the men struck the woman. When the police came to that scene, they immediately assumed the men were the perpetrators of the crime reported earlier across town. The police never looked for anyone else.

The case involved Thalia Fortescu Massie, twenty-year-old wife of Thomas Hedges Massie, a Naval Academy graduate in the submarine service. Through her father she was connected to Theodore Roosevelt; her mother, Grace Fortescu, was a socialite. The couple lived in Mānoa Valley, and in pre–World War II Hawai'i were part of a small, closed group of Caucasian navy officers and their families of whom the women were treated in the society sections of the newspapers as members of the haole elite.

It is instructive to place the *Massie* case into historical newspaper context. Peter Nelligan's meticulous study, "Social Change and Rape Law," points out that from the nineteenth century until recently, what has mattered most to the legal system and the newspapers is "who was raped by whom" (Nelligan 1983). Women have been divided into "respectable" and "unrespectable" based on their observance or nonobservance of norms of sexual exclusivity. From the 1850s on, the mainstream papers, backing the legal system, demanded the control of dangerous sexual proclivities of the non-white underclass. "Lynch law," however, was not a component. Nor were manufactured "crime waves" (Sutherland and Cressey 1980).

In the early years of the twentieth century, ethnic relations deteriorated due to a changing class structure, urbanization, and a diffusion into the Territory of mainland racial attitudes through the growth of a military presence (Fuchs 1961; Nelligan 1983). Honolulu papers from the 1910s through the 1930s adopted the mainland pattern of reporting sex crimes, the papers escalating a few spectacular or particularly brutal ones to a "crime wave" for which "lynch law" was the solution. The *Advertiser* was an "agent of change" in this, according to Nelligan. During a so-called crime wave in 1910, non-Caucasian perpetrators of rape were labeled subhuman "brutes . . . reeking of bestiality." The "honor of womanhood and the sanctity of virtue" were at stake (*Adv.*, July 28, Aug. 24, 1910). Editorials calling for "the lash" for rapists set off a pro-whipping campaign by haole men and women.

In 1931, the papers labeled the alleged attackers "gangsters," "degenerates," and "thugs": that is, five dark-skinned youths from the lower socioeconomic neighborhoods of Kalihi, Pālama, and 'Aiea. The papers stressed the "criminality" of the young men—"ex-convicts with prison records"—in that one had been previously charged with "fornication involving a minor" and another had served time for robbery.

The victim by contrast was called "a woman of the highest character" and "a white woman of refinement and culture" (*Adv.*, *Star-Bull.*, Sept. 14, 1931). Although she remained unnamed in the mainstream papers until after her mother, husband, and two accomplices murdered one of the youths, her identity was immediately disclosed by *Hawaii Hochi* and was soon widely known (Sept. 14, 1931).

There was an immediate sharp division among the public as to the men's guilt or innocence, mostly dependent upon the source of information. Most Caucasians and navy personnel who read the English language dailies and had a "haole grapevine" assumed the men's guilt. Hawaiians, Japanese, Portuguese, and other local groups who read *Hawaii Hochi* or were informed by a non-haole grapevine, which included members of the police force in which many Hawaiians served, felt that the youths were being railroaded.

In newspapers, selection and placement of stories and photos is always informative. Reflecting their own and the navy's fear that justice would not be done, the *Advertiser* and *Star-Bulletin* printed messages that can only be called an invitation to lynch law. Rear Admiral Yates Stirling Jr., commandant of the Fourteenth Naval District at Pearl Harbor, was quoted and requoted as saying that whites were "under attack in Hawai'i" and as advising the public to "seize the brutes and string them up in trees." Front page *Advertiser* editorials declared that no woman nor child was safe because of "emboldened sex offenders." During the trial, the papers repeatedly displayed the same staring "mug shot" photos of the young men. During jury deliberation, the *Advertiser*, using a layout device almost as attention getting as a photo, boxed and placed top center on the front page a wire press story from Maryland: "Mob Lynches Negro Slayer, Burns Body" (Dec. 3, 1931).

Jurors first returned a "no bill," the equivalent to finding insufficient evidence to warrant a formal charge. Judge Albert Cristy sent them back to reconsider their decision. They did so, and the trial went forward. The jury, however, deadlocked. Composed of a cross section by employment and ethnic backgrounds of Honolulu males, they were not convinced beyond a reasonable doubt that a rape had occurred. Thalia Massie's clothing was intact, and who beat her was in question. A later private report by the Pinkerton Agency for Governor Lawrence Judd supported the time element that placed the youths miles from the scene and would have vindicated them (Wright 1966).

Establishment papers were furious. They blasted John C. Kelley, prosecuting attorney, and the criminal justice system for not having done their jobs. They cited "known outrages" and reported that white women were having to arm themselves. Moreover, the entire situation was bad for tourism and the defense economy of Hawai'i— an "unbearable state of affairs." Under the headline, "Something Must Be Done," one editorial stated that tourists who left Hawai'i told others that it was not safe for women and children. The good name of Honolulu was being sullied, the community "virtually at the mercy of gangsters" (*Adv.*, Sept. 29, 1931). Another declared that any cancellation of naval fleet activities would bring great financial loss to the business community (*Star-Bull.*, Dec. 11, 1931). Picking up on both points, a national news magazine, under "Lust in Paradise," opined that "yellow men's lust for white women had broken bonds" and that Honolulu was "unsafe" for Navy wives (*Time*, Dec. 28, 1931).

After the trial, Horace Ida was seized on the street by several men, driven into the country, and severely beaten. The *Advertiser*'s recommendation? Vigilantism: "Hysteria in Favor of Law Observance is Wholesome" (Jan. 7, 1932). The next day, crime news again rocked the Islands. On January 8, Joseph Kahahawai was forced into a car. Kahahawai's cousin alerted the police, and patrol cars stopped the auto near Koko Head. Police arrested the driver, Lieutenant Massie, Mrs. Fortescu, who had come from the East Coast to be at her daughter's side, and Albert O. Jones, a navy enlisted man who had a gun and was seated beside the dead body of Kahahawai. They also arrested Edward J. Lord, a sailor who had been present at the Massie house where Kahahawai was taken, shot, and killed, and his body stuffed into the Massie car for disposal.

National attention zeroed in on the murder trial. Mrs. Fortescu hired the famous criminal lawyer, Clarence Darrow, for the codefendants, and the New York papers sent reporters. The papers warned of the "mongrel mixture of races in Hawaii" where there was a "Melting Pot Peril!" (*New York News, New York Post,* Jan. 11, 1932). The Hearst papers demanded that Hawai'i be placed under martial law (*New York American,* Jan. 12, 1932). The *Star-Bulletin*'s worst fears seemed to have been realized—"Fleet Coming; Shore Leave Barred"—for in the meantime, it was reassessing the situation because of the obvious damage to Hawai'i's mainland image. Riley Allen editorialized, "People who take the law into their own hands always make a mess of it." He cautioned Islanders to follow the orderly process of the law and said that what had happened was a "horrible example of what hysteria and lack of balance will do" (*Star-Bull.,* Jan. 9, 1932).

At the trial of Kahahawai's murderers, Darrow pleaded temporary insanity for his clients. The jury brought in a verdict of manslaughter with a recommendation for leniency for Lieutenant Massie "for all he'd suffered." Nevertheless, Judge Charles S. Davis sentenced each of the four to ten years at hard labor in O'ahu Prison. Significantly, however, the perpetrators, who were not held in jail during the trial, which was the custom, but stayed aboard the USN *Alden* at Pearl Harbor, served exactly one hour of their sentences, in Governor Lawrence Judd's chambers.

Surprisingly, considering its control of the Islands, the oligarchy itself came under attack. A highly vocal *Hawaii Hochi* had expressed outrage when the case originally broke, suggesting that the five suspects might have a "water-tight alibi" (Sept. 14, 1931). After the second crime, *Hochi* stated: "The crime [of killing Kahahawai] is the logical consequence of events. . . . To this end, the local hysteria and impatience with 'due process of law' contributed no small share." *Hochi* expressed disatisfaction with the navy, as well, stating that those in command "surely have something to answer for" (Jan. 12, 1932). *Hochi* blasted the haole leadership as "traitors to Hawaii in the eyes of the common people" and of having acquiesced to a reign of terror and intimidation (May 10, 1932). Years later, former Governor Judd admitted to having been pressured from Washington, D.C., to release Kahahawai's killers (Wright 1966).

A good many people, including those running and reading the English language dailies, were sobered, as reflected in a spate of letters to the editor. Few could abide lynching, and a number of letters spoke of the necessity to be "law abiding." In addition, oligarchy control was threatened by serious talk in Washington, D.C., of a commission government and the removal of residency requirements for appointed officials to the Territory, a remedy the oligarchy most emphatically did not want. The oligarchy had its own answers: a reorganization of the criminal justice system and a change in the penalty for rape from life imprisonment to death, both backed by the main dailies.

In the aftermath of the *Massie* case and Hawai'i's unfortunate national exposure, the papers sought stories that would place the Islands in a good light and would continue to divert attention from economic hard times, which establishment papers on all the Islands generally denied. Visits by a U.S. president and a Hollywood megastar helped to do this. The Hilo daily said when Franklin Delano Roosevelt arrived in 1934, "The greatest newswriters in America will accompany the nation's executive. . . . They will get a true picture of modern-day Hawaii" (*Trib.-Herald*, Apr. 18, 1934). The 1935 visit of Shirley Temple, may have been even more of a diversion. "Into the Hearts of All Honolulu" came the blond, curly-haired moppet to monopolize the front pages for her entire three-week visit, one headline declaring, "Depression in U.S. Is Shown to Be Ended," and another announcing "Thousands on Hand to Greet Shirley Temple" (*Star-Bull.*, July 29, 1935).

But the *Massie* case was not forgotten, just dormant. It was déjà vu in 1948. Two young Hawaiian men who were prisoners walked away from a work crew and broke into Mrs. Theresa Wilder's Nu'uanu home. Mrs. Wilder was a sixty-eight-year-old Caucasian "kamaaina widow and a member of one of Hawaii's best known families" (*Star Bull.*, Mar. 16, 1948). Her body was discovered bound and gagged. She had been strangled, and she may have been raped.

Using the same old tactics, the dailies tried and convicted the accused and cued the public. The press cried, a "crime wave" of postwar "lawlessness," an "outrage against decency," the "blood lust of

a killer [who] slew a woman mercilessly and savagely" (*Star-Bull.,
Adv.*, Mar. 17, 18, 1948). The *Advertiser* called for the death penalty.
Although premeditated first degree murder could not be proved, the
jury convicted James E. Majors, twenty-one, and John Palakiko,
nineteen, and they were sentenced to be hanged.

Post–World War II Hawai'i, like post-1900, was undergoing
change, but this time for the better. With a shift in the demographics
of power from a small haole oligarchy to a broader based and ethnically mixed middle class, public sentiment was changing (Hormann
1950). Criticism of the oligarchy spread through the community
(Nelligan 1983). Another opposition paper, the *Honolulu Record*,
drew the comparison to the *Massie* case, pointing out that Majors
and Palakiko, like Joseph Kahahawai, were underprivileged Hawaiians, that the crime was likely unpremeditated, and that there was a
double standard of class and race that would hang the Hawaiians but
had freed Kahahawai's Caucasian murderers.

The Honolulu dailes had not yet changed, however. Because "left
wing" lawyers and a "radical" newspaper—that is, labor attorney
Harriet Bouslog and the *Honolulu Record*—had taken up the *Majors-
Palakiko* case, the *Advertiser* refused to print any letters to the editor on the subject. Claiming there were too many, the *Star-Bulletin*
limited those it printed.

More than six years after the crime's date and many appeals, Governor Samuel Wilder King, himself part-Hawaiian and sensitive to
the racial issues, commuted the sentences to life imprisonment
(*Star-Bull.*, Aug. 14, 1954) and signed legislation in 1957 abolishing
the death penalty. Majors and Palakiko were pardoned by Governor
John Burns in 1962. "Governor Paroles Two Island Slayers," headlined the *Advertiser* (Dec. 12, 1962).

The power of the Massie story to arouse emotions resurfaces at
regular intervals, and rape is still viewed as injurious to the visitor
industry. The race of offenders is less important, but "sexual exclusivity" or lack of it in the victim is still a primary consideration. In
1979, when local youths gang-raped a Finnish dental student who
had smoked marijuana with them, a jury refused to convict the
assailants. The *Advertiser* commented on the "Nanakuli Rape
Case": "The recent sexual assault on a Scandinavian tourist is a
reminder that such violent attacks are unusually damaging to
Hawaii where the economy depends largely on a well earned international reputation for the Aloha spirit" (July 15, 1979).

24. Hilo's "Bloody Monday": The *Tribune-Herald* and the *Voice of Labor*

Murder, rape, visits from a president and a megastar—these did not for long distract people who could not meet the costs of living during the Great Depression. In Hilo, a long simmering labor-management dispute erupted on August 1, 1938, into what some have called "Bloody Monday," others the "Hilo Massacre." Two very different kinds of newspapers were there to record this, but more than that, to impact upon the way people felt about the episode from then to now. The *Hilo Tribune-Herald*, owned by the *Star-Bulletin*, spoke for management; the *Voice of Labor*, backed by the International Longshoremen's and Warehousemen's Union (ILWU), represented labor.

The *Tribune-Herald* was Hawai'i island's only daily paper. (The Honolulu dailies were shipped in overnight.) Its circulation of 3,010 on weekdays and 3,475 on Sunday resulted in a distribution that was quite low considering its territory covered the entire Big Island, with a total population of 77,833. The *Voice of Labor*, a weekly published in Honolulu and aimed at a Territory-wide population of 388,336, claimed a paid circulation of 1,000, an apparently smaller distribution ratio. But the *Voice* had a press run far beyond that, of 4,000 to 5,000. Free copies were passed from hand to hand and house to house, as well as on street corners, at union halls, cafes, pool halls, and other places where workers congregated. The *Voice* was probably read by more people than the *Tribune-Herald*.

How did these papers respond to August 1? How much influence did they wield? It is possible to view the *Tribune-Herald*, as does professor of labor studies William J. Puette, as a management accomplice to Bloody Monday (Puette 1988). It is also possible to view it as being ambivalent and thus inadvertently helping labor. The *Voice of Labor*'s position was unambivalent. In a contest between uncertainty and clarity of purpose, the latter usually prevails. The *Voice* was also in the vanguard of the shaping of modern Hawai'i.

Several things are clear today. Bloody Monday or the Hilo Massacre occurred in a unique community that over the years has placed a premium on harmony. In Hilo, members of management and labor

were often intimately connected through work, family, and friendships. Periodically threatened by lava flows from active volcanoes
and devastating tidal waves, residents have also developed an attitude against "playing it safe." In 1938, there were feuds, as is usual
in small towns; but regardless of differences in social, political, or
economic backgrounds, Hilo residents met daily at the post office
and corner drugstores and expected to get along with each other.
Bloody Monday is part of Hilo's social history when its social fabric
was ripped apart, then mended.

Hilo Tribune-Herald Responds

The Big Island's first paper, the weekly *Hilo Tribune*, in 1895,
merged with other papers to become the daily *Hilo Tribune-Herald*
in 1917. In turn, it was bought out by the *Honolulu Star-Bulletin* in
1925, cementing its economic dominance but ceding its position as
a "hometown" paper.

Management practice was to exchange staff between the two
papers. The *Star-Bulletin* in 1934 sent Kenneth S. Byerly from Honolulu to Hilo where he became vice president and general manager, a
post he held for more than ten years. Byerly, who joined the Hilo
Chamber of Commerce that took Big Five positions, and editor Virginia Bennett Hill were Republican in politics and conservative in
outlook. Hill, however, was from Hilo, and a gregarious Byerly made
friends among many community groups, including rising Democratic party leaders such as Judge Delbert Metzger and attorney Martin Pence.

Moreover, after new federal laws in 1933 and 1935 legalized labor
organizing and labor-management mediation by the National Labor
Relations Board, the Star-Bulletin Printing Company in July 1938
signed an agreement with the International Typographers Union,
covering pressmen and bindery workers, and the ILWU for its circulation department. This somewhat moderated the *Star-Bulletin* and
Tribune-Herald hard-line antiunion stance, although both opposed
picketing and favored antiunion laws.

The *Tribune-Herald* was in many ways the typical mainstream
periodical that poorly informs the public about the reasons behind
social upheavals and emphasizes the threatening behavior of those
who protest against the system. The status quo represents "order";
changes advocated by those outside the power structure typify "disorder." But in 1938, departing from earlier practice, neither the *Tribune-Herald* nor its Honolulu parent tried to black out news of labor

agitation. They acknowledged that the workers were American born and educated and that strikers and sympathizers were homegrown dissidents.

Another departure was that the *Tribune-Herald,* in its total support of Hilo business, unintentionally strengthened labor's cause. Before regular air transport, Hilo depended upon shipping for supply lines. Business complained that Hilo was not getting its share of tourists. The *Tribune-Herald* frequently expressed the feeling that Honolulu viewed Hilo as a "branch town" and asked that Hilo be treated fairly and with dignity.

The news in the mid-1930s was filled with union organizing and strikes demanding fair treatment for labor. What labor had learned from the 1909 and 1920 strikes was to build a nonracial organization (Beechert 1985). A young Hawaiian-Chinese Hiloite, Harry Lehua Kamoku, was the primary organizer in November 1935 of the Hilo Longshoremen's Association (HLA) that represented an ethnic spectrum. Kamoku had worked on the San Francisco waterfront when West Coast maritime strikers, who battled police and the National Guard, won a closed shop hiring hall in 1934. Kamoku, thirty years old in 1935, came home to fight for the same benefits. By 1937, laundry, cane, and railroad workers were organized and opposing battle lines were being formed. Indicative of the community's intimacy in spite of battle lines, Kamoku and Hilo Sheriff Henry K. Martin were half brothers.

The *Tribune-Herald* in 1937 at first tried to blame "outsiders"—the usual establishment response—for the ninety-eight-day strike. The Inland Boatmen's Union, a Congress of Industrial Organizations affiliate, organized crews of the two ships that carried all light freight and passengers from Honolulu to Hilo. Inter-Island Steam Navigation Company, controlled since 1925 by Matson Navigation Company and Castle & Cooke, owned the ships. The Hilo daily reported the arrest of three "Coast Union Men" who allegedly beat up a "scab" seaman in the union hall (Jan. 25, 1937). But it also ran a photograph of picketers whose signs stated, "Hawaii Is an Integral Part of the U.S.A. So Are We," and "Uphold Democracy in the Hawaiian Islands." The caption stated, "Members of the Hilo Longshoremen's Association tell their story with . . . forceful placards in their peaceful demonstration along Kuhio Wharf" (Jan. 13, 1937).

The HLA won this strike, and the newspaper thanked Hilo for a return to "normal conditions" (*Trib.-Herald,* Feb. 5, 1937). When another strike surfaced in 1938, the paper this time blamed local labor for letting a "strike epidemic" spread from the mainland to Hawai'i but again adopted a community line, expressing "a sincere desire to be mutually helpful in its endeavor to bring about a better understanding between the men and the company than is now apparent" (May 20, 1938). Editorials were condescending and paternalistic, but they reminded Hilo that life would continue beyond any strike: "Most of us islanders are proud of the reputation which we have enjoyed over a long period of years to the effect that the bond between master and man has been made of a pretty fair brand of material, and, as strikes cannot possibly last forever, the fewer nasty spots left over to be rubbed out, the better for the future relations . . . of the daily contacts between employer and employe" (*Trib.-Herald*, May 29, 1938). Because merchants lose business and newspapers lose advertising during a strike, the paper almost daily expressed the hope, "Strike Settlement Nearer" (*Trib.-Herald*, July 16, 1938).

But settlement was not near, and real trouble loomed. Inter-Island, determined to keep the ships moving, sent the SS *Waialeale* from Honolulu to Hilo in late July. A large crowd assembled at the Hilo wharf on July 22. When the crowd moved toward the ship, Lieutenant Charles Warren from the Sheriff's Department lobbed a tear gas canister into the middle of the gathering. Warren, a World War I veteran, had a reputation for hotheadedness and brutality. The bomb exploded in the face of Onson Kim, an eleven-year-old child, who was rushed to the hospital. Her injuries were minor, but reactions were strong. The paper printed an agreement between Kamoku and Thomas Straithern, Inter-Island Hilo manager (who later issued a denial), that the union would not demonstrate against passenger and mail service and that the company would not unload cargo in Hilo (*Trib.-Herald*, July 22, 1938).

A "dynamite plot" surfaced, allegedly against the *Waialeale*, and was headlined throughout the Islands. The *Advertiser* immediately assumed the guilt of seven American Federation of Labor men who had been arrested (July 18, 1938). But the *Star-Bulletin* and *Tribune-Herald*, although positing that it could be a "sinister conspiracy," added that it might only be "a clumsy scheme to discredit labor, or merely a shallow farce originating in some dimwit's brain" (*Star-Bull., Trib.-Herald*, July 23, 1938). The court dismissed the charges for lack of evidence.

On August 1, Inter-Island management sent the *Waialeale* back to Hilo, and Sheriff Martin armed sixty county officers with riot guns fitted with bayonets. Some 200 protestors, mostly young men and women belonging to several local unions, marched down Kūhiō Road to Pier 2, where they sat down. Some sang "Hail, hail, the gangs all here"; others shouted to the crew to stop "scabbing" and taunted "tear gas Warren." The police panicked. Unlike the Hanapēpē Massacre of 1924, in which twenty men were killed, Hilo's Bloody Monday produced no deaths. In five minutes time, however, the police gassed, hosed, shot, and bayoneted fifty-one of their fellow citizens who received most of their wounds in their backs as they fled (Beechert 1985; Puette 1988).

The *Tribune-Herald*'s reflex reaction in its "Extra" edition was to speak for the establishment. It called the protestors a "mob" and halved the numbers of injured—"36 Injured During Riot." A front page editorial invoked the usual plea, "Let True American Citizenship Prevail" on "the side of law and order" (Aug. 1, 2). But the Hilo daily also provided accurate details of the event. A first-page account of August 1 by a young reporter, Donald Billam-Walker, stated that the union group had made no attempt to molest disembarking passengers:

> They . . . sat down about 150 feet from the entrance to the Inter-Island shed. The police attempted to disperse them without success and it appeared to be a "sit-down" strike for the next hour. Then slowly the group edged closer toward the entrance to Pier 2 and sat down about 15 yards from the entrance. Police officers were closing in around the group, using their clubs to keep them back.
>
> At this time, . . . one group rushed at Charlie Warren, police officer . . . [who] reportedly used his bayonet, stabbing . . . Kai Uratani in the back. An order to fire was given by Deputy Sheriff Peter N. Pakele, and the police fired into the mob, shooting toward the ground.

The *Tribune-Herald* not only let authorities speak—the usual practice—but let workers speak for themselves and did not refute them, likely a first in establishment papers:

> Kai Uratani . . . said he was half lying on the ground on his right side and that Police Officer Charles Warren approached:
> "He carried a gun. There was a bayonet fixed.
> Warren said to me: 'You get the hell out of here.'

With that, Warren brought the butt of his gun up and with it struck the side of my face three times. I began to get up and retreat.

It was while I was moving off I was bayoneted in the back by Warren." (Aug. 2, 1938)

The *Tribune-Herald* reporter objectively quoted other participants. Warren claimed that Uratani refused to obey his order to move. David Furtano, ILWU clerk, differed, stating that Warren hit Uratani "who was sitting down, with the butt of his gun on the side of his face. . . . As Kai retreated he was bayoneted in the back by Warren." Others confirmed this view. Charles Martin, Hilo weatherman, who was related to both unionist Harry Kamoku and Kamoku's half brother Sheriff Henry Martin, called the actions of brother Henry a "disgrace" and said that he "fell down in his job." To Harry Kamoku, this was "a massacre of the workers by police who used murderous bullets. . . . a bunch of mad men under their uniforms" (Aug. 2, 1938). Sharp photographs reinforced Kamoku's account, for they showed unarmed men and women seated on the docks, then attempting to flee from the police by leaping from the pier into the water.

The *Tribune-Herald* departed from establishment practice in another significant way. During the strike, it provided a public forum for letters to the editor from both sides. At the strike's end, it asked for the community to draw together, expressing

a profound sigh of relief that the minds of men have been restored to their normal level.

The main duty for each one of us to follow from this day forward is to see to it that we meet every gesture of friendship with a corresponding advance. . . .

Mutual goodwill stands out as the greatest need of the hour. Mutual respect will follow. (Aug. 15, 1938)

In the aftermath, the Territory officially whitewashed the entire episode through an attorney general's "investigation." The *Tribune-Herald* continued its campaign to bring tourist ships directly to Hilo and to boost Big Island business. Yet in 1938 it covered the first Labor Day parade in Hilo's history.

Another Hilo paper followed the *Tribune-Herald*'s lead. Put out by John A. Lee and Harold W. Ching, the *Hawaii Press* (1932–1949), was against the strike but didn't blame either side. It welcomed

Hilo's return to "normalcy" because "everyone loses, the community the most of all" (*Haw. Press*, Aug. 16, 1938).

The *Voice of Labor* Responds

The *Hilo Tribune-Herald* attempted in its own limited way to present both sides. This was not the goal of the *Voice of Labor* (1935–1939). In 1936, "Hawaii's only working class newspaper" became the ILWU's official organ. In the words of Jack Hall, synonymous with the *Voice:* "There is no excuse for an impartial paper. People are not impartial" (Zalberg 1979).

The first labor papers in Hawai'i, *Ookala Shuho* (1902) and *Rhoda Shinbun* (1904), were unaffiliated, short-lived journals in Japanese published in sugar camps (Sakamaki 1928). Some sixty labor newspapers have appeared since the early 1900s, from semiweeklies to monthlies, bearing such descriptive names as the *Hook* (1939), put out by the Honolulu Longshoremen's Association, and the ILWU's *Soapboxer* (1977–1978). The *Voice of Labor* has likely been the most influential because of the important years in which it appeared and because it clarified labor issues for the workers, provided communication among them, and boosted their morale. Not only union members, but legislators, university professors, and other opinion-makers read the *Voice.*

Corby Paxton, the first editor, raised forty dollars to start the *Voice* and was the only paid staff member, at ten dollars per week, when he was paid (Zalberg 1979). In contrast to the professionally printed *Tribune-Herald*, whose editor made ten times that figure, the *Voice* originally appeared on mimeographed, stapled sheets. It was produced at ILWU headquarters, first at 918 Maunakea Street, and then from 184 Merchant Street. Within six weeks, enough money was raised by union members and from advertisements and subscriptions—two dollars per year or five cents per single copy—to buy an old printing press and produce the *Voice* on newsprint. Advertisements mirrored labor's support, such as: in Honolulu, the Dew Drop Inn at 'A'ala Park, the Anchor Cafe "opposite Pier 19," Aala Fish Market, and No-D-Lay Cab, in which "4 can ride for the price of one"; in Hilo, the Kuhio Grocerteria and Union Bar, "Jimmy Kealoha, Prop."

The *Voice* came out in English, with occasional columns in Japanese and Hawaiian. In mid-1936, the union bought better press equipment with photo engraving capability. Rather typical of a seat-of-the-pants opposition operation, publication days were erratic, shifting from Saturdays to Mondays to Thursdays. But the small staff never missed an edition.

Some *Voice of Labor* staff, as union activist Bob McElrath pointed out, had previous newspaper experience. Edward Berman covered sports for the *Philadelphia Record*, and McElrath, a fireman aboard a Matson vessel and a labor organizer, wrote for the the American Newspaper Guild journal in Seattle. Although his name did not appear on the masthead until April 1938, union organizer Jack Hall was the main editor. He occasionally slept on the office floor or on a cot to arise early to help print the paper and to hawk copies on the street. Because equipment lacked an automatic folder and the *Voice* had no mailing permit, Hall and McElrath would fold each paper and individually lick each one-cent stamp for the mailings. McElrath wryly stated that they took delight in mailing copies to the Honolulu FBI office (McElrath 1987).

As a weekly, the *Voice* did not compete for the breaking news. Rather, it delved into root causes and went to unofficial sources to dig up information that the "Sugar Press," as it called the establishment papers, would not print. It issued special "Strike Bulletins" to apprise workers of developments.

The *Voice* seemed to take special pleasure in catching "the bosses" in contradictions. At the height of the depression, it published the substantial earnings of the Big Five companies while wages of workers dropped. Cartoons depicted bloated capitalists lighting cigars with dollar bills. A front page column, "This Day in Paradise," highlighted child labor and poor pineapple cannery working conditions. The paper reported plots against union hiring halls and organizers.

The *Voice*'s reporting of the events on August 1 was unabashedly pro-labor: "They Even Shot Men in the Back." The story, "By Harry Kamoku. As Told to Edward Berman," was an amplification of the *Tribune-Herald*'s and was accompanied by the same photos, but its language was far more condemnatory. "They shot us down like a herd of sheep. We didn't have a chance. . . . They just kept pumping buckshot and bullets into our bodies. They shot men in the back as they ran. They shot men who were trying to help wounded comrades and women. They ripped their bodies with bayonets. It was just plain slaughter . . . of unarmed, defenseless workers" (*Voice*, Aug. 4, 1938). Finally, the *Voice*, quoting Harry Kamoku, contributed the word "massacre" to history (Aug. 11, 1938).

The *Voice of Labor* is gone. The paper accompanied union organizing activities first to Kaua'i, as the *Kauai Herald* (1940–1941), then to Honolulu as the *Herald* (1941), where after the onset of World War II it became the *Victory* (1942). With union activities dead for the war's duration, the lively paper that made history closed up shop.

The *Tribune-Herald*, however, is still here and regularly revisits the memory of August 1, 1938. Upon the episode's fiftieth anniversary, the *Hawaii Tribune-Herald* (its name since 1964) gave front-page coverage to commemorative services led by ILWU Local 142 and the unveiling of a monument at the Hilo dock. Reporter Maxine Hughes interviewed the most severely injured person of that day, Bert Nakano, a twenty-seven-year-old longshoreman at the time: "ILWU retiree recalls 1938's 'Hilo Massacre.'" The quotes within quotes illustrate the conflicting viewpoints between management and labor that still exist. But Hughes' account also reflects Hilo's ongoing ability to agree to disagree and its community mindedness.

As in 1938, the paper let Nakano speak for himself: "I took four buckshot; one passed through my forearm, another through my thigh, and two through my groin, severing an artery." He described his long recuperation, his career as ILWU secretary-treasurer and business agent, and his appointment to president of the County Planning Commission and member of the County Board of Appeals. Retired, Nakano concluded, "I try to look on the good side of life, and keep myself busy" (*Trib.-Herald*, July 31, 1988).

Nakano's summary aptly summarizes the merging of labor and management into the social, political, and economic mainstream of Hawai'i. Its labor and management papers in 1938 pointed toward this goal.

PART V

"Passed for Publication"—
1941–1945

25. A Wartime Press and the Paradox of Censorship for Freedom

The attack by Japan on Sunday, December 7, 1941, at 7:55 A.M. lasted less than one hour but affected the papers' relationship to the public as no other event in Hawaiian history has. The newspapers were indispensable as the primary source of public information during the four years of the war. They also confirmed the Territory as an integral part of the United States, a fact previously not always understood or acknowledged by the forty-eight states.

At the center of their function in this critical period was a series of paradoxes. An inherent paradox is that war itself stimulates news while other forces, mainly shortages and censorship, curtail its reporting. Another is that most of the Territory's papers were shut down in 1941, thereby leaving to the censored few the enormous task of keeping a civilian population of 423,340 informed about the war (1940 census figures). Newspapers allowed to remain in business—whether establishment, opposition, or independent—in effect merged into an official press. As it developed, other unusual paradoxes contributed to how the papers interacted with history.

Getting Out the News in Wartime

To an *Advertiser* staff member, Pearl Harbor was by far the most important experience in her forty-five years as a newspaperwoman. Irva Coll attests to the strong motivation shared by newspeople everywhere, to get out the news regardless of uncertainty or danger. The *Advertiser* printed and delivered its Sunday edition before the Pearl Harbor attack. Coll went to the Kapi'olani Boulevard building Sunday morning to work on Monday's edition: "I arrived about 7:30. When we realized we were being attacked, we ran up on the roof of the building, but all we could see were billowing clouds of smoke over Pearl Harbor. People were saying we should go down into the basement for safety, but I wouldn't go. That's where we kept the huge rolls of newsprint, and I could imagine if a bomb struck those rolls would crush us. I sat on the stairs on the first floor for a while, then decided to go up to the second and go to work" (Coll 1991).

Publisher Lorrin Thurston arrived at the *Advertiser* just after a shell burst close by (later identified as American antiaircraft fire). Editor Riley Allen, at his desk at the *Star-Bulletin* on Merchant Street and working on Monday's paper, immediately called in reporters and production people who got out three "Extra" editions, the first within two hours, making the *Star-Bulletin* the first newspaper in the world with details of the attack (Pratte 1966).

Radio stations KGU and KGMB carried immediate reports of the attack. Within two hours military censors delivered explicit wartime instructions to the stations, banning giving details of places or speculations on the size of attack. These orders were then distributed to the newspaper offices.

At 11:30 A.M. on December 7, Governor Joseph Poindexter invoked the Hawaii Defense Act, adopted in 1941, and at 3:30 P.M. proclaimed a state of martial law. The commanding general of the U.S. Army took over as governor. The military, assuming all executive, legislative, and judiciary powers, issued comprehensive directives as to what exactly the newspapers could print. These reached the papers' offices on Monday morning.

The newspapers only briefly gave sensationalist or wrong information, as when the *Advertiser* erroneously headlined: "Saboteurs Land Here! Raiders Return in Dawn Attack" (Dec. 8, 1941). In its excitement, the *Maui News* forgot to change Saturday's date line and printed its "First War Extra" on "December 6."

Except for a few such errors, the papers from Līhu'e to Hilo provided essential news and instructions and calmed the public—no small feat in an atmosphere of total nightly blackouts and curfews and uncertainty as to when and if there would be another attack. *Maui News* editor Ezra J. Crane, who shortly went on active duty with the army, remembered to give Maui readers all-important news. Punahou School was to have played Baldwin High School on Sunday for the final game of the interscholastic football season. "Game Off," headlined Crane, followed by "Japan Planes Attack Oahu" (Dec. 6 [*sic*], 1941). On Kaua'i, Charlie Fern, *Garden Island* owner and director of Civilian Defense for the island, gave useful instructions for several weeks: "Keep Calm—Keep the Peace" and "What to Do in Case of An Air Raid Warning." The *Garden Island* ran columns in Japanese, Tagalog, and Visayan. Fern and Civilian Defense issued a *Garden Island War Daily* (Dec. 10, 1941–Jan. 14, 1942) that blanketed the island daily with 5,000 copies.

A military "Governor's Proclamation" went into effect under

General Order No. 14: "By virtue of the authority vested in me as Military Governor, I hereby order and prohibit, effective at 8:00 A.M. December 12, 1941, the publication, printing, or circulation of all newspapers, magazines, periodicals, the dissemination of news or information by means of any unauthorized printed matter, or by wireless, radio, or press association."

Another paradox surrounds December 7. On the day of the attack, there were about thirty newspapers publishing in the Territory, including seventeen foreign language journals in Chinese, Filipino, Japanese, and Korean.

Those allowed to continue to publish without interruption were the *Honolulu Star-Bulletin* and *Honolulu Advertiser*, the *Hawaii Chinese Journal*, the *Hilo Tribune-Herald*, and *Hawaii Press* renamed the *Hawaii Filipino News*, the *Maui News*, and the *Garden Island*. Also permitted to operate were the wire press services and Transradio Press, along with four radio stations on O'ahu, Kaua'i, and Hawai'i (*Adv., Star-Bull.*, Dec. 12, 1941). The *Hawaii Chinese Journal*, a weekly that called itself "The Voice of 29,000 Chinese," identified how Hawai'i's complex racial mix affected its residents. When James Lum Akana, a sixty-year-old fire warden and bootblack, was "mistaken for a parachutist" by other wardens who beat and killed him, the paper reminded readers: "Unfortunately we look like Japanese. We must be on the alert for enemy spies, saboteurs and parachutists, but we must also guard against overzealous, unwarranted 'defense' measures against friendly civilians" (*Haw. Chinese Journ.*, Dec. 11, 1941). General Order No. 40 later permitted publication with English translations of two Chinese papers, *Hsin Chung-Kuo Jih Pao* (New China daily press) and *T'an Pao* (Hawaii Chinese journal) as well as religious journals such as the *Catholic Herald* and the *Hawaiian Church Chronicle*. Other orders allowed trade, school, and similar papers to operate (Richstad 1970). Although in March 1943 and October 1944 restoration of government powers to civilian authorities was phased in, the entire press remained under martial law and censorship to the war's end in August 1945.

But the papers were not the same. They were cut in size: for example, the *Star-Bulletin* went from up to fifty-four pages to eight to twenty-four. Sections were eliminated or reduced, although comics, at first removed, were restored for morale's sake. Home delivery ceased for the duration: the papers were only sold on the streets.

It was the most recent instance of censorship of the Islands' press—the Republic had suppressed press freedom in the 1890s. The

Newspaper, Radio Censorship Set Up

TERRITORY OF HAWAII
OFFICE OF THE MILITARY GOVERNOR
FORT SHAFTER, T. H.

10 December 1941.

Newspapers and Radios

GENERAL ORDERS NO. 14.

By virtue of the authority vested in me as Military Governor, I hereby order and prohibit, effective at 8:00 A. M., December 12, 1941, the publication, printing, or circulation of all newspapers, magazines, periodicals, the dissemination of news or information by means of any unauthorized printed matter, or by wireless, radio, or press association, except as follows:

1. NEWSPAPERS. Until further notice the following newspapers may, if they so desire, continue to be published and circulated under such conditions and regulations as shall be prescribed from time to time by the Military Governor:

NEWSPAPERS	Location
Honolulu Star-Bulletin	Oahu
Honolulu Advertiser	Oahu
Hilo Tribune-Herald	Hawaii
Hawaii Press	Hawaii
Maui News	Maui
Garden Island	Kauai

2. RADIO STATIONS. Until further notice the following radio stations may, if they so desire, continue to broadcast under such conditions and regulations as shall be prescribed from time to time by the Military Governor:

Radio Station	Location
KGU	Oahu
KGMB	Oahu
KTOH	Kauai
KHBC	Hawaii

3. PRESS ASSOCIATIONS. Until further notice the following press associations may continue to operate under such conditions and regulations as shall be prescribed from time to time by the Military Governor:

PRESS ASSOCIATIONS

Associated Press
United Press
International News Service
Transradio Press

By order of the Military Governor:
(S) THOMAS H. GREEN,
Lt. Col., J.A.G.D.,
Executive.

Gasoline Stations

OFFICE OF THE
TERRITORIAL DIRECTOR OF CIVILIAN DEFENSE
HONOLULU, T. H.

December 10, 1941.
Time: 3:40 p.m.

GENERAL ORDER NO. 27.

By virtue of the authority in me vested by the Governor of Hawaii, I do hereby order as follows:

1. Under paragraph 15 of Section 3 of Rule 4, business establishments dispensing gasoline may remain open at all hours until further notice. provided such establishments fully comply with all Blackout and other regulations.

By Order of

EDOUARD L. DOTY,
Territorial Director of Civilian Defense

From December 10, 1941, until the war's end in 1945, the military government, through General Order No. 14, imposed upon the Islands the most complete censorship ever practiced in the United States. Yet the papers remained the chief source of information for the public in the Territory during the war. (Hawai'i State Archives)

1940s censorship was the most complete ever imposed upon American newspapers. Initially, the military government cut off all incoming cables, radiograms, and telephone calls, imposing a total blackout on outside information—with one fortunate oversight. According to Hugh Lytle, Associated Press bureau chief who as a reserve officer was immediately ordered into uniform, had it not been for the United Press receiving station outside of town, the Islands' newspapers and radio stations would not have known of America's declaration of war on the Axis powers. All communications were restored in midweek (H. Lytle 1992).

From December 12 on, the Army's G-2 Section of the Hawaiian Department of Military Intelligence administered the censorship. Initially, a red-stamped notice, "Passed for Publication US Army Press Censor," was required on the front pages, but this was soon abandoned as cumbersome. The Federal Office of Censorship retained William Norwood, *Star-Bulletin* reporter, to oversee the application of directives (Pratte 1976), and the G-2 Section appointed two civilians to assist at the office located at the Sacred Hearts Convent on Nu'uanu Avenue. (A separate postal censorship was located in the post office building on Richards Street.)

An absence of news can be significant. During World War I, America's newspapers showed little of war's reality. No photos of dead bodies ever appeared (Fulton 1988). During World War II on the mainland, censorship under the War Powers Act of December 19, 1941, developed into a "Code of Wartime Practices for the American Press." Adherence to the code was voluntary (Emery and Emery 1992; Hynds 1980). Even so, newspapers, printed photographs of American casualties only after September 1943, but seldom of their faces.

Unlike the mainland, the Territory had total and mandatory censorship. At first, all the papers patriotically supported this. But because the military government extended censorship to cover its own conduct, doubts arose over contradictory and irrational directives. These doubts spread to questioning the necessity of military rule itself and the constitutionality of press censorship. The *Star-Bulletin* led in this questioning.

Although *Advertiser* publisher Lorrin P. Thurston was "happy to comply" with all censorship (*Adv.*, Dec. 13, 1941) and the morning paper had a cozy relationship with the military—Thurston became public relations adviser to the military government, and the powerful business leader, Walter Dillingham, part owner of the *Advertiser,* testified before Congress on the oligarchy's willingness to go along with military rule (Anthony 1975)—the *Advertiser* was the first to discuss the problems of putting out a paper in wartime. Editor Ray Coll Sr. also raised the larger issue of "higher-ups" delaying or prohibiting material that mainland papers freely disseminated (Dec. 21, 1942). It was difficult, too, "to adjust to radical, almost revolutionary changes in its methods of news-gathering, editing and circulation" (Mar. 29, 1942). For all that, the morning paper defended military rule even after the U.S. Supreme Court in 1946 declared its imposition on Hawai'i to have been unconstitutional.

By contrast, *Star-Bulletin* publisher Joe Farrington and editor Riley Allen early on were critical of censorship. *Star-Bulletin* leaders raised concerns about their reduced ability to inform the public and about the loss of press freedom. In 1942, territorial Attorney General J. Garner Anthony authored a legal brief in the *University of California Law Review* questioning the legality of the military government. Riley Allen connected Garner's brief to press freedom, and the *New York Times* picked up the story (*Star-Bull.*, May 16, 1942; *New York Times*, May 17, 1942). In December, Delegate to Congress Farrington made the first of several requests to return civil authority and constitutional government to the Territory. The military government was not happy. When Urban M. Allen, editor of the *Star-Bulletin*-owned *Hilo Tribune-Herald*, editorialized on the inordinate pressures being brought to bear on Americans of Japanese ancestry if they did not join the armed forces even though many had jobs essential to the war effort (*Trib.-Herald*, Feb. 9, 1943), the G-2 Hilo officer, Joseph O'Donnell, declared the Hilo daily harmful to the war effort and padlocked its doors. *Star-Bulletin* leaders protested, and the padlock was removed five hours later. But Riley Allen received a warning for the papers to not criticize the military government (Pratte 1966).

In 1944, when the war had long since moved westward and it was obvious that the United States was winning, Hawai'i was still considered a combat zone for censorship purposes. In a memo of June 5, Riley Allen outlined just what the papers were not allowed to print (Allen 1944; Pratte 1966). The catalog illustrates the vagaries of censorship. Weather conditions could not be printed until one week after these conditions disappeared and then only with the approval of G-2. News of the spectacular 1942 Mauna Loa eruption was suppressed although the glow could be clearly seen on O'ahu. The papers were not allowed to publish any military unit number except the Pacific's Seventh Air Force—but not its fighter command, unless in an official communiqué from Washington, D.C., or from a war theater. The papers could not reveal the name of any soldier killed in an accident, as in an auto accident, until the army notified next of kin, but "the Navy was not so particular on this point," Allen commented. They were denied access to police files and could not report murders and rapes. "Pen Pals" columns were eliminated because they might provide the enemy with "information of value." Nor could the papers in 1944 report government construction, such as the new Naval Air Station at Ke'ehi Lagoon, although the official ceremony opening the facility was reported in mainland papers. The *Star-Bulletin* had to remove a photo of the arrival of mainland wives to take jobs that the *Pearl Harbor Banner* (1943–1944), a civilian navy yard publication, printed.

What could the papers print during these four years? Much of importance. In the two Honolulu dailies alone, there appeared 140 separate articles on the blackout and another 50 on the curfew. There were at least 150 items on civilian defense, plus hundreds on the issuance of gas masks and the availability of food supplies and gasoline. In a lighter vein (now, but not at the time), the *Garden Island* urged Kaua'i residents to eat poi and taro and to ride on horses instead of in cars. Carrying sad news, too, the papers were the vehicle for casualty lists of Island men wounded or killed in North Africa, Europe, Asia, and the Pacific.

When a Presidential Proclamation finally terminated martial law and Hawai'i regained its powers of self-government, on October 24, 1944, the *Star-Bulletin* declared this the most significant day since annexation. Paradoxically, however, the army, through the Office of Internal Security, again took over censorship and continued it to the war's end.

Another kind of censorship continued over military papers. These papers were considered to be such an important means of communications and morale building for a service population that had burgeoned to almost one million that they were fully subsidized. Officers supervised the sixty or so published, but enlisted personnel put them out—editors, staff artists, reporters, cartoonists—who often had been professional journalists in civilian life. The papers ranged from mimeographed, stapled bulletins to tabloids on newsprint, and from bland officialese to the highly imaginative.

A small newspaper, the *SeaBeecon* (1943–1944), the monthly voice of the Third Naval Construction Regiment at Pearl Harbor, was involved in a censorship battle that reached the U.S. Supreme Court. The Seabees were members of the U.S. Navy's construction battalion. (Their clever name is attributed to a Honolulu newsman, William (Bill) Ewing, who headed the Associated Press bureau and later became editor of the *Star-Bulletin*.) Its New Year's 1944 edition placed the paper at the center of a censorship storm.

In 1943, the postmaster general brought charges of obscenity against *Esquire* magazine for printing allegedly harmful material that was not fulfilling a public service or need. The U.S. Post Office had sweeping powers to exclude "offensive" material from the mails. The material in question was an airbrushed drawing by Vargas, a famous illustrator, of a blond, voluptuous, scantily clad female. The post office attempted to rescind *Esquire*'s second-class mailing privileges; *Esquire* would have to pay a half million dollars a year in additional postal charges.

A small military paper, the *SeaBeecon*, found itself embroiled in a large national censorship case when, on January 1, 1944, it printed a Varga (sic) girl "pin-up" that the U.S. postmaster general declared to be "obscene." (University of Hawai'i, Hawaii War Records Depository)

While the magazine was fighting the charges through the courts, Vargas donated a copy of the drawing inscribed "To the 'Seabeecon.'" With the approval of the navy chaplain who oversaw the paper, the *SeaBeecon* reprinted it, to the delight of its readers. *Esquire's* mailing privileges were upheld: "*Esquire* Ban Lifted: 'Abhorrent Power'" (*Ed. & Pub.*, Feb. 9, 1946). *Esquire* reaped invaluable publicity, and the *SeaBeecon* edition became a collector's item.

Looking back on those war years, Alfred Pratte, scholar-journalist formerly on the *Star-Bulletin* staff, believes that censorship, "ranging from cables to carrier pigeons," amounted to "Orwellian rule" with "Big Brother" watching over the Islands' residents in a "1984-like atmosphere" (*Star-Bull.*, Mar. 17, 1967). There is evidence, too, that the newspapers took advantage of the war to make huge profits. Pages were swollen with advertisements for war bonds by businesses wanting to unload excess profits and by Japanese merchants who felt pressured to buy advertising with patriotic themes (MacDonald 1944). The combined circulation of the two major dailies skyrocketed to an estimated 200,000 in 1944. The *Star-Bulletin's* share of more than 100,000, according to business manager Porter Dickinson, was "the largest circulation west of Chicago" (obituary, *Star-Bull.*, July 10, 1984).

Jim Richstad, who studied the press' role during wartime, warns that martial law and censorship could happen again. But he adds with some justification that the military did "a good job helping the newspapers function under wartime conditions" (Richstad 1970). Furthermore, the local press worked well in that the *Advertiser* printed some twelve military publications, including two that reached military units throughout the Pacific: the *Midpacifican* (1942–1945), and *Stars and Stripes* "Pacific Edition" (1945–1946). As to whether the military had the lawful authority to license, censor, and otherwise control the press in Hawai'i, it simply claimed "necessity."

The Japanese Language Papers

The most severely affected by the December 12 proclamation were the Japanese language papers. The most repressive national policies against any foreign language press since World War I, which destroyed the German-American press, were aimed against them.

Contrary to popular opinion, the Japanese papers were not immediately suspended nor retitled in English. Several appeared on December 8 and 9. When *Advertiser* equipment broke down early Sunday morning, December 7, staff cried, "Sabotage!" Pressmen discovered a worn-out metal piece. They sent the plates for Monday's edition to *Nippu Jiji* for printing (by Tuesday, Honolulu Iron Works replaced the necessary part). The *Maui Record* (1916–1941) in Wailuku, a four-page weekly in English and Japanese with occasional columns in Filipino, printed through December 9.

In Honolulu, reporter Ryokin Toyohiro recounts how he arrived at the *Nippu Jiji* building at 928 Nu'uanu Avenue on Sunday morning and saw planes and smoke overhead. Assuming maneuvers were taking place, he continued to play Go (a Japanese form of chess) with fellow staff members. When military police ran up the stairs, announced the attack, and ordered them to go home, he did so, but others got out a four-page edition (*Haw. Pacific Press*, Dec. 1, 1983). Editor Yasutaro Soga focused on what he sensed would affect many, including himself: "U.S. Congress Declares War Against Japan As FDR Accuses Her of Treachery." Like the English language papers, *Nippu Jiji* implored readers, "Let's Be Calm!" (Dec. 8, 1941).

Soga, an issei, along with several other newsmen, was shortly arrested and interned for the war's duration in "relocation centers," a euphemism for prison camps. This was his second incarceration: the first, for "conspiracy" when he supported labor in the 1909 strike (Shiramizu 1986). In neither case was there one shred of evidence that he was disloyal to America. His fate was sealed by the years in which he expressed pride in Japan as a world power and the belief that good citizenship required that the homeland be honored, too. It counted against Soga that he had traveled to Asia in the 1930s and that the paper had maintained a correspondent in Japan.

Ever the newspaperman, the interned Soga helped to produce camp papers, thus alleviating what Kazuo Miyamoto, in *Hawaii, End of the Rainbow* (1964), called "the hardest blow to endure," the "deprivation of printed matter and newspapers.... History was being made everyday all over the world," wrote Miyamoto, and internees "were denied ... hearing the news." Soga's son, Shigeo Soga, an alumnus of Punahou and the University of Missouri School of Journalism, took over as president and editor of *Nippu Jiji* and continued after his father's return at the war's end.

The far more confrontational Frederick Makino, an issei like Soga, was spared arrest and imprisonment. Makino had opposed the 1930s military buildup of Japan, and his editorial after the attack stated, "This is our war." Regardless of citizenship or race, "all must swear allegiance to the United States" (*Hochi*, Dec. 8, 1941). The military government, however, placed George Wright, English language editor, in charge of the *Bee* and *Hawaii Hochi* (Richstad 1970).

A month after the December 12 proclamation, the military government, having no way to communicate with issei residents who could not read English, had to reverse itself. It ordered *Nippu Jiji* and *Hawaii Hochi* to reopen and operate under its directives, which they did on January 9. After some resistance by Makino and Wright, *Hochi* was finally renamed *Hawaii Herald* on October 23, 1942, and *Nippu Jiji* became the *Hawaii Times* on November 2, 1942.

When the Japanese language dailies resumed publication, the censorship office sent Bill Norwood and Kenneth Barr, a former *Seattle Times* newsman in the Honolulu insurance business, to *Nippu Jiji* and *Hawaii Hochi* respectively. Neither knew Japanese but read the English versions of the articles, many of which were written by Hugh Lytle and other newsmen who sometimes used the pejorative word "Jap." The articles were translated into Japanese by staff members, then read by army or FBI language experts. The English version was usually printed a day ahead of the Japanese version. These two papers' assigned role was not just to provide essential information, but to exhort the Japanese community to American patriotism.

Nippu Jiji's Toyohiro, the Go-playing reporter, who was raised on a plantation and graduated from 'Iolani School, draws a graphic picture of "Life on a Newspaper During World War II." The reporter felt demeaned by *Nippu Jiji/Hawaii Times* having to publish cartoons and articles showing the Japanese emperor as a clown. Mourning the loss of reportorial freedom and camaraderie, Toyohiro stated that "we had to write like a mouthpiece all the directives indicated by the U.S. Army not unlike a phonograph. Our daily hours at the editorial office were rather dreary" (*Haw. Pacific Press*, Jan. 1, 1984).

Yet again paradoxically, the contents of these papers, whether written by their own staff or others, demonstrated that the Japanese were proud and loyal Americans. *Nippu Jiji* felt "A Deep Responsibilty" toward its constituency "to live and work on American soil that warrants their loyalty as much as though they had received citizenship." It assured the Territory that the trust given the paper "is rightly placed" (Jan. 8, 1942).

Hawaii Hochi took a further step. It reminded the new rulers, the military government, of America's democratic foundations. *Hochi* defended the military government because of the "unprecedented emergency" but warned of possible abuses. In reply to the government's praise for the Japanese community's response to the war and martial law, *Hochi* stated, "We Return the Compliment," adding that "the record is clean" and "we are convinced that we will be able to keep it so. . . . It is in all essential respects a military dictatorship—but it is built up and administered under the framework of a democracy by those who believe in . . . our democratic form of government. . . . The power and authority we have delegated to the armed forces we will expect to be returned to us when the emergency of war is over" (Jan. 13, 1942).

The influence of these two dailies was enormous. Their combined circulation in 1942 topped 20,000. They were very much in the tradition of the immigrant press in America in expressing pride in its roots yet simultaneously helping to Americanize its ethnic group. Furthermore, under extreme wartime duress, the Japanese language papers showed strong survival powers and became "unique symbols in American journalism" (*Adv.*, Nov. 29, 1959).

As to their more recent history, *Nippu Jiji/Hawaii Times*, after a long, vital life, shut down in 1985. *Hawaii Hochi*, its original name reclaimed by Frederick Makino in 1952, continues and is owned by *Shizuoka Shimbun* newspaper in Japan. Printed in Japanese with a page in English expertly edited by Jim Brown, and still a daily, *Hochi* has a circulation of 10,000 and reaches Japanese-speaking visitors and residents. Publisher Paul Yempuku also sponsors the *Hawaii Herald* (1969–1973, 1980–), "Hawaii's Japanese American Journal." The *Herald*, a twice monthly tabloid in English, enjoys a circulation of 6,000. Editorial leadership, like that by island-born Arnold Hiura, sees that it maintains an independent stand from *Hochi*, fosters pride in heritage, and, as Makino did, promotes social activism.

26.   AJAs: American Patriots

Even before America's entrance into World War II, war was continuously on the front pages of the Islands' papers, from Japanese aggression in Asia to spreading European conflicts. The papers communicated public anxiety and apprehension that war would eventually engulf America. Nevertheless, the attack on Pearl Harbor was a profound shock that galvanized the Territory as no war fought thousands of miles away could have.

The story of how Americans of Japanese ancestry, the AJAs, had to fight to join the military—one of the most powerful symbols of loyalty in the United States—and their subsequent courageous record in the 100th Infantry Battalion and the 442nd Infantry Regiment has been ably recounted by Thomas Murphy in *Ambassadors in Arms* (1955). Here, a brief recap of enlistment and casualty figures is appropriate in that they underscore why nisei were to become a force in reshaping the social and political structures of postwar Hawai'i. In the Territory during the World War II, inductees numbered 32,197 through selective service and an additional 4,580 through other means. AJAs made up 50 percent of those numbers and constituted 80 percent of those killed and 88 percent of the wounded.

The difference in the newspapers' coverage of the AJAs is less well known. A study by John Tamashiro outlines how the big Honolulu dailies before and during World War II mirrored community attitudes toward local Japanese. The *Advertiser* represented the more "conservative" and the *Star-Bulletin* the more "moderate" positions (Tamashiro 1972). Others, like Larry Kaya and Ralph Miwa, from a plantation town and Kalihi respectively, have said that the *Advertiser* was considered the "aristocrat" and "business" newspaper for the Caucasian upper and middle classes, the *Star-Bulletin* the paper of the "common folks" (Larry Kaya 1994; Ralph Miwa 1985). Japanese Americans remembered those positions for a long time and contributed to the *Advertiser*'s postwar drop in circulation and revenue until that paper changed its image.

By the late 1930s, as U.S.-Japanese relations deteriorated, the papers abandoned their earlier strategy in which they had attempted to connect discontented laborers to sinister plots from Japan. Mainstream papers became primarily concerned with the Islands' Japanese, not much with their mainland counterparts, and separated both groups from Japan. When 305 Japanese returned from Japan to Hawai'i in October 1941 due to the imminence of war, the *Star-Bulletin* advised, "Give Them a Hearty Welcome," and the *Advertiser* observed, "Good to be in Hawaii" (*Star-Bull.*, Oct. 22, 1941; *Adv.*, Oct. 25, 1941). The two major Honolulu dailies, the *Hilo Tribune-Herald, Maui News,* and the *Garden Island* shared a similar view of Japanese loyalty. They generally adopted the "positive stereotype," in Tamashiro's words, of viewing the Islands' Japanese as cooperative, diligent workers. The *Advertiser* urged calm, fair treatment of issei in the event of war (Sept. 10, 1941).

After the attack, only the *Garden Island* among establishment papers immediately came to the defense of Japanese American citizens. Publisher Charles Fern, also director of Civilian Defense, asserted that he was convinced of their loyalty and that in the future they would be "designated as Americans without any hyphenation" (*Garden Isl.*, Dec. 9, 1941).

The Honolulu papers were less generous and clear-sighted. The *Advertiser* editorialized against Japanese "clannishness" in celebrating the New Year, a popular holiday among them (and every other group). In the daily "Honolulu War Diary" column, items reflected misgivings about the Territory's security. The dailies supported military directives for Japanese to turn in all firearms, ammunition, and explosives (*Adv.*, Feb. 21, 22, 1942; *Star-Bull.*, Feb. 22, 1942). The two papers reverted to their position of the 1920s, advocating abolition of the Japanese language schools and other "alien" organizations.

The *Star-Bulletin* and *Hilo Tribune-Herald,* however, had already separated themselves from the *Advertiser* regarding the necessity of military censorship. The *Star-Bulletin* soon had second thoughts on Japanese Americans. It declared as false the rumors that local accomplices had abetted the attack on Pearl Harbor (*Star-Bull.*, *Trib.-Herald*, Dec. 16, 1941, Jan. 5, 1942). By August 1942, the *Star-Bulletin* was editorially asking for the release of local internees held at Sand Island, which at least partly influenced the government's decision to release 400 of the 1,400. The other 1,000, however, were sent to mainland camps for the duration.

As to internees, the papers significantly differed on Executive Order 9066 of February 10, 1942, the authorization by President

Roosevelt that permitted the wholesale evacuation and imprisonment of 120,000 West Coast Japanese, aliens and citizens alike. A
hysterical American press, particularly on the West Coast, champi-
oned this blatant injustice. The *Star-Bulletin* in August reprinted a
four-part series from the always moderate *Christian Science Monitor*
that criticized the internment order. The *Advertiser* infrequently
mentioned the subject, and then only to criticize the camps' civilian
administration, accusing Dr. Miles Carey, the widely respected Mc-
Kinley High School principal on leave to work as education director
at the Poston (Arizona) Relocation Center, of "pampering" internees
(*Adv.*, Aug 11, 1943). When a University of Washington professor
suggested that the decision to relocate 120,000 Japanese residents
might have been linked to selfish economic purposes and race
hatred, the morning daily vilified the professor (*Adv.*, Mar. 12, 1944).

It was about the AJAs, however, that the principal dailies came
to most clearly differ. Both papers in February 1942 praised the formation of the Varsity Victory Volunteers, formed from nisei University of Hawai'i students who worked for the U.S. Army Corps of
Engineers, and both endorsed an all-nisei fighting unit when the
United States in January 1943 finally permitted them to volunteer
for active military service. After that, editorial attitudes sharply
diverged. With the departure of the young men to the mainland for
training in March 1943, the *Advertiser*'s position was that the appel-
lation "AJA" was ridiculous. It asked, "why label them in any way?"
(Feb. 6, 1943). Editorials stated that the nisei should not be singled
out for distinction because mainlanders would gain the impression
that only Japanese soldiers came from Hawai'i and thus inflate
"Nisei egos" (*Adv.*, Feb. 1, 6, 1943).

The *Star-Bulletin* sent John Terry, its Washington, D.C., correspondent, to Camp Shelby, Mississippi, where the 442nd was in
training. Terry wrote admiring accounts of the men and their eager-
ness to fight for the United States. The *Star-Bulletin* approved of the
AJA tag, predicted that it would carry a patriotic flavor, and stated
that the nisei soldier projected a democratic America as the land of
fair treatment. Mainland papers, finding AJAs very good copy,
picked up *Star-Bulletin* stories of their valor through Associated
Press dispatches (Pratte 1976).

As news reached home of their participation in North African
and European battles, Lieutenant Colonel Farrant L. Turner, head of
the 100th Infantry Battalion, met in Honolulu with a large gathering
of families who feared that AJAs were being assigned to unnecessar-

Less Limelight, Please

"This army today has praise for the 'guinea pigs from Pearl Harbor,' a unit of American infantry composed of men of Japanese descent," begins a routine press dispatch from an American army headquarters in Italy. The item goes on to describe how this outfit has been in action ("Officers said they never saw any troops handle themselves better . . ."), quotes at length an account of the fighting as related by Capt. Taro Suzuki of Honolulu, and says in part: "They probably are a criterion of the loyalty of all Americans of Japanese blood . . ."

It is natural that a war reporter, casting about at the front for a piece of news with an "angle" or of some special interest, might pick out American soldiers of Japanese blood who are fighting the Germans and Italians; an even better "angle" would be such troops fighting against the Japanese forces in the Pacific. The moral seems to be that such troops are, surprisingly, loyal to the U.S.A. and are fighting our enemies even though some of those enemies are Japanese.

Such publicity may be interesting, but it does, in a rather subtle way, more harm than good. A great deal of praise has been written and published about the AJA's. The results include (1) an impression on many Mainland readers that the only fighting men from Hawaii are Japanese, and (2) a distorted impression of their own role in the war for the local Japanese themselves.

Capt. Suzuki is doing no more in this struggle than Lieut. Amorosi, an American of Italian descent, or Pfc. Schultz, an American of German descent. And there are a lot of men in the American forces on land, sea and in the air in the European and Pacific theaters who are Hawaii boys of Chinese or Portuguese or Scotch descent, though you don't read very much about them. They are no more unusual than the Suzukis—they are just doing a hard, dirty job for their country. There are millions of them.

Less pointed publicity about the boys of Japanese descent will be to their benefit in the long run. Being fixed continually in a spotlight makes a fellow unhappy and self-conscious.

An example of losing influence because of editorial policies, the *Advertiser,* in this editorial of October 18, 1943, asked for "Less Limelight" to be bestowed upon the AJAs even as the young men were sacrificing their lives for America during World War II. This negative attitude contributed to the morning daily's decline in readership and profits into the 1960s. (Hawai'i State Archives) ily dangerous, if not impossible, missions. Turner attempted to console them by saying that the 100th was not alone in fighting the war (Murphy 1955). The *Advertiser* twisted the speech to demonstrate that the soldiers and their families through excessive publicity had gained a distorted view of the young men's role in the national war effort: "Less Limelight Please," the *Advertiser* requested. (Oct. 18, 1943). The long lists of casualties printed in the *Advertiser*, in which Japanese names predominated, belied its small-mindedness. In Tamashiro's understated observation, there was no doubt that by this time, although the *Advertiser* went in more for occasional journalistic outbursts than for sustained attacks, that the *Star-Bulletin* was the "friendlier" paper (Tamashiro 1972). In 1945, the *Star-Bulletin* sent another correspondent, Washington, D.C.-based Lyn Crost, to cover the AJAs. Crost was accredited to the 442nd Regional Combat Team in Italy and France and followed the team into Germany, sending back almost daily reports from the front.

In addition, throughout the war, the *Advertiser* carried the syndicated columnist Westbrook Pegler who relentlessly attacked American Japanese as spies and defended relocation on the basis of national security. By contrast, the *Star-Bulletin* carried the column "My Day" by the racially and politically liberal Eleanor Roosevelt.

What was behind this treatment of AJAs? Back in the 1930s, there was already recognition that social changes were coming. This recognition was noticeable in the neighbor islands papers that wrote up social events of all residents, not just of Caucasians. In fact, all incorporated non-Caucasians on their staffs before the war, hiring Japanese, Chinese, and Filipino reporters. With less visibility, the *Star-Bulletin* hired a few Asian American journalists in the 1930s.

But it was the Honolulu papers in the 1940s that openly debated change under the great political question: Who should govern Hawai'i after the war? Here, too, they differed. Whatever private doubts *Advertiser* editor Raymond Coll Sr. had of his employer's policies, and he apparently did, he publicly expressed the views of publisher Lorrin Thurston and owner Walter Dillingham. *Advertiser* leadership feared the loss of oligarchy control in postwar Hawai'i and the gain in power of a Japanese electorate. The *Advertiser* recommended suspending all elections for the war's duration (Mar. 28, 1942). Elections continued, but Island Japanese chose to withdraw from campaigning for political office and from office itself. The *Star-Bulletin* agreed with their temporary actions but stated that elections were an essential part of democratic principles for which the war was being fought (Oct.

15, 1942). *Star-Bulletin* leaders were well aware that the AJAs were determined to make changes at home after the war.

What did this add up to? In essence, *Star-Bulletin* management anticipated and positioned the paper for political and social changes in postwar times that would affect circulation and readership. The *Advertiser* did not. It continued to pursue outdated policies into the 1950s and not surprisingly went downhill economically as Hawai'i became democratized with the "Democratic Revolution" of 1954. This was the historical result of AJAs uniting with Caucasians and Hawaiians to challenge a discredited Republican oligarchy of which the *Advertiser* was the major voice. The *Star-Bulletin* conversely gained advertising, circulation, and community clout. Although owner Joe Farrington was a Republican, he had long recognized racism as counterproductive. It was no accident that he was invited in 1948 to speak on the occasion of the birthday of the AJAs 442nd Veterans Club.

Advertiser leaders did not receive any such invitations. In fact, on the eve of statehood, upon assuming the *Advertiser* editorship in 1959, George Chaplin faced a Japanese American community that heartily disliked his paper. Chaplin recalls that an influential nisei physician told him, "I will not have the Advertiser in my house" (Chaplin 1985). Chaplin, aided by Thurston Twigg-Smith's ouster of his uncle Lorrin P. Thurston from the publisher's post, was instrumental in changing the morning daily's policies and practices. Yet as late as the 1980s, internal readership surveys revealed that Japanese had among the lowest subscription rates of all ethnic groups.

There is a final word on the power of journalism. The AJAs themselves were journalists, having gained experience on their high school and college papers. They produced *Varsity Victory Volunteer* (1942–1943) during the war as a weekly mimeographed news bulletin. After the war, veterans created *Puka Puka Parade* (1946–), a full-fledged newspaper—the 100th Infantry Battalion called itself "One puka puka," *puka* indicating a "hole" (in Hawaiian) or a zero. Its editors have been community leaders, such as Ted T. Hirayama, Sparky Matsunaga, Al Palans, and Ben Tamashiro. The paper is distributed throughout the Islands to enthusiastic readers, like Hilo resident Haroo "Porky" Furuye who states that he reads every issue completely (Furuye 1993). It serves up a popular mixture of the chatty with the serious, uses readers' nicknames such as "Angel" and "Spider," and runs news items and photos of those who served in the justifiably famous 100th and 442nd companies.

PART VI

The March toward Statehood— the 1940s and 1950s

27. "Dear Joe": Lorrin Thurston Writes to Joe—Stalin or Farrington?

On May 4, 1949, a "letter" appeared in the *Advertiser*, spread across four columns on the front page. Three days earlier, 2,000 stevedores had walked away from the piers, initiating a strike by the ILWU that would last 177 days and be among the most bitter in Hawai'i's history. The strike precipitated the "Dear Joe" letters, almost fifty over a period of six months, that addressed a supposed ILWU/Communist takeover of Hawai'i.

The letters' impact was both immediate and long lasting. As *Advertiser* editor Raymond Coll Sr. expressed it, "We felt the community needed to be aroused and the community has been aroused" (*Ed. & Pub.*, June 25, 1949). Sandy Zalberg, *Advertiser* staff member and author of *A Spark Is Struck! Jack Hall and the ILWU in Hawaii* (1979), believed that the letters set "a strident tone" for the struggle that "tore at the fabric of the community, stirred up passion and hysteria, set people against people. . . . and established the ILWU as an entrenched power."

What is unusual, and less well known, is that, rather than operating in a cultural lag behind the mainland, Hawai'i's newspapers took the lead in the national "Red scare." The "Dear Joe" letters were created by *Advertiser* publisher Lorrin P. Thurston, who had assumed the paper's leadership in 1931 upon the death of his father, Lorrin A. Thurston. Lorrin A., missionary descendant, attorney, and newspaperman, hated and feared the monarchy, abetted its overthrow in 1893, and was a key player in bringing about U.S. annexation and cementing the power of the Republican oligarchy and the Big Five, the companies that dominated the Territory's economy. He controlled the *Advertiser* from 1900 until his death in 1931. Lorrin P., born in 1899, despised and feared the ILWU and intended to drive it from Hawai'i. He believed the union to be part of an international Communist conspiracy, led by Soviet dictator Joseph Stalin, that was determined to destroy the Territory's economy. Lorrin P. was a prime factor in making Red-baiting and anti-Communism paranoia acceptable. The specter of Communism was a handy target, for this

In post–World War II Hawai'i, establishment papers achieved the doubtful distinction of contributing to the rabid anti-Communist paranoia of the era. The *Advertiser* through 1949, as in this example of May 4, ran a series of "Dear Joe" letters. Supposedly written by an ILWU labor organizer to his "boss" in the Kremlin, Soviet leader Joe Stalin, the letters were actually the creation of publisher Lorrin P. Thurston. (Hawai'i State Archives)

was, in historian Theon Wright's words, "the last gasp of the Big Five in its long domination" of Hawai'i and part of the battle between labor and management, postponed by World War II, that led to the social revolution of the 1950s (Wright 1972).

Although they did not bear Lorrin P.'s signature, the public soon attributed the letters to Thurston who, in turn, proudly acknowledged he wrote "every damn word" himself (Zalburg 1979). Thurston adopted the persona of a half-literate, wily union leader who ostensibly was reporting to Stalin on the strike's progress. The effects were sometimes odd: meticulous punctuation attached to ungrammatical colloquialisms and Hawaiian phrases, along with an English cockney dropping of the "H," as in "'arry" for Harry Bridges, ILWU leader.

But to whom were they addressed? In a postscript to his seventh letter, the writer discounted that they were meant for anyone but Joe Stalin: "Some people here got mixed up and thought we was referring to another Joe in these reports. . . . maybe Joe also referred to Joe Farrington. But you and I know better. Where we're concerned, there's only one Joe and he lives in the Kremlin" (May 10, 1949). Hugh Lytle, former *Advertiser* managing editor, and Bud Smyser, former *Star-Bulletin* editor, have confirmed that the missives were also aimed at Joe Farrington, president and general manager of the *Star-Bulletin*, who Thurston thought was soft on unions and Communism (H. Lytle 1992; Smyser 1991). Farrington had been endorsed by the Political Action Committee (PAC) of the ILWU in his 1946 race for delegate to Congress against Democrat William Borthwick. Up to election day, the *Advertiser* printed a daily box score of those endorsed by the PAC under the heading, "Moscow Supports These Oahu Candidates."

As to the letters themselves, Thurston's opening salvos set the basic themes. "What Are Your Next Orders, Joe?" the writer asked. He bragged about "hiding behind the Stars & Stripes" and "free speech" to wage a war on capitalism. He had no interest in the well-being of the general public—"The Hell with them"—and he assured "Joe" that "we've got Hawaii all set up for you." The average worker was a "dupe"; and the battle over wages—a 42¢ wage differential between West Coast stevedores, paid $1.82 an hour, and the Islands' stevedores, paid $1.40 an hour for the same work—was a phony issue (May 4, 1949).

Subsequent letters reported "progress." "Divide and rule! Does it work! We're dividing 'em fast. We'll rule 'em before too long. . . . See you in China" (May 5, 1949), the last a reference to the Communist revolution in that country. As to when a Communist takeover succeeded, the writer stated, "I'd make a pretty good Governor, Joe—wouldn't I? I'll get all my boys in the topside jobs when Hawaii becomes a state." He ended one letter with a Russianized sign-off, "Alohaski Gunghoski. Aufwieder-schednski—or whatever it is you say over there" (May 7, 1949).

The letters were placed side by side with political cartoons and heavily slanted "news" stories. One letter appeared in the Hawaiian language on Kamehameha Day, illustrated by a cartoon of the great king holding his nose (June 11, 1949). Accompanying articles on this and other days stated that the strike was a move to aid China's "Red Regime."

The letters clearly had an impact. Union members left the waterfront picket line to march in front of the Advertiser building on the corner of Kapi'olani Boulevard and South Street. Not taking Thurston entirely seriously, or, at least, showing a sense of humor, picketers' signs addressed him in local idioms as "Joe": "We forgive you, Joe, you lolo" (feeble-minded); "Wassa mala Joe! You pupule" (What's the matter! You crazy.) (June, 1, 1949). The *Advertiser* responded by mounting loudspeakers that emitted sounds of jeering and laughter from the building's windows.

A less likely group also took to the streets. Some 300 women, predominantly Caucasian, organized a "Broom Brigade" to "clean out" the unions. Carrying brooms with signs attached that urged strikers to go back to work, the women on May 31 marched at Pier 11 in front of ILWU headquarters, then walked over to Merchant Street and picketed the "pro-ILWU" afternoon paper.

Letters to the editor flooded in, the *Advertiser* only printing those that agreed with "Dear Joe." The *Star-Bulletin*, however, although fervently anti-Communist—but not enough so for the *Advertiser* or the more extreme segments of the community—ran letters on both sides of the issue. To editor Riley H. Allen, Communism was "an idea and can be defeated only by a better idea, not by force" (*Star-Bull.*, May 2, 1949). When the Broom Brigade picketed the *Star-Bulletin* building, Thurston likely expressed his true feelings through his union persona: "If we could just bust that lousy sheet it would help us lots" (*Adv.*, June 5, 1949).

The *Star-Bulletin* and the *Advertiser* began to realize that the anti-Red campaign had unexpected and unwelcome outcomes. National publications picked up the controversy, and mainland papers, like the *St. Louis Globe-Democrat*, depicted a grim Territory, with shipping shut down from the West Coast, infants and children on vastly reduced rations, and mothers foraging desperately for canned milk. The *New York World Telegram* and other Scripps-Howard papers reprinted the *Advertiser*'s front page of August 3, 1949, on how a nucleus of trained Communists was conquering Hawai'i. U.S. Senator Wayne Morse, Oregonian Republican, stated that if Hawai'i were in the grips of Communists, it was not ready for statehood (*Ed. & Pub.*, June 25, 1949).

Star-Bulletin leaders became alarmed. The paper defended the statehood cause. Editor Riley Allen, for example, was quoted in the *Philadelphia Inquirer* as saying that the Communist issue was trumpeted so loudly that it had largely obscured the wage issue (Zalburg 1979). Thurston, who had assumed the chairmanship of the Hawaii Statehood Commission in 1947, faced unpleasant reactions. Union newspapers accused Thurston of labor hating and union busting. The *ILWU Reporter* (1949–1960), produced by Jack Hall and sponsored by the union, revealed that Thurston had secretly asked the Federal Communications Commission to investigate radio station KHON, which in the interest of fairness aired opposing viewpoints during the strike.

When "Dear Joe" retaliated by accusing the union of "fraud and corruption" in conducting strike votes—"phoney, crooked, unfair, un-American, dishonest and rotten to the core" (*Adv.,* June 14, 1949)—the ILWU filed a $500,000 libel suit against the morning daily. The *Advertiser* filed a counter libel suit for $250,000 against the union for radio broadcasts in which Bob McElrath accused the paper of being untrustworthy and unreliable. After the strike was settled, the suits were sensibly dropped.

In the meantime, there is no doubt that the economy was hurting. The newspapers felt the strike's impact at a most basic level. There was less newsprint to cover more news. They cooperated with each other in attempting to get in new supplies, but the union declared the cargoes "hot" and selectively unloaded them, refusing to recognize newsprint as an "essential commodity" (*Ed. & Pub.,* July 30, 1949) such as food, medicines, hospital supplies, and mail. Eleven weeks into the strike, the dailies reduced printing to twelve to sixteen pages weekdays and twenty to twenty-four on weekends. The *Star-Bulletin* allowed no more than 200 words per story; the *Advertiser* cut work hours for its composing crews.

The "Dear Joe" letters elicited another strong reaction. The more rabid anti-Communist merchants instituted an advertising boycott against the *Star-Bulletin,* the Big Three retailers—Liberty House, McInerny's, and Sears Roebuck—withdrawing their advertisements from the afternoon paper. When the Associated Press local bureau proposed doing a national article on the boycott, the merchants had second thoughts and reinstated their ads (*New York Times,* June 29, 1949). Nevertheless, with the prolonged strike, businesses had fewer goods to sell and consumers had less money to buy. Ad lineage in the dailies was reduced by almost 30 percent.

In spite of newsprint shortages and space reductions, the "Dear Joe" letters continued. The *Advertiser* devoted its entire front page to an editorial in favor of the dock seizure act that put the Territory in charge of stevedoring operations. But behind the scenes, there were feverish efforts by business, government, labor, and newspaper leaders, including Joe Farrington in Washington, D.C., to settle the strike. The "Dear Joe" letters tapered off in August and September. The strike, begun on May 1, was finally over October 23, 1949.

The *Advertiser* declared, "Waterfront Strike Tops Year's 10 Big Stories in Hawaii" (Jan. 1, 1950). The *Advertiser* did not but could have laid claim to its publisher following in his father's footsteps in the practice of slanted, unethical journalism.

28. The *Honolulu Record* and the Art of Muckraking

The 1950s have the image of being the last era of quiet acceptance by a "silent generation" chiefly interested in living the good life and making money. Koji Ariyoshi and the *Honolulu Record* (1948–1958) belie that image. Ariyoshi (no relation to the later governor), a vocal critic of the establishment, was the epitome of the tenacious investigative reporter. His campaigns for justice stretched over ten years in his muckraking journal and achieved a high standard of journalism.

The term "muckraking" comes from the man with a "muck-rake" in John Bunyan's seventeenth century novel, *Pilgrim's Progress*, who always looks downward to the filth on the floor. In 1906, Theodore Roosevelt derisively applied the word to journalists who exposed the corruption of the sociopolitical system in attempts to reform it. "Muckrakers" adopted the word as a badge of pride for those upholding the conscience of society (Leonard 1986; Miraldi 1990).

In 1950, the *Honolulu Record* revealed that a prominent University of Hawai'i faculty member had been systematically denied promotion. "The Strange Case of Dr. Sakamaki," headlined the weekly (*Hono. Record*, Sept. 28, 1950). The *Record* stated that Shunzo Sakamaki, Ph.D., a popular University of Hawai'i teacher and a productive scholar whose work on nineteenth century U.S.-Japanese relationships was said to be the fullest, most well-documented account on the subject, would never be promoted from associate to full professor for one reason—he was Japanese. Ariyoshi added that not one "local product" had ever received a full professorship at the University. Ariyoshi's dogged determination in a four-year campaign resulted in the professor's promotion.

Although circulation figures were not officially compiled, the *Record* probably printed about 5,000 copies per week, compared to the dailies' 45,000 and 77,700 for the *Advertiser* and *Star-Bulletin* respectively. Regardless of its lower distribution ratio, Honolulu residents recall how they looked forward to the latest edition of the tabloid. Journalists on the mainstream dailies regularly read the *Record*

The *Honolulu Record,* a small weekly, had a big impact. One successful crusade, illustrated in this issue of September 28, 1950, culminated in the promotion to full professorship of Dr. Shunzo Sakamaki, the first Asian American to be promoted to that rank by the University of Hawai'i. (University of Hawai'i Hawaiian and Pacific Collection)

for news tips, too, although if the stories were too combative, they might ignore them, as they did this one.

The *Honolulu Record* was very much Ariyoshi's creation. From the time he was young, he seemed to prepare himself for the role of muckraker. Born in Kona on the Big Island in 1914, he was the son of immigrant contract laborer parents. As a boy he walked three miles each way to borrow books from the public library. Two series he later wrote for the *Star-Bulletin* (bought from him at reduced rates) recounted the hard lives suffered by coffee farmers and their families. Farmers braved possible eviction by the company by bootlegging coffee for cash to provide school clothing for their children or occasional meat for the family dinner table (*Star-Bull.*, July 16–27, 1938).

Ariyoshi, who described himself and his life in a *Record* series (1951–1952) entitled "My Thoughts," signed on in 1936 as a longshoreman at the Castle & Cooke terminals in Honolulu. While stevedoring, he attended the University of Hawai'i and wrote for *Ka Leo o Hawaii*, the student newspaper. He named as a turning point in his life YMCA sessions where participants discussed trade unionism. He completed a degree in journalism from the University of Georgia through a scholarship; it was in the South that he witnessed brutal racism firsthand and identified himself as a person of color with Negroes. The depression and the New Deal further forged his conscience, and crusading Japanese-English language editors, Frederick Makino of *Hawaii Hochi* and Yasutara Soga of *Nippu Jiji*, became his models.

Returning to the waterfront, Ariyoshi was one of two stevedores of Japanese ancestry arrested in San Francisco after December 7, 1941, for possessing a "dangerous weapon"—a cargo hook that stevedores used for handling sacks of plaster. Only a San Francisco Communist journal defended the two men. Ariyoshi was interned, then left the internment camp by volunteering for the U.S. Army. He attended Military Intelligence Language School and spent three years in the China theater as an intelligence officer, including nineteen months at Chinese Communist headquarters.

Back in the United States, Ariyoshi completed a book on China that was unpublishable because it expressed sympathy for the Mao Tse-tung revolutionary government. Ariyoshi, age thirty-four, returned to Hawai'i in 1948 with his wife, Taeko Ito, a native Californian whom he had married while they were interned at Manzanar, and their two children. Because of his union connections, no stevedoring company would hire him.

While the *Honolulu Record* was Ariyoshi's conception, its gene-sis was made possible by Jack Kimoto, who edited the *Hawai Suta* (Hawaii star) (1947–1952), an ILWU-sponsored weekly in Japanese and English. Kimoto helped Ariyoshi set up an old hand-fed press at 811 Sheridan Street. The ILWU partially backed the *Record,* but Ariyoshi invested his own savings of $3,000. He drew the modest salary of $200 a month from the paper's earnings. Never fully accept-ing ILWU leadership or Communist theory, Ariyoshi ran the *Record* as a general circulation newspaper rather than a labor organ. While his cause was social injustice, he offered a lively mix of features, sports, cartoons, and photos of pretty girls.

As any number of papers have done over the years, Ariyoshi timed the inauguration of his paper with Independence Day, the Fourth of July, stating that it would be "an independent voice" for those whose views are today "not properly presented . . . by the existing newspapers" (*Hono. Record,* July 1, 1948). Early issues included Governor Ingram Stainback's list of nominees for the draft board, who were all "haole businessmen," and an "Employer's Who's Who," and statistics showing that Honolulu electricity rates were among the highest in the United States (Dec. 30, 1954). Ari-yoshi saw himself as a thorn in the side of the power elite. He enjoyed tweaking the big papers in his column "In Our Dailies," in which he reprinted their false claims and errors. In return, they attacked him. Charles E. Hogue of the *Star-Bulletin* called the *Record* the "incidental press," and the *Advertiser* labeled it a "pipsqueak . . . vituperative little party-line weekly" (*Star-Bull.,* Nov. 8, 1948; *Adv.,* May 12, 1951).

Ariyoshi pursued a wide variety of international and national top-ics, like opposition to the Korean War and the exclusion of American Indians from mainland college fraternities. It was his local crusades, however, for which he did his own research, that gained him reader-ship: for example, police brutality against locals and African Ameri-cans, and illegal dog and cock fights, and gambling. Another exposé reported a "shocking stag party" at a Junior Chamber of Commerce convention on Maui, with police in cahoots with the Jaycees to have strippers perform at a Wailuku clubhouse (June 17, 1954).

He consistently defended civil liberties, particularly freedom of speech and the press, to him, a holy cause, even speaking up for an establishment reporter, *Advertiser* columnist Bob Krauss, whom the *Advertiser* took to task for writing a negative review of an exhibit at the Honolulu Academy of Arts. It is our "democratic right" to speak out and say what we think, said Ariyoshi (*Hono. Record*, July 28, 1955).

As to Professor Sakamaki, like his defender he was an idealist with an interest in journalism. Also from the Big Island, from the plantation town of 'Ōla'a, Sakamaki attended the University of Hawai'i, and as editor of *Ka Leo o Hawaii* supported "free speech." In some ways, the two men's lives were parallel, but as the grandson of samurai, Shunzo Sakamaki came from somewhat better economic circumstances.

While in Japan pursuing graduate studies, Sakamaki served as a "special correspondent" for the *Star-Bulletin* and contributed "An Oriental Journey" on his experiences in the Far East (June 8–9, 1931). The *Star-Bulletin* carried news items on Sakamaki over the decades, like his winning of honors at Columbia University for his doctorate and the award of a Rockefeller Foundation Fellowship. But the paper relegated news of his marriage to Miss Yoshiko Ikeda to the fifth page of the Saturday Society section: "A wedding of two popular members of the Japanese community" (July 22, 1933). Sakamaki's appearance in the society pages at all reflects that, unlike his defender, he was acceptable to the establishment. An ardent Christian generally uncritical of America, he wrote a series during World War II on Japan's state religion, entitled "Shinto: Fake Religion" (*Star-Bull.*, Apr. 18–25, 1942). In 1952, the Chamber of Commerce named Sakamaki "American of the Week."

During its fight to gain justice for Sakamaki, who had joined the University faculty in 1936, the *Record* highlighted other applicable cases of discrimination. One was that of a student of Japanese ancestry to whom chemistry faculty voted an award but were overridden by the department chair Leonora Bilger, who gave the award to a Caucasian student (*Hono. Record*, Oct. 5, 1950).

The University took four years from the time of the first exposé to promote Sakamaki to the rank of full professor. The mainstream papers then buried the information in a larger story: "UH Regents Confirm Advancements for 24." At the same time, the Board of Regents announced the creation of a new category above "full professor," that of "senior professor," to which Professor Bilger was named (*Star-Bull.*, May 19, 1954). Two months later, another small story announced that Sakamaki was named chairman of the history department (*Star-Bull.*, July 19, 1954). By contrast, the *Honolulu Record* highlighted his photo and the story of his promotion on the upper right front page under "Sakamaki Promotion Reflects New

Trend" and commended the University for recognizing "a 'local product' of non-haole ancestry" (Oct. 7, 1954).

After the underfinanced *Record* shut down, Ariyoshi turned to small-business enterprises and to promoting friendship between the People's Republic of China and the United States. Happily, his public image improved with age, and before his death in 1976, the State House of Representatives recognized the former Kona farm boy for his "dedication to truth and social justice." Vicki Ong, *Advertiser* staff writer, observed that the *Record* had had a great influence on the newly emerging Democratic party leadership and on unionized workers (obituary, *Adv.*, Oct. 25, 1976).

The *Honolulu Record* was not around to comment upon the University's final recognition of one of its most illustrious homegrown professors. Professor Sakamaki died in 1973. A general classroom building, completed in 1977, was finally named "Sakamaki Hall" in 1979. An appropriate testimony to its namesake and his champion, Sakamaki Hall today houses the history and philosophy departments and is one of the more beautiful Mānoa campus buildings, with its inside garden courtyards planted in bamboo and illuminated by sunlight.

29. The Hawaii Seven: Journalists in Jeopardy

The "Red scare" of the late 1940s, in which the mainstream dailies played a principal role, widened in the 1950s to enfold four opposition journalists. In 1951 and 1952, the fear that Communists would take over Hawai'i was the alleged reason behind the headlined arrests and trial of the "Hawaii Seven" under the Smith Act (Holmes 1994). Making the connection to another trial that had consumed public interest, award-winning newsman Keyes Beech observed, "Not since the celebrated *Massie* case twenty years ago has any trial commanded such wide interest in these islands" (*Chicago Daily News*, Sept. 2, 1952). A Honolulu paper would name the Hawaii Seven the biggest news story of 1953 (*Star-Bull.*, Dec. 26, 1953).

Four of the Hawaii Seven were journalists connected to the *Honolulu Record*: Koji Ariyoshi, Jack Hall, Jack Denichi Kimoto, and John Reinecke. The other three were Dwight James Freeman, construction worker and union organizer who had served in the U.S. Navy for two years; Charles Kazuyuki Fujimoto, from a Kaua'i plantation family, a former University of Hawai'i research chemist and the only admitted Communist; and his wife Eileen Fujimoto, ILWU secretary. But it is the journalists who are the subject here.

The post–World War II Smith Act case was another low point in Island journalism that had sunk dismally in the 1920s with its anti-Japanese campaign. In her master's thesis, Ernestine Enomoto points out that the 1950s witch hunt, again in the name of "patriotism," had an anti-Japanese cast to it in that four of the Hawaii Seven were Japanese and two of the three Caucasian men were married to Japanese women (Enomoto 1971). The current case, however, was broader than the earlier one, taking on a life that extended far beyond the arrests on August 28, 1951, a five-month trial from November 10, 1952 to May 23, 1953, convictions, appeals, and final acquittal in the Ninth Circuit Court in San Francisco on January 20, 1958. Beyond that, memories of the Smith Act case have haunted the public almost to the present.

In 1951, the establishment papers and the territorial and federal governments rushed to judge "Reds" and "Commies" guilty. Nor did opposition papers come to their defense, except for the *ILWU Reporter* (1949–1960) and Koji Ariyoshi's *Honolulu Record*. Union leadership was engaged in jurisdictional struggles, so that Arthur Rutledge's *Hawaii Labor News* (1953–1957), for example, representing teamsters, hotel and restaurant employees, bartenders, and transit workers, could not be counted on for support. Too, most labor newspapers were not strictly speaking "radical." Rather than wanting to overthrow the system, most were more interested in ameliorating the condition of the working class (Altschull 1990). Nor was support forthcoming from the two main Japanese-English language journals, the *Hawaii Herald* and the *Hawaii Times*, that in the past had been critical of the establishment but were now more cautious.

To place this case in context, as Robert McNamara's careful thesis has done, the "Smith Act" came into being as the Alien Registration Act of 1940 but was popularly named after its author, Congressman Howard Smith of Virginia (McNamara 1960). After World War II, this statute enabled the Justice Department to prosecute Communist party leaders and journalists (on newspapers like the *Daily Worker*) and to fine and imprison them for conspiring to overthrow the U.S. government by force. The act was amended in 1948 to broaden punishment for conspiracy. Conspiracy theories that the Soviet Union was plotting to take over the U.S. government were rife. The rise of Communist China in the 1940s and the Korean War in the early 1950s intensified American fears of the USSR. A press furor accompanied Wisconsin Senator Joseph McCarthy's unsubstantiated allegations in 1950 that there were 205 Communists working in the State Department. "McCarthyism" became the label permanently attached to witch hunting.

At the time of the Smith Act trial in the Islands it was not illegal to be a Communist. The U.S. government argued, however, on the basis of the Justice Department's position, that the writings of Marx, Engels, Lenin, and Stalin promoted the violent overthrow of all capitalist countries, and that if people were members of the Communist party, that in itself meant they would encourage others to become familiar with these works, thus forming a "conspiracy" (McNamara 1960). In 1951, the government claimed that the Hawaii Seven defendants had engaged in a "conspiracy" that continued until their arrests. The court's determination that all seven be tried together reinforced the idea that a conspiracy had taken place.

In the decade following World War II, the newspapers, still the

dominant source of news, nationally produced thousands of anti-
Communist stories, features, editorials, and cartoons (Aronson
1970). Locally, hundreds of items in the mainstream press ignited
suspicion and paranoia of a "Red menace." In 1947, Hawai'i's own
Governor Ingram Stainback, along with former newspaper editor
and unionist Ichiro Izuka, beat Joe McCarthy to the anti-Red punch
by launching a "Crusade against Communism" and asked the U.S.
Justice Department for a "sweeping investigation of Communist
activities in Hawaii" (*Adv., Star-Bull.,* Oct. 24, 1947), setting off a
decade of vague charges and pseudo evidence. The *Advertiser* featured a series of six articles by Alfred L. Castle, "There Can Be No
Compromise With Communism" (Dec. 28, 1947–Jan. 2, 1948), that
it reprinted and distributed in pamphlet form as "a public service."
The *Star-Bulletin* ran a series from *Newsweek* by FBI Director
J. Edgar Hoover on "How to Fight Communism" (*Star-Bull.,* Apr.
14–20, 1948.) In the comics, heroic Steve Canyon battled the mysterious and sinister "Ivan," and kindly plutocrat Daddy Warbucks
educated "Little Orphan Annie" on capitalism's virtues. The "Society" section highlighted University economics professor Boris Stan-
field who lectured to the American Association of University
Women on "Who Is Winning the Cold War?" (*Star-Bull.,* Apr. 1,
1950). When the U.S. House Un-American Activities Committee
(HUAC) traveled to the Islands to "investigate" Communism, editor Ezra J. Crane of the *Maui News* called union members engaged
in labor battles against management and their allies "communist
parlor pinks, self-impressed liberals and the rest of the deprecators
of our Island standards of living" (Jan. 4, 1950). Not surprisingly,
William Puette's comprehensive documentation of the national
media contains a chapter on the Islands' establishment papers holding a prevailing bias against labor and unions (Puette 1992). At the
conclusion of the nine-day hearing, which accomplished little, the
Star-Bulletin thanked HUAC for a mission "Well Done" (*Star-Bull.,*
Apr. 20, 1950).

Neighbor Island management-sponsored plantation papers, specifically aimed at the workers, got into the act. The *Naalehu News*
(1944–1970), representing the Hutchinson Plantation (of C. Brewer
and Company) at Ka'ū under manager James Beatty, adopted anti-
Communism as its major theme: "Mr. Beatty . . . is deeply concerned over the possibility of a strike . . . and also over communistic
leaders who are trying to destroy our American Way of Life"
(*Naalehu News,* June 1949). Myrtle T. Hansen, among the few

women plantation newspaper editors (her husband, H. A. Hansen, headed Hutchinson's Industrial Relations Department and was the paper's "adviser"), exhorted readers in the English and Ilocano sections to "Join the Anti-Communist League of Hawaii." Another plantation paper, the *Paauhau News* (1943–1960), ran slogans above its title, "Today Communism is Treason" and "You Cannot Help the Poor By Destroying the Rich."

The hysteria even spread to Moloka'i, where editor Marie Gallard of *Ka Leo o Molokai* (1950–1955) and the *Friendly Isle News* (1955–1957) warned Moloka'i residents to beware of "fanatics" sent from all over the world to subvert them (*Friendly Isle,* July 20, 1956).

The most extremist paper was the Honolulu-based *IMUA* (1949–1976), under various titles—*IMUA Spotlight, IMUA Newsletter,* the *Criterion,* and *Fact Finder. IMUA* had high visibility, despite a circulation of less than 3,000 by direct mail to subscribers. It was likely the brainchild of the wealthy Mrs. Walter Dillingham and claimed to represent the "Hawaii Residents Association," by innuendo implying its critics were "outsiders." Its board of directors included business and professional leaders, such as physicians Clarence E. Fronk, Lyle G. Phillips, and Philip M. Corboy, former Governor Lawrence Judd, and businessman Thomas G. Singlehurst. *IMUA* featured "The Plot to Sovietize Hawaii" and "The Communist Grip in Hawaii." Incredibly, to *IMUA* the *Wall Street Journal* was "Communist" because it reported on the Islands' labor problems (*IMUA,* Mar. 1954).

IMUA writer Tony Todaro is an interesting example of a vulnerable person catching the anti-Communism virus. A native Pennsylvanian and a talented writer of *hapa haole* (Hawaiian-English) songs, Todaro was employed as a skilled machinist at Pearl Harbor for nine years until a reduction of forces caused his layoff. He turned to promoting a "United Nations Institute of Peace" as a living war memorial (obituary, *Adv.,* July 29, 1976). But by 1949, infected with fear, he abandoned his peace efforts, joined *IMUA,* and assailed the Honolulu dailies for being "soft" on Communism. He addressed a series of "open letters" in *IMUA* to Ariyoshi: the *Record* was a "subtle and vicious tool of Communism" and the Hawaii Seven "The Seven Moles of Moscow" (*IMUA,* Sept. 26, 1951, Nov. 12, 1952.)

What about the Hawaii Seven journalists? Koji Ariyoshi, whose small paper's circulation never exceeded 5,000, was named by John S. Wood, Georgia congressman and chairman of HUAC, as "probably one of the best qualified persons in Hawaii to propagandize the Communist Party line through the medium of the press." Ariyoshi's denial of direct connection to the Communist party U.S.A. "is no proof otherwise," for the *Honolulu Record* was "within the orbit of control of the Communist Party" (*Hono. Record*, Oct. 1, 1950).

The second newsman, Jack Denichi Kimoto, born in 'Ewa, O'ahu, had lived in Japan and California. He returned to Hawai'i in 1938 during the depression, worked for *Hawaii Hochi*, drove a taxi, and served as a union business agent. Like Ariyoshi, he served the United States during World War II as a translator of Japanese documents. After the war, he helped form a short-lived Japanese-English labor paper and then joined the *Record* as business manager and compositor. In an astonishing exercise in improbability, the U.S. attorney general called the taxi driver and compositor "one of the six most dangerous people in the United States."

ILWU leader Jack Hall was the third of the accused. Hall, whose boyhood was spent in Wisconsin, signed on as an ordinary seaman out of San Francisco in 1932 at the age of seventeen. He came to Hawai'i to stay in 1935 as a labor organizer and *Voice of Labor* editor and after the war continued to write for labor journals. Hall's unparalleled successes in organizing labor included the sugar strike in 1946, the pineapple strike of 1947, and the dock strike of 1949. At the time of his arrest, he was in the midst of sugar and pineapple negotiations (Zalburg 1979).

But it was not the charismatic, brilliant Hall who earned the most newspaper publicity as a dangerous subversive. That was the fate of the fourth journalist, John Reinecke, Ph.D., who along with his wife, Aiko Reinecke, also suffered the most. A Yale University graduate in philosophy, Chinese scholar, and public high school teacher, Reinecke wrote for the *Record* and worked in its back shop. The Reineckes' access to youth (she was an elementary school teacher but was not arrested) made them especially suspect. Under the flimsiest of pretexts, the Reineckes were targeted for attack by mainstream newspapers in 1947: "Affiliation With Reds of Isle Teacher Hinted" (*Trib.-Herald*, Nov. 18, 1947). Within eight days, they were suspended from their jobs by the Department of Public Instruction (DPI) for "not possessing the ideals of democracy" and because their loyalty to the United States was in doubt (*Adv.*, Nov. 26, 29, 1947). Fully ninety separate articles on them appeared on the dailies' front or editorial pages in an eleven-month period, from November 1947 to October 30, 1948 when their dismissals by the DPI were upheld. During this same period, Jack Hall was featured about ten times.

In 1951, the arrest of the Hawaii Seven was announced in language that assumed their guilt: "7 Nabbed as Reds Free on Bail" (*Adv.*, Aug. 29, 1951). And at the start of their trial: "Red Trial Jury Is Seated" (*Star-Bull.*, Nov. 8, 1952). The *Star-Bulletin* summarized the trial's daily events in a column titled " 'Red' Inquiry in Brief." Occasionally placing quotes around "Red" was a subtlety probably lost on most readers. Only the *Honolulu Record*, in an attempt to bring the facts to the public, printed the full text of the trial.

Defense attorney Harriet Bouslog unsuccessfully moved for a mistrial on the basis that the *Advertiser* and *Star-Bulletin* linked ILWU activities with Communism and thus misinformed and prejudiced the public. Bouslog challenged the government to find any treasonous passages in Kimoto's or Ariyoshi's writings and pointed out that there cannot be a conspiracy if material is publicly printed, such as Koji Ariyoshi's quotations from Thomas Paine, the Declaration of Independence, and other public documents readily found in books and libraries (*Hono. Record*, Sept. 13, 1951).

The result shows how much or how little evidence was needed to convict in federal district court in 1953 (McNamara 1960). Ariyoshi drew the analogy between his situation and the one in 1909 when Frederick Makino of *Hawaii Hochi* and Yasutara Soga of *Nippu Jiji* were arrested in "Hawaii's First Big Conspiracy Trial." There was no overt act to overthrow the plantations then, Ariyoshi said, nor any overt act to overthrow the American government now (*Hono. Record*, Aug. 5, 1954). Only one person actually identified Ariyoshi as having attended "six or seven" party meetings but admitted that Ariyoshi had not spoken. The Honolulu dailies refused to print a resolution by ILWU workers on Maui that interpreted Hall's arrest as an act deliberately detrimental to their union. The jury decided that Ariyoshi intended to advocate the violent overthrow of the United States. Character witnesses for those on trial stepped forward, including Honolulu Mayor Johnny Wilson for Jack Hall. The amount of space the dailies gave to these witnesses, however, was far less than that accorded to those testifying against the Hawaii Seven.

Arresting, convicting, and jailing journalists is always a blow to freedom of speech and the press, not to mention their wallets. Hall did not receive a prison sentence, but Ariyoshi, Kimoto, and Reinecke spent a week behind bars before they could post bail. On the day of Ariyoshi's arrest, Honolulu Paper Company, a Big Five subsidiary, cut off the *Record*'s credit. Upon release, Ariyoshi called the company and argued that the *Record* had never been in debt, but a company spokesman said that the move "was an order from the top." Ariyoshi printed on book paper until another supply of newsprint could be located and continued his series, "My Thoughts For Which I Am Indicted."

After the men were released, the *Advertiser*'s fair-minded Sandy Zalberg visited the *Record* back shop for a story. The staff was at work as usual. Reinecke, "in a torn shirt smeared with printer's ink," was taking proofs, while Ariyoshi operated a Linotype machine, and Kimoto worked on page makeup (*Adv.*, Jan. 20, 1958). Jack Hall continued to write an occasional column.

The reversals of all seven convictions in 1958 led to somewhat more balanced coverage. Back in late 1952, under the growing realization that Red baiting was delaying statehood, the *Star-Bulletin* had already begun to back away from insisting that the Territory was in the grips of a Communist conspiracy. In Hilo, the *Star-Bulletin* affiliate under Harry M. Blickhahn editorialized, "Red Influence Waning" in Western Europe" (*Trib.-Herald*, Dec. 13, 1952). Yet the *Star-Bulletin* played it safe. Publisher Joe Farrington, on *IMUA*'s fourth birthday, sent a congratulatory message to *IMUA:* "Our country's security and Hawaii's welfare demand that no effort be spared to expose and eradicate enemies who operate under the guise of Communism" (*IMUA*, Aug. 1, 1953).

The *Advertiser*'s Lorrin Thurston distanced himself from his earlier Red-baiting tactics and threw himself into the job of chairman of the Hawaii Statehood Commission. By the end of 1957, "Thurston Says Communist 'Bunk' Hurting Statehood" (*Adv.*, Dec. 13, 1957). City editor Buck Buchwach prepared a booklet, "Hawaii, U.S.A.—Communist Beachhead or Showcase for Americanism?" and came down in favor of "Showcase" (*Adv.*, Apr. 14, 1958). Plantation papers became more reasonable as management was forced to sit down with labor at the negotiating table.

But the Communist smear was far from over. George Chaplin, who became *Advertiser* editor in 1959 and had a well-earned reputation for racial liberalism, maintained an anti-Communist hard line for years. In 1960, John Reinecke complained in a letter about the morning daily's slanted coverage. The paper alleged that ILWU officer Antonio Rania was "following the communist line" by saying there was vice and corruption in the Philippine government, but when it wrote up the same story it considered this "just good straight reporting." Editor-in-chief Chaplin responded the same day with a signed editorial. Could Reinecke have touched a nerve? "The practice of you and your friends," Chaplin lashed out, is to "emphasize what's 'wrong' in the democracies and what's 'right' everywhere else." The *Advertiser*, by contrast, is "an honest newspaper" that does not go into a story with preconceived ideas as to what it will find. Ignoring the fact that the Hawaii Seven convictions had been overturned, Chaplin added: "And frankly your background is not one to inspire confidence.... You were one of the Hawaii Seven.... You were a proofreader for the now-defunct, Red-lining Honolulu Record and you were a teacher whose license was revoked by the Commission of Education in 1948" (*Adv.*, Sept. 22, 1960). *IMUA* went further, insisting well past the advent of statehood that the Hawaii Seven's final acquittal increased the menace of Communism in Hawai'i.

Back in 1953, Koji Ariyoshi had predicted, "McCarthyism will have spent itself like a destructive tornado.... and will rot on the garbage heap of history" (*Hono. Record*, Aug. 6, 1953). By 1979, the *Advertiser* agreed, staff writer Peter Rosegg recapping "the Hysteria of the Cold War and the Early McCarthy Era" (Jan. 2, 1979).

30. *Ka Leo* Reports on the *Golden Rule*

In the rabidly anti-Communist decade of the 1950s, a college paper, *Ka Leo o Hawaii* (1922–), the University of Hawai'i student publication, rose above the low level of mainstream press discourse to distinguish itself.

The university or college newspaper is different from other mainstream journals in that it is subsidized and only partly commercial (by selling advertisements). As a vehicle for student expression and a training ground for future professionals, it makes up a significant segment of the U.S. press (Hynds 1975; Atkins 1982). It is also an anomaly in that within itself it may contain all four newspaper categories: establishment, opposition, official, and independent. The paper usually is housed on school property and exists at the sufferance of the establishment that would like it to be its official voice. Critics may view the paper as oppositionist. Student producers usually want it to be independent.

When two small ships entered Hawaiian waters on 1958 on their way to the Pacific nuclear testing grounds, in protest of the experiments, *Ka Leo* provided the most independent coverage. In print during the height of the cold war years, and in the face of an enormous public relations effort or nuclear boosterism by various government agencies to make nuclear testing palatable to Americans—it was in the 1950s that the judicious Douglas Cater named his study of the press *The Fourth Branch of Government* (1959)—*Ka Leo* was among the few local newspapers to let divergent voices speak in the news section and reserve opinion for the editorial page. A partial ban on testing nuclear weapons would be achieved in 1963, and it may not be too much to claim that *Ka Leo* contributed to an informed public supporting that.

The ideal of fairly and objectively presenting the news was formulated in 1947 by the Hutchins Commission under guidelines to "A Free and Responsible Press" (Chafee 1947; Marquette University 1962). Led by University of Chicago president Robert Hutchins, the commission's study was a response to widespread public dissatisfaction with the commercial press and the press' fear, in turn, of government regulation and control. The report painted a picture of sensationalist, irresponsible papers in the hands of "big business." The study concluded, among other points, that the press should widen its outreach and provide a forum for exchange of comment, that goals and values of the society should be clarified, and that the public had the right to expect accurate, comprehensive accounts of the day's news. The report was vilified by editors, including Henry R. Luce, of *Time*, who had helped to finance the commission's work. Its work nonetheless contributed to raising public expectations of how newspapers should behave.

In 1958, *Ka Leo* was a semiweekly sponsored by the Associated Students of the University of Hawai'i (ASUH). It appeared during the main academic year, from September through May. Money for the operation came from student fees and ads sold by the paper's business staff. After appointing the editor and business manager, ASUH mostly had a hands-off policy. Faculty and staff, too, attempted to leave students alone. *Ka Leo* reporters and editors were not required to enroll in journalism classes taught by the English Department, although they often did. Bob Scott, who taught journalism classes and was faculty adviser to *Ka Leo*, sometimes saw copy ahead of printing but usually only critiqued the paper for errors in fact and writing after it appeared (Scott 1992). *Ka Leo*'s circulation was a modest 4,000. But a university newspaper reaches large numbers of readers because it is widely distributed free on the campus, as well as at downtown newspaper offices, the legislature, and other seats of influence.

In 1958, the climate of opinion in which *Ka Leo* existed favored nuclear testing and was hostile to a ban. In 1945, there had been initial shock over the detonation of the atomic bomb on Hiroshima and Nagasaki. Editorials stated that it was "the most terrible device to come out of man's reign on earth" and would be "mankind's greatest advance toward a new and better world or toward chaos and destruction" (*Star-Bull.*, Aug. 6, 7, 1945; *Adv.*, Aug. 9, 1945).

Even so, the widely held mainstream press view was that dropping the atomic bomb was necessary and that testing was essential to national security. Over the next decade, as atomic weapons were detonated underwater in the Pacific and in the atmosphere, establishment papers responded with expressions ranging from respectful awe or jocular dismissiveness to what a really big story this was. Prior to new tests at Bikini atoll, the *Star-Bulletin* approvingly stated, "Honolulu Prepares to Welcome Bomb Test Observers" (Mar. 14, 1946). In the only hoax the paper ever admitted to having perpetrated, except for an occasional April Fool's Day prank, the *Star-Bulletin* produced a phony "Extra" for atom-test observers attending a stag cocktail party at the Royal Hawaiian Hotel. The 700 men were momentarily stunned when "bright-capped newsboys dashed through the genially chatting crowd shouting, 'Extra—Star-Bulletin Extra! A-Bomb test called off.' " Tiny print between each line gave the exact opposite information. Everyone had "a good laugh" when they got "the joke" (*Star-Bull.*, June 19, 1946).

The commercial press uncritically printed government releases verbatim. Test sites seemed remote. Part of a United Nations–sponsored trusteeship administered by the United States beginning in 1947, Bikini and Eniwetok were some 2,700 miles southwest of Honolulu. Only 100 or so of the 2,000 islands in the area were inhabited, principally by Micronesians. On the anniversary of Pearl Harbor, the papers ran U.S. Navy photos of evacuated Bikini children on Ujelang atoll. The accompanying caption described them as "pretty husky and happy and much like happy-go-lucky Hawaiian children when they were asked to smile for the photographer" (*Adv.*, Dec. 7, 1947).

As ever more powerful weapons of destruction were invented, an ambivalent note began to intrude into the news. When Lorrin P. Thurston traveled at government invitation to the Bikini zone in 1948, along with other newsmen, photographers, and assorted experts, he speculated in his "Bikini Diary" on possible long-term radiation effects (*Adv.*, July 8, 1948). But even as tests of the hydrogen bomb on March 1, 1954, moved closer to home, and radiation victims were flown to Tripler Army Medical Hospital for checking, the dailies, with little comment, printed official releases aimed at allaying public fears, such as the Board of Health's assurance that the Hawaiian Islands were "safe from contamination" (*Adv.*, Mar. 20, 1954). In 1956, after a particularly stunning test, the *Advertiser* opined that Honolulu could be "erased . . . from earth" but reflected a general public apathy, reporting that people during a civil defense "alert" seemed more concerned over the traffic tie-ups than about the alert (*Adv.*, May 6, 1956; *Star-Bull.*, July 21, 1956).

On April 18, 1958, when the *Golden Rule*, a thirty-foot ketch, arrived in Honolulu on its way to the Eniwetok nuclear testing zone, establishment papers trivialized what was a bold idea. In the grand tradition of local photojournalism, the commercial press created an aura of tourism, posing the *Golden Rule* and crew at Ala Wai Yacht Harbor against a Diamond Head background (*Star-Bull.*, Apr. 20, 1958). Reporters only superficially addressed the reasons behind the actions of the "pacifist" crew of four (later five) and asked loaded questions. Why weren't crew members opposed to Russian testing? Didn't America have to catch up to Russian tests? Why were the crew "pacifists"?

Golden Rule skipper Albert Bigelow, a former World War II naval officer, attempted to place the crew's actions within a larger frame. The crew was opposed to all testing; America to date had conducted 150 tests, the Russians 75, the British 25; Bigelow and crew members were Quakers and Methodists who believed in solving problems nonviolently (*Adv.*, Apr. 21, 1958). The group represented a growing skepticism on the mainland and throughout the world of the U.S. government's testing program.

But there was little effort to explain the American principle of civil disobedience, an idea as old as the Boston Tea Party, or to go beyond official sources. Occasionally the dailies reported opposition to testing if doubters held prominent positions, such as Delegate to Congress John Burns and territorial legislators who in 1957 objected to British atmospheric testing near Kiribati, formerly Christmas Island, less than a thousand miles south of the Hawaiian Islands. In 1958, the papers quoted territorial legislator Patsy Mink who upon the arrival of the *Golden Rule* decried "public apathy" and asked people "to stop and think" (*Star-Bull.*, Apr. 9, 1958). But the commercial press in 1958 then resorted to guilt by association. One editorial stated: "Much of the nation's military machinery is geared at the moment to extending knowledge of this weapon. . . . The very act of hindrance will add some fuel to the propoganda fires. . . . Red Chinese already hail the Quakers as heroes for peace, which puts the American voyagers in very bad company indeed" (*Adv.*, Apr. 19, 1958). Church leaders, who supported Bigelow and his crew, were "well-meaning" but misguided: "Latching on to their efforts are assorted pinkos, super pacifists, zealots and professional squawkers" (*Adv.*, May 7, 1958). When the *Golden Rule* crew defied a court order not to sail into the testing zone and were subsequently picked up by the navy and returned to Honolulu to jail, the *Advertiser* wrote: "Theirs was a minor act of civil disobedience. It was a defiant and completely un-American example of law violation" (May 10, 1958). The *Star-Bulletin* observed editorially that Judge Jon Wiig's sentence of sixty days was a "lenient" and "compassionate penalty" (May 10, 1958).

Placement of news stories further violated objectivity. It is always instructive to see how layout subtly reinforces editorial opinion. On Apr. 19, 1958, on page six, next to a "jump" story on the *Golden Rule,* the *Advertiser* placed a two-column photo of La Rance C. Sullivan, who with twenty other American soldiers had refused repatriation from China where they were detained after capture during the Korean War. The *Advertiser*'s Buck Buchwach identified Sullivan, who was passing through Honolulu, as "the first Negro of nine turncoats to return from China." The *Star-Bulletin*'s front page on April 24, prominently featured "Court Blocks Sailing of Golden Rule" next to a headline, "U.S. Intercontinental Missile Is Hurled 5,000 Miles" at Cape Canaveral, Florida. Below the front-page fold was the government announcement that missiles with nuclear warheads would be fired during the atomic tests: "H Missiles to Roar from Johnston Isle."

Recognizing the need for fairness toward a subject of such importance, it was *Ka Leo* that responsibly addressed the "stop and think" plea, sought objectivity in content and placement, and achieved a leadership role in questioning knee-jerk patriotism. Staff arranged for the crew to speak to the student body, and the paper gave its April 22 front page over to the *Golden Rule*'s mission.

Having conducted a campuswide opinion poll, student editor Elsie Loo reported that opinion was "split" on the necessity of continued testing. An extensive story by Marilyn Vause—"4 Men, a Boat, an Ocean and a Principle"—ably summarized the mission. It gave background information omitted by the daily press: for example, Bigelow in 1957 had attempted to present a petition with 17,411 signatures to President Dwight Eisenhower to cancel the test, but the White House had refused to accept the petition. Another student interviewed two University presidents, past and present, and reported their differing views. President Emeritus Gregg Sinclair, in whose honor Sinclair Library was named, remained unconvinced of the danger of radiation in the atmosphere and stated, "The U.S. must catch up with the Russians." President Laurence H. Snyder, who developed the first course in medical genetics to be required in a U.S. medical school and had served as president of the American Association for Advancement of Science, had another view: he knew that nuclear testing caused genetic harm and thought that testing would eventually have to be stopped by all countries. Snyder said of the *Golden Rule*'s crew, "I don't think they will do any good, but I admire them" (*Ka Leo,* Apr. 22, 30, 1958).

Golden Rule-Issue of an Era?

Ka Leo O Hawaii
THE VOICE OF HAWAII

Dr. Snyder States Case As Campus Opinion Splits

By Winifred Leong

XXXVI, No. 42   UNIVERSITY OF HAWAII   TUESDAY, APRIL 22, 1958

...Her Meets ...Golden Rule'

By Stephen Vause

FROM LEFT to right, Bigelow, Willoughby, Sherwood, Huntington.   Photo by Bob Young

Crew To Speak Today

Because of the controversial nature of the questions involved, Ka Leo O Hawaii has arranged for the crew of the Golden Rule to speak to the UH student body from the steps of Hawaii Hall facing the main quadrangle today at 12:30 p.m.

Men, a Boat, an Ocean and a Principle

By MARILYN VAUSE

(Continued on page 2)

Among the few truly independent papers in the Islands' history, *Ka Leo o Hawaii,* the University of Hawai'i student publication, in its edition of April 22, 1958, evenhandedly reported protests against nuclear testing in the Pacific. (University of Hawai'i Hawaiian and Pacific Collection)

Ka Leo in subsequent editions carried letters on both sides of the issue and sponsored a debate between students and faculty (Apr. 30, May 7, 1958). Expressing a more conventional view, Pablo Isawa, the student editor who followed Elsie Loo (a new editor takes over at the end of the spring semester for the following academic year), admitted to being more cautious on the subject and editorially asked if the crew might have "overstepped their boundaries" in defying the court injunction. He added that *Ka Leo*, however, would remain "unbiased" editorially on the subject (May 21, 1958).

When the *Phoenix* arrived to add its support to the *Golden Rule*, it was more of the same by the dailies. The *Phoenix* was skippered by Earle Reynolds, a noted anthropologist who had conducted a study of radiation effects on children in Hiroshima and Nagasaki for the National Academy of Science—"Scientist Notes Atomic Victims Growth Change" (*Adv.*, Dec. 31, 1954)—and became dedicated to peace causes. Reynolds and his family sailed toward the Eniwetok atoll that he asserted was in international waters, were arrested, returned to Honolulu by the navy, and were convicted in Honolulu District Court (a conviction declared illegal by the U.S. Court of Appeals in 1961). The *Phoenix* story appeared next to a submarine commander's statement that the radiation on a Nautilus sub was lower than at Waikīkī Beach (*Star-Bull.*, July 3, 1958).

In the aftermath of 1958, crew members of the *Golden Rule* and *Phoenix* applied their energies elsewhere. In 1959, the *Star-Bulletin* belatedly confirmed what residents already knew from observation that flashes of two 1958 blasts were visible from Honolulu—"Last Summer's A-Blasts 800 Miles From Honolulu" (Mar. 12, 1959). Still, in 1962, the *Star-Bulletin*'s headline for a hydrogen bomb explosion was "N-Blast Produces Colorful Display," and the story assured readers of "little fallout" from the test (July 9, 1962). Finally, a test ban agreement between the United States and Russia was reached on July 25, 1963. *Ka Leo*, not in print during the summer, could not comment.

An interesting footnote is that after the test ban treaty and as the 1960s progressed, the commercial papers appeared to tolerate more dissent. Or perhaps what had been dissenting views were edging toward the mainstream. Lyle Nelson, for instance, in his column "The Armed Forces," matter-of-factly informed readers of the origins of the peace symbol, which had been created by Earle Reynolds of the *Phoenix* by combining the Navy signalman's *N* and *D* signs (nuclear disarmament) to form the bisected circle and inverted *Y* (*Star-Bull.*, Oct. 16, 1969).

As to *Ka Leo*, the university administration recognized the value of an independent student press and responded to an era of increasing criticism of the establishment in general by students and faculty by institutionalizing *Ka Leo*'s autonomy. In 1974, journalism became its own department under John Luter, distinguished journalist and a former faculty member of the Columbia University Graduate School of Journalism. *Ka Leo*, by then a daily, was completely separated from administrative or faculty oversight to be overseen by an independent Board of Publications.

Ka Leo's influence reaches even further. Having garnered a host of national honors and awards, many of its staff have gone on to careers in journalism, joining the local downtown dailies. And working journalists, in turn, have joined the Journalism Department as faculty members and lecturers.

31. Watch Them Grow: Tourism and Suburban Oʻahu

There was another kind of fallout in the 1950s, a more benign one than that from nuclear bomb tests. The appearance in Hawaiʻi of community newspapers was the fallout from the explosive growth of community papers on the mainland (the Suburban Press Foundation would be formed in 1960) (Sim 1969; Lister 1975). Occurring prior to statehood and coinciding with a rapid expansion of population and commerce on Oʻahu, community papers grew in the following decades to become important vehicles of communication and enormously profitable. The inceptions of the *Waikiki Beach Press* (1955–1993) and the *Pali Press* (1958–1966) were significant indicators of the growth of Honolulu's tourist industry and a burgeoning Windward suburbia.

Community papers have their detractors. To those on general circulation papers that charge for the product, the community paper does not present "what is going on in the world," as the late Buck Buchwach of the *Advertiser* expressed it, but, rather, relies for content on entertainment and advertisements (Buchwach 1985). These critics call them "throwaways" and vehicles for shopping mall advertising.

This view of the "free" papers misses several points (Brandsberg 1969). Community papers are admittedly commercial enterprises, just like their competition. Beyond that, they form a distinctive type of mainstream press because, unlike the regional dailies, they do not aim at a mass audience but target defined geographic areas (Thorn and Pfeil 1987). The best combine advertising with neighborhood news of which the metropolitan papers carry little. Readers outside the central city thus have a sense of belonging to a distinctive locale. Targeted audiences possess higher than average education and income levels—the average suburban inhabitant, for instance, purchases 50 percent more goods than does the urbanite and does so in suburban stores or malls. Unlike shopping guides and "penny-savers," which are almost entirely advertising and are distributed on a saturation basis at places like supermarkets, community papers

220

have controlled circulation and are delivered to every household and to newspaper racks within their zone. Some are offered on a voluntary pay basis but continue delivery even if the customer does not pay. Community papers, like other establishment papers, may also have joint operating agreements. A company will print several neighborhood or community papers under a single operation. Today community papers reach an estimated 30 million readers nationwide and almost 300,000 in the Islands.

The *Waikiki Beach Press*

Stewart and Lee Fern were entrepreneurs who saw the future of community papers. Their first effort, the *Waikiki Beach Press,* served a constituency that would not appear to be a community—those visitors arriving from all over the world to savor the pleasures of the "Paradise of the Pacific." Yet it was aimed at a particular locale and selected readership.

Exclusively tourist newspapers for Waikīkī surfaced briefly in the 1930s, to fall victim to the depression and, in 1952, to again fail. It was in 1955, on the eve of jet flight to Hawai'i from the mainland and Asia, an event directly leading to ever-increasing numbers of visitors, that the Ferns began the paper that stayed in print for thirty-eight years.

There has been an intimate relationship between tourism and newspapers since the first English language journal in the Islands carried advertisements for accommodations for transients. In the 1870s, the first tourist guidebooks were written and printed by newspaperman Henry Whitney. By the century's end, newspapers considered tourism to be a "national asset," with 500 to 750 visitors spending $500,000 yearly (*Daily Bull.,* Feb, 18, 1888). Any threat to the economy elicited editorials promoting tourism as the cure-all, as in 1891, during a sugar market slump, when the *Advertiser* declared that the hope for a prosperous Hawai'i lay in a tourist industry "capable of an almost indefinite expansion" (*Adv.,* Oct. 20, 1891). The *Advertiser*'s Lorrin A. Thurston led the effort to found a tourist bureau in 1892. Between 1893 and 1895, the turmoil following the overthrow of the monarchy brought a response that would continue to the present—any negative publicity hurt the industry. The *Hawaiian Gazette,* in "A Word To Tourists," asked residents to inform their friends abroad that the Islands remained peaceful and were still "the Paradise of the Pacific" (June 11, 1895).

The "paradise" of the Pacific benefited from others' ill fortunes.

It was considered to be a wonderful opportunity when World War I closed Europe to tourists: "The tourists are coming—hooray, hooray," and "Tourist Season Is Open and the Influx Will Be Large" (*Adv.*, Nov. 10, 1914). World War II only temporarily stemmed a rising tide of tourists or, the preferred term, "visitors." After the war, new energy was poured into the third largest industry (sugar and pineapple were first and second).

Stewart E. Fern was the archetypal combination of journalist, public relations person, and businessman who saw an opportunity and seized it. An Ohio native, he arrived in Hawai'i as a captain and photographic chief for the Seventh Air Force. Fern next taught public relations in Orlando, Florida, to air force officers. In 1946, he returned to the Territory with his wife, Natalie "Lee" Florsheim, whom he met in a journalism class at Kent State University. Lee Fern edited a Westchester County (New York) paper and an industrial magazine during the war. Fern joined the Hawaii Visitors Bureau (HVB) as a publicist. Chairing HVB in 1948 was *Advertiser* president Lorrin P. Thurston, who named Fern as the bureau's acting executive secretary. Fern's publicity releases regularly appeared as "news" items in the paper during these years, such as, "Tourist Industry Held Key to [Territory of Hawai'i] Prosperity" (*Adv.*, Jan. 9, 1949). Reminiscent of Henry Whitney in the nineteenth century, Stewart and Lee Fern authored the *Hawaii Travel Handbook and Vacation Guide* (1950).

Fern then formed his own public relations firm. Public relations is the planned effort to influence favorable opinion. Press agents or "flacks" today call themselves "public relations directors" and "information specialists" and perform "news management" services. They move back and forth with ease between the newspapers and positions in government, business, and nonprofit agencies (Cater 1959; Rivers 1982).

When the Ferns took on the *Waikiki Beach Press* in 1955, they operated from certain basic premises. One was that visitors read newspapers as their primary source of information. Another was that the newspaper should be easily available on ships and planes arriving in the Islands, as well as in Waikīkī hotel rooms. Stewart Fern recalls how he initially met resistance: the Matson steamship company would not "let me in" on their ships or hotels, and United Air Lines would only place the newspaper "in the coach sections of their planes but not in first class." Others "went all the way with me," however, like Pan American Airways, a major carrier, and Roy

Kelley, owner of the Outrigger Hotel chain. Kelley had the *Beach Press* placed in every hotel room (Fern 1991). It quickly gained favor with industry people by printing favorable items about them and by running their press releases, or, as they came to be called, "advertorials." Articles ballyhooed tourism itself, as in an interview with author James Michener advising the industry to plan for the future (*Beach Press*, Sept. 6–12, 1955).

Another premise was to be a good neighbor. The *Beach Press* campaigned for improvements that would enhance the industry, such as a new Waikīkī post office and better street lighting. It helped organizations reach visitors by promoting places and events, like 'Iolani Palace, the Bishop Museum, Chinatown shops, fashion shows, lū'au, and cultural and sports events.

Tourist publications always put a positive spin to the news. Hawai'i was presented as the exotic land of hula girls, palm trees, and tropic tranquility, laced with excitement. The Ferns introduced an attractive, readable format of big print, bold headlines, lots of pictures, and lavish use of color, the last well ahead of its use by the dailies. The weekly expanded into a semiweekly.

The Ferns' business methods were another key to success. The *Beach Press* employed few reporters and repeated the same stories and features several times for a revolving clientele. There was no separation of the editorial from the business side of the house; the Ferns tightly controlled every facet of production. Stewart Fern even charged more for ad space than the dailies: $3.95 per column inch, he recalls, versus $2.00 for the major papers. Lee Fern managed the newspaper and its allied job printing operation at the Kō'ula Street location near Ala Moana Boulevard.

By 1959, almost a half million visitors were spending $109 million annually. Advertisements rolled in from every phase of the industry and filled up to 70 percent of any issue. The paper rode the statehood tidal wave: "Vast Hawaii Statehood Publicity to Attract New Capital, Tourism" (*Adv.*, Apr. 12, 1959). By 1960, the paper's circulation on Mondays and Fridays rose to almost 13,000 free and 350 paid or mailed out (Ayer 1960).

In 1964, the Ferns, who had invested in real estate and acquired several papers, divested themselves of actively running the latter. The *Waikiki Beach Press*, however, had taken on a life of its own. Japanese columns were added. In 1971, Obun Company in Japan instituted the Japanese version of the *Beach Press*, *Waikiki Bichi Puresu*, and distributed it on airlines and in hotels and travel agencies in Hawai'i and Japan ("The Waikiki Beach Press Goes Japanese," *Hawaii Business*, January 1976). By 1974, with approximately two million visitors arriving for at least an overnight stay, the *Waikiki Beach Press* under Gerald P. Fisher advertised itself as the world's largest tourist newspaper (Mar. 4–7, 1974). To meet changing tastes of readers, it added soft porn, such as a photo of an entertainer clad in a *malo* (loin cloth) twirling knives and "hot balls of fire!" in the air, one fireball extending between his separated legs (June 10–13, 1974). Circulation reached 50,000 in English and 35,000 in Japanese, and the paper expanded to editions on Maui and Kaua'i. The Aloha State, with the premier publication in an industry that reaps billions of dollars yearly, led the world in the number of tourist publications.

But times changed again, unfortunately, making a postmortem necessary. Bad news began to creep into the paper. The *Beach Press* proffered advice on what to do in case of accidents and warned readers about robbery and theft. There was a rising skepticism, too, about the value of Hawai'i's main industry. Social historian Noel J. Kent, for example, has said that with the decline of sugar and pineapple and the rise of multinationals and external ownership, tourism is "the new plantation" with "its own newspaper, the Waikiki Beach Press" (Kent 1983). More importantly, a downturn in the visitor industry led to decreased advertising. This, with the installation of television in every hotel room complete with local advertising, led to the demise of the *Beach Press* on O'ahu and Maui. (Only the Kaua'i *Beach Press* is still alive.) When the Virginia-based owner, the Scripps League, shut the papers down (*Adv.*, Apr. 4, 1993), managing editor Larry LeDoux and publisher Bill Paul both said, and they spoke for many, that it was "a very sad day" (LeDoux 1993; Paul 1993).

The *Pali Press*

Another kind of community paper took off in the 1950s, the suburban journal. Anticipating this growth were neighborhood papers like the *Kaimuki Courier* (1947), published by Emmett A. Cahill and William Ellis Jr., and the *Waikiki-Kaimuki Chronicle* (1948–1949) by Benet Costa. In the 1950s, as housing tracts spread out from the Honolulu district, papers appeared in Kailua and Kāne'ohe, 'Āina-Haina, Hawai'i Kai, Waipahu, and Mililani. Awareness of the opportunities linked to population and business growth spread to the neighbor islands, to Kailua-Kona in 1951 with J. B. Dixon's *Koko*

The Islands have fostered one of the most diverse presses in the world, including the premier tourist publication, the *Waikiki Beach Press*, here featured in its Christmas publication of 1974.

Nuts and *Dixon's Big Islander*, followed by Homer Hayes's *West Hawaii News* in 1952.

Some suburban papers were small operations, like the *Windward News* (1947–1950) whose publisher, Neil Sutherland, used his living room as an office. Others, like the *Rural Oahu Reporter* (1950–1955), employed a dozen men and women as well as carriers for home deliveries. Marion Sexton, radio and print media entrepreneur, produced several, including the *Windward (Oʻahu) Reporter* (1951–1960) out of Kailua. His papers typically ran promotional features next to paid advertisements, such as the opening of a new Dairy Queen or a branch bank, as well as neighborhood news in columns like "Bundles from Heaven" (new births) and photos of little league teams.

According to Stewart Fern, the birth of the *Pali Press* was in his learning that advertisers felt they weren't getting enough service from the *Windward Reporter*. Believing that the area could support two papers, the Ferns started the *Pali Press*. "The word around town," said Fern, was that "we'd go bust." But the *Waikiki Beach Press* carried the *Pali Press* during its first year, and after that the Windward paper sailed along on its own.

The *Pali Press*, whose mission was to serve the "windward wonderland" (*Pali Press*, June 13, 1958), was mailed to 10,000 homes from Waimānalo to Kahuku. It carried a combination of personal items, "Community Events," school lunch menus, fashions, recipes, and photos of beauty queens. Furthermore, it successfully lobbied for community projects, like getting the City and County to provide lifeguard service for Kailua Beach. (July 18, 24, 1958; Nov. 7, 1958).

Because it was tied to Windward growth, early issues featured the construction of the two pairs of tunnels, the Wilson-Kalihi and the Pali, that would physically link the Leeward area and Honolulu to the Windward side. In its soon recognizable punchy style, a front page headline welcomed the "relief" in sight for Windward traffic woes: "Traffic Tensions, Tranquilizers Now But Pep Pills Soon for Pali Passers" (June 13, 1958).

Easing Pali traffic was not a new topic. In fact, newspapers in the 1830s asked for improvements of the footpath, and in the 1850s for a tunnel. With annexation and development in the offing in 1897, the papers strongly supported legislation for a $40,000 appropriation to improve the Pali Road. A twenty-five-year-old engineer, Johnny Wilson, oversaw the project—the same Wilson who would become the colorful mayor of the City and County of Honolulu (1929–1930, 1947–1954) and with the dailies push through his pet project, tunnels through the Kalihi side of the Koʻolaus. The *Pali Press*, like its mainstream peers, cheered the latest improvements and the formal opening of the tunnels to two-way traffic on August 1, 1961.

Population growth continued, and success bred success. New weeklies, including military papers, sprung up from the North Shore to the Leeward Coast and to the east end of the island, and achieved a combined circulation of 100,000. With such competition, it was inevitable that the regional press would try to curb the free circulation papers—which they have periodically tried to do since 1962 by influencing legislative action. In 1963, a five-months-long strike by Local 37 of the Honolulu Typographers Union struck the Fern papers. The Ferns sold them shortly thereafter and comfortably retired.

In spite of some setbacks, there is no postmortem needed for the community journals. In 1972, at least ten, including military papers, banded together under a joint operating agreement, a cost-effective cooperative for advertising, printing, and circulation (Sim 1969). Called Community Publications, but popularly known as the Sun Press, each newspaper adopted its own distinctive title for the district where the paper appears and carries content about that specific area. The papers, however, are similar in format with one notable exception, *MidWeek* (1984–). This is a magazine-newspaper hybrid and is distributed islandwide on Oʻahu. It is today Hawaiʻi's most successful publication. This success is due in part to *MidWeek* outperforming the Hawaii Newspaper Agency in its management of the business operations of the two urban dailies. *MidWeek* has more favorable volume prices and superior color reproduction for advertising. Too, editors have deliberately developed content that rests exclusively on the output of popular weekly columnists. Current circulation is about 280,000, which outstrips that of the combined dailies by 80,000.

The Sun Press enterprise today, published by RFD Publications, is the state's largest commercial printing business. It is owned by the immensely profitable Newhouse Publications. Publisher Ken Berry, who oversees all publications, like Fern, has a military, journalism, advertising, and public relations background.

Berry and former editor Vera Benedek have pointed out other influences of Sun Press publications, whose slogan is "Hawaii's Leader in Local News." Occasionally, a story will break first in a

The Sun Press newspaper of February 2, 1972, is an example of the "free" newspaper, a type of weekly community periodical that is distributed free within a designated zone and has enjoyed a phenomenal growth in the Islands. (University of Hawai'i microfilm)

Sun Press paper, to be followed up by the dailies, as the heptachlor or tainted milk scare in the late 1970s. The major dailies will also sporadically try to include some neighborhood news. There is crossover employment, too. Journalists who began their careers on community weeklies have been hired by the dailies (Berry 1992; Benedek 1992).

32.   Statehood and the *Star-Bulletin*

The Islands' newspaper history is marked by milestones since the advent of the first American-style newspapers of the 1830s to the present. Statehood, long sought over two centuries, was the milestone in 1959 that placed Hawai'i on an equal footing with the rest of the states.

"STATEHOOD!" shouted a banner headline above an enormous fifty-star flag in the *Honolulu Star-Bulletin* of March 12, 1959. The front page, wholly given over to the event, featured reports of special prayer services of thanksgiving and photos of smiling residents, "Now First Class Citizens." A month later, the afternoon daily produced the largest issue in its history, a Fiftieth State edition of 178 pages (Mar. 12, Apr. 14, 1959). On Admission Day, August 21, the *Star-Bulletin* again joyously greeted the occasion, its euphoria understandable considering it was the principal newspaper crusading for statehood for over five decades.

The *Star-Bulletin* in its March 12 edition recapped the history of the statehood movement from the time the subject first arose, in 1849, when the *Northern Journal*, a Lowville, New York, paper broached the subject of making Hawai'i part of the United States. The idea of annexation appeared sporadically through the nineteenth century but lost specificity as to what form it would take until, on the eve of annexation, Wallace Rider Farrington gave it form and force.

Star-Bulletin leadership by the Farrington family illustrates the powerful impact of newspaper ownership united to a political agenda. Newspaper scholar Alfred Pratte, admittedly favorable to the paper that employed him for many years, nevertheless has accurately assessed the *Star-Bulletin*'s and the Farrington family's role over the decades of preparing and organizing public opinion in Hawai'i and Washington, D.C. (*Star-Bull.*, Mar. 2, 1979).

Wallace Rider Farrington, from Maine and an experienced newsman, led the campaign from his first arrival in the Islands in 1894, through his tenure as governor from 1921 to 1929, until his death in

The *Star-Bulletin*'s sustained crusade for statehood, from the beginning of the twentieth century to 1959, resulted in this banner-headlined victory of March 12, 1959. (Hawai'i State Archives)

1933. Farrington, who was working for the *New York Commercial*, was recruited for the position of managing editor by Henry Castle, principal owner of the *Pacific Commercial Advertiser*, when Castle stopped in New York on his way to Europe. In Hawai'i, Farrington moved on to become vice president, business manager, and then editor of the *Evening Bulletin* in 1898. A vocal proponent of annexation, Farrington was disappointed when statehood did not accompany annexation, and he declared territorial status a mistake, for "democracy can be achieved only through the practice of self-government"

The *Star-Bulletin* and its highly respected longtime editor Riley Allen, shown here at his desk, helped to shape modern Island history. (Hawai'i State Archives)

(*Evening Bull.*, Sept. 1, 1898). In 1912, when that paper merged with the *Hawaiian Star* to form the *Star-Bulletin*, the paper's leader elevated statehood to a cause (Pratte 1976).

Son Joseph Rider Farrington, who was born in Washington, D.C., while his parents were visiting there, took up the campaign even while in college. A later *Star-Bulletin* editor, A. A. "Bud" Smyser, recalls the story that Joe Farrington told on himself, that when he was courting his future wife while both were journalism students at the University of Wisconsin in 1919, he explained that if she married him she would have to be for statehood, too (Smyser 1991). At his father's death, Joe Farrington assumed leadership of the *Star-Bulletin*, and two years later, in April 1935, proposed formation of a Hawaii Equal Rights Commission to lobby for the same rights for Hawai'i as those held by the forty-eight states (*Star-Bull.*, Sept. 27, 1935). He carried his advocacy of statehood from the paper's Merchant Street headquarters to Washington, D.C., where he was delegate to Congress from 1943 to his death in 1954. Farrington succeeded Samuel Wilder King, another statehood advocate, but King did not own a newspaper that could keep the issue before the public. It was during his tenure as delegate that Joe Farrington gained the sobriquet, "statehood's champion." Many attributed Farrington's fatal heart attack in his capitol office to the demanding schedule he followed. At his death, the rival *Advertiser* paid tribute to Farrington as "Newsman, Delegate" and "leader of the movement for Hawaiian statehood" (*Adv.*, June 19, 20, 1954).

His widow, Betty Farrington, continued the fight as the paper's publisher, as the appointed delegate to complete her husband's term, and through a two-year term of her own. Betty Pruett, the daughter of American missionaries from Tennessee who had lived in Japan, was a leader over the years in Republican women's national organizations and lobbied steadily for statehood from that vantage point. Although she was defeated for reelection in 1956 by John Burns in the Democratic sweep of that year and was not present at the ceremonial signing of the proclamation making Hawai'i the fiftieth state, President Dwight D. Eisenhower sent her the principal pen he had used for the signing (*Star-Bull.*, Aug. 15, 1980).

Over the years, members of the Atherton family, who were the financial angels of the *Star-Bulletin*, fully backed the cause: Charles H. Atherton purchased control of the *Hawaiian Star* in 1908, and brothers Charles H. and Frank C. and father Joseph Ballard Atherton became owners of the *Star-Bulletin* in 1912. W. R. Farrington acquired stock, and the Athertons turned over controlling interest to him after he concluded his second term as governor. Joe and Betty Farrington inherited that financial interest. An important factor in the long drive for statehood was to build circulation, which grew from approximately 4,000 in 1912 to 104,000 in 1959.

Much of the history of the *Star-Bulletin* can be read within the context of how a particular issue or employment practice fit into the statehood drive. For example, the ugly chapter of its 1920s' campaign to shut down the Japanese-language schools was waged in part because Farrington feared that mainlanders would view Hawai'i as harboring an alien spirit. In the 1930s, to make amends, and also as a response to the increasing clout of nisei at the polls, editor Riley Allen hired Japanese reporters and writers. Later, during World War II, Allen and the Farringtons threw the paper's total support behind Hawai'i's Japanese.

Riley Harris Allen, who was born in Texas and worked for a Seattle, Washington, newspaper, joined the *Evening Bulletin* in 1910. In 1912, W. R. Farrington elevated Allen to editor in chief of the *Star-Bulletin*. Allen held this position until 1960, giving him the longest tenure of any local editor, only absent from 1918 to 1921 as a relief worker with the Red Cross in Russia. Temporary setbacks did not discourage him. For example, when Governor Lawrence M. Judd vetoed a joint territorial legislative resolution on statehood, Allen editorialized, "The governor's action may temporarily delay the appeal to Congress but cannot long prevent it" (May 1, 1931). From the 1930s through the 1950s, the *Star-Bulletin* maintained a Washington, D.C., bureau, a practice usually confined to much larger metropolitan dailies. The paper never failed to publicize any favorable story on statehood, such as national Gallup polls showing public opinion in favor of it, or, a local slant, "Molokai Asks 'Statehood and Water'" (Jan. 17, 1948). Allen's enthusiasm for statehood was so well known that colleagues, in an annual Gridiron Roast sponsored by the Honolulu Press Club, lampooned him as demanding to know of the newly published *Kinsey Report on Females* (1953), a study of the sexual habits of women: "Kinsey Report? What's it got to do with statehood?" (*Adv.*, Dec. 8, 1953).

Accounts by other staff members throw additional light upon the paper's single-mindedness, such as Bud Smyser's recollection of his employment (Smyser 1991). A former Pennsylvania newsman newly discharged from the U.S. Navy after World War II and attracted to the Islands, Smyser called both dailies, but it was the weekend, and *Advertiser* editor Ray Coll Sr. was not available. Riley Allen was at his desk and asked, "Where are you?" Smyser agreed to work for $225 per month as the paper's political reporter, traveling with Joe Farrington through the Islands during his reelection campaign in 1946 because "I believed in what Joe stood for—statehood."

Statehood was also an article of faith with Hilo-born Urban Allen who began his career on the *Star-Bulletin*-owned *Hilo Tribune-Herald* in 1927. After stints as city editor and editor in Hilo, Urban Allen (no relation to Riley) in 1946 moved to the city editor's desk of the Honolulu afternoon paper with responsibility for the editorial page. His obituary noted his dedication, adding that "the proudest moment in his career" was the "day he was asked by Riley Allen . . . to write the editorial comment when Hawaii became a state" (obituary, *Star-Bull.,* Aug. 2, 1975).

The *Star-Bulletin* was not alone over the years in its campaign. It was a popular newspaper cause across the political and economic spectrum. The Japanese-English *Maui Record,* calling itself a Democratic party organ, and the *Maui News,* proudly identifying itself as "A Republican Paper," both supported it. *Maui News* editor Ezra Crane served as a member of the pre–World War II bipartisan Maui County statehood committee. Editor Kengi (Jimmy) Yamada of *Hawaii Hochi* in Honolulu spoke up for statehood, and upon its achievement echoed the widely held view that finally "we are first-class citizens in every sense of the word" (*Hochi,* Mar. 13, 1959). The confirming plebiscite was carried by 17 to 1, only the island of Ni'ihau voting against ratification, by 70 to 18.

Because there was such intense activity in its favor, there must have been opposition. There was, and it caused statehood's delay. Interviewed on the subject, Betty Farrington said that, nationally, Southerners and Dixiecrats—a spin-off party by those opposed in 1948 to the nomination of Harry S. Truman for president—feared two things, Communism and racial mixing (*Star-Bull.,* Aug. 15, 1980). She offered as evidence various statehood bills that were held up for years in the southern-dominated Rules Committee and thus could never reach the floor of Congress for a vote.

Locally, a private opinion poll, commissioned in 1958 by historian Lawrence Fuchs, revealed haole and Hawaiian opposition to be at 23 and 27 percent respectively (Fuchs 1961). A more recent analysis by another historian, John S. Whitehead, posits that substantial internal opposition, including that by Governor Ingram Stainback, the anti-Communist newspaper *IMUA,* and Alice Kamokila Campbell, contributed to the delay (Whitehead 1993). This opposition focused on supposed Communist infiltration of the Islands.

Racial fears were another factor. Alice Kamokila Campbell, a territorial legislator and an heiress of James Campbell, nineteenth-century landowner, sugar grower, and financier, spoke for those who feared runaway development and cultural decline (Whitehead 1993). Kamokila, as she was called, was excellent copy as—lei-bedecked at public hearings and with a regal bearing—she lashed out at the

Islands' Japanese and Communists: "Kamokila Pulls No Punches" (*Adv.*, Jan 18, 1946).

But even more formidable and sustained opposition came from the *Advertiser*. Lorrin Andrews Thurston, publisher from 1900 to 1931, spoke for the oligarchy that guarded territorial status because this allowed the haole elite to keep its power and kept Asian labor subservient. In the 1920s, Thurston was noted for front-page editorials attacking any proposal for statehood. One memorable headline announced, "Hawaii Needs Statehood As Much as a Cat Needs Two Tails." A follow-up story alluded to the "ultimate ideal" of statehood remaining just that—an ideal and not a reality "until the moral standards of our electorate have been raised to a standard commensurate with our political needs"—a thinly veiled allusion to Asians and Hawaiians (*Adv.*, July 10, 17, 1927). Thurston periodically trotted out his "credentials"—that as a member of the Annexation Commission in 1897 he secured privileges of American citizenship for Native Hawaiians.

Lorrin Potter Thurston, upon his father's death in 1931, took up the anti-statehood battle, and after World War II engaged in anti-Communist diatribes against the ILWU and Joe Farrington. But in 1947, Thurston suddenly and inexplicably reversed himself, at least publicly. The territorial legislature named him chairman of the newly created Hawaii Statehood Commission, a position he held for five years. Had he been co-opted? He still attacked the pro-statehood *Star-Bulletin*, and in turn that paper cited the *Advertiser*'s principal stockholder, industrial giant Walter Dillingham, on his opposition to statehood: "Chicago Sunday Tribune Interview: Walter Dillingham Opposes Statehood (*Star-Bull.*, July 7, 1952).

But according to Theon Wright, former *Advertiser* reporter, editor Ray Coll Sr. convinced Thurston of the inevitability of statehood (Wright 1972). Another reliable source states that Thurston retained private doubts, not about race or Communism, but on economics. With statehood, Thurston feared, "haoles from the mainland" holding big money would swoop in and "buy out Hawai'i." "He got the people wrong," states the informant, who wishes anonymity, "but he was right otherwise."

Regardless of opposition, and as Coll knew, the future lay in statehood. The Democratic party sweep of elections in 1954 and 1956 had broken the Republican oligarchy's hold. Coll editorially swung the *Advertiser* behind it. Like Riley Allen, Ray Coll Sr. had a long term in the editor's chair, from 1922 until 1959. As editors, the two together totaled an impressive eighty-five years. Upon their retirements, both men were designated "dean" of Hawai'i's newspapers. Coll's pioneering newspaper background in Pennsylvania, where he covered the coal field campaigns of socialists Samuel Gompers and Eugene Debs, and in the Arizona territory, as well as his careful postmortems with staff every morning, earned him the respect of those to whom he was "boss." Hawai'i was "ready" for statehood, Coll believed, because "One-third of the 500,000 population is of Japanese or Chinese ancestry . . . but they are fully Americans. In 70 years they have progressed further than any group I know" (*Adv.*, Aug. 31, 1956).

In 1957, as city editor, Buck Buchwach prepared a series of articles for the International News Service, the *Denver Post,* and other mainland papers, and the series was then printed as a twelve-page pamphlet entitled "Hawaii, U.S.A." In it, Buchwach presented his impeccable credentials as a correspondent accredited to the Defense Department and as wartime city editor of the *Stars and Stripes* Pacific edition. His basic premise was that Hawai'i was a "Showcase for Real Americanism."

Too, Lorrin P. Thurston as president and general manager hired George Chaplin in December 1958 and promoted him to editor in chief on March 1, 1959. (Coll, eighty-four, became editor emeritus.) Chaplin, not to be outdone by the afternoon daily, ran a 300-page *Advertiser* Statehood edition, "the largest newspaper ever published in Hawaii" (June 23, 1959). By the end of the 1950s, Stainback was history, *IMUA* declared that it had fought Communism, not statehood (*IMUA*, Sept. 25, 1958), and Mrs. Campbell graciously accepted the new arrangement.

But the story isn't over yet. Surprisingly, after statehood was achieved, the *Star-Bulletin* tarnished its own sterling record. Could it have lost its focus once it achieved the glorious victory? There seemed little point in Red-baiting John A. Burns, who, as delegate to Congress in 1959, helped to plan the bipartisan strategy that allowed Alaska to become the forty-ninth state and Hawai'i the fiftieth. Little point, except that Jack Burns had defeated Betty Farrington in the delegate's race in 1956.

Spread across the top of the front page of the afternoon daily on Thursday, July 16, 1959, was a photo of Jack Burns, lined up with separate photos of ILWU leaders Harry Bridges and Louis Goldblatt, and Teamsters President James R. Hoffa. The accompanying story read, "Burns Silent on Star-Bulletin Bids for Statement on Bridges

and Hoffa." Attending an ILWU convention in Seattle, Burns allegedly said in a speech, "The foundations of democracy were laid by
the I.L.W.U." The *Star-Bulletin* asked for amplification, and Burns
delayed answering for several days (July 16, 1959). The *Star-Bulletin*
not only gratuitously placed Burns's photo beside the others, but
indulged in guilt by association by recounting the history of charges
against Hoffa for racketeering and against Bridges for lying in his
application for naturalization that he had never been a Communist.
By implication, Burns was a crook and a Communist.

The *Star-Bulletin* continued mudslinging through the 1959 campaign in which Burns ran against William F. Quinn for the governorship. It editorialized almost daily for Quinn as "the better
candidate." The day before the election was "A Time for Sober
Thought and Prayer" (July 27, 1959). The election day front page
showed the two opponents at the polls: an unsmiling Burns with
head lowered, his eyes barely visible over his glasses; a smiling
Quinn standing tall and looking straight into the camera (July 27,
1959). The *Star-Bulletin* exulted over Burns' narrow defeat. Jack
Burns, to become governor in 1962, "never forgave the *Star-Bulletin*," according to his biographer Dan Boylan (Boylan 1992). Burns'
admirers to this day resent the implication that Burns was traffick-
ing with Communists and racketeers.

If the *Star-Bulletin* suffered a brief regression from its pro-statehood position, the *Advertiser,* by contrast, wrenched its editorial eye
around to look at the future. In 1953, distancing himself from his
father Walter's position, Ben Dillingham asked for immediate statehood because it would "rid Hawaii of Communism" (*Star-Bull.,
Adv.,* July 2, 3, 1953.) But when Ben Dillingham ran for the U.S. Senate in 1962, the *Advertiser* endorsed his opponent, Daniel Inouye
(July 19, 1962). *Advertiser* political editor John R. (Jack) Teehan
joined Inouye's campaign, and Inouye won by a two-and-a-half to
one margin. Feeling betrayed, Walter Dillingham, who had poured
money into the paper, and several other members resigned from the
board in December 1962. Dillingham died in 1963. Power had
already passed to those who supported statehood.

PART VII

The Turbulent 1960s

33. The Business of Newspapers

Events of 1962 and 1963 vividly illustrate a basic function of the commercial or establishment press—to be profitable. The first, on June 1, 1962, was a joint operating agreement between the *Advertiser* and the *Star-Bulletin* and the formation of the Hawaii News Agency (HNA). The second was a forty-six-day general strike in 1963, the first in the Islands' newspaper history. The third, on March 18, 1963, was the formation of the *Pacific Business News* (1963–), a "special interest" weekly devoted to business.

The Joint Operating Agreement

A joint operating agreement (JOA) was not new in 1962. In fact, in the 1890s the *Advertiser* and the *Hawaiian Gazette* shared a printing plant while maintaining separate editorial staffs. In 1934, a JOA became formally operational in Albuquerque, New Mexico. By 1963, there were twenty such agreements in mainland cities (Compaine 1982). Special state and federal legislation exempted newspapers from antitrust laws. That is, two papers operating in one town or city—usually one in the morning and one in the afternoon—could form a joint agreement to insure that both could stay in business and provide the public with competing viewpoints, believed to be essential to a free press.

HNA centralized all business functions of the two dailies, while each paper maintained its own editorial staff. In 1962, Honolulu actually had more than a dozen newspapers, but the *Advertiser* and *Star-Bulletin* were the large general interest periodicals that commanded the bulk of circulation and readers. Facilities were consolidated in the *Advertiser*'s structure that was renamed the News Building and was extensively remodeled and enlarged to accommodate two newspaper staffs, two wire services, radio station KGU, production operations, and HNA personnel.

Leading up to the agreement were years of financial problems for the *Advertiser*, whose circulation had slid downhill from a World War II figure of 100,000 to about 48,000 in 1959. Measures such as adding a special youth tabloid, hiring a new editor, and adding, in 1960, the first Asian Americans to the Board of Trustees, financier Chinn Ho and attorney Katsuro Miho, did not help. According to former publisher Thurston Twigg-Smith, the *Advertiser*'s woes were made more severe by the rival *Star-Bulletin*'s aggressive tactics, such as its introduction of a Sunday edition in 1959 (Twigg-Smith 1992).

Advertiser money and circulation struggles led to the most monumental struggle of all, control of the paper itself. In 1961, brothers Thurston and David Twigg-Smith, with the support of Thurston family members, forced the retirement of their uncle, Lorrin A. Thurston (their mother was Lorrin A.'s sister), publisher for thirty years. Twigg-Smith, called "Twigg," had been away in the army during World War II and was not tainted with the paper's outdated policies and, moreover, had learned the business by working his way up from the advertising to the editorial departments. By 1961, in an islandwide population of 632,772, *Advertiser* circulation had risen to 64,300 weekdays and 81,400 Sundays but still lagged far behind the *Star-Bulletin* with its 105,000 weekdays, 95,800 Saturdays, and 112,600 Sundays (Ayer 1961). The *Advertiser* earned only 37 percent of the two dailies' advertising revenue. Twigg-Smith assumed control on December 31, 1961, although Lorrin Thurston continued for several years to battle his nephews in the courts.

It was not smooth sailing for the *Star-Bulletin* either. Betty Farrington as president was very competitive. According to several sources, Mrs. Farrington wanted to drive the morning daily out of business. But in spite of higher circulation, the *Star-Bulletin* earned lower profits than the stockholders considered acceptable—"declining profits" meant that the paper would have to cut dividends.

As early as 1956, Atherton financial interests in the *Star-Bulletin* commissioned a feasibility study on a joint operating agreement (Pratte 1976). Betty Farrington and editor Riley Allen both strongly opposed such an agreement. Allen retired in 1960. A lengthy, bitter fight over Farrington family stock led to the ouster of Betty Farrington soon after. Trustees took over the paper's management, and the *Star-Bulletin* went on the market. Although Farrington took court action to halt its sale, the trustees accepted one of several offers—that from a *hui* (organization) led by Chinn Ho and other major players in local financial circles, including two Athertons, John T. Waterhouse, William H. "Doc" Hill of Hilo, and attorney William H. Heen. The purchase price in November 1961 of $11 million included three broadcasting stations, the *Hilo Tribune-Herald,* the Star-Bulletin Printing Company, and 50 percent of Honolulu Lithograph Company (*Ed. & Pub.*, Nov. 25, 1961). Ho, having conveniently been named earlier to the *Advertiser* board, resigned from that board and took the helm of the *Star-Bulletin*. He became president on May 1, 1962.

"Joint Production Plan Arranged for Honolulu" was the next big news (*Ed. & Pub.*, June 2, 1962). Officials of the two papers hammered out the plan: for the *Advertiser*, Twigg-Smith and editor George Chaplin; for the *Star-Bulletin*, president Chinn Ho and executive vice president Porter Dickinson. The *Star-Bulletin*, in the stronger position, was assigned 60 percent of future profits, the *Advertiser* 40 percent.

Porter Dickinson became HNA's first president and has been credited by many for its successful operation. He had arrived in the Islands in 1927, joined the *Star-Bulletin* advertising department that year, and quickly rose to management positions in civic and financial circles. (Dickinson retired in 1972.) The agreement carefully spelled out nonconflicting operational practices, from a single print shop to a single library, thus sharply cutting overhead. The JOA divided the labors of a combined Sunday edition. A single advertising rate meant that customers had to pay to advertise in both newspapers.

Within a year, and prior to court dismissal of Lorrin Thurston's final lawsuit in May 1964, the *Advertiser* began its upward climb out of the economic basement, while the *Star-Bulletin* increased its profits. To this day there is a good deal of cynicism privately and publically expressed about the timing of Ho's appointment to the *Advertiser* board, about Twigg-Smith's timing of his uncle's ouster, and about the *hui*'s buyout of the *Star-Bulletin* that all led to the JOA.

The Strike

Operationally, the transition to a JOA appeared to be smooth. Then employees struck. In 1963, 850 employees belonging to seven unions shut down the papers for forty-six days, from June 21 to August 7. The unions had gone along with the JOA plan in 1962. They negotiated under what national unions called the "Hawaiian pattern," with all unions negotiating at the same time instead of bargaining individually. But in 1963 new contracts had not yet been signed. The question is, why did the unions initiate the first general newspaper strike in the Islands' history in 1963?

Called the "aloha strike," it remains to this day an anomaly in a labor history noted for rancor and hard feelings. Publically, the

Advertiser labeled the strike "a disaster." It was for the public. The strike brought to a virtual halt for forty-six days the dissemination of information peculiarly the province of newspapers: detailed reports on state and local government and international events, statistics on deaths and births and stock market returns, schedules of community events, legal notices, ads for employment. Based on an estimate of a two-to-one ratio of readers to subscribers, the 1963 strike affected a daily readership of about 300,000 out of a population of 632,700. This was a total disruption of the only business that (still) provides the public with door-to-door service every day of the year.

Other media not on strike tried to fill the gap by expanding their outreach, like a Honolulu edition of the *Hilo Tribune-Herald* and larger editions of the *Hawaii Times* and *Hawaii Hochi.* But the three combined reached far fewer readers, or about 75,000. Television and radio distributed two-page headline sheets, but due to the nature of the technology, TV and radio are constricted to what can be said within short time blocks.

The aloha strike deserves a further look regarding the business of newspapers being business. Management and labor previously had amicably worked out disagreements. For example, the Hawaii Newspaper Guild successfully negotiated raises. The guild, organized February 2, 1934, was always mild in comparison to the national organization, launched in 1933 during the Great Depression and the tumultuous period of massive union-organizing campaigns, strikes, and violence at the picket line (Seldes 1938; Udell 1978). The Hawai'i guild was "too far away" geographically to unite with the national union, according to Roy C. Kruse, local guild leader (Kruse 1992). It was also co-opted. Ray Coll Jr., for example, *Advertiser* business writer and waterfront columnist and the son of senior editor Ray Coll Sr., became guild treasurer (*Adv.,* Feb. 3, 1934). Even after national affiliation in 1956, affability prevailed. In 1963, for example, *Star-Bulletin* president Chinn Ho "stood and chatted" with union employees "who were picketing his plant" (*Hawaii Times,* June 22, 1963). "Strike—with Ukuleles," summarized a national periodical, describing how picketers strummed ukuleles and sang and danced impromptu hulas (*Columbia Journ. Rev.,* Fall 1963).

Was the strike a disaster for the newspapers? Apparently not. The "aloha" spirit of the strike may have been management's cleverest tactic of all. At the strike's end—"Aloha Dere! It's Sure Great

To Be Back" (*Adv.*, Aug. 7, 1963)—the public purchased 7,400 more copies than usual of the morning paper and 3,000 more of the evening *Star-Bulletin* (*Ed. & Pub.*, Aug. 17, 1963). The guild succeeded in raising wages and in resolving sick pay and other benefits, but the papers emerged from the strike in a stronger position than ever, with HNA and the joint operating agreement firmly in place and profits on the rise.

The story continues, for other dynamics were at work that affected Hilo. The outcome, however, was to be the same. Pressmen, typographers, photographers, photoengravers, reporters—all knew that their livelihoods were disappearing because of joint agreements that decreased the numbers of newspapers and jobs and an electronic technology that was driving the hot lead, labor-intensive printing trade out of business. All this coincided with new corporate ownership. In January 1964, the *Star-Bulletin* sold the *Hilo Tribune-Herald* to the Donrey Media Group, a company based in Las Vegas, that renamed the paper the *Hawaii Tribune-Herald*. Because the *Tribune-Herald* had installed a new offset press, management proposed to lay off four Linotype operators, some with twenty years service, and to cut the pay scale of other workers (*Star-Bull.*, May 22, 1967). In 1967, from May 21 to July 16, International Typographers Union (ITU), Local 37, a newer pressmen's local, and the American Newspaper Guild struck for fifty-six days against the Big Island's only daily. Supervisory personnel put out the first edition to come off the new equipment (*Trib.-Herald*, May 23, 1967). The paper stayed in print the entire time, and Donrey emerged in a stronger position than ever.

There have been no further walkouts on the dailies. All today employ fewer workers in the editorial and production departments, estimated to be one-half of the personnel required thirty years ago. A. H. Raskin, for many years chief labor columnist and correspondent for the *New York Times*, in the 1980s chronicled a shrinking American Newspaper Guild (*Columbia Journ. Rev.*, Sept.–Oct. 1982) that today represents only about 20 percent of U.S. working journalists. Salaries for those employed are high—locally in 1992, thirty-five to forty-six dollars per hour for a seven-and-a-half-hour work day for reporters. According to Kit Smith, former financial reporter for the *Advertiser*, the fiercest debates appear to be over the cost of yearly union dues, about $600 and no longer tax deductible (Smith 1991).

The *Pacific Business News*

An event in 1963 that received less notice than the strike was the
inception of the *Pacific Business News* (PBN). A small story in the
Star-Bulletin signaled its appearance: "Pacific Business News To Be
Published by Crossroads Press, Inc." with George Mason named as
the publisher and president (*Star-Bull.*, Feb. 7, 1963). Yet *PBN* was to
prove very important to the business of newspapers.

PBN's first edition of Monday, March 18, an eight-page tabloid,
preceded the strike by two months, but the strike gave the new
weekly an unexpected boost. The popular television newscaster Bob
Seavey held up the paper for viewers on his nightly show. During the
strike, *PBN* issued daily editions, and Mason hired striking workers.
While the strike was still on, however, *PBN* returned to the weekly
status it was meant for.

Many believed that *PBN* would not succeed. Mason had set up a
dummy copy to show to potential advertisers at a lunch he hosted at
the Willows restaurant. "They were unimpressed," he states (Mason
1985). But he found a few backers, principally Woodson Woods, heir
to the Ralston Purina fortune, and Walter K. Collins, president of
Belt, Collins and Associates, and started with an offset press on
Waiakamilo Road. His own expertise ensured the success of the
enterprise.

Mason came to Hawai'i in the fall of 1947 with a background in
journalism and public relations. Interested in economic planning
and development, he became the Territory's director for the Economic Planning and Coordination Authority and the State's first
director of Economic Development. Mason had another invaluable
asset in his wife, Eleanore Mason. Mrs. Mason worked in radio on
the mainland and in the Islands was an industrial relations writer for
the Hawaiian Pineapple Company.

The Masons set up sound business practices and hired capable
staff, such as University of Hawai'i journalism interns. John Ram-
sey, the first editor, was an honor graduate of the University of Missouri journalism school, a former *Newsweek* correspondent, and an
assistant to the editor at the *Star-Bulletin*. George Mason himself
performed every job on the paper so that he understood the entire
operation.

In the first year, the paper only had a circulation of 1,563 paid and
1,180 free. Its modest total capital outlay was $985. It was four years

before the Masons drew salaries. After this, *PBN* was on a pay-as-you-go footing with a profit-sharing plan.

Mason has observed that when he began *PBN* the big dailies did not have business sections and that they underreported small businesses (Mason 1985). Business reporting consists of stories about earnings, dividends, financing, economics, corporate developments, meetings, management interviews, reports on executive and managerial positions, and stock market quotations (Kirsh 1978). In 1963, the *Star-Bulletin* still had only two pages of Business, placed between the women's page and the "funnies." It was not until 1986 that Gerry Keir set up the first business section, called Money, in the *Advertiser* (*Adv.*, Apr. 1, 1986). This might demonstrate what Louis Rukeyser, columnist and moderator of Public Broadcasting System's *Wall Street Week*, has said is the "No. 1 failing of journalism." Rukeyser states that despite its pervasive influence on American life, business has received less coverage in most newspapers than have politics, sports, or women's news. Moreover, the space provided is often devoted to "mere surfaces and facades, an unstructured flow of executive promotion announcements, earning reports, speeches and press conferences" (*Time*, Jan. 20, 1975). Another critic, Chris Welles, has stated that there is little hardheaded analysis but much about the strategy and tactics of a sports team ("The Bleak Wasteland of Financial Journalism," *Columbia Journ. Rev.*, July–Aug. 1973).

That is one point of view. There is another. American newspapers were founded in colonial times as journals of commerce and were emulated in the Islands from 1836 on. From that time to the present, the newspaper's central topic may be said to be business and economics. The topic is not relegated to the financial pages but is spread throughout the paper, from page one that features stories on the rising price of homes, the effect of possible cuts in defense spending on local workers, and how many tourists visited Hawai'i last month, to the sports section that reports the salaries of baseball stars, to the last multiple pages that display the Help Wanted ads. But in the final analysis, this very diffusion of business reporting could also illustrate Mason's and others' point that business reporting is diluted.

PBN definitely filled a niche. It did not dilute business news, and it built a reputation for accuracy and fairness. For instance, during the strike, the paper introduced the "PBN Exclusive" that

PACIFIC BUSINESS NEWS

ROUTE TO:

See Victor Riesel's
'Inside Labor' on Page 4

Volume 1 Number 1   HONOLULU, HAWAII • MONDAY, MARCH 18, 1963   25c a Copy

WORTH EVERY PENNY of the $50,000 it cost, the Credit Bureau of Hawaii's new direct-dial phone method of record-checking—shown in operation here—cuts the time it takes to look up an individual's credit for a business member from hours or even days to just a few minutes. The Bureau invited its members to an open house over the week-end to see the installation.

Local Products Push Started by Ogata Bill

Support in strategic places is shaping up for Senate Bill 780, a key piece of legislation for local manufacturers who are advocating it in the strongest terms.

If the bill passes, state and county agencies will have to specify Hawaii-made products for all public works projects if they match imported items in quality and aren't costlier by more than 5 per cent delivered.

Maui's Senator Thomas S. Ogata, who tossed the bill in the hopper without fanfare last week, will give it an early hearing in his Economic Development Committee.

Ogata predicts a sympathetic House reception for the bill and believes all senators would have signed it had there been time to circulate it fully before introducing it.

Said Ogata: "If we can by this means get more jobs, get more business going, I'm for it."

Benefits would outweigh any costs involved, he said.

IF THE bill passes:

The state's chief purchaser will list Hawaii-made products that government units must buy if they cost within 5 per cent more than imports.

Items not made locally but available through dealers will have to be bought from someone in business here at least three months, with the 5 per cent differential applying.

Government-called bids must specify whether materials are locally-made or imported.

Members of a special Hawaii Manufacturers Association committee found in developing the bill that price advantages to local producers go as high as 10 per cent elsewhere.

They contend every 100 new hirings in manufacturing create 65 jobs for others and bring $331,000 in new retail sales.

Many industrialists believe the bill could mean up to 500 new manufacturing jobs for Hawaii.

Here's a New Face—Make it Familiar

This first issue of Pacific Business News is being mailed only to selected business firms and professional people—and to those who subscribed before seeing an issue.

If you've already subscribed, you'll receive six issues before your paid subscription begins.

If you've been singled out as a reader we think will be especially interested, you'll receive an additional five issues as a courtesy subscription.

But after this six-issue introductory period, PBN will be available by paid subscription only.

You'll find the order form on Page 2.

Please note that the special Charter Subscriber rates are good only until May 25. After that, our regular rates—higher by $1 than the Charter Subscriber rates—will apply.

Every subscription is guaranteed refundable for any unused portion.

Avery Appointed To Executive Post

Alden I. Avery has been appointed executive vice-president and general manager of Frazier, Inc., representative for a number of Mainland manufacturers of commercial and household products.

Avery recently left the Honolulu Iron Works Co. as manager of its industrial supplies department.

During the last seven years, Avery he held several key executive posts there, including that of corporate secretary.

Charles R. Frazier, Jr., the corporation's president, announced the appointment.

Modern New Barge Is Being Built For Young Bros.

Young Bros., Ltd., is having a new barge built in California to put into inter-Island service.

Men in shipping circles describe the vessel as ultra-modern, with automated equipment to handle cargo.

They also point out that the vessel may well be intended to compete with a $2 million, 2,900-gross-tonnage container vessel that Matson is talking of putting into service here next fall.

Plans call for Matson to use its semi-automated vessel only for transshipment of cargo originating on the Mainland.

But there's speculation in some quarters that Matson might be tempted to cut into the locally-generated traffic that has for years been Young Bros.' almost exclusively.

If that should happen, it would mean not only competition but would add up to competition with some of the most modern equipment available in maritime service.

All equipment aboard the Matson vessel except a crane on deck will operate automatically or by remote control.

The ship will be capable of carrying 750 containers.

It's believed in some quarters that using the vessel for locally-generated cargo may eventually become too attractive a proposition to resist.

Informed sources say Young Bros. expects delivery of the new

Canadians Plan Wax Museum As New Waikiki Attraction

A Canadian group intends to bring Waikiki a new attraction: Hawaii's first wax museum.

Such museums have been highly profitable on the Mainland, particularly in resort areas.

Waikiki's version is intended to feature wax figures depicting Hawaiian history and personalities.

The group, headed by Frank L. Jeckell of Ottawa, began investigating the market more than a year ago.

Until now, the project was kept under wraps.

But the group filed incorporation papers last week to operate as Hawaiian Wax Museum, Ltd.

One source indicated the museum will be located near the Princess Kaiulani Hotel and that lease arrangements have already been made.

The corporation's paid in capital is $2,000, with authorized capital stock of $20,000 and future capitalization limited to $2 million.

Jeckell was in Honolulu earlier but returned to Canada last Tuesday.

C. Dudley Pratt is vice-president of the firm and its local attorney.

Small Contractor Outbids Them All

The big operators are gnashing their teeth.

Not only does a small outfit—W. T. Chang Contractors—look likely to get the State's coveted Magic Island peninsula extending job.

But it was Chang who tackled the seawalls for Kaiser as subcontractor in the first increment —and Chang has underbid Kaiser as well as Hawaiian Dredging in the cost-range most likely to be accepted.

What really rankles is that nobody underbid anybody else by much. The estimates were the closest officials have seen in a long time.

Plan-drafting for Nuclear Electric Plant May Be Less than a Year in Future

Hawaiian Electric may find itself drawing plans for the Pacific's first nuclear plant even before its newly-contracted-for second conventional unit at Kahe Valley starts humming.

Heco just awarded E.E. Black, Ltd., a $2.7 million contract to complete that conventional unit by November 1, 1964.

But Heco needs to know within months whether a nuclear plant would cut generating costs and be dependable if it's to make a space-age unit out of a plant

that's earmarked for operation in 1968.

Mainlanders who operate too-costly nuclear units expect to find ways to make later projects pay off, and it's this prospect that Heco's eyeing.

It's like building a car, says Heco's Lewis W. Lengnick, vice-president and executive engineer.

The first one is prohibitively expensive. But mass production slashes the costs.

TAX TIPS

Your 20 per cent first-year depreciation allowance can be taken on the full cost of equipment, and you needn't reduce the base by investment credit you're claiming.

For instance, if you bought $20,000 worth of machinery last summer, the new 7 per cent investment credit lops $1,400 off your 1962 tax bill and cuts the basis for regular depreciation to $18,600.

But your extra first-year write-off still comes to 20 per cent of $20,000, not 20 per

A Statement from the Publisher

We can predict that the birth of Pacific Business News will be met with mixed emotions.

We know many Hawaii businessmen who have felt a need for a business-oriented newspaper and will welcome this weekly as a boon.

We're just as aware of others who, with raised eyebrows, will wonder at this audacious attempt to sail into the perilous

Mason

Crossroads Press, Inc., was formed—as are all firms—with the hope of someday earning a fair return on invested capital. The directors know that serving a useful purpose for its readers and obtaining results for its advertisers are essential to realizing that fair return.

WE BELIEVE we will accomplish both ends through sound business practices and unflinching editorial integrity.

Pacific Business News will be pro-business, but it will not be blind to the weaknesses of business.

cover commerce throughout Hawaii and the Pacific. Our objective is to furnish a substantial amount of useful information each week that is not otherwise easily obtainable.

We will always welcome criticism and suggestions, correct our mistakes openly, and seek to constantly improve and be of greater service.

We seek no favors. We expect to stand or fall on what we deliver.

George Mason
Publisher

The *Pacific Business News,* from its inception on March 18, 1963, has played a significant role for over thirty years in reporting the business news in the state. *(Pacific Business News)* reported expert opinions from both sides of controversial subjects. *PBN* ran unedited statements side by side by management and the unions. Mason chastised both sides for hurting the State's economy: "Settle That Strike—and Fast!" (July 8, 1963). In addition, *PBN* has made itself a newspaper of record, carrying weekly lists that many readers turn to first, such as bankruptcies, building permits, cases docketed in the Supreme Court, federal and state tax liens, and foreclosures.

As much as anything, *PBN* has transmitted Mason's conviction that the State is antibusiness and anticompetition. He has widened the charge to include the Honolulu dailies. While there is another view of this, too—the high-rise skyline of Honolulu and the expansion over the major islands of real estate developments and shopping malls would make it appear that big business has been all too successful—Mason has articulated what many feel. Even Buck Buchwach's statement that newspapers are "capitalist enterprises" (*Adv.*, Apr. 2, 1970), meant to refute Mason's charge, may reinforce Mason's and many others' belief that the JOA is an uncompetitive arrangement.

But as much to the point, Mason, who has professionally and personally demonstrated his devotion to business, has also profited by it. Mason helped to attract the Laurence S. Rockefeller development of the Mauna Kea Beach Hotel and was on the payroll of Waimea Properties, the company that joined the Rockefeller project "to supervise the island development program" (*Star-Bull.*, Feb. 7, 1961). Mason said approvingly in 1969, ten years after the writing of the State General Plan that outlined future development from Kaua'i to the Big Island, that the "boom has just begun" (Feb. 1, 1969).

PBN under Mason was an exemplary model of a small business. It is now a symbolic and real example of the post-statehood urban development he promoted that threatened to overwhelm small business enterprises he touted. *PBN* was bought out by American City Business Journals, a Kansas City–based chain of eight business tabloids in 1984, which in 1995 sold out to Advance Publications, a communications empire led by S. I. Newhouse Jr.

A feature of its continued success, *PBN* retains its hometown flavor. On any given Monday, downtown Honoluluans may be seen reading *PBN* from the first to the last page. Its extensive job printing operation puts out from 12 to 18 separate titles a year, including the *Hawaiian Realtor, Hawaii Medical Journal,* and *Hawaii State Bar Directory.* Its circulation remains at about 12,000, a healthy figure for a special interest publication. The operation, among the most technologically advanced of Island press operations, is situated (for the present) in the large, buff-colored, two story building on Hale-kauwila Street in Kaka'ako, on prime development land. Mason interests have retained ownership of the land.

34. The Popular Columnist

The columnist is always one of the most popular features in any newspaper. Columns average about 750 words and appear in a fixed place at regular intervals (Weiner 1979). They are a mainstay in any newspaper and range from the staid and conventional in union and church newsletters to the extremist in political periodicals.

Early columnists in the Islands specialized in religion, education, and shipping news. Today they vary widely in their subject matter, from sports, bridge, politics, horoscopes, child raising, and stamps to medical problems, gossip, art, fashion, and entertainment. Some columnists trade on being witty; others on what they know; still others—the three-dot . . . or "gossip" writers—on whom they know. An accompanying picture of the writer helps to personalize the material. Many have begun as unknowns but have gained a certain fame by becoming a habit to readers who phone and write in tips.

In 160 years of publication, Hawai'i's periodical press has produced hundreds of columns, including the longest continuously running one in the United States, "Down to Cases." It also produced the phenomenally successful Heloise, whose column was syndicated for publication throughout the country.

When Heloise Cruse quietly broke into print in the *Advertiser* on Monday, February 16, 1959—"If You Have Questions Write Readers Exchange"—there was no indication she would become famous. The "Readers Exchange" format was a simple one: readers submitted their problems to her, Heloise ran them, and the answers from other readers were then printed. The column might ask how to keep lizards out of the house and "Should a 12-Year-Old Be Allowed to Wear Lipstick?" (Feb. 16, 17, 1959). Heloise sometimes commented from personal knowledge but just as often asked readers to give their responses, as in "Parents of Adolescent Need Help Desperately": "Please be patient. I know this is hard for you. I am sure that some mother or father who has solved this problem will see your letter and write to this column with good answers for you" (June 1, 1959). Readers perceived her as sympathetic and levelheaded. The six-days-a-week column with her picture moved to the top of the Advice Page in the section for "Women." Heloise also mentioned commercial products.

Letters streamed in at the rate of 1,000 per week, and the *Advertiser* hired a staff to deal with the avalanche (Mar. 10, 1960). High-school girls met at her house to fill readers' requests for recipes and household hints. The morning paper sponsored "Heloise Day" attended by Mayor Neil Blaisdell and the town's top business leaders for the "Friendly Woman Next Door" (May 25, 1961). There were "Heloise" days on the neighbor islands.

As successful columnists do, Heloise adroitly created an image. Born in 1919 in Fort Worth, Texas, she briefly attended college, married, and lived in several countries before arriving in the Islands. In 1957, she and her husband, Lieutenant Colonel Marshall (Mike) H. Cruse, and their two teenage children took up residence in Foster Village. Heloise Bowles Cruse claimed she was not a writer but had learned when young how to cook and run a house. After she became famous, an apocryphal story made the rounds that she had left a proper calling card with the *Advertiser* managing editor, Thurston Twigg-Smith, who hired her for fifteen dollars per week. She actually approached Twigg-Smith with sample columns of material she had gleaned from acquaintances and was hired on a thirty-day trial basis (Mary Cooke, "Who Is Heloise? Just a Housewife Who Wanted to Write," *Adv.*, Sept. 27, 1959).

Heloise attracted national attention. *Time* magazine ran a two-column spread on her (*Adv.*, June 21, 1961). King Feature Syndicate began handling Heloise in September 1961. The *Advertiser* was paying her $600 per month plus expenses, but after being picked up by the syndicate, her earnings rose to $50,000, then $100,000 annually. *Advertiser* editor George Chaplin credited her for contributing to the morning paper's increased circulation (June 21. 1961). *Newsweek* called the column "one of the hottest properties in the newspaper business" (*Newsweek*, Apr. 16, 1962). Her endorsement of an insect repellent that a reader recommended, for example, brought 20,000 orders in a single day to the company. In assessing her astonishing popularity, Bill Ewing, editor of the rival *Star-Bulletin*, explained to columnist Cobey Black: "Abby, Ann and Heloise all use the same formula: they let their readers write their columns. . . . With the whole country's populations to draw from, the material is always fresh" (*Honolulu Beacon*, Sept. 1963).

Maintaining her modest, low-key style, she insisted in interviews that she still had dinner every evening with her family and attended church with them every Sunday. She seldom mentioned being on the road for weeks out of each year promoting her column and books.

Heloise continued to write after leaving Hawai'i. After her death in 1977 in San Antonio, Texas, her daughter, Ponce Cruse, successfully continued the column.

And what of other columnists? Although not nationally famous like Heloise, they, too, are a staple and help to sell papers. The record for being the oldest continually run column in the country—fifty-five years—belongs to "Down to Cases" by Howard D. Case. A McKinley High School graduate, Case joined the *Star-Bulletin* in 1912 as a $12.50 a week cub reporter. He started the column in 1922 and carried it with him when he moved over to the *Advertiser* as city editor in 1946. His daily output was a brief 100 words on the editorial page. Case commented humorously in two- or three-line squibs on the foibles of the times and concluded with "Your Hokum for Today" and a nonsense item, such as "When I went to school I NEVER played hookey" (*Star-Bull.*, Apr. 1, 1936). A fellow columnist, Bob Krauss, verified how Case wrote up until the day before he died, at age eighty-three, on May 4, 1977 (obituary, *Adv.*, May 6, 1977).

A much-beloved columnist was *Advertiser* sports editor Vernon "Red" McQueen. A Honolulu native and an outstanding athlete at Saint Louis College and Punahou School, McQueen joined the morning daily in 1928. He was an habitué of the old Smile Cafe in Waikīkī where sports figures hung out and where the Quarterback Club met. McQueen's "Hoomalimali" (to flatter, to persuade with soft words) column appeared off and on for almost fifty years. Colleague Monty Ito described McQueen: "Red would sit down at his battered typewriter, light up a cigar, and begin to pound away with those gnarled, arthritic talented stubby fingers of his and he wrote it straight" (obituary, *Adv.*, Nov. 18, 1984).

Personal rectitude does not necessarily coincide with a columnist's popularity, however. In spite of, or perhaps because of it, Samuel Crowningburg Amalu gained fame as Hawai'i's "favorite rascal." Amalu was involved in various scams, such as one in real estate that almost victimized *Star-Bulletin* president Chinn Ho ("The Story of the Big Hoax," *Star-Bull.*, May 17, 1962). Amalu's column originated while he was behind bars in Leavenworth, Kansas, for passing bogus checks. He sent funny and interesting letters describing prison life to Punahou classmate Twigg-Smith, and the morning paper ran "the world of sammy amalu" as columns. Trading on Amalu's claim of descending from royalty, the paper, tongue in cheek, acclaimed him upon his being paroled as a "social and literary lion" (obituary, *Sun. Bull. & Adv.*, Feb. 23, 1986). Amalu had a wide readership among admirers and critics alike.

Amalu was colorful. But Bob Krauss may be the most original of the Islands' columnists because of the range he covers. Any topical event provides material for "Our Honolulu." Krauss, the son of a German Lutheran minister in Kansas, majored in music education. After a stint in the U.S. Navy during World War II, he graduated from the University of Minnesota in journalism in 1950. His local career started as a general assignment reporter on the *Advertiser* in October 1951; he wrote his first column, "In One Ear," in 1953. What would become a typical Krauss item appeared under "Kuhio Beach Department." A "poi" dog shooed away by a couple, got scared, jumped, and landed on top of a sunbather: "She screamed—and leaped to her feet before she remembered she was minus the top of her bathing suit" (Feb. 24, 1953). The column's logo of an ear, on the first page of the second section, quickly gained reader identification.

Krauss wrote both spoofs and serious material from that day on. His whimsy produced "Windward Ho," a "scientific expedition" to test Hawaiian hospitality. Krauss walked around the island with a pack mule. People lined Kamehameha Highway to greet him, and Governor Samuel King met the "expedition" at 'Iolani Palace upon its return (May 5–15, 1955). Another stunt that drew a big response was "Calorie Counter Anonymous." The Royal Hawaiian Hotel chef prepared the menu for this diet, and the *Advertiser* estimated that one out of ten Honolulans, including twelve prisoners at O'ahu Penitentiary, followed the diet (Mar. 19. 1956). Krauss' serious material included a column on behalf of statehood asking for readers' response (July 8, 1958). He received 5,000 replies. The column was distributed to thirty mainland papers, and 15,000 were sent out to businesses and civic groups.

Other popular longtime columnists include Wayne Harada and Ben Wood. Harada started writing columns for the *Advertiser* as a Farrington High School student, continued while attending the University of Hawai'i, and worked during the summers for the paper (Harada 1992). He is a one-man entertainment department. George S. Kanahele, historian of music, credits Harada with bringing public awareness to Hawaiian music and culture and being a major factor in the Hawaiian Renaissance of the 1970s (*Adv.*, Nov. 20, 1971). He has also been influential in attracting top names in entertainment to appear in the Islands. By reporting on celebrities, Harada himself has become a celebrity who is widely known in national entertainment circles. Ben Wood, a Roosevelt High School graduate, has been the longtime entertainment editor for the *Star-Bulletin*. His "For Your Leisure" column in the 1970s was followed by "Ben Wood's Hawaii" in the 1980s and 1990s, its longevity attesting to its drawing power.

MidWeek (1984–), the weekly hybrid newspaper-magazine, has carried the popularity of columns to a logical conclusion. Its entire editorial content, except for a cover feature, is composed of them. Three or four columnists are nationally syndicated, and the rest are locally prominent experts on topics that range from cooking and fashions to sports and politics. *MidWeek* contains the town's most popular three-dot . . . columnist. Eddie Sherman arrived in the Islands as a naval shipyard worker during World War II, authored a book on Pearl Harbor, did radio and television work, and wrote columns alternately for both Honolulu dailies. Each of Sherman's columns of a thousand or more words contains a pithy item on someone famous, near famous, or just plain interesting.

35. Sports and Journalism: "The Social Fabric"

Revolution, war, strikes—newspapers have played a key role in reporting and participating in these events. But it is another kind of event that mesmerizes readers and accumulates the most column inches and headlines. Since the turn of the century, sports have garnered an estimated 10 to 20 percent of the total "news hole"—the space allotted to news and editorial content—on a typical weekday, and more on weekends (Hynds 1975).

Sports contain the essence of news value: conflict and human interest, progress and consequence, and the twin spectacle of disaster and victory. And even though they involve losers as well as winners, sports journalism is basically upbeat. As former *Star-Bulletin* sports editor and public relations veteran Jim Hackleman has stated, "Certainly we accentuate the positive . . . but it's understandable." There is a winner and a loser, and "the peg is usually on the winner—ergo: the positive approach" ("The Game's the Same," *Hawaii Journ. Rev.*, July 1971).

Sports, too, are an outlet for local, regional, and national pride and appeal to the most loyal, even fanatical, fans whose adrenalin flows in response to the vicarious thrills. It is these fans, not the athletes, for whom the sports pages are written. Although television has replaced the newspaper as the primary source of news, the sports fan, after having been glued to the electronic screen, still turns to print journalism for the intricate details and postmortems.

Modern sports journalism developed out of nineteenth-century American industrialism and urbanization, accompanied by mass circulation, advertising, wireless communications, and photography. The *Polynesian* in 1840 reported a "good old bat-and-ball" game (Dec. 26, 1840) and in 1860 a baseball game "between Punahou boys and the Town Boys" (Apr. 7, 1860). By the century's end the papers regularly wrote up and ran box scores of games played in the Hawaii Baseball League.

Occasionally, a newspaper might resist, as when a religious journal wanted to prohibit Sunday games (*Friend*, Dec. 1889). But public interest and growing advertising revenue won out. By the century's end, too, advertising was all important to the promotion of sports, as in the notice that "Japanese Wrestling" would take place at a vacant lot on Smith Street (*Adv.*, Nov. 26, 1891).

With the advent of the Pacific cable in 1903, providing instant wireless communication with the the West Coast and the rest of the world, the fabric of sports and journalism was even more tightly woven. Single and double columns of sports news expanded into whole pages, then into sections in weekend editions. Coverage included an ever-widening range of events, among others: auto racing and archery, boxing and basketball, canoeing and cycling, fishing and football, pole vaulting and polo, roller derbies and roller skating, soccer and surfing, sumo and softball, tennis and track, water skiing and weight lifting.

Other factors contributed to the explosion of coverage, but none so important as the rise of photojournalism. Photojournalism arose out of the nineteenth-century invention of photography (Fulton 1988). The *PCA* in 1899 first used halftone engravings—photographs transferred onto plates that were locked into the cylindrical presses. The refinement of camera speed, light, shutters, and film has meant that events can be photographed as breaking news. Photography has become such a basic medium of mass communication and so pervasive a form of social documentation that we think in the images presented to us (Sontag 1973).

Photojournalism helped to create the Islands' first sports idol, Duke Kahanamoku. The six one, 200-pound Native Hawaiian captured the front pages in 1912 when he smashed swimming records at the Olympics in Stockholm, Sweden. "The Duke," "this son of the soil" who carried "the American colors to victory" (*Adv.*, July 7, 1912), became an international culture hero whose authorized biography was printed by the *Advertiser* in 1966.

Shorter ships' crossing times brought in mainland teams to play local groups. A multiethnic culture provided a wide range of participants and audience; the camera produced the images that would become the hallmark of the trade. Just for one example, a five-day crossing made possible "The Big Game Saturday," the first intercollegiate contest staged in the Islands, on Christmas Day, 1920. Sunny K. Hung bylined the 14 to 0 victory of the University of Nevada over the College of Hawai'i (the future University) (*Star-Bull.*, Dec. 27, 1920). In the days before and after the event, entire pages were devoted to photos and stories. Illustrative of the multicultural

essence of sports, Hung, of Chinese ancestry, was among non-Caucasians whom the haole establishment papers hired as sports writers
from the early 1900s on, long before they were employed in other
departments such as society or business. Non-Caucasian photojour-
nalists also captured sporting events on film. "Extra" editions fueled
the public's interest, such as a special Football edition on Friday
nights during the football season and another on Saturday following
the afternoon game. Fans would call the sports departments of the
newspapers to get results (and still do).

Papers across all categories—establishment, opposition, official,
independent—have promoted athletes and athletics since the Duke
captured public attention. The Japanese-English *Maui Record* featured letters written from abroad when Maui swimming star, Keo
Nakama, and his great coach, Soichi Sakamoto, competed in swim
meets (Feb. 14, Mar. 28, 31, 1939). *Hawaii Hochi* and *Nippu Jiji* carried at least two pages each of sports news from the 1920s onward.
Plantation newspapers gave affectionate coverage to hometown little league teams and AJA baseball. After World War II, the *Garden
Island* literally filled up half of its pages with sports stories and photos. Union and military papers employed sports columnists. Special
interest papers have made their contribution, such as the *50th State
Bowler* (1960–1964) and *Hawaii Fishing News* (1975–).

Hardly a football or baseball season passes without a write-up
about the old Honolulu Stadium, the former sports center. Located
on South King Street in the Mōʻiliʻili neighborhood, the stadium,
which opened November 11, 1926, and was phased out in 1975, had
real grass and wooden bleachers. "Only the Memories Remain,"
lamented Bill Gee. Or as sports writer Ferd Borsch described it, the
stadium was "a big part of the social fabric of this town" (*Sun. Bull.
& Adv.*, July 11, 1976, Aug. 10, 1986).

Journalists were among those promoting a new stadium. Sports
editors Tom Hopkins of the *Star-Bulletin* and Red McQueen of the
Advertiser joined Mayor Neil Blaisdell's committee for this purpose.
The *Star-Bulletin* sponsored a "Star-Bulletin Stadium Name Contest." The opening of Aloha Stadium in September 1975 produced a
special *Advertiser* souvenir edition. The two Honolulu dailies alone
in 1975 yielded more than 150 separate items on Aloha Stadium.

Sports journalism requires a special idiom. It speaks in an excited
voice dependent upon adjectives, metaphors, and hyperbole. Its writers are allowed greater informality and freedom in expressing their
opinions than in more sedate kinds of reporting. Writers may even

occasionally criticize the home teams. But essentially they build readership on being accurate, fair, colorful, and positive. Not much has changed in style since 1914, when the *Advertiser* promoted two mainland teams, the All-Nationals and the All-Americans, to appear on the old Mōʻiliʻili field: "Today will inaugurate the greatest sporting event in the history of the Hawaiian Islands, for . . . twenty-eight of the world's greatest baseball players will set foot on the . . . Paradise of the Pacific to prepare for the biggest and most wonderful series played anywhere in the world" (*Adv.*, Dec. 1, 1914).

In 1965, fifty years later, another event demonstrates how the excitement, special idiom, and the social fabric of sports merge. When asked to name the story that he felt had made the greatest impact during his long career, Jim Becker did not hesitate. The former Associated Press bureau chief and world correspondent who has covered revolutions, holocausts, and space launchings named "The Farrington High School-Kamehameha 'Turkey Day' game of 1965" as "the biggest contribution of my career." The game, asserted Becker, illustrated an important Islands dynamic: public versus private school, the less privileged versus the more privileged, David versus Goliath. Furthermore, it has particular significance, for "Hawaiʻi is the only place in the country where people tell you what high school they went to" (Becker 1991).

First played in 1926, the Thanksgiving Day game became a grid classic between the top two high school teams who competed for the title to the Interscholastic League of Honolulu (ILH). For eight years, Punahou and Kamehameha, both private schools with selective enrollments and scholarships, had a "stranglehold" on the championship. In 1965, it looked like the team from Farrington High School, in the rough Kalihi district of Honolulu, had a chance to break that record. Drawn to the human interest elements of the story, Becker thought, "It would make an interesting column if I reported what kind of boys these were, and how they reacted the day of the big game."

Prior to the game, Farrington Coach Tom Kiyosaki invited Becker to the Coco Palms Hotel in Waikīkī where the team was staying, "three boys to a room and two rooms for the coaches." Kiyosaki, a former University of Hawaiʻi football player who won two Purple Hearts in World War II, was also a counselor at the school. Kiyosaki "a blunt, unemotional man," thoroughly understood the social environment. He explained to Becker, "The kids had had a lot of crank calls. . . . I wanted to get them all together and keep them together."

And he wanted to get the boys away from the Kalihi housing area where many of them lived and "to keep the gamblers away from them." Kiyosaki sequestered his team. Becker only planned to spend an hour or two with them on Thursday but "was so impressed with the boys" that he spent the whole day and took fifty pages of notes.

Becker's riveting account describes how during the season Kiyosaki arranged with the school cafeteria to save leftover milk while he purchased cartons of cereal to feed the team. He gave the boys food and money from his own pocket. The team bus was "a wheezing, rusted hulk of a 1942 model," driven by a city garbage collector who volunteered on his day off. The trainer was a merchant seaman "who does not ship out" during the football season. Becker's story strikes all the chords. Out of a poor, tough neighborhood come "the 1965 champions of the violent world of prep football, the Farrington Governors." Because most are seniors, "this is the story of their last day together." The coaches and boys demonstrate their pride and mutual respect—the boys wear shirts and ties and the coaching staff jackets and ties. The boys dedicate this last game to their coaches. The Farrington team wins, 16 to 6.

If they had lost? "It would probably have been a different story," Becker muses in retrospect. He went home after the game, ate dinner, started writing at 3:00 A.M., and finished at 8:00 A.M. "The day the Govs won it all" appeared on the *Star-Bulletin*'s front page that afternoon (Nov. 26, 1965). Photos in the Sports section show the underdog Kalihi boys and the "blunt, unemotional" Kiyosaki weeping at the game's end.

Becker received more than 360 letters plus 150 phone calls including those from Mayor Neil Blaisdell, Governor John Burns, and everyday citizens "thanking me for writing about people who they wouldn't have known otherwise—underprivileged kids." His follow-up described how "the Govs got to me, and the story obviously got to a lot of the people" (*Star-Bull.*, Dec. 3, 1965). He has since traced the careers of the former team members; he proudly reports that they have "15 to 20 college degrees among them" and are "successful members of the community."

If the Turkey Day game played out the drama of what's right with sports, there is another aspect that points to what is wrong—that is, the fraying of the social fabric. Sports were once the purview of "gentlemen" and "ladies." In 1909, however, the very first newspaper-recorded pennant race carried a reporter's complaint of "dirty" playing. Punahou School beat High School (later named McKinley),

6 to 0. Both teams engaged in "ungentlemanly and unsportsmanlike conduct" with the players shouting at each other and trying "to cripple players by the tackling methods" (*Adv.*, Nov. 25, 1909). In 1969, worried about fairness and wishing to equalize the competition, sports writers supported a move by public school principals, to split the ILH league into two divisions (*Star-Bull.*, Dec, 4, 1969). But fairness has been difficult to maintain with ever more fierce competition tied to ever larger stakes.

In recent years, collegiate sports have suffered the most scandals. Scandals rocked the University of Hawai'i basketball program after coach Bruce O'Neil brought in a series of winning seasons, the "Fabulous Five" team, and a trip to Madison Square Garden in 1973. Rumors of illegal activities swept through the community, and the program came under heavy investigation by various groups from the University and the state government. Coach O'Neil had his defenders, like sports writer Hal Wood, who praised him for his uncompromising "honesty" (*Adv.*, Nov. 10, 1974). But others had second thoughts, such as attempting to "deprofessionalize UH athletics" (*Star-Bull.*, Oct. 6; *Adv.*, Nov. 7, 1976).

The National Collegiate Athletic Association's (NCAA) subsequent report documented sixty-eight specific violations of NCAA rules, like improper recruiting inducements, payments for automobiles and rent, loans, money for meals and clothing, and complimentary season tickets (*Sun. Bull. & Adv.*, May 8, 1977). Tom Kiyosaki lived in a simpler era when he could give team members cash from his own pocket. The NCAA censured the University program and placed it on two years probation.

The social fabric of sports and journalism was woven too tightly to be more than temporarily frayed by such negative aspects of the social dynamic (including gambling, as alluded to by Coach Kiyosaki in the Becker interview). The positive, upbeat side survives. When Jim Becker, twenty-five years later, went to the Blaisdell Arena box office to buy tickets to an all-star basketball game, the man behind the ticket booth recognized the former sports writer and repeated verbatim the headline to him, "The day the Govs won it all." He gave Becker a free pass to the game.

36.   Above Ground:
The Battle for Diamond Head

The name "Diamond Head" was prophetic. British sailors in the nineteenth century, who found crystalline rocks, or olivines, on its slopes and mistook them for diamonds, gave it a name that suggested the future value of that real estate.

In 1967, Diamond Head was at the center of a conflict that found Honolulu's major dailies on opposing sides. On one side was the ownership of the *Star-Bulletin,* the Islands' largest newspaper, speaking for those who wished to build hotels and apartments on the Diamond Head shoreline. On the other was the second largest, the *Advertiser,* speaking for those who opposed the development. The disagreement followed by only a few years the joint operating agreement (1961) that had led to the charge that the two papers did not just "go to bed" together in one production facility, but were editorially too cozy as well. Former *Advertiser* publisher Thurston Twigg-Smith cites the conflict as proof that the two papers had independent editorial policies (Twigg-Smith 1992). It should be noted, too, that journalism scholar David Shaw in *Press Watch* (1984) cites many examples of how the national establishment press is not monolithic in its treatment and presentation of major topics.

Prior to 1967, the dailies held similar positions on development. Each demonstrated the basic and profound tension that has existed among the mainstream papers for decades, a tension produced by being in a place that is heavily dependent on natural beauty to feed its primary industry, tourism, and the competing interests that seek profit through development, called "progress," that generally makes the land less beautiful.

American-style newspapers from their earliest days expressed the fundamental American creed that yoked profit to progress. By the century's end, they represented how intrinsic both were to their existence. Large real estate advertisements announced "Land For Sale" in the new subdivisions opening up from Kaimukī to Kalihi. By 1900, Diamond Head's shoreline on O'ahu's beautiful southeast coast, only three miles from Honolulu's center, had become the real estate of choice for charming resort hotels and the large, sumptuous homes of *haole kama'āina* (Hawai'i-born Caucasians).

Assaults on Diamond Head began in earnest after annexation, fully supported by mainstream papers. In 1904, the new federal government purchased Diamond Head's 729 acres from the Territory for $3,300. In the 1910s and 1920s, "reclamation" projects took place on the land that stretched along Kalākaua Avenue to the foot of the mountain so that development could commence (Nakamura 1979).

All kinds of proposals for the use of Diamond Head crater have appeared over the years. The morning paper approved of the crater as an Olympic Games site; the afternoon daily advocated "Put Sports Arena in Crater" (*Adv.*, Mar. 21, 1950; *Star-Bull.*, Dec. 7, 9 1960). Still others proposed a golf course. To its own question, "Golf in Diamond Head?" the *Advertiser* replied, "Yes," and staff editorial cartoonist Harry Lyons depicted harried golfers wailing over "insufficient courses" (Mar. 28, 1966). These were unsuccessful. Successful proposals included building a National Guard and Federal Aviation Administration (FAA) air traffic control center in the crater and auctioning off home lots on the mountain's slopes by the State Department of Land and Natural Resources. By 1967, Diamond Head land was worth $1 million an acre.

But competing arguments caused complications. From the nineteenth century on, the papers also embraced and promoted the idea of the "paradise of the Pacific" as a tourist attraction. (In 1888, that title belonged to a newspaper that became a magazine.) By 1900, Diamond Head had become an international symbol of the unique beauty of the Hawaiian Islands. In that year, *Evening Bulletin* editor W. O. Smith was among the first to articulate an environmental view of city development connected to "planning" to preserve this beauty: "There is no doubt that Honolulu will grow very much." Smith proposed, "There is a magnificent opportunity to lay out the future Honolulu. A broad and complete plan should be made, covering the area from Diamond Head to Moanalua." The *Evening Bulletin* urged the enactment of a city charter for this purpose (June 16, Nov. 20, 1900).

Both dailies backed the founding of the Outdoor Circle in 1912 and supported its watchdog position against billboards and other advertising that blighted the natural scenery (Schmitt and Ronck 1995). Both did photo features showing enormous billboards that hyped cigarettes, chewing gum, and pickles and blocked out the landscape; the *Advertiser* devoted an entire edition to the subject (*Adv.*,

May 10, 1913; *Star-Bull.*, May 13, 1913). They endorsed in 1915 a City Planning Commission, among the earliest municipal government organizations of its type in the country.

As promotion of a tourism economy intensified and population grew, there emerged a greater sense of urgency to reconcile development with preservation. After World War II, the *Advertiser*, joined by the chamber of commerce and other civic agencies, called for a master plan for Honolulu (Jan. 7, 1949). There seemed to be "a grand new chance to set a planned course," as city historian Donald D. Johnson expressed it (Johnson 1991). But the public and the newspapers could not agree as to the meaning of "planned growth." Would there be urban renewal to replace old slums and blighted areas with more beautiful residential and business districts? How would Honolulu's distinctiveness be preserved? Would there be a new wave of private, largely speculative building producing urban and suburban sprawl and increasing congestion, especially in Waikīkī?

In Johnson's understated opinion, there again seemed to be "more emphasis on private than public satisfactions" (Johnson 1991). "Gold" was the central metaphor in the greeting of Honolulu's first high-rise apartment building, on Ala Wai Boulevard in Waikīkī:

> Gala Events Mark Opening of Rosalei Apartments
> The second Alaska gold rush is on—and this time it's away from the far Northern Territory.
> More than 70 Alaskans are in the City awaiting the formal opening Thursday of the Rosalei Apartments. . . . The big, modern, 12-story apartment building . . . is filling rapidly. (*Star-Bull.*, Mar. 8, 1955)

Classified ads held out the promise of Waikīkī real estate investment: "Waikiki! Priced Right. Sold in 1 day! 2 Bldgs. Exc. Cond.— 4,500 sq. ft. Fee simple $33,500." The papers ran press releases from the Honolulu Realty Board that recommended street widening and off-street parking and positioned these alongside ads by builders, roofing companies, and other development-related businesses (*Star-Bull.*, Mar. 5, 8, 1955). Statehood in 1959 ushered in increasing pressures for development, and news columns carried "puffs," or free ads, that glowingly described new luxury condo units. The stories were enhanced by photos of smiling inhabitants lounging on lānais (porches) and enjoying "a panoromic view from the ocean" (*Star-Bull.*, Sept. 15, 1959).

Simultaneously, the papers revealed increasing pressure for controlling growth. The morning daily backed temporary moratoriums on building until an overall plan could be approved (*Adv.*, Oct. 25, 1960). The afternoon paper's publisher Mrs. Betty Farrington and editor Bill Ewing specifically opposed the development of Diamond Head along its face and base. Under the headline, "This Is Progress?" the *Star-Bulletin* stated that those who would profit would not be the people, nor the City or State. "We're for progress, too. We're even in favor of money. Diamond Head is an asset just the way it is." The *Advertiser* urged a restudy of the whole question (*Star-Bull.*, June 18, 1961; *Adv.*, Oct. 30, 1961).

Even after the *Star-Bulletin* changed hands, in November 1961, when financier Chinn Ho and powerful business associates bought it—Mr. Ho and his Capital Investment Company were the developers of the Ilikai Hotel in Waikīkī and Mākaha Valley in Leeward O'ahu—editorial policies supported city planning. In the meantime, multistoried apartment dwellings sprung up on Diamond Head's slopes, and high-rise condos and hotels arose on its shoreline at Sans Souci.

A growing public environmental consciousness began to make itself heard. A grassroots movement to Save Diamond Head took hold and was joined by the Outdoor Circle, the Hawai'i chapter of the American Institute of Architects, Mayor Neil Blaisdell, and business interests who looked at long-term costs.

The *Advertiser* mounted its campaign in 1962. Editorial writer John Griffin pointed out with disgust that Hawai'i sent politicians, not planners, abroad to planning sessions and that the Islands' representative to the World Planning Congress in Paris "may be the only politician in the 150-member American delegation" comprised of architects, city planners, and the like. Harry Lyons drew an accompanying cartoon of city councilman Richard Kageyama and France's president Charles de Gaulle standing by the Eiffel Tower. Kageyama, flicking cigar ashes with one hand and pointing to the Paris landmark with the other, explains to a puzzled de Gaulle, "Back in Hawaii, Charlie, We Hide Things Like That Behind High-Rise Buildings" (*Adv.*, Apr. 3, 1962).

In 1963, the *Star-Bulletin* condemned city administrators for trying to rush "half-baked" plans into existence. "And for what reason? So that developers with dollar signs gleaming in their eyes won't be inconvenienced." Reminiscent of its precursor in 1900, the *Star-Bulletin* stated that with proper planning Honolulu could save its natural heritage and become one of the most beautiful resort cities in the world (Aug. 16, 1963). A new establishment paper, *Pacific Business News*, highlighted the problem, stating that a Honolulu landowner could obtain "a zoning variance almost as easily as he buys coffee from a City Hall vending machine" (July 29, 1963).

In 1965, both dailies ran public forums. Letters to the editor expressed a passionate commitment by residents and "disappointed visitors" to "please, please save the beauty" of this "beloved landmark" and "symbol of paradise" (*Adv.*, Oct. 20, 1965). The *Star-Bulletin*'s Inquiring Reporter revealed (or, in any event, the paper printed) only assent from those who were asked if they were in favor of "protecting Diamond Head" (Oct. 11, 1965). It ran a two-column photo of the "disappearing view of Diamond Head ... fast being blotted out by new high-rise buildings in Waikiki" (Feb. 2, 1966). Both papers appointed full-time planning reporters to cover city council meetings, in which angry citizens demanded a halt to any further building along the shoreline.

Then, in 1966, *Star-Bulletin* editorial policy abruptly flip-flopped. In March, Chinn Ho and associates organized the Diamond Head Improvement Association—the word "improvement" is often adopted by those advocating a change that others doubt is an improvement—and produced a plan to develop Diamond Head. The association attempted to sell the public on the idea that there were careful architectural controls on planned twin high-rise apartments. These were "one planned unit" of "low density" that would "beautify the shoreline." The association sent out press releases and placed large ads in the papers. Ho himself attended public meetings in which he presented "legal planned growth"—that is, architectural sketches purporting to show how the buildings would be no higher than those already located at the Kalākaua Avenue end of the strip.

As the *Star-Bulletin* stepped up publicity favoring development, the *Advertiser* counterattacked. Another Harry Lyons cartoon depicted "High Rise" positioned between a pair of huge booted legs trampling on Diamond Head. The title asked, "Good Grief, You Again?" An accompanying editorial asserted, "Hawaii's great and beloved landmark ... is too precious an asset to be sacrificed" and asked the critical question, what will "the world think of us?" as a tourist destination (*Adv.*, Apr. 5, 1967). The grassroots Save Diamond Head Association was formed in 1967.

The *Star-Bulletin* now couched the issue as a "controversy," lending credibility to the idea that each side's view held merit, as in a photo essay entitled, "Diamond Head Controversy." The *Star-Bulle-*

"Good Grief, YOU Again?"

Editorial cartoonist Harry Lyons, on April 5, 1967, assisted the *Advertiser* in its battle to save Diamond Head, the world-famous landmark, from high-rise development. (Hawai'i State Archives)

tin's editorial page under Bud Smyser loyally supported President Ho's project: "The issue is beauty. . . . We have labored for a long time to encourage tourism and encourage economic development. . . . Some of us are more than a little dismayed about what is happening. . . . We may think nostalgically of the past—coloring it quiet and beautiful, . . . but we know that it is the busy future with which we must cope" (May 10, 1967). The paper urged the City and the public to stick with "Planned United Development," or business as usual.

The public wasn't buying. As the *Advertiser* predicted, the world did have an opinion. The prestigious *New York Times* stated that the "mid-Pacific's most famous beacon" was in danger (*New York Times*, July 13, 1967). More telling was the view of visitor industry writers, as in an article by Kenneth Lamott:

I once lived almost in the shadow of Diamond Head myself, and when I discovered recently that this celebrated symbol of the

aloha spirit was in trouble, I paused during a trip to the Islands
to look at the matter.

I found Diamond Head, which has been declared a state monument, in imminent danger of turning into a monument for the
fast buck, its craggy profile threatened with disappearance
behind a palisade of tall concrete buildings. (*Holiday Magazine,*
July 14, 1967)

The *Star-Bulletin* fought back, with Ho charging that emotionalism
was carrying the day and that he was being misrepresented. But the
battle was already lost. The *Star-Bulletin*, struggling to be perceived
as evenhanded, reprinted the *New York Times* editorial (July 14,
1967) and presented a forum of "opposing views" (Dec. 9, 1967).

In December, after a packed four-hour public hearing, five members of the nine-member city council voted in favor of retention of
the present single-family residential zoning; the other four members
abstained (*Star-Bull.*, Dec. 13, 1967). In 1968, Diamond Head was
designated an official landmark and then a national landmark.

How influential were the papers in the Diamond Head issue?
Both dailies and the *Pacific Business News* gave the story a lot of
space. It might have been an unintended result that by keeping the
issue open in support of shoreline development, the *Star-Bulletin*
contributed to reminding the public of what was at stake.

When Diamond Head was designated a national landmark, both
the major dailies expressed civic pride: "Diamond Head today joined
a highly select group of National Natural Landmarks as a worldwide volcanic phenomena." This was a "rare national honor" (*Star-
Bull.*, Sept. 28, 1968). The afternoon paper loyally continued to
defend its president's position, Bud Smyser stating that Ho had been
"viciously misrepresented as wanting to build skyscrapers on the
famous slopes" ("The Saga of Chinn Ho," Apr. 18, 1972). Ho interests later presented other proposals for development, but Diamond
Head was never one of them.

37. Underground: The Battle for Hawai'i's Soul

Save Diamond Head was not just a grassroots movement but was backed by a major daily representing the economically and socially powerful. Dissent against developing the shoreline of that famous landmark was exercised within the perimeters of acceptable behavior. The movement was in essence reformist.

During the same period, dissent by an underground press was initiated by relatively smaller numbers of university students and former students, campus activists, church and other support groups, as well as by members of the military. The term encompassing their dissent was simply called the Movement or the New Left, and was nationally in action from 1964 to 1975 (Peck 1985), and locally from 1967 to 1980. The underground press' central causes were opposition to the U.S. involvement in Southeast Asia and to the military draft that the papers alleged made pursuit of the Vietnam War possible. The papers attacked allied issues, principally the social ills of poverty, racial prejudice, and environmental degradation. Movement journalists, disavowing professional status and the profit motive, were not just antiestablishment, but antiestablishment media. Underground papers filled another important purpose, that of organizing sit-ins, protest marches, and boycotts. They were the extreme expression of an increasingly skeptical view of establishment organizations. Unlike the Save Diamond Head movement, the Movement wanted to save American society itself, in essence a radical position.

Nationwide, during the era, an estimated 1,500 underground dailies, weeklies, and monthlies (Peck 1985) were published out of a total of more than 11,000 newspapers (Ayer 1968). There is the general notion that resistance to the Vietnam War was exercised locally by a vocal but small minority. To the contrary, Hawai'i, which was a staging area for the war, generated a higher ratio of underground papers than the national average, or about fifteen out of some seventy-five newspapers published during the period. Readers' numbers were also high, an estimated six readers for each copy, because underground journals were passed from hand to hand.

Vol. 1, No. 1
May 13, 1968
Honolulu, Hawaii

TENURE vs CENSURE

What is the Lee case all about? Aside from details of who did what and when, what is its significance for the University? What will it mean if the Regents accept the second Faculty Hearing Committee Report of if they reject it?

THE REAL ISSUES

Chronologically, the first issue is the right of students to form, express, and be held responsible for their opinions on controversial matters. The Administration's ap-

Former E-W Center Grantee Kidnapped, Jailed, Needs Aid

This is Chen Yu-hsi. He is a former East-West-Center grantee and assistant in the UH economics department. While here he made friends with some well-known opponents of the Vietna War.

However, he came from Taiwan, sometimes called "Free China." In a place where 85% of the national budget goes to military expenses, anti-war sympathizers are not popular. Hence, Chen was spied upon here and in Japan where he had been continuing his studies. It was learned recently that he had been kidnapped and deported from Japan back to Taiwan on Feb. 9th. There he has been imprisoned. According to his landlady, a Mrs. Kuwata, even his father has been denied permission to see him.

Apparently, it is only his political beliefs that are the source of his detention, since he is not a criminal. But his case is not uncommon. A Japanese newspaper describes a round-up of some 150 Taiwanese students to be returned to Taiwan. There are grounds for fearing for Chen's life. But rumor has it that sometimes the Taiwanese government simply locks up suspected opponents without charges to intimidate them into conformity. The more adamant the refusal of Chinese consul general Johnson Chun-ti Pao to investigate the matter, the greater the credibility for the reports on Chen and the more it is necessary to fear for Chen's safety. The con-

CHEN YU-HSI

parent assumption is that Dr. Lee is responsible for the SPA statement. Students resent this paternalism, convinced that they have never yet come to grips with this question in its presentation of the case. Instead they have focussed on Dr. Lee. This issue of student academic freedom brings into question the entire role of faculty advisors. If the community does not like the views expressed by some students, then let them direct their criticisms at the students not to a father-figure who neither wrote nor approved the opinions.

Secrecy is the second point. The community was given a good deal of the Administration's evidence right from the start: the radical nature of the SPA statement itself which was printed in full in the local press the incidental and irrelevant fact that Lee had used his department's mineograph machine to duplicate the statement, suggesting erroneously that he was anxious for its dissemination, and the very public act of President Hamilton resigning as if in righteous indignation. Meanwhile, the evidence supporting Lee's case was bottled up by the initial agreement to keep the case secret, an agreement originating in a request by HAMILTON, not Lee. Why the Administration wished secrecy can be seen in the evidence presented below. Even if it made sense to keep hearings secret while they were in progress, how can the continuance of secrecy as intended by the Administration be justified? In short, why were the completed reports not given publicity? It is as if by the hand of a just God that we the public now have access to these formerly secret documents. The Press has done a major service to democracy in Hawaii by publishing the evidence which convinced the Faculty Hearing Committee of the two main weaknesses in the Administration position: lack of evidence for the revocation of tenure and violation of due process. "Due process" is akin to the labor union phrase "grievance procedure" in that it makes it possible for persons in subordinate positions to have guaranteed rights that they will not be fired arbitrarily without a fair hearing on the part of the Administration before revoking tenure is the third significant issue. The prolonged hearings

LIBERATED BARRACKS

DOD DIRECTIVE no. 1325.6, SECTION IIIA;
"The mere possession of unauthorized printed material may not be prohibited."

This is your personal property and CANNOT be confiscated.

"If our people fight one tribe at a time, all will be killed. They can cut off our fingers one by one, but if we join together we will make a powerful fist." Little Turtle, 1791

Vol. II, No. 11   Phone: 261-4855   July-Aug., 1973

RESIST TO EXIST!

We at LIBERATED BARRACKS know that drugs, especially heroin, have damaged and continue to damage the lives of thousands of people in the military. We also know that many GI's are only doing dope in order to put up with the day to day harassment and oppression of military life. The military neglects the real reasons people turn to dope and does little to relieve the situation.

Therefore:

1. We demand a REAL drug amnesty program, NOT a farce used to search out and prosecute people and force others to drop dimes on friends. The military should return to the REAL concept of amnesty for drug users.

2. We demand an end to the illegal search and seizure policies of the brass, CID, NIS, and MP's.

3. We demand an end to the CIA and brass involvement with the drug traffic in South East Asia.

4. We demand that the military begin REAL efforts to provide medical and psychiatric care to those who need it, to start REAL rehabilitation programs, and NOT COURT MARTIALS OR JAIL for people trying to survive in a world of oppression.

The only answer is for all of us to get together to learn just what our rights are, and make the military stick to their own rules. Learning our legal rights in reference to drugs is our only protection against illegal search and seizure, selective drug prosecution, incriminating Service Record Book entries, unjust punishment, plants, harassing tactics by the brass—against the whole biased way the military looks at dope and why people do dope.

The LIBERATED BARRACKS is trying to let people know those rights. We are also a drug referral center and have contacts with people and programs that will really try to deal with drug problems and/or questions. Call us at 261-4855, or drop by to see us.

Liberated Barracks, in this issue of July–August 1973, counseled and spoke for those who resisted the war. (University of Hawai'i Hawaiian and Pacific Collection)

Newspaper critics occasionally have yoked together underground and counterculture papers in that they are both types of alternative journalism (Hynds 1975; Armstrong 1981). But there is a difference. The counterculture New York *Village Voice*, founded in 1955, and its new journalism—a style of writing categorized by the writer's direct and evaluative expression of an event in which he or she may be a participant—heralded the youth culture and an evolving national consciousness (Johnson 1971; Dennis and Rivers 1974). It is irreverant, having broken the four-letter-word barrier and taboos against writing about sex and illegal drugs (Emery and Emery 1978), but essentially it operates within the system.

Some of these qualities exist in the underground press. But "underground," by contrast, connotes a clandestine group that attempts to conceal itself from what it perceives as a repressive civil order. It operates outside the boundaries of acceptable behavior and is vulnerable to harassment, surveillance, even sabotage (Peck 1985). It is the underground press allied to the movement in Hawai'i that helped to heighten public awareness on the military draft and the war, deeply influenced the lives of those involved, and contributed to changing social norms and behavior.

Hawai'i's underground press had its roots in two California periodicals, the *Los Angeles Free Press* in 1964 and the *Berkeley Barb* in 1965. These and their successors were usually printed by offset, a quick and cheap process. Their producers needed only a typewriter, a glue pot to paste up copy on flat sheets for photographing, and an old press. *Carrion Crow* (1967–1968) was the first local effort, appearing in mid-1967, "anonymous . . . through modesty and cowardice."

At the protest movement's onset, the reaction of the establishment papers to the Vietnam War and the draft was to cite official sources, present superficial analysis, and de-emphasize the number of protesters. In his "Hawaii begins drafting 19-year olds for the first time since Korea," reporter Gene Hunter interviewed four puzzled but compliant high-school graduates. Hunter's chief source was the State director of Selective Service, Colonel Henry Oyesato, who observed that the draft was going smoothly (*Adv.*, Dec. 10, 11, 1965). A series by military reporter Lyle Nelson pointed out the draft's oddities: there were no Ni'ihau men in uniform, for example, because the Native Hawaiians from that island "cannot speak understandable English." Nelson went a step further on sources and quoted "deferred students"—college or trade school students with passing grades were exempt—on the draft's "unconstitutionality" (*Star-Bull.*, Mar. 25–31, 1967). Establishment journalists' basic premise, however, was that the draft was necessary.

As the war escalated, mainstream papers continued to report symptoms, not causes, and invariably focused on the confrontational aspect of an event even while attempting to de-emphasize its importance. A young historian, Noel Kent, and an assistant professor of political science, Oliver Lee, led a "teach-in," an attempt to educate the public about the war, held at the East-West Center on the University of Hawai'i campus. This drew the response from the morning daily's Bob Krauss, beneath the headline, "Kent, Lee Are Nobodies," that the majority of students were studying for exams and were indifferent to the "latest University of Hawaii flap" (*Adv.*, June 2, 1967). The *Star-Bulletin* splashed a story on a draft protest across eight columns below the page one fold: "Draft Cards Burned at U.H." The story emphasized the illegality of the card burners' action but did not analyze motives nor the risks to the protestors who faced arrest, imprisonment, even exile. The paper reported 200 in attendance (*Star-Bull.*, Dec. 6, 1967); those present in the auditorium recall the number as closer to 300.

The dailies, nevertheless, dramatized and gave visibility to the movement. "Nobody" Oliver Lee became a household name—813 separate items on Lee appeared in the two major dailies in 1967 and 1968. In fact, Lee and a mimeograph machine were catalysts in an academic freedom case that grabbed headlines and propelled the *Roach* (1968–1969), the Islands' most flamboyant underground journal, into public awareness.

Editor Jon Olsen and about a dozen fellow activists began the *Roach* in May 1968. It recapped the Oliver Lee case: "Tenure Vs. Censure." University President Tom Hamilton had initially defended Lee's academic freedom when the professor spoke out against the war. But when Lee, on department equipment, ran off an inflammatory statement by a student group to which he was an adviser, Hamilton revoked the letter of intent to grant tenure. Criticism against Hamilton mounted from on and off campus for not following due process.

In 1968, the *Roach* called the University Board of Regents the "Board of Rejects" and accurately predicted censure of the University by the nationally influential American Association of University Professors for violating free speech and due process (*Roach*, June 18, 1968). The Board of Regents' official termination of Professor Lee set off an eleven-day sit-in at Bachman Hall, the University administration building. *Roach* editor Olsen was among 153 arrested by police coming onto the campus. Other newsmakers the police scooped up included two future underground editors, two Associated Press reporters, and a TV cameraman. Olsen passed out copies of the *Berkeley Barb* in the paddy wagon on the way to the police station, where he spent the night. The *Star-Bulletin* printed the arrestees' names and occupations in long columns (May 22, 1968). The *Roach* ran photos of policemen in riot gear on the Bachman Hall lawn and printed the list of arrestees as a "Roll of Honor" (June 4, 1968).

The underground papers and their creators reflect how closely tied they are to social action. *Roach* editor Jon Olsen arrived in the Islands from Maine in 1966. A twenty-five-year-old self-styled liberal and a graduate student in philosophy, he was radicalized by the draft and escalating war and infuriated by the government's "big lie," which mainstream papers accepted, that Vietnam was two countries. And Olsen had always liked to write—he had contributed to his high-school and college papers (Olsen 1992).

Olsen wrote letters to the dailies and passed out leaflets. He then ran for the U.S. House of Representatives in 1968 on the Peace and Freedom ticket. With the *Roach,* he literally went underground, printing on an old offset press in the basement of an unidentified house. The name was a whimsical reference to both the Islands' pest and to a marijuana cigarette. Volunteers wrote, typed, pasted up, printed, sold ads, and distributed the paper. The *Roach* ran "Comix" and contributions from high-school students. Liberation News Service, a graduate student-run outfit on the mainland, modeled after United Press International, provided packets of news stories, essays, poetry, and photos.

But money was short—a chronic condition of these journals—so that the nominal cost of about $160 per edition for 300 to 500 copies was hard to raise. Sometimes sold for ten or fifteen cents, the *Roach* was mostly given away on the campus and at nearby churches and stores. Although the paper pleaded for more advertisements (*Roach,* Mar. 23–Apr. 1, 1968), the downtown dailies reaped revenue from advertisements for cigarettes, liquor, automobiles, clothing, and furniture, while the *Roach*'s were for food cooperatives and an occasional used Volkswagen or bicycle. The *Roach* introduced the first explicit sex advertisements in the Islands' newspapers, the photo of a naked, embracing couple and an invitation to join the "Heterosexual Freedom League" with "Tarzan and Jane" (June 4, 1968).

In 1968, the Bachman Hall sit-in was on the dailies' front pages from May 21 to May 31. Jane Evinger, *Advertiser* education writer, straightforwardly reported unfolding events. But the paper otherwise sent mixed messages. Staff writer Gerry Keir downplayed the event and estimated only 600 participants at Bachman Hall (*Adv.*, May 22, 23, 1968), while those present placed the number at closer to 1,000, which the paper's own photos seemed to confirm. Headlines on May 23 announced Hamilton's resignation.

The rift between the viewpoints of the underground and mainstream papers is underscored in an interview run by the *Star-Bulletin*. Appearing in the Young Ideas section, two student editors, Olsen of the *Roach* and Jerry Burris of the University paper, *Ka Leo*, debated the merits and demerits of the two kinds of papers. Burris (who would serve in the army after graduation and then join the *Advertiser*) dismissed the New Left journalism and characterized the *Roach* as "a tenant of the arm of social change." By contrast, "we in the establishment newspapers are obligated to display as much straight information as possible." Olsen in turn rejected the idea of establishment objectivity: "it is very hard for someone with my view to get a fair hearing because of the quarter truths and half truths that sneak into a story and then get read by thousands and thousands of people." He believed "there should be a full spectrum of communication" (*Star-Bull.*, Oct. 3, 1969). When it was pointed out to him that the underground press got a lot of attention, Olson replied that this was "quantity" coverage, not "quality."

Whether underground papers even had a right to exist was a question. Burris, and most of the working press, although critical of them, believed that all newspapers had the constitutional right to freedom of speech. Others wanted to deny this right to dissenters. Ted Adameck, former *Star-Bulletin* make-up man who produced *That Other Paper* (1969–1971), an expression of the extremist John Birch Society, believed that the *Roach* should be abolished—a "pornographic ... filthy publication" edited by a "notorious left-wing student agitator" (*That Other Paper*, Apr. 1, 1969).

Attacks on dissenters by agencies of the federal, state, and city governments, ostensibly the protectors of citizens' rights, were more damaging, such as surveillance of leafleting efforts or newspaper distribution by the Honolulu Police Department, the FBI, and the 710th Military Intelligence Unit (Emery 1975). It is of record, as investigative reporters Angus McKenzie and Geoffrey Rips have documented, that on the day Richard M. Nixon was elected to the presidency in

1968 FBI Director J. Edgar Hoover sent a memo to all FBI offices instructing them to "immediately institute a detailed surveillance concerning "New Left type of publications." (McKenzie, "Sabotaging the Dissident Press," *Columbia Journ. Rev.*, Mar.–Apr. 1981; Rips 1981). Even earlier, under Lyndon Johnson's administration (Kessler 1984), Olsen was sure his phone was tapped (Olsen 1992). The *Roach* folded in mid-1969.

Although the papers were difficult to sustain because of little money and much harassment, the mobile technology lent itself to new ventures. Activists, including Olsen, brought out *Hawaii Free People's Press* (1969–1970), sponsored by Students for a Democratic Society (SDS). The FBI labeled SDS as subversive, to which the journal replied, "They call us a conspiracy, and we are. Conspiring to end hate, end hunger, and bad vibrations" The paper wanted to "liberate the media" into "a new world." It urged young men to "F—— the Draft" by refusing induction into the military (June, Nov. 1969).

In the impassioned rhetoric of new journalism, *Free People's Press* also attacked development and raised environmental concerns. It argued against widening Waikīkī Beach at the Queen's Beach end, against a proposed development on Magic Island at Ala Moana Park, and for making a public park out of Sand Island near central Honolulu:

To ALL PLANNER$, LEGISLATOR$, AND DEVELOPER$, including GOVERNOR BURN$—we swimmers, divers, bathers, fishermen, conservationists, and park users outnumber you "decision-makers." . . . So be forewarned: there will be no high-rises, no construction on the reef at Kewalo! . . . There will be no more killing of Hawaii's reefs for someone's private profit. No more polluting swimming areas with dredging! No Waikiki at Ala Moana! This entire Ocean Beach Park from the green grass to the harbor . . . belongs to the people. . . . AND THIS WE WILL DEFEND! (Aug. 1969)

John Kelly, active with *Free People's Press,* was also instrumental in organizing the grassroots organization Save Our Surf (SOS). The combination illustrates how effective the underground was. Kelly, a social worker, musician, and printer who worked on union newspapers, was surfing at Ala Moana one day in 1969 when heavy trucks drove to the shore and dumped rocks into the ocean. He learned that this was part of the Oʻahu General Plan, approved ten years earlier on the eve of statehood, that was to fill in the shoreline and extend it from central Honolulu around to the east end of Koko Head. Dillingham Corporation had been awarded the $56 million contract.

Kelly, who did not believe that corporate powers were monolithic, and another printer, ex-*Star-Bulletin* employee Tony Van Kralingen Jr., found a discarded high-school press and with volunteers at an undisclosed location produced leaflets, and brochures filled with photographs, eye-catching graphics, and sharply focused stories. Kelly explains, "You target your audience and you don't distract them." If Kāhala residents are being affected—the Dillingham project included building a tunnel from Kāhala to Hawai'i Kai—then "you leaflet Kāhala, and they'll pick up on the issue" (Kelly 1992).

Some 1,500 citizens marched on the State capitol. Not all of the *Free People's Press* or the SOS agenda was enacted. But plans for the development of Magic Island died and Sand Island became a public park. In the words of the *Star-Bulletin*, "Save Our Surf Group Makes Some Waves" (Apr. 13, 1970).

Other underground papers, though less influential, should be mentioned for the view they afford of a changing society. *Right On* (1970–1974), its title the slang exclamation for encouragement and approval, blended pro-Christian fundamentalism and antiwar zeal with another cause, in which it was almost alone—anti-dope. The monthly *Gathering Place* (1971–1972) carried the more usual mix of drugs and sex, gay news, and psychedelic art. Several high schools produced subterranean papers, including Roosevelt, Farrington, and Punahou.

A paper that rivaled the *Roach* in visibility and extended its influence into the mainstream was *Another Voice* (1972–1975). The Reverend Lawrence S. "Larry" Jones first functioned within conventional bounds, then lost confidence in the establishment. A Californian, the idealistic Jones arrived in the Islands in 1956 as a pastor at a Wai'alae Kāhala Congregational church. In 1963, Jones became president of the Honolulu Council of Churches—"To Take Church Out To People," an approving Honolulu daily said about the ministry of social activism and projects such as civil rights, poverty, and affordable housing (*Adv.*, July 18, 1964). Jones wrote a weekly column for the combined Sunday paper from 1967 to 1972.

With the assassinations of Martin Luther King and Robert Kennedy and the riot-torn Democratic National Convention, the years of hope turned to days of rage—social historian Todd Gitlin's phrase for 1968 (Gitlin 1987). The military itself was a target of internal disaffection. In Hawai'i alone, thirty-six soldiers, sailors, marines, and airmen sought asylum in three churches between August 6 and September 12, 1968. Honolulu's Church of the Crossroads, on University Avenue near the Mānoa campus, became the largest sanctuary in the nation.

An ancient custom across many cultures, sanctuary has no legal sanction in contemporary societies (Tillich 1977). The *Star-Bulletin* was its most vocal critic, supporting city officials who cited the church for zoning and health infractions—"unhealthy," "over-crowded," "operating a hotel" (Aug 15, Sept. 2, 1969). Military police battered down the doors—they were unlocked—broke into the Unitarian Church on Pali Highway and the Society of Friends (Quakers) in Mānoa Valley and arrested the men for being "absent without leave." The Church of the Crossroads produced a single edition of a newspaper, *Sanctuary of Servicemen* (Aug. 14, 1969).

Escalating his activities, Jones indirectly became involved in the 1971 burning of the university ROTC building. *Advertiser* editor John Griffin fired Jones, asserting that he presented "a narrowing viewpoint" and that space was limited (*Adv.*, Jan. 30, 1972). Larry Jones then created another pulpit, *Another Voice.* He virtually wrote the entire contents of the biweekly and specialized in investigative reporting. In the meantime, reporters from the major media had founded the iconoclastic *Hawaii Journalism Review* (1971–1973), in which they could run stories rejected by their employers. Dianne Coughlin, a *Star-Bulletin* reporter, praised Jones for his unsentimental analysis of the economics of the new Kuilima resort on the North Shore that "most of the town's press treated like a big new Barbie Doll" (*Haw. Journ. Rev.*, Nov. 1972).

Another Voice folded, a one-year teaching stint at the university ended, and Jones was unemployed. He joined the *Revolutionary Worker* (1975–1979), among the most radical of the underground papers. Sponsored by the Revolutionary Communist party, it had mainland connections. Ardent Maoists passed out copies at gates leading into military installations.

It is generally acknowledged that police in Hawai'i, both military and civilian, were usually more restrained in handling protestors than their mainland counterparts; that means that few protestors were beaten up. But the police responded forcefully to the *Revolutionary Worker.* They arrested the paper's distributors on several occasions for not having a license and for tacking the paper to utility poles. The Honolulu city attorney found the arrests to be unconstitutional: "Maoist newspaper needs no license" (*Adv.*, Feb. 7, 1980).

In the meantime, another type of underground publication appeared. As Murray Polnar explains in "The Underground GI Press," to the authorities the "GI paper" was the most dangerous of all. Penalties for participants were the most severe (*Columbia Journ. Rev.*, Fall 1970). The "GI paper" began nationally with the *Bond*, the Voice of the American Servicemen's Union (Berkeley, 1967–?), which by 1971 claimed a circulation of 100,000. There were some 100 GI newspapers across the mainland (Armstrong 1981). These called for reforms, including the election of officers, racial equality, and the right to disobey illegal orders, and printed material on Vietnam that could not be found elsewhere, like stories of soldiers turning guns on gung ho officers. Illustrative again of the heated antiwar movement, there were at least four GI papers in the Islands and another two or three connected to them in the Philippines and Japan. An exact count of these most subterranean of journals is impossible to make.

Eric Seitz, Honolulu attorney, participated in the GI papers: *Liberated Barracks* (1971–1974) on O'ahu, *Semper Fi* (1970–1971?) in Japan, and *Below Decks* (1970) in the Philippines. *Liberated Barracks* was printed on an offset press in a Kailua, O'ahu, residence as part of a program that sponsored houses—"liberated barracks"—near military bases where service personnel could discuss the war or any other topic. Copies surfaced on troop ships bound for Vietnam.

Seitz was not in the military himself: he had a student deferment, then was classified 1-A, but was never called up. He lent his considerable legal skills, honed in law school at the University of California Berkeley in the crucial years from 1966 to 1969, to counseling those in conflict with the military. Raised by parents who worked with the Works Progress Administration (WPA) projects and unions during the depression, Seitz had a heightened social conscience and was deeply opposed to the war. He wrote articles giving legal advice, always careful never to recommend, only to present options, and he forswore drugs—these were mostly marijuana and LSD—because drug busts and imprisonment were weapons used against protestors. Seitz recalls traveling overseas to Japan to defend soldiers and only learning upon his return that he'd been under surveillance the whole time (Seitz 1992).

In 1969, the U.S. Army issued a "Guidance on Dissent," which all the services supposedly followed. This stated that the "publication of underground newspapers by soldiers off post, and with their own money and equipment, is generally protected under the First

Amendment." On-base military commands paid little attention to the directive (Kessler 1984). *Below Decks* was produced near Subic Bay Naval Base by two young seamen, Barry Meadow, twenty-three, of New York City, and Mark Flint, twenty-four, of Ashland, Oregon, who were careful to work on the paper while off duty. They ran articles critical of official releases on Laos and on policies that allowed officers to have overnight women guests in their quarters while guests of enlisted personnel had to leave by 11:30. Philippine police raided the *Below Decks* office, and navy investigators seized the papers' files. The sailor-journalists were discharged from the navy ("Paper Without a Future," (*Star-Bull.*, July 16, 1970).

In the short run, underground papers seemed to be "without a future," for they began to lose strength with the dismantling of the military draft beginning in 1972 and the culmination of U.S. withdrawal from Vietnam in 1975. In the long run, their influence as catalysts for change has been extensive. The first to defend attacks on those who protested the draft and the war, they were instrumental in building the groundswell that eventually encompassed a middle-class majority that, in turn, affected the mainstream press (Aronson 1970; Hertzgaard 1988). In a sense, they set the agenda.

Both Eric Seitz and John Witeck, another contributor to several underground papers, emphasize this press' importance as an organizing tool and, using Witeck's phrase, getting "the word out" (Witeck 1992). Seitz adds, "We helped to create public opinion" (Seitz 1992). Furthermore, the papers changed the language of the conventional press. One has only to recall former taboo subjects, like drugs and sex, gay rights, and the rock and roll culture, that filtered into establishment papers by the mid-1970s. By this time, the *Star-Bulletin* and *Advertiser* no longer referred to those opposed to the draft as "draft dodgers" or "draft evaders" but used "draft resisters," the term of choice for those involved (*Star-Bull.*, Jan. 22, 1977).

Official military papers changed, too. Army papers, in the view of reporter Melvin Gee, were no longer "staid and stodgy" (*Sun. Bull. & Adv.*, Apr. 7, 1974). It was still off-limits to seriously question God and country, but by congressional action the military services no longer ran military papers. By 1970, the Fifteenth Infantry Division's publication, called *Hawaii Lightning News* (1957–1966), then *Tropic Lightning News* (1966–1969), stated, "Views and opinions expressed are not necessarily those of the Department of the Army." A more liberal agenda means that military papers run frank discussions on such topics as substance and family abuse. Humorously, and an indication of the adoption of underground press language, a military monthly put out in the "tunnel" beneath the pineapple fields near Schofield Barracks calls itself the *Kunia Underground News* (1984–).

As to influencing the people involved, informants have expressed in a number of ways the significance of their underground years. Lifetime friendships and marriages were formed. To many, this was the defining time of their lives, and they have retained strong social consciences and civic activism. Olsen, for example, writes for the Green party, which backs environmental candidates for political office. Larry Jones also continues to be involved, writing for international publications dedicated to human rights.

Seitz, who defended the Revolutionary Communist party people, still takes difficult cases on a pro bono basis. When the producers of the tiny Moloka'i publication, *Ke Kukini,* a biweekly that criticized developers of a luxury Moloka'i hotel, were sued for libel for $10 million, Seitz defended *Ke Kukini*'s editors and got the suit dropped (*Adv.,* Feb. 23, 1985). The mainstream press has compared Seitz to the nationally famous attorney for the underdog, calling him the "William Kuntzler of Hawai'i" (*Adv.,* July 17, 1992).

John Witeck, who stayed with resisting servicemen inside the Church of the Crossroads sanctuary and married Lucy Hashizumi of Wahiawā at the church, has continued a career in journalism as editor of several union journals. Witeck was among the first members appointed to the Honolulu Community-Media Council, a volunteer organization formed in 1970 to mediate disagreements between a public critical of the press and the press itself (Rivers 1982). Witeck continues to work to improve society, although as a family man and a union officer he is no longer, as he states, "quite as willing to get arrested" (Witeck 1992).

As the system has changed, others have merged into it. The list from the May 22, 1968, *Star-Bulletin* of those arrested in the Bachman Hall sit-in includes names of present-day government, labor, and business leaders; a sports director; stock and real estate brokers; journalists; medical doctors and nurses; legislators; and tenured University professor Oliver Lee.

38. Women in the News: From Society to Social Causes

The role of women in newspapers in the 1960s was twofold and interlocking: as producers of the product and as subjects within its pages. When newspapers were still a major influence, women journalists, acutely aware of this double strain, altered the kinds of work they were engaged in and the images they projected. They were a part of the larger struggle against social and sexual pigeonholing. In the 1960s, women moved from producing and appearing in the society pages, to getting rid of those pages, and to taking primary positions on major topics of the decade: the Vietnam War and legalizing abortion.

Women as Producers

Women have produced newspapers since the colonial period in America when they were editors, typesetters, and printers. As a rule, a woman took up the trade in what was a family business (Emery and Emery 1992; Mills 1988). Americans imported this practice to the Islands where a few women actively engaged in producing papers in the nineteenth and early decades of the twentieth centuries, but their involvement was still dependent upon the goodwill of male owners (Chapin 1985).

It is only since the 1930s that increasing numbers of women have been recognized for their own journalistic talents. Editors include Virginia Bennett Hill of the *Hilo Tribune-Herald* in the 1930s, Ella Chun of the *Waikiki Beach Press* in the 1950s, Jean Holmes of the *Garden Island* in the 1970s and 1980s, and Nora Cooper on the *Maui News* from the 1970s into the 1990s. In Honolulu, the *Star-Bulletin* has employed Asian American women as editors or publishers (a public relations position): Catherine Shen in 1986, Arlene Lum in 1989, and Diane Chang in 1993.

More often, however, women have functioned at lower-paying levels. When newspapers expanded in size and numbers after 1900, and more women began to be hired, they usually were assigned to the business department as clerks, or, if reporters, to the Society and homemaking sections. A handful of determined women in the 1920s and 1930s succeeded in joining news departments where there was more prestige and better pay—although they were routinely paid less than men holding the same jobs. Their very scarcity made them noticeable. At the *Star-Bulletin*, Gwenfread Allen and Louise "Loujo" Hollingsworth were highly respected general assignment newswomen. The *Star-Bulletin* in the 1930s hired the first Asian American women on establishment papers: May Day Lo Walden and Ah Jook Ku (Leong) were both graduates of the University of Missouri School of Journalism. On the *Advertiser*, Millie Bennett Mitchel was a police reporter and Elaine Fogg Stroup a general assignment writer.

World War II broadened women's opportunities when the men left to join the military services. Clarice Taylor replaced Charles Fern for the duration as editor of the *Garden Island* on Kaua'i. Gwenfread Allen of the *Star-Bulletin* became official territorial historian for the war years (Allen 1950). The *Advertiser* introduced its first action-line columnist, Ilona Adams, writing under the name of "Miss Fixit." Making a living was essential. But by everyone's account another strong motivating factor was to have interesting and challenging work. "We loved our jobs," states Irva Coll, who moved from the *Advertiser*'s commercial printing department to the city desk at the war's onset and remained there until retiring in 1977 (Coll 1991).

In 1945, Bonnie Wiley was the first wire service female war correspondent in the western Pacific. After high school, Wiley worked on papers and taught herself to take photos for the stories she was assigned. Making several attempts, she finally, in 1945, was attached to the U.S. Navy for the Associated Press. After the war, and in spite of a threat by back-shop pressmen that they'd walk out if she got "temperamental," Wiley became managing editor of the *Yakima* (Wash.) *Herald*. They didn't and she didn't (Wiley 1991). Wiley earned a doctorate and joined the University of Hawai'i journalism faculty when such faculties were dominated by Caucasian males. (She is now retired.)

When the men returned after World War II, and unlike many of their mainland counterparts, women kept their jobs, even when married to colleagues. They continued, however, to be underrepresented as reporters and in news management, not to mention the back shop that is still largely male. When they were represented, they were often trivialized, as in the *Star-Bulletin*'s description of its excellent reporters, Helen Altonn and Harriet Gee, as "little jewels in [the] newsrooms" (Aug. 14, 1962).

By the early 1970s, national statistics showed them composing only 26 percent of the newspaper workforce, decreasing to 10 percent at the upper levels (Hynds 1975). Recognizing that sexual stratification works both ways, *Advertiser* women in 1971 called for the Hawaii Newspaper Guild to look into why there were no women city editors, no female copyboys, and no males in the family or women's sections (*Adv.*, July 30, 1971). This campaign, to increase hiring and advancement of women and eliminate discriminatory practices in pay and assignments, was well ahead of the national Wire Service Guild suit in 1973 and the American Newspaper Guild program from 1974 on (Marzolf 1977).

Women as Subjects

Employment practices undoubtedly impacted upon how women were portrayed. In the 1960s, with the second wave of American feminism, the numbers of women increased in the general work force, as well as on newspapers, and their image changed.

Women had appeared infrequently in newspapers until late in the nineteenth century. The assumption was that men were the main buyers and readers. The rise of department store advertising aimed at women and the recognition that they were out in public in jobs altered this assumption (Hynds 1975). From 1900 on, women regularly appeared in women's sections, to which, however, they were largely confined, with one exception: sports pages included "girl" athletes. Yet there were no full-time women sports writers until the 1960s.

The *Advertiser* Society section, begun in March 1901, by 1903 constituted several pages on Sunday as it did for the *Star-Bulletin* after 1912 on Saturdays. The weekend editions were the most prestigious ones for women to appear in. Island women's sections were similar to those on the mainland except that they portrayed a somewhat different socially and economically dominant group. Added to the Caucasian privileged and well-to-do were upper- and middle-class Hawaiian women: that is, the pages were never entirely limited to white women. The ethnic papers, like the *Hawaii Chinese Journal*, also had society and women's pages.

"Socially prominent" visitors and women connected to military officers received special treatment, too, as in "Society Events in the Services." The *Star-Bulletin*, with the largest interisland circulation, devoted a page to "Society on the Other Islands." Society in the *Hilo Tribune-Herald, Maui News,* and *Garden Island* was even narrower in scope, focusing mostly on the few Caucasian female residents and fewer visitors.

Women's satellite relations to powerful men were at the heart of society news. Engagements and weddings were thus the most lavishly developed features. As eminent sociologist Gaye Tuchman has wryly observed in her book on images of women in the mass media, a Martian reading the traditional women's pages would conclude that every female earthling spent at least several days a month getting married (Tuchman et al. 1978). Photographs heightened the subjects' prestige—the more affluent and socially prominent, the larger the photographs. It was always noted, too, if the bride or groom were descendants of missionaries and if they had attended Punahou School. Of all the schools, the repeated appearance in society news of Punahou, the school begun in 1841 by American Protestant missionaries from New England and representing but a fraction of the total school population, reinforced the status of attendees.

Other topics deemed proper for society sections were club meetings, fashion, beauty tips, food, volunteer work for benefits and bazaars, home and child care, entertainments like luncheons and dances, and "cultural" events such as musical recitals and art shows. A typical Saturday section might feature a three-column photo and caption, "A lovely bride of the week and her attendants," with the story detailing the fashionable dress of the participants, the beautiful floral decorations, and the sumptuous buffet. An "Aloha Luncheon" describes a "charming" matron leaving on the SS *Malolo* for a trip to San Francisco with her "delightful" children. Another story features "Tennis Party Followed by Supper at Dillingham Home" (*Star-Bull.*, Mar. 1, 1930). The Dillinghams, in the parlance of the times, were "a prominent kama'āina family," and all their activities and those of others in this category, no matter how minor, were minutely reported. No one reading the society sections in these years could have perceived that there was a depression.

The society editor who epitomized the role was Edna B. Lawson. Edna B., as she was known, was in charge of the *Advertiser* Society section from 1932 until her retirement in 1952. Born in South Dakota when it was an Indian territory, she was widowed and taught English and drama at the old Honolulu Normal School before joining the morning daily. By all reports, she was tough and determined, but she was known for being "a lady" who wore hats in the newsroom while typing up her stories. During her reign, coverage occasionally was extended to Japanese and Chinese women honorees connected to well-to-do merchants or professional men—but relegated to the fourth or fifth pages of the section.

As to race, class, and gender, the papers followed the national, even international, norm: morning papers were the more prestigious, appealing to business men, government leaders, and the like; afternoon papers have been aimed more at the working classes. Daughters of immigrants thus gained employment earlier on the *Star-Bulletin* and on neighbor island afternoon papers where, for example, Harriet Albao was news editor of the *Garden Island* during World War II.

After World War II, women's sections document and reflect the changes and accompanying tensions as change accelerated; or as *Advertiser* editorial writer Hugh Lytle described it, the "spectacular transformation from a silly society section to broad, comprehensive coverage (H. Lytle 1992)." The shift from "Society" to "Women" did not eliminate stereotyping, however, as in the description of how women in the 1950s have "branched out" in interests: "Over her morning coffee the busy mother can relax with six-day-a-week pages" devoted to such topics as bridge, "The Mature Parent," "Your Horoscope," and "Secrets of Charm" (*Adv.*, July 1, 1956). "Petticoat Politics" headlined an article on women who assisted political party organizations with tasks like mailings (*Star-Bull.*, May 23, 1959).

Drue Lytle, Edna B.'s successor, the staff she hired, and topics she covered illustrate the transition period. Lytle wrote about fashions for men and women and covered shows in New York, Washington, D.C., and Paris. "I worked hard," she said, pointing to the competitive reality behind what appeared to be a glamorous assignment. After attending shows all day and into the evening, she would retire to her hotel room and write up the stories into the early morning hours (D. Lytle 1992). Under Lytle, in the late 1950s, but only after lengthy discussions behind the scenes, Filipino brides finally made it into the "Soc" pages of the *Advertiser*.

Under Lytle, too, the *Advertiser* in 1961 won the prestigious University of Missouri School of Journalism award for the second best women's pages in the country for papers with 25,000 to 100,000 circulation. Her staff included two capable non-Caucasians: Patsy Matsuura, trained on the McKinley High School *Daily Pinion*, and Lynette Chung, a Radford High School graduate (*Adv.*, May 17, 1961). Yet Lytle and the staff who garnered this national honor were conveniently transformed into soft news. Mary Cooke and Nancy Harlocker were tagged as "Punahou graduates." Cleo Evans, who had worked on the Roosevelt High School paper and the *Garden Island*, was described as "a picture of fashion herself," from "her high-heeled pumps to the top of her French twist coiffure ... pressed, polished, groomed and chic!" (*Adv.*, Oct. 4, 1959). To the national honorary fraternity for newswomen, they were "the ladies of the press," and Lytle was "Sweet Drue" with a "sweet smile" (*Alpha Theta*, winter 1962–1963).

Changes escalated. Lois Taylor has described the mid to late 1960s as "an enormous watershed" that raised questions as to "what was superficial and what wasn't" (Taylor 1992). Beverly Creamer observes that journalism majors carried the rising consciousness and activism of these years from campuses to the newspaper workplace (Creamer 1993). A generation separates Taylor and Creamer, but both their careers demonstrate the times.

Lois Taylor made her mark by subtly extending her scope from weddings and parties to issues of government, education, and social welfare. She recalls that being on the *Daily Californian*, the Berkeley student paper, during World War II when the men were gone, gave her a clear sense of what she could accomplish. The *Star-Bulletin* introduced its "new Society columnist" as "the wife of Stanley Taylor, prominent Honolulu businessman. . . . She and her husband lead a gay social life in addition to bringing up their four children. . . . Her bright style of writing is familiar to readers of the Junior League magazine, the Mynah Bird, of which she has been the editor" (Sept. 3, 1961).

Taylor's "bright style" developed a bite. She attended a formal dinner at Washington Place given by Governor John Burns for members of the State legislature, and her witty description memorialized the event that featured a red carpet that "stretched the length of the lanai to the two bars set up on the lawn." To critics who accused her of going "uninvited" and of flippancy and disrespect, Taylor pointed out that the press was entitled to cover a government function (*Star-Bull.*, Mar. 18, 23, 1963). She admitted to occasionally tweaking the powerful but never made fun of those who couldn't fight back.

Taylor recalls a rich irony. She discovered that the most devoted readers of her "About People" column, in which she mentioned those taking trips and the guest lists for upcoming parties, were burglars. This was before burglar alarms were a household appliance. Understandably, people no longer wanted their absences from home

288288288288 *The Turbulent 1960s*

mentioned. Taylor turned to such topics as day care, children having children, rape, alcoholism, hunger, and human rights. The 1970 census verified readers' changing interests: 41 percent of the state's civilian labor force was female, and two-income families were widespread. In 1971, Lois Taylor was appointed to the first State Commission on the Status of Women. Later, as a widow, she felt "working saved my life." She is proud of retiring in 1992 at the "top of the union scale" (Taylor 1992).

Beverly Creamer arrived at the University of Hawai'i campus in 1965 from Canada. Her mother had worked for the *Winnipeg Free Press* before taking up homemaking and raising children, and Creamer observed her parent's deferred desires for a larger sphere of action. A journalism major during the activist 1960s, Creamer was provided with the kinds of subjects she would develop as a professional journalist into the 1990s: changing family structures, changing lives, and coping. She considers her profession to be her contribution to society—with a small *s*. She recalls that when she joined the *Star-Bulletin* as a cub reporter and was assigned to the legislative bureau, it was difficult to gain access to newsmakers. Men called her "dear" and took her less seriously than male reporters who were "automatically given their legitimacy" (Creamer 1993).

Women seized the opportunity to write about genuinely interesting subjects. Mary Cooke's long piece in the Family section, "The Suzukis of Kahuku," described the closing of Kahuku Plantation and what that meant to one family: the immigrant parents, their sons, and the younger Suzuki women whose lives and livelihoods were subsumed in the North Shore community. Photos showed the Suzukis in work clothes, standing by their pickup truck at *pau hana* time (work is done) (*Adv.*, Mar. 22, 1970). In the *Hawaii Tribune-Herald*, women's page editor Maxine H. Hughes reported on such topics as nursing homes and the aging.

Many were happy to witness a new day for women and family pages. Others longed for the old Society. Among the former is Peggy Bendet. Named editor of the afternoon paper's women's page in May 1969, Bendet bid "Goodby Society (Pages)" with relief. They were "an ego trip" and "an escape" for the wealthy and the middle class who could believe that "the only crises were social gaffs and the only problems were servants." She was glad to get rid of having to determine length of coverage—society editors lived in fear that some woman assigned little space "might turn out to be more important than she seemed" (*Haw. Journ. Rev.*, Apr. 1971). Bendet herself embodied the changing times. She left journalism to study Eastern religion and meditation. But she is credited, as is her successor Barbara Morgan, with being especially helpful in the training of younger women journalists.

To Barbara Morgan goes credit for helping to carry the fight for equality to the governor's office. In 1973, only 15 percent of the total number of 700 seats on State boards and commissions were filled by women. Morgan asked David Paco, assistant to Governor Burns, why no applications by women were being processed and why there weren't any women's names on the lists to fill vacancies. Her open letter to "Dear Gov. Burns" directly quoted Paco's answers: " 'We Can't Have a Bunch of Women's Libbers on State Commissions.' " The *Star-Bulletin* reprinted a copy of the official application form and invited "Ladies" to apply (Oct. 4, 1973). Applications poured in, processing sped up, and the number of women appointed doubled within two years.

Among those who mourned the passing of society sections was Samuel Crowningburg Amalu, who claimed royal descent. His lament may seem frivolous—"My god, how I do miss the late Edna B. Lawson" who could "recognize quality when she saw it." But he also identified a substantive alteration. Gone was the glamour; here was "dealing with a vaginal cyst and what to do about it"—a reference to Pat Hunter, who shifted from *Advertiser* "homemaking editor" to medical reporter. To Amalu, "These pages are as dull and grim as our lives" (*Adv.*, Sept. 12, 1972).

War and Women Journalists

The Vietnam War was a tragedy for the men and women who served in it. But for women correspondents, it was another watershed. For the first time in history, the U.S. Defense Department allowed them to participate in covering combat on an equal footing with men (Edwards 1988). If men gained power through the military and war, then many women were no longer willing to be left out.

Hawai'i's Denby Fawcett was among ten women correspondents in Vietnam. Her story graphically shows changing roles and images. Fawcett as a young girl felt lucky to earn her own money—fifty cents a column inch for a teenage column she wrote for the *Star-Bulletin* while at Punahou. A Columbia University graduate, she made the most out of her consignment to women's subjects, such as the Military Debutantes' Ball. She states that this made her think about the military, and finding society assignments "boring," she asked to be sent to Vietnam. The *Star-Bulletin* refused her, but she got a "yes" answer from *Advertiser* managing editor Buck Buchwach (Fawcett 1992).

First she was employed on a freelance basis, but her outstanding dispatches from Saigon quickly earned her regular status. She was part of the only newswoman-newsman Vietnam staff combination—the newsman was Bob Jones. United Press International photographed her in a jeep in combat fatigues with a camera around her neck. In spite of that, to the *Advertiser* she was "our girl, Denby," and "certainly the prettiest correspondent in Viet Nam" (Sept. 12, 1966).

Jones went north, but Fawcett remained in Saigon. Women correspondents could not go into the field overnight. They protested, struck a deal with the U.S. Military Assistance Command by agreeing to police themselves, and Fawcett joined the Twenty-fifth Tropic Lightning Division from Schofield Barracks in the north. She recalls that it was "hard for women, we were treated as kids." But she identified with the young soldiers and ignored personal danger (Fawcett 1992). And there was danger: forty-five correspondents were killed in Vietnam.

Like her male colleagues, Fawcett initially believed in the Vietnam War. A study by Mark Hertzgaard in shifts in public opinion posits that there is a sphere of opinion like a doughnut. At the center or hole there is consensus on such issues as motherhood, apple pie, and the need for a strong national defense. In the middle lies an area of legitimate controversy, like the two-party political system. In the outermost region are those views rejected by mainstream society and journalists, like getting out of Vietnam (Hertzgaard 1988). Journalists and public opinion shifted almost simultaneously and pulled that outer area toward the center. Consensus may not have been achieved, but what had been unthinkable became acceptable.

One can trace the evolution of opinion in Fawcett's eighteen-month stint. Her early dispatches were largely descriptive:

> Da Nang, Viet Nam—
> Bits of jagged glass and hundreds of rusty nails scream through the air as someone trips a land mine.
>   Fragments strike with a force that bites, stings, shocks and in many cases results in either death or an injury that may require amputation of a limb. (*Adv.*, Sept. 12, 1966)

She earned placement on the first page of Section B, the best spot after the front page to draw readers. The army awarded Fawcett a citation for "outstanding coverage of the American soldier as an individual in combat" (Dec. 31, 1966), but she began to think, "It wasn't a good war." She chronicled the easy availability of marijuana, accompanied by photos of neatly packaged cigarettes—"Marijuana is about as easy to buy as candy in Vietnam" (Oct. 5, 1967)—and the sordid life of bar girls. Her "farewell look" took up the entire op-ed page:

> Vietnam: Confusions
> And Self-Deceptions
> Destruction of a Society
> As I leave after the long months, I see the slow destruction of the Vietnamese rural society.
>
> When villages can't be won to the side of the Saigon government, they will be burned and their inhabitants moved to hot, dusty resettlement camps. . . . More luxuries will be available for the rich Saigonese who can afford to keep their sons out of the Army, while more anguish awaits the peasants who can barely afford rice and who are caught between the brutal vise of the Americans and the Communists.
>
> More valiant Americans will die with fewer of them believing in what they're dying for. (*Sun. Bull. & Adv.*, Dec. 17, 1967).

The *Advertiser*, the most establishment of papers, moved from total support to skepticism: "The war that Denby Fawcett depicts . . . is quite different from the war that the President and his Secretary of State talk about" (Dec. 22, 1967).

Fawcett's professional career broke with the past, but, again like so many of her contemporaries, she chose a traditional personal life—with alterations. When Hugh and Drue Lytle married, their wedding appeared in the Society section: "Tall candles burned at the altar and graceful white gladioli adorned the rails. . . . Mrs. Lytle was becomingly gowned in an aqua linen suit with hat to match" (*Adv.*, Apr. 19, 1947). When Fawcett and Jones wed, a photo and write-up in the news section stated, "Robert O. 'Bob' Jones and his bride, the former Denby Fawcett. . . . both won praises and awards for their coverage of the war in Vietnam for the paper" (*Adv.*, Mar. 21, 1970). Fawcett and Jones helped to sponsor the *Hawaii Journalism Review*.

The New Topic—Abortion

No topic so much reveals the changes in opinion as that of abortion, described by researchers Patricia Steinhoff and Milton Diamond as a

remarkable transformation of public opinion, whereby the community became aroused, informed, and mobilized about an issue which
had been obscure" (Steinhoff and Diamond 1977). The abortion topic
was not just obscure, but taboo, except in euphemisms, as in nineteenth-century advertisements for "female monthly regulating
pills" or when reported as a crime. Even then, coverage was buried
in inside pages, and victims' names were withheld: "Mother of 3
Dies After Abortion Try" (*Adv.*, Mar. 28, 1955). The watershed years
were from 1969 to 1971. The Honolulu dailies were in the vanguard
of the U.S. movement.

In the early 1960s, male reporters began to attack the taboo. This
may seem odd because abortion is often seen as a "woman's" issue.
Men, however, have had more opportunities to legitimize subjects.
Spence Brady reported that the Honolulu Police Department had
recorded five arrests for abortions the previous year. Another male
reporter found abortion "a growing Honolulu problem" that leads
"to the hospital and, not infrequently, to the morgue" (*Sun. Bull. &
Adv.*, Sept. 16, 1962, Apr. 14, 1963). Heavily reported medical factors
contributed to the new openness, such as a rubella epidemic and the
thalidomide tragedy. Medical doctors in favor of abortion law reform
were given ample newspaper space.

From the mid-1960s on, the subject moved to the women's pages
where it was frankly discussed, now mostly by women. Critics have
charged that this move indicated a trivializing of the subject. A later
study, however, by the national Bureau of Advertising, found that
the topic had a general appeal, with 90 percent of women and 80 percent of men readers reading the women and family pages (*Ed. &
Pub.*, Apr. 21, 1973).

There was an upsurge of articles: from 1968 to 1969, there were
190 items in the Honolulu dailies; in 1970, approximately 400. The
Star-Bulletin Family Today section ran specials, as on the practice of
Honolulu travel agencies conducting a regular business in women
passengers seeking legal abortions in Japan. The topic was aimed at
high-school students, too, in the Young Ideas section: "Abortion: An
Old Issue Seen Through New Eyes" (*Star-Bull.*, June 20, Oct. 6, 1969).

There was also an upsurge of polls and editorials. The *Star-Bulletin* ran a front-page questionnaire, "Speak Up," urging readers to fill
out and return the form to the newspaper office. Although not a controlled sampling, the poll showed a 20 to 1 pro-choice support for
"Abortion Repeal" (Oct. 25, Nov. 7, 1969). A *Star-Bulletin* editorial
stated, "The consciences of the woman and a trained physician

should prevail. Morality cannot be legislated." A supporting cartoon showed a parade of maimed women and "unwanted" children following a coffin labeled "Blackmarket Butchery" (Oct. 22, 1969).

A particularly frank series in the Family Today section by reporter Judy McKnight protected her subjects' identities but emphasized that their experiences with illegal abortions "are real," as one about a hastily performed "operation" for $300 on a newspaper-covered table—the last detail the touch of a novelist. Another was on "Sandy Downes," eighteen and alone, who was "lucky to be alive" because the abortionist was a "butcher," but "Sandy" will never be able to bear children (*Star-Bull.*, Nov. 12, 29, 1969).

In 1970, during legislative hearings, coverage moved to the front pages as a political issue. Polls were prominently displayed: "Survey Indicates Abortion Repeal Favored by 55% of Voters"; "HMA poll of MDs lists 90% for repeal." The *Star-Bulletin* asked for passage of "a Humane Law" (*Star-Bull.*, Feb. 13, 19, 25, 1970).

Such obvious advocacy drew a heated reaction. Honolulu Mayor Frank Fasi charged that the papers did not fairly represent the opposition. The Catholic Church protested in the pages of the *Hawaii Catholic Herald* (1936–). Published by the diocese, the weekly was distributed free to all parishes and had a considerable readership, an estimated 25,000 to 30,000. From 1969 to 1970, the bishop of Honolulu John J. Scanlon, the publisher, and Monsignor Francis A. Marzen, the editor, launched a major campaign against "the secular press" for its support of "this unspeakable crime" (Oct. 31, 1969). A boxed front-page story, for example, "told" by a fetus, stated, "Mother Let Me Live." Supporting editorials and advertisements appeared on every page (Feb. 6, 1970).

The Abortion Reform Bill passed on March 10, 1970, without the signature of Governor Burns, a Catholic who had agonized over his decision. (*Roe v. Wade* would be decided by the U.S. Supreme Court on January 22, 1973.) It might seem that critics claiming bias by the Honolulu dailies had a point. A review, however, shows that these papers assigned prominent space to *Catholic Herald* positions and carried many letters to the editor, such as "Shadow of a Doubt" and "Equal Time," as well as op-ed pieces, including an extensive one by former congress woman and ambassador Claire Booth Luce, "Dissent—Decries Abortion Bill" (*Star-Bull.*, Feb. 12, 1970; *Adv.*, Mar. 4, 1970). As to Mayor Fasi's charge, the papers, as was their wont when attacked by the mayor, felt obligated to give him space: "Fasi Blasts Newspaper Coverage of Abortion Law Controversy" (*Star-Bull.*, Feb.

20, 1970). Beverly Creamer, who reported the legislative hearings and was pro-choice, remembers that while it was difficult to keep one's reportorial balance because it was "a very emotional time," she made an extra effort to present a balanced account, as in writing up the pro and con testimony presented at the hearings (Creamer 1993; Star-Bull., Feb. 4, 10, 1970).

In summary, women have not yet entirely succeeded in their drive to move "from the women's pages to the front pages" (Mills 1988). They continue to appear in far greater numbers as both producers and as images in the feature sections, like Living and Food, than they do in the news. There are studies, too, that document that of the photographs run of women and men, women's bodies appear much more frequently, while men's faces are usually shown.

Still, change continues. On the *Advertiser* in the 1970s, Ann Harpham was assigned to the business pages, a major breakthrough, and rose to managing editor, a powerful position that impacts upon budget, hiring, content, and production. Susan Yim, heading up the Living section in 1986, found it "a dream assignment" for the autonomy she had and the creativity she could bring to its pages (Yim 1993). In the 1990s, the number of women in the local newspaper workforce is about 40 percent, decreasing to 15 to 20 percent at the upper levels. Pay equity for them seems to have been achieved.

PART VIII

From Satellite City Halls to a Satellite Universe— 1970–1976

39. Memories of Maui

The newspaper is the memory of the community.
Gail Bartholomew, *Maui News* indexer

Until the 1960s, the *Maui News* (1900–) was either the only general circulation newspaper on that island or completely overshadowed smaller ones like the Japanese-English *Maui Record* (1916–1941) and the *Valley Isle Chronicle* (1922–1950). Before regular air service, the Honolulu dailies arrived by boat only twice weekly. As a single continuous entity, the *Maui News* is second in age only to the *Honolulu Advertiser*. Today, it has an islandwide circulation of about 17,000 weekdays and 10,175 Sundays, and a Friday edition is mailed to mainland subscribers.

Up into the 1960s, Maui was overwhelmingly agricultural, sugar and pineapple dominating a vast countryside only sparsely settled by small towns. More than any other island, except for privately owned Ni'ihau, Maui was economically and socially ruled by a handful of haole families led by the Baldwins who were descended from missionaries. Beginning in the 1960s, the arrival of new residents, predominantly young Caucasians from the mainland who were tagged as "hippies, "surf bums," and worse, meant that by 1970 Caucasians composed 27 percent of a population of 38,691; by the 1980s, 33 percent of 63,823 (*State of Hawaii Data Book* 1970, 1980). Those of Japanese ancestry made up another one-third, and Filipinos, Hawaiians, and Portuguese another third.

Accompanying in-migration was a rise in construction, tourism, the retail business market, congestion, and a drug culture. Each year from 1970 on broke the previous year's construction record. All of Maui County in 1960 contained only 247 hotel units. In 1970, there were 2,643, and visitors reached a half-million (*State of Hawaii Data Book* 1970). Maui epitomized the state's shift from an agricultural to a service economy.

In the 1970s, a number of newspapers burst into life to capture new readers and a share of the advertising market. In this turbulent decade, Maui underwent the most dramatic and rapid changes since Lahaina's whaling days. Perhaps a dozen papers were published out of more than 100 throughout the state. The most notable were two

297

counterculture or alternative papers: the first, the *Sun*, as the *Lahaina Sun* (1970–1973) and its successor the *Maui Sun* (1973–1981) came to be collectively called; the second, the *Valley Isle* (1977–1978).

The *Sun*, alive for eleven years, may best reflect contemporary Maui. The *Valley Isle*, the shortest lived—just eighteen months—had the most startling impact. Repercussions from the edition that asked, "Does Hawaii Have a Godfather?" still reverberate through the Islands. But together, the venerable *Maui News*, the lively, young, upstart *Sun*, and the brave, rash *Valley Isle* presented a range of opinion not previously offered. They are textbook cases of periodicals making history even as they react to it.

The *Maui News*

The *Maui News*, anticipating growth and prosperity, began the year of formal U.S. annexation. George B. Robertson, its first proprietor and editor, who was assisted by Mrs. Robertson as business manager, prophesied that the paper's reception "indicates that it is destined, if worthy, to live a long and useful life" (*Maui News*, Feb. 17, 1900).

The paper's personality was immediately evident. A booster with conventional values, this was the hometown weekly or semiweekly that carried essential information, such as the Kahului Railroad timetable, passenger and shipping times of interisland steamers, and sugar production figures. It would breathlessly announce what was always of interest: a snowfall on Haleakalā. It proclaimed its political affiliation on the masthead, "A Republican Newspaper."

In 1924, J. Walter Cameron married missionary descendant Frances Baldwin and began a Cameron family dynasty that was to last through the century. With a background in journalism and advertising in Massachusetts, Cameron had arrived in the Islands in 1923, worked for the *Advertiser*, then moved to Maui. In the 1930s, Cameron joined the board of directors of Maui Publishing Company, owner of the *Maui News*. He became president in 1939 and took over as the paper's publisher in 1965. By this time he had financial holdings and directorships in sugar, pineapple, ranching, banking, utilities, hotels, and airlines. Demonstrating the economic and demographic shifts underway, J. Walter and son Colin in the 1970s diversified into resort development.

In the meantime, changes were affecting the *Maui News*. Nora I. Cooper, a Canadian married to Howard Cooper, a Hāna native, moved to Maui. In 1954, she joined a Cameron radio enterprise where she wrote advertising and editorials. Cooper became an assistant to *Maui News* editor Richard E. Mawson, and upon Mawson's death in 1969 assumed the behind-the-scenes position of managing editor although William O. Paine was the titular head. In 1970, the paper increased printing to three days weekly and upgraded its press equipment to offset. Walter Cameron, near death at the age of eighty, officially put the paper into the hands of Cooper. He died on January 2, 1976, and her name appeared on the masthead on January 7. Since then, the publishers have also been Camerons: Colin Cameron (now deceased), Mary C. "Maizie" Sanford, and Richard Cameron.

Supported wholeheartedly by the Cameron family, and like them, dedicated both to the establishment community and to the newspaper, Cooper brought the paper into the late twentieth century. The *Maui News* moved from old wooden buildings in downtown Wailuku to Quonset huts at the town's edge, then into a handsome modern plant on the same property ("The New Maui News," *Hawaii Business,* May 1982). In its November 1983 issue, *Hawaii Business* named Cooper among the twenty most influential people on Maui. Others placed her in the top three.

To Cooper, the "bottom line" was that the bills must be paid. With a reputation for political conservatism, she nonetheless set an industry-wide standard, according to Hawai'i Newspaper Guild leader Roy Kruse, of top worker benefits. Her paper was never struck (Kruse 1992). She was ably assisted for many years by Earl I. Tanaka, who joined the paper in 1939 after high school and rose to news editor. He was noted for an excellent memory, accuracy, and dedication. Cooper is respected throughout the community and industry, even by those who have disagreed with her strong views. (She retired as editor emeritus in 1992 and still writes editorials. David Hoff succeeded her as editor.)

Cooper has expressed what mainstream editors know so well, that one can't be ahead of the community: "the people won't advertise in or buy the product." Nor can one lag behind, because "you won't be where they are" (Cooper 1992). Reporter Tom Stevens has said of Cooper that she has had as good a sense as anyone of the "daily pulse of Maui life" (*Maui News* special insert, January 1988). The masthead tag, "A Republican Paper," is long gone (since April 8, 1950), and the *Maui News* is one of the few Hawai'i papers that does not endorse political candidates. There are enough "divisive issues," Cooper has stated, "without adding to them."

The late 1960s and early 1970s were certainly filled with divisive issues. New arrivals flooded in, mainly the young who rejected the dress, personal habits, and living arrangements of conventional soci-

The *Maui News* since 1900 has wielded enormous influence upon Maui business and social life. Managing editor Nora Cooper, described as "a conservative with a liberal staff," successfully led the paper from 1976 until her retirement in 1992. *(Maui News)*

ety. In her distinctive style, Cooper castigated the rising counter-culture and editorialized for "Middle Class Morality": "Repeatedly, in recent months, we have been coming across the phrase, 'middle class morality.' Each time we see it in print it is like a wet mop in the face. The hippies head for a Haight-Ashbury in San Francisco to rid themselves of it; movie reviewers find enlightenment in movies which portray persons trying to escape it." Stating that three out of four Americans still come from the middle class, the editor laid out the code to be followed: "Work a full day for a day's wage, save for a rainy day, fear God, defend the Flag, help the sick and the poor, preserve the family. . . . Middle class morality isn't a sickness of our society; it is the spine of it" (Feb. 5, 1969).

Doing its part for middle-class morality and Maui's economy during escalating protests against the Vietnam War and the draft, the *Maui News* ran photos and stories of earnest Scout troops, smiling golfers, Hilton Hotel executives and guests, Rotarians, pretty brides in white satin, and scrubbed and handsome families. The paper welcomed mainstream visitors with an insert, "Holiday Maui," which was also distributed in every hotel room on the island. It was filled with advertisements for car rentals and real estate aimed at the investment-minded *malihini* (newcomer). Editorials urged readers to "Buy on Maui" and warned against "Overdoing the Gloom and Doom": "So clamourous have grown the complaints of America's detractors . . . that many of us have begun to doubt our essential decency and competence and to wonder if our system is near collapse from moral decay and economic decadence. . . . America . . . remains one of the most favored of all the world's nations. . . . Let's not allow ourselves to be brainwashed into agreeing with the virulent few who profess to believe otherwise" (Nov. 21, 1970).

Early in 1971, the *Maui News* departed from its practice of not running "canned" material, or reprints from other sources, and filled a page with a *Wall Street Journal* article on the "hippie problem." Maui was the destination, according to the New York journal, of "hairy young dropouts who live off welfare," "shun haircuts," and try to "beat the system" by not working (repr., *Maui News*, Jan. 9, 1971). This article coincided with a brochure put out by the Maui County Police Department and the office of Mayor Elmer Cravalho warning Maui's newest citizens against trying to sell products without a license, hitchhiking, or camping without a permit: "Aloha. In Hawaiian, aloha means hello, but it also means goodbye. The type of aloha you get on Maui depends on how you conduct yourself and how you obey our laws" (repr., *Sun*, Dec. 23, 1970).

Here Comes "The *Sun*"

Even as the *Maui News* was defending traditional culture, a counterculture paper challenged it. The *Sun*, rising in 1970, had a staff of mostly newcomers who were themselves part of the counterculture. They believed that the old order was crumbling and a fresh, alternative "lifestyle"—that overworked phrase was itself then fresh and new—was in the making.

The *Sun* was part of the Aquarian or new age media (Armstrong 1981; R. Goldstein 1989). Like underground papers, new age papers contained stories on music, art, drugs, sex, and the environment, and aimed at raising people's consciousness about themselves and society. They were marked by hip language and eye-catching graphics. They tended to appear in small cities, were locally oriented, and, unlike their underground counterparts, accepted commercialism.

While sometimes satirizing capitalism and materialism, these alternative papers survived by turning to "over-the-counter culture," or "hip capitalism" (Krieger 1979; Peck 1985)—that is, building circulation upon advertising by retail merchants. As counterculture papers edged toward the mainstream, mainstream papers moved closer to them by absorbing their subject matter, style, and even staff members. Alternative journals proved to be a bridge to the establishment.

Some journalism patterns repeat themselves, like the roving printer editor who in the nineteenth century washed up on island shores. After various stints at newspapering and public relations, thirty-year-old Don Graydon built a trimaran in California and set sail around the world. He named the boat *Yellow Submarine* for the Ringo Starr song he listened to while building it. Don and Sharmen Graydon got as far as Moloka'i where Sharmen landed a teaching job at Moanaloa and Don single-handedly put out a semimonthly, the *Molokai Reporter* (1969–1970). He was also a "stringer," or part-time writer, for the *Advertiser.*

Opportunity beckoned from across the channel where Sharmen could teach and Don could widen his sphere of influence. In Graydon's view, no paper presented competition to the *Maui News* that "was inadequate to the community" (Graydon 1992). Dubbing his new enterprise the Yellow Submarine Press and the publication the *Lahaina Sun,* Graydon opened for business on November 11, 1970.

The *Sun's* logo was a bright yellow sun to the left of the title. Although at times it called itself a newsmagazine—it did not have to report the breaking news—the *Sun* functioned as a topical newspaper. Its hallmark was serious journalism interacting with clever features and handsome photography. Early issues of the tabloid covered such topics as the Kā'anapali hotel strike, which affected jobs, and also featured a front-page photo of a surfer in the curl of a beautiful wave and the caption, "Surf's Up" (Nov. 11, Dec. 2, 1970). The seventh issue carried the full text of Mayor Cravalho's and the Police Department's "Hippie Brochure," as the *Sun* labeled it. Another issue printed a "Hello-Goodby Game," ostensibly a board game played on a map of Maui island. The game could be "turned into a real trip." Players drew cards for Hitchhiking, Get Out of Jail in Lahaina, and Selling Without a Permit (Feb. 24, 1971). Graydon moved the enterprise to Wailuku, renaming it the *Maui Sun* to indicate its islandwide coverage. The *Sun* had its own tradition, an "April Fool" edition with an upside down logo, in which it spoofed the public, as in one that featured a superimposed monorail on concrete pilings gliding past and dwarfing Maui's beloved scenic 'Iao Needle (Apr. 6–12, 1977).

The *Sun* and the *Maui News* reported many of the same events, but their approaches were quite different. While the *Maui News* tended to quote official sources, like the mayor's office, Graydon interviewed newcomers at Kahului airport and "Gays on Maui" (July 20–26, 1977). Both discussed land and water use, but the *Sun* additionally reported annually on the numbers of condominium units and hotel rooms being built and printed maps that detailed escalating development.

The *Sun*'s answer to "Holiday Maui" was the "Maui Goodtimes Guide." The guide eschewed puffery and aimed at younger "with it" readers by featuring offbeat film and TV reviews by Bob Green, a comparison shopping column, and a restaurant guide. This last, "The Phantom Diner," praised or condemned eating places and listed health and sanitation violations by official inspectors, which caused a great deal of comment.

Maui News circulation held steady at 10,000, but new readers enabled the *Sun* to reach 4,500 to 5,000. The *Sun* maintained an editorial to advertising ratio of 50 percent and charged the same rates as the *Maui News*. Patrons included shops like the Leather Loft and the Lahaina Beer Garden and up-and-coming young realtors like Mike McCormack and Hugh Menefee. The *Maui News*, however, was the more profitable with a ratio of 35 percent editorial to 65 percent advertising that came from the larger businesses like hotels, automobile agencies, and supermarkets.

If the *Maui News* was a traditional family operation, employing over a hundred people, the *Sun* was that of the recreated or alternative family, with about fifteen including part-timers. Several were literally related, like Sharmen Graydon and her sister-in-law, Luann

Graydon; others called themselves "a family" who, in Don Graydon's words, went "80 percent on spirit and did not count up sixty-to eighty-hour weeks" (Graydon 1992).

A number had journalism backgrounds. Jill Engledow, for example, was "third generation in newspapers"—her father and grandfather were newspapermen. From California, in her early "hippie days" on Maui, as she called them, Engledow mopped floors and did odd jobs. When the *Sun* began, she thought, "I know how to write," and submitted a story on lush, ripe, delicious homegrown tomatoes. Engledow became a full-time reporter (Engledow 1992). Cynthia Conrad, a graduate in fine arts from the University of California at Berkeley, designed many of the *Sun*'s graphics. Others learned the trade through Graydon—"a great teacher," "patient, careful, and very positive" (Conrad 1992). Sandy Zalburg, *Advertiser* city editor, described the *Sun* as "one of the brightest, most imaginative newspapers in the state" (*Adv.,* Feb. 18, 1972).

The *Sun* developed a devoted readership. But it had its critics and problems. A local group told reporter Jeanette Foster that the *Sun* was too haole and did not cover what was important to local people (Apr. 3–9, 1977). Still others said that it was "too effete, too epicurian, too in-groupy" (Conrad 1992). Nor did the *Sun* thrive in the business sense. Graydon scrupulously gave everyone, including himself, the same wages of $140 to $160 weekly. There were benefits to pay, however, like health, dental, and unemployment insurance. And some advertisers were scared away by the *Sun*'s far-out image. Another problem was libel suits. Although the *Maui News* and other establishment papers are regularly sued, they have greater resources and access to expert legal opinion. Smaller, undercapitalized papers have a harder time surviving (Forer 1987).

Producing the paper under difficult conditions took its toll. In 1975, Graydon took time out in Seattle. He received offers to sell and finally did, in 1979, to radio station owner Kirk Monroe who ran the *Sun* more as a bottom-line operation. A strike by disgruntled employees and a drop in advertising revenue hastened its demise ("A Melancholy Maui Sunset," *Hawaii Business,* May 1982).

The *Sun*'s story is not over, attesting to the ability of a newspaper to make history even after its death. Stephanie Austin, former office manager, points out that the *Sun* led in hiring a significant ratio of women—up to 50 percent of its staff (Austin 1992). Too, a number of women and men have gone on to excellent careers with other publications, including Graydon himself who joined the *Seattle Post-Intelligencer* as copy editor.

Looking back, Graydon believes that the *Sun* provided competition that "improved" the *Maui News*. Nora Cooper disagrees with this assessment. Interestingly enough, however, the *Maui News* in these years began to shed what some called its "Maui snooze" image and, in fact, hired a number of those it once looked askance at as "hippies," including Jill Engledow and Tom Stevens.

The *Sun*, too, was a model for other alternative papers, like the *Hilo Rain* (1976) and Steve Omar's *Universe Sun* and *Maui Moon* (1975–1977). Like Graydon, another young Californian found her way to Moloka'i. Linda Crockett published the *Molokai Free Press* (1976–1980) on that island, then moved to Maui. Linda Crockett Lingle became mayor of Maui County in 1990.

The *Valley Isle*

> A journalist is a grumbler, a censurer, a giver of advice, a regent of sovereigns, a tutor of nations. Four hostile newspapers are more to be feared than a thousand bayonets.
> Napoleon Bonaparte

Not four, but one hostile newspaper appeared from 1977 to 1978 to frighten establishment leaders more than a thousand bullets might have. With a life of only thirty-six issues, the *Valley Isle* had an impact that continues to be felt.

In the late nineteenth century, the haole oligarchy used libel suits against Hawaiian nationalist papers to silence them. In the late twentieth century, when the *Valley Isle* asked, "Who is Hawaii's Godfather?" (June 15–28, 1977), an ethnically mixed power structure used libel suits to force the paper out of existence. What became known as the "godfather edition" raised questions about a member of the newer power structure. Larry Mehau, Big Island rancher, was a member of the State Land Board, a political supporter of Governor George Ariyoshi, and head of Hawaii Protective Agency, a security guard firm doing business with the state.

Lawsuits filed on behalf of Mehau by attorney David Schutter, one of the most formidable legal talents in the state, totaled $51 million; subsidiary suits amounted to another $30 million. Had the legal actions only been against the *Valley Isle* people, the story would be shorter. But they were also against the establishment press that, simply by reporting the charges, repeated them: among others, the *Honolulu Star-Bulletin*, the *Hawaii Tribune-Herald*, and several television and radio stations.

The *Valley Isle* was the brainchild of two Maui newcomers, Rick Reed and Mike Durkin from Washington State. They were joined by

The Valley Isle

Maui's Feature Newspaper

June 15–28

Were Helm and Mitchell Murdered?

Who is Hawaii's "Godfather"?

The Pakalolo Raids– A Syndicate Number?

Acupuncture · The Straight Shooter

Special Edition: 40,000 copies

& More

A small counterculture paper with a big impact, the semimonthly *Valley Isle* grabbed statewide attention and reshaped the lives of many people with its "godfather issue" of June 15–28, 1977. (University of Hawai'i Hawaiian and Pacific Collection) several local residents. Durkin, an organic farmer, had worked on the *Sun,* but Reed was without journalism experience. To Reed, Watergate and the Vietnam War "upset my stomach." He took up meditation and moved to Maui in 1977 (Reed 1985). In a long line of newspapermen who have combined adversarial journalism with political ambitions, Reed began a paper as a vehicle for change.

Like Graydon, Reed thought the *Maui News* was a corporate journal still tied to the past. But Reed had a different view toward the *Sun:* "It made me think of Lahaina yacht people and tourists with the news chosen as something to put above the ads catering to hippies, haoles, and the beautiful people." Reed put up $400 from his savings, others about $1,000, and a friend provided a 35-millimeter camera. Volunteers operated out of a workroom in a small house. Each edition of the free semimonthly cost from $300 to $500, so staff had to sell advertisements. Staff included Kathy Hoshijo, a volunteer social worker and a fashion designer who had run for state lieutenant governor in 1976, and Wayne Nishiki, who had attended Maui Community College and was a farmer and small businessman.

No one paid much attention to early editions. These contained well-written interviews with entrepreneurs, like Dewey Kobayashi of Maui Potato Chips, and profiles on Native Hawaiian musicians (May 4–19, 1977; May 18–31, 1977). Reed claims he was not looking for sensationalist material. Hawaiian acquaintances, he said, tipped him off to the "godfather" story (Reed 1992).

The reaction was delayed, then explosive. *Advertiser* editor George Chaplin, who did not print the allegations for ten days, explained in a boxed front-page editorial that it was his paper's "responsibility to be fair" and that "allegations that a man is the No. 1 criminal in a state . . . are of the most serious nature." He cited "the question of possible libel" and his paper's "written code of ethics" requiring that "we reach the individual and give him or her the opportunity to respond simultaneously with the publication of the allegations"—Larry Mehau was reportedly out of town (June 24, 1977). The *Advertiser* was not sued.

The *Valley Isle* doubled its printing, to 20,000 copies, and ran more inflammatory material. In an interview with Frank Fasi, it quoted the Honolulu mayor as saying that Goveror George Ariyoshi knew who the "godfather" was. The paper reported death threats against its staff and moved to an unspecified location. Copy was hand carried to Honolulu for printing ("Hiding Out from the Syndicate," *Sun,* June 29–July 5, 1977).

Frightened, outraged, or both, the conventional press, but principally the *Advertiser*, visited its wrath upon the Maui alternative
paper, blasting it out of the Maui waters. It found the hook upon
which to hang the *Valley Isle*—an alleged connection with a political party called Independents for Godly Government (IGG). The
IGG, a splinter group from the International Society for Krishna
Consciousness, or "Hare Krishna," replaced 1950s "communists"
and 1960s "hippies" as the latest scapegoats in whom all the demons
of society lurked.

Advertiser politics writer Jerry Burris in 1976 reported on the
IGG in his ironic and sensible style. He identified IGG's eccentric
ways but did not view it as sinister: "If you can live on a poverty-
level salary, accept no gifts, commit no crimes and abstain from
intoxication and illicit sex, there may be a political party for you"
(June 30, 1976). After the "godfather edition," the *Advertiser's* tone
bordered on hysteria. Reporter Walter Wright's overwrought three-
part series treated the *Valley Isle* group as a dangerous cabal and
malignant force whose members were "participants in a powerful
but little-known spiritual movement whose devotees win thousands
of votes in politics, handle millions of dollars in business and follow
a black sheep guru chanting the name of Krishna." Wright stated
that Hoshijo and other 1976 IGG candidates—John Moore, Robert
Gleason, and Bill Penaroza—had "hidden" religious names. IGG
money came from "32 big donors: giving and chanting more than 80
percent of the 1976 political campaign." The second article was
headlined, "The Secret Spiritual Base of a New Political Force."
Wright "broke the news" in the third; the *Valley Isle* and the *Kauai
Sun* (1977–1978)—the latter owned by Penaroza—were both connected to the IGG and that "many of the individuals . . . share a common form of worship—chanting the 'Hare Krishna' mantra" (*Adv.*,
Aug. 21–23, 1977).

How powerful was this "new political force"? The "millions of
dollars" amounted to IGG having collected all of $43,090. No IGG
candidates were elected. In a letter to the *Advertiser* editor, Hoshijo
charged that the paper was engaged in a "smear attempt" that
amounted to "political and religious persecution." Even more to the
point, Hoshijo wondered if she was singled out because, like Mayor
Fasi, she opposed the Hawaii Newspaper Preservation Act that
"sanctions a newspaper monopoly" (*Adv.*, Aug. 23, 1977). She posed
the same question asked by Channel 2 newscaster Ray Lovell, is it
"front page news" if Kathy Hoshijo chants Hare Krishna? Why,

Hoshijo asked, had no one mentioned that Lieutenant Governor Nelson Doi and editor Chaplin were both "students of Maharishi Yoga and Transcendental Meditation" or that the daughter of the editorial page editor, John Griffin, was a member of the Hare Krishna group (*Valley Isle*, Aug. 24–Sept. 6, 1976).

The virulent attacks upon it were one indication of the *Valley Isle*'s impact on the establishment. Another was that when the lawsuits entered the legal system, nine out of thirteen circuit court judges refused to hear "the Mehau case" (*Star-Bull.*, Oct. 27, 1978). The *Valley Isle* managed to stay in print irregularly until 1978. Unrepentant to the end, the final edition listed organized crime killings since 1962 (Nov. 1, 1978).

There were continued reverberations. Scott Shirai, one of the TV reporters sued, left the mainstream media. Nishiki, a Democrat eventually elected to the Maui council, has had to run outsider campaigns with little money. Republican Reed was elected to the state senate from the Fifth District and served from 1986 to 1994 but has called the libel suits a "nightmare." Reed believes that the whole business was meant to intimidate not just him but also the establishment media people. He thought initially that the working press would identify with the issue of organized crime and challenge "what has happened in this state." But they have not (Reed 1985). Reed has never backed off of his allegations. When a jury in the early 1990s refused to convict Reed of libel—although not an attorney, he represented himself to save legal fees—the judge, to the surprise of many, overturned the jury's decision and kept the case open.

For Larry Mehau, too, who has returned to private life, the experience has been costly and difficult. Unable to prove absolutely that the reports were false, he has stated that his reputation has been ruined and that the "stigma of the allegation" has hurt his children (*Adv.*, Dec. 12, 1991). It may be, too, that the publicity he has found so disruptive and unwelcome has increased even as his lawsuits claiming invasion of privacy have continued.

40. Corporate Economics and Chain Papers

> The daily newspapers of the United States are being put in chains, newspaper chains.
>
> Lione Ghiglione, *The Buying and Selling of America's Newspapers*

What does it mean for a hometown newspaper to be bought out by a chain, or in today's parlance, a newspaper group? When newspapers no longer have their primary ties to their communities, who records the daily births and deaths and the myriad activities of our lives between those two events? Does this mean that they—and we—stand to lose our collective memory?

The 1970s have been called the period of the "Newspaper Acquisition Binge" (*Business Week*, Feb. 21, 1977). In 98 percent of U.S. cities, a handful of corporations assumed control of the daily news business, the nation's tenth largest industry and fifth largest industrial employer. Hometown papers were rapidly consumed by billion dollar conglomerates headquartered in New York City or Miami, Florida, concentrating financial power in the hands of relatively few people. The usual pattern has been "death in the afternoon" (Benjaminson 1984)—the afternoon dailies fall victim to traffic congestion, which makes it difficult to deliver them to households, and to the television evening news. Nor do the more viable morning papers gain in circulation.

The "chain" newspaper, with its connotations of a series of links or a number of organizations under one ownership or management, is not new to the Islands. One was formed in the nineteenth century by Walter Murray Gibson, who controlled five newspapers. But Gibson's papers were firmly connected to King Kalākaua and the Native Hawaiians. Stewart Fern's Hawaii Press Newspapers group in the 1950s and 1960s was also locally based. Disconnectedness begins in the Islands' newspaper offices in 1963 when, because of tax laws, Fern found it lucrative to sell his company to the Scripps League of Newspapers, headquartered in San Mateo, California.

This buyout began what can be called a chain reaction. In 1964, the Donrey Media Group out of Las Vegas bought out the dominant Hawai'i island newspapers, the *Hilo Tribune-Herald* and the *Kona Tribune-Herald*, now *Hawaii Tribune-Herald* and *West Hawaii Today* (1968–) respectively. In 1965, the *Garden Island* was sold to the Scripps League and Hagadone Newspapers of Coeur d'Alene, Idaho, a partnership that was dissolved in 1977 making the Scripps League the sole owner.

Only passing comment greeted the Fern deal, likely because his papers were weeklies viewed by many as "shoppers." The *Hilo Tribune-Herald*'s sale mainly caused internal disruption. The Star-Bulletin Printing Company had bought the paper back in 1924. Because "it was controlled out of Honolulu," many Hilo residents, according to Lou Pujalet, former general manager, did not view the *Tribune-Herald* "as a Hilo paper." But behind the scenes, publisher William H. "Doc" Hill, felt "torpedoed" (Pujalet 1992). Hill was the Big Island political and business leader with interests in hotels, laundries, retail stores, banking, utilities, and the *Star-Bulletin*. Soon after the sale, Hill was out of the newspaper picture altogether. There was a strike, which Donrey won, and staff on the Hilo paper found that long-distance corporate decisions made for shaky tenures. Pujalet was let go overnight in 1967, and editor Ray Yuen retired abruptly in 1974 after thirty-five years with the journal. Yuen, according to longtime Hilo residents like Leo Lycurgus, had done more to give the paper a local flavor and respect than any editor before or since (Lycurgus 1992). For example, his series on the aged from December 1971 through February 1972, a subject that concerned every family, is credited with improving care and facilities for Hilo's senior citizens.

Nor did Kaua'i react strongly to the buyout of its hometown paper. But there were internal struggles there, too. Upon consummation of the sale to Scripps League, Charlie Fern passed the publishers' mantle on to his son, Mike Fern, who resigned from the paper in 1966.

The event that sent shock waves out into the community was the sale, in 1971, of the *Star-Bulletin* to the Gannett Corporation out of Rochester, New York (later, Washington, D.C.). The *Star-Bulletin*, which had closely identified with citizens' concerns for decades, was Hawai'i's premier daily. A mainland "newspaper broker," Vincent J. Manno, put together the two sales of the *Star-Bulletin*, the first purchase in 1961 by Chinn Ho and associates, and the second in 1971 by Gannett. To be called the "dean of newspaper brokers" (obituary, *Ed. & Pub.*, Jan. 19, 1980), Manno also brokered the sale of the *Hilo Tribune-Herald* to Donrey.

During the 1970s, "three themes" were mandatory in "the ritual speech" hailing the acquisition of a hometown daily by a distant corporation. Media critic Ben Bagdikian, former managing editor of the *Washington Post* and a Pulitzer Prize winner, describes the speech in *The Media Monopoly* (1990): "The new acquisition is a splendid paper that the outside company has no intention of changing; the chain acquired the paper in order to offer its larger resources for even greater service to the community; and the new owner believes, absolutely, completely, and without mental reservation in Local Autonomy." The *Star-Bulletin* proclaimed that the paper "will remain the same locally-directed, community-oriented paper that it has been since Alexander Atherton's father helped to establish it in 1912." Disregarding the situation's inherent contradictions, the *Star-Bulletin* assured the public of both "local autonomy" and closer ties to the mainland that would provide "greater resources" for the paper's benefit (*Star-Bull.*, Aug. 3, 1971). In response to the question of why he had decided on the merger, Atherton said, "Well, the climate for such a merger is so much better right now. And we got to know the Gannett bunch of people over a period of time. They are an excellent clan" (*Adv.*, Aug. 3, 1971).

Earlier, speaking to the International Press Institution in Helsinki, Finland, Chinn Ho had expressed the ideal that newspapers should help humankind. But, he added, in practical terms "change is inevitable" (*Star-Bull.*, June 7, 1971). What were the "inevitable" changes? They illustrate another meaning of chain—to confine and restrict. Former *Star-Bulletin* staff writer Denby Fawcett listed the changes in "What Happens When a Chain Owner Arrives" (*Columbia Journ. Rev.*, Nov.–Dec. 1972). In essence, the *Star-Bulletin* was placed "on a diet." The bulging fat newspaper of one year ago was gone, replaced by a lean new version. The new publisher, claiming cuts were necessary for "economic reasons," canceled a dozen columns and features. Russ and Peg Apple's "Hawaiian Heritage" column was reduced from daily to Saturdays only. The longtime Washington, D.C., bureau was closed, and the final edition was canceled. Gannett eliminated neighbor island bureaus and drastically cut distribution to those islands. Three engravers were laid off, and thirty printers lost regular positions and were put on a "daily basis" without full-time benefits. A cartoon accompanied another Fawcett story and displayed a newsboy hawking a tiny *Star-Bulletin*, "GANNEXTRA! GANNEXTRA! READ LESS ABOUT IT" (*Haw. Journ. Rev.*, May 1972).

Gannett Corporation refers to its papers as "units." It has a profit plan, which it calls a "progress plan." Top editors and executives are

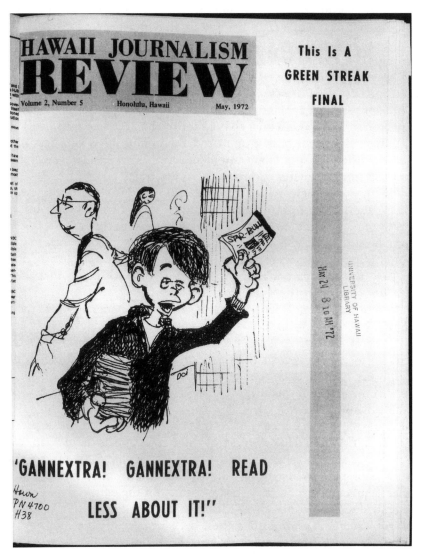

The *Hawaiian Journalism Review,* an alternative voice to establishment papers, cast a cool eye, in May 1972, on the Gannett buyout of the *Star-Bulletin.* The acquisition of a local paper by a chain was not the first in Hawai'i, but it had the most far-reaching effects. (University of Hawai'i Hawaiian and Pacific Collection)

chosen with corporate needs in mind. The local publisher is told exactly how much he or she must produce in profits in each three-month period. Managers who meet the quotas have considerable freedom. If they don't, they may lose their jobs or the chance to be promoted in the national organization. Such juggling is called "executive realignment," as when HNA president Philip T. Gialanella became the *Star-Bulletin* publisher (*Star-Bull.*, Nov. 1, 1975).

Not that local personnel are totally out of the picture. Longtime employees will remain on a chain after the buyout, and new hires at the lower levels usually come from the community. Gannett has also made it a point in Honolulu to place an Asian American woman in a top slot for greater community acceptance.

In 1971, Gannett owned fifty papers. The Honolulu "unit" was "fourth from the bottom" in performance, that is, in making money. Performance considerably improved, to the extent that the *Star-Bulletin* became a "cash cow," with Gannett pumping money out to the corporation. While decreasing in size and circulation (from 124,000 in 1971 to under 90,000 in the early 1990s), the brilliantly managed *Star-Bulletin* sharply gained in profitability.

Some hold benevolent views of corporate ownership. To John Simonds, *Star-Bulletin* senior editor with the longest local tenure for a Gannett executive, Gannett is a "solid corporate citizen" well known for its "generosity" in the form of grants and scholarships and other funding and support. The paper is firmly "middle class," representing and respecting mainstream community interests and traditions (Simonds 1992).

Stuart Ho, who joined the Gannett organization after the death of his father, Chinn Ho—"Stuart Ho Named Chairman of Gannett Pacific" (*Star-Bull.*, June 2, 1987)—has stated that Gannett has "a very strong policy regarding editorial autonomy in its units," and that in practical terms it is good business for the editorial and managerial sides not to cross lines. Too, the paper must appeal to readers to get advertisers. Like his father, he is active in civic affairs. An attorney and former state legislator, he believes, "The newspaper doesn't create its times, it lives in its times" (Ho 1992).

On Kaua'i, former *Garden Island* editor Jean Holmes has insisted that off-island ownership never interfered in any way, even when the paper was battling political and economic forces that were pushing for development (Holmes 1990).

Ben Bagdikian, however, casts a cold eye on the purported goodness, philanthropy, and civic-mindedness of the media giants, whom he calls cold-blooded businessmen with an eye on Wall Street. The chains upgrade the papers with "cosmetic alterations" of page design and makeup and reduce the amount of news by 8 percent below that of independently owned papers (Bagdikian 1990). And according to Tom Brislin, journalist and a professor of journalism, "middle class" orientation boils down to coverage of seawalls at Lanikai in front of the homes of the well-to-do, but no coverage of the bus barn moving from the center of town to Kalihi, which affects the less well-heeled public (Brislin 1992).

Postscript

What has been said of Gannett's relationship to the *Star-Bulletin* may be applied to the surprising development of its 1992 acquisition of the *Advertiser*. Prevented by law under a joint operating agreement from owning both papers in the same town, Gannett found a buyer for the *Star-Bulletin* in Rupert E. Phillips of Destin, Florida. Phillips is an investor and broker who formed Liberty Newspapers Limited Partnership, an Arkansas company, to make the purchase. The back-to-back sales were worth altogether more than $250 million, the lion's share going to the *Advertiser* for the paper and the prime land it sits on adjacent to a developing Kaka'ako district. In the words of Thurston Twigg-Smith, who led the sale, "It's a good deal all the way around" (*Sun. Bull. & Adv.*, Jan. 31, 1993). Gannett in the 1990s had annual net earnings of $2.5 billion, its holdings including the phenomenally successful *USA Today* (1981–). The purchase of the *Advertiser*, the tenth largest among Gannett dailies, gained the chain a solidly solvent "unit."

Information of the buyout of the *Advertiser* broke on the evening television news (Sept. 2, 1992). The follow-up newspaper story explained, "People asking how to pronounce Gannett—whether to put the accent on the first or second syllable (it's the second)—were told simply to pronounce it 'Money' " (*Adv.*, Sept. 3, 1992).

Advertiser staff had been proud of being family owned and had become accustomed to looking down upon the afternoon paper as a lesser vehicle. "All of a sudden, they are us," Jerry Burris states (Burris 1993). Determinedly upbeat about their new owners in public, several *Advertiser* people are privately cynical. A retired reporter believes that "layoffs will come," along with "executive realignments." The blow was somewhat softened for longtime employees who had taken advantage years ago of a stock ownership plan offered by Thurston Twigg-Smith and the Persis Corporation, the corporate owner of the *Advertiser*.

As to *Star-Bulletin* employees, the 1992 sale burst like a bombshell on them, causing consternation and bitterness. "We had been sold on being corporately loyal," explains one longtime employee, "then we were dumped." Employees unsuccessfuly tried to put together a purchase plan. Publicly, their leaders, like editor and publisher John M. Flanagan, express confidence. Privately, by and large, *Star-Bulletin* staff are not optimistic about their future.

There was little fanfare, however, among the jaded public. Mayor Frank Fasi expressed the hope that the *Star-Bulletin* would return to local ownership. Others have called the two transactions a "smoke and mirrors deal" to get around the joint operating agreement and to insure Gannett, which owns HNA, control of both Honolulu papers. Phillips by agreement is not to "sell" the afternoon paper for twenty years, but nothing precludes the *Star-Bulletin* from being shut down. Will there be "death in the afternoon" for the *Star-Bulletin*?

In yet another chain reaction, in 1993 the Donrey Media Group sold controlling interest in its Big Island papers to the Arkansas-based Stephens Group. Donrey, in the meantime, has acquired a limited partnership in Liberty Newspapers, which acquired the *Star-Bulletin* (*Adv.*, Aug. 30, 1993).

At this moment there is only one major paper in Hawai'i, the *Maui News*, that is still home owned. Publisher Mary Cameron Sanford states that from the day her father J. Walter Cameron died, in 1976, to the present, there have been phone calls from brokers asking if the *Maui News* is for sale. She says it is not (Sanford 1992).

Stay tuned—to the television news.

41. Fighting the Newspapers to a Draw: Frank Fasi and the Dailies

Frank F. Fasi's battles with the two major Honolulu dailies are the exception to the old adage, never get into an argument with a newspaper unless you own it. But they also bear out the truth of another adage: even bad publicity can be good. From the front page to the editorial section, from Living or Today to the business pages, the man who has been the longest serving mayor of the City and County of Honolulu—from 1968 to 1994, except for one four-year term (which he lost to Eileen Anderson)—has been the subject of an enormous number of news stories, features, editorials, letters to the editor, columns, cartoons, and photographs. His former wife, the present Mrs. Fasi, his children, and his springer spaniel, "first dog" Gino, have received voluminous coverage. The national press has followed his career. The record shows that he has garnered more column inches in Hawai'i than any other single person from the first newspaper to today. His first name standing alone is enough for people to instantly identify the subject.

Frank Fasi was not the first mayor to be the focus of the mainstream papers' unhappiness. That distinction belongs to the Islands' first mayor. The Republican Honolulu dailies kept James Joseph Fern, a Democrat and a Native Hawaiian, under attack from 1908 until his death in 1920. In fact, the *Advertiser*, falling prey to its own pre-election propaganda, headlined Fern's defeat on election day in 1908 and had to print a retraction the following day (*Adv.*, Nov. 4, 5, 1908).

Skirmishes between Fasi and the dailies began in the 1950s and heated up in the 1960s. Hostilities reached fever pitch in the 1970s, when he was the focus of forty, fifty, even sixty editorials yearly, mostly unfavorable. This took its toll in the short run. In 1974, when he ran against George Ariyoshi for governor, more than 300 items plus 20 cartoons, mostly negative, appeared about Fasi in the two major dailies. By contrast, some 200 entries plus editorials, mostly positive, appeared on his opponent. Fasi lost that race and another to Ariyoshi in 1978.

317

Mayor Fasi, as it turns out, has been part of a national pattern in which powerful political figures claim to be underdogs unfairly treated by the media. Particularly during the Nixon years, government figures and the media engaged in a credibility duel. One outgrowth of the feuding was increased public dissatisfaction with both sides. Although Fasi would continue to win most of his campaigns, public disgust led to the formation of the Honolulu Community–Media Council in 1970 to mediate between the public and the press.

Frank Fasi's background is well known: his immigrant parentage and impoverished childhood in Hartford, Connecticut; his Marine Corps service; his journey in Hawai'i from *malihini* (newcomer) small businessman to the upper ranks of the Democratic party; his elections in 1964 to the Honolulu City Council and in 1968 to mayor (and his later splits with the Democrats to become either an Independent or a Republican).

What is less known is the history of his masterful use of the press to gain and solidify his influence with the public. The papers would periodically attack him for his quarrels with the city council, his use or misuse of campaign funds, his awarding or not awarding of contracts, his language, dress, and demeanor. The dynamic was that he would accuse the press of attacking him when it questioned or criticized him; the press, automatically responding, would repeat the charges; his image as the little guy fighting the power structure would be strengthened.

The battle began in earnest in 1964 when the *Star-Bulletin* obliquely attacked Fasi, one editorial stating, "Frank Fasi, a two-time loser in previous races for Honolulu mayor, said today he is 'very seriously' thinking about getting into the November race" (Jan. 29, 1964). Another negative story reported on a Fasi business enterprise in scrap metal, headlined "Fasi Holds Lease on Land," followed by "A Junkyard Grows in Waimalu" (July 24, 1964). The accompanying photo to this showed junked cars, buses, and vans with the caption reading, "This is the view of Pearl Harbor that tourists now get from Kamehameha Highway across from Waimalu Shopping Center." In this instance, the afternoon daily "overstepped itself," according to Brian Sullam in the *Hawaii Observer* (Sept. 24, 1974), in that it armed Fasi with his favorite weapon—the accusation that the newspapers, principally the *Star-Bulletin,* were unfair to him because they singled out his misdemeanors while ignoring others' same shortcomings.

The mayor's race in 1968 brought the battle between Fasi and the establishment papers to front center stage. The *Star-Bulletin*, throwing its editorial weight behind Fasi's opponent, stated:

> The gloves are off in the mayor's race and it is about time . . . [State Sen. D. G. Andy] Anderson and those who want to see Anderson elected need to come out and swing and swing hard. Fasi has grown too strong under the Marquis of Queensbury rules that seemed to have shielded him from attacks through the Democratic primary until now. Anderson has wisely turned it into the slugging match that it will have to be if the better man—Anderson—is to win. (Oct. 16, 1968)

Fasi slugged back; the *Star-Bulletin*, trying to defend itself, repeated Fasi's accusations and leant them further credibility:

> As re-told by Fasi to a downtown rally: The Honolulu Star-Bulletin has said in effect to my opponent, 'Forget the rules of good conduct. Forget the laws of decency. If you want to get in this race get in the gutter, kick and cheat and lie and do anything possible to win.'
>
> The Honolulu Star-Bulletin, of course, said nothing of the sort. (Oct. 28, 1968)

Fasi won, but his unhappiness with the *Star-Bulletin* deepened, especially with editor A. A. "Bud" Smyser. In June 1969, Fasi accused *Star-Bulletin* reporter Toni Withington of a deliberate attempt to discredit his administration. The offending story stated that an attorney for a developer who proposed a tramway on Koko Head crater was an active campaigner for Fasi. The mayor barred Withington from his office (*Star-Bull.*, June 4, 1969), then expanded the ban to all *Star-Bulletin* reporters. They could no longer attend press conferences nor interview City department heads. The *Star-Bulletin* retaliated with charges of censorship. When he learned the *Star-Bulletin* was filing stories on him with the Associated Press, the mayor extended his boycott to the wire service.

There was an uproar. Protests poured in from the American Civil Liberties Union (ACLU), Hawai'i Newspaper Guild, Hawai'i Newspaper and Printing Trades Council, the *Advertiser*, several radio and television stations, the Republican party, the AFL-CIO of Hawai'i, the ILWU, the American Society of Newspaper Editors, and the Associated Press Managing Editors. After an eleven-month ban, lifted in May 1970, Fasi allowed *Star-Bulletin* reporters back into city hall. There appeared to be a temporary truce: "Newsmen

Hope for Better Relationship with the Mayor" (*Star Bull.*, Dec. 27, 1971).

The battle, however, continued through the 1972 campaign and into 1973, with Fasi dominating the front pages. In November 1973, the mayor banned the afternoon daily's politics reporter, Richard Borreca. The mayor charged that Borreca had boasted, "Every chance I get I'm going to give the Mayor of Honolulu a shafting in my stories" (*Star-Bull.*, Aug. 24, 1973). Borreca strongly denied he'd said this and claimed that for the first month after the election his relations with city hall were okay. This changed when he wrote stories that "the Mayor didn't like," such as: "On Duty Firemen Sold Tickets for Fasi, Did Campaign Chores" (Sept. 16, 1972).

This story, bylined by Borreca and Dave Shapiro, claimed that City employees sold tickets to the mayor's $100 a plate stew and rice dinner. It added, but only at the end, that this had been going on among mayors for years on a "volunteer" basis. After that, Borreca said, "the entire City Hall operation was closed to me" (Aug. 24, 1973).

The Sunday paper added an unfavorable comparison of the mayor to President Richard Nixon: "While Fasi's administration is not in Nixon's kind of trouble and the Mayor has not surrounded himself with the same number of media-haters . . . At least Nixon was willing to go into a no-holds-barred press conference and not restrict attendance to those newsmen he thinks are 'fair'. . . . perhaps, his Nixonish behavior should raise even more concern about his potential for abusing power" (*Sun. Bull. & Adv.* Nov. 4, 1973).

The stakes rose higher in the media-mayor poker game. The *Star-Bulletin* took the mayor to court, and Federal Judge Samuel P. King ruled that the mayor could not exclude the newsman: "King Calls Fasi Edict a Form of Censorship" (*Star-Bull.*, Jan. 22, 1974). Fasi countered by banning reporters from both dailies and announced that he would make all major announcements through the electronic media. To Tuck Newport, publisher of the *Hawaii Observer*, "Mayor Fasi Routs the *Star-Bulletin*": "As the gubernatorial campaign enters 1974, Honolulu Mayor Frank Fasi has once more demonstrated his ability to dominate Hawaii's political terrain" (*Observer*, Feb. 19, 1974).

In 1974, the *Advertiser* brought suit in U.S. District Court. Even the City's attorneys agreed that the mayor's actions to bar reporters violated the First and Fourteenth Amendments of the U.S. Constitution. Federal Judge Martin Pence urged both parties to work out guidelines to cover appropriate relations between officials and the media. The mayor allowed reporters into his office, and the *Star-Bulletin* dropped its suit (*Adv., Star-Bull.,* Jan. 23, 1974). Both sides claimed victory, but the mayor exacted "conditions" under which his news conferences could be covered, and ACLU called the settlement a "compromise" by the papers.

The mayor again raised the ante by having bills introduced into the state legislature that would have put the two dailies under the control of the Public Utilities Commission. Although Fasi claimed that only advertising rates, and not editorial content, would be regulated under the new arrangement, the press again charged censorship. The bills were not enacted.

A number of people close to the action are convinced that there was another, hidden scenario behind this tug-of-war. Rather than indignation over Fasi and fear of censorship, "self-interest" was at the core of the dailies' attacks on the mayor. As a veteran journalist put it, "The papers went after Fasi when he attacked their joint operating agreement."

Fasi and members of the state legislature charged the *Advertiser* and *Star-Bulletin* with "monopolistic" practices, chiefly because of the single advertising structure, a charge Fasi periodically has raised from that day to this. *Advertiser* publisher Thurston Twigg-Smith and *Star-Bulletin* president Chinn Ho issued denials, claiming that mutual production facilities would "permanently assure Honolulu of two locally-owned competitive newspapers with independent voices" (*Star Bull., Adv.,* June 1, 2, 1962.) Other publicity releases repeated the assertion that without the JOA Honolulu would have become a one-newspaper town: "Twigg-Smith Says 'Tiser Faced Ruin," and "Publisher Says Newspaper Plan Saves Honolulu From Monopoly" (*Adv.,* June 13, Sept. 26, 1962).

In 1970, the federal Newspaper Preservation Act provided the formula whereby advertising, sales, production, and distribution would be put into the hands of a third corporation, while competitive editorial and news staffs would remain under separate ownership (Compaine 1982). There was an antitrust exemption that legalized price setting by agencies like the Hawaii Newspaper Agency. The entire Hawai'i congressional delegation in Washington, D.C., plus a host of the Islands' community and business organizations, supported the act.

In 1971, a state Newspaper Preservation Bill, identical in language with the federal law, was steered through the legislature by the Democratic leadership of Senate President David C. McClung

and House Speaker Tadao Beppu. The dailies openly lobbied for the
bill. *Advertiser* editor in chief George Chaplin praised it under the
headline, "State Newspaper Bill Commended" (*Adv.*, Mar. 10, 1971).
Twigg-Smith on page 1 told "our side on the newspaper bill" (*Adv.*,
Apr. 18, 1971). It is the period between the formation of the JOA in
1961 and the enactment of legislation in 1971 and 1972 that has
given Fasi his ammunition—that the dailies operated illegally for
almost a decade.

   A neutral third party assessed the situation somewhat differ-
ently. *Editor & Publisher*, the national journal for the industry,
agreed with Fasi that the dailies operated out of "self-interest" and
had sought out the state bill, not because of "legal need," but to discourage suits by the mayor against them. The journal predicted that
much of the mayor's mayoralty campaign in 1972 would be built on
attacks on the media and that he was expected "to win easily"—
which he did. (July 8, 1972). During the campaign, Honolulu witnessed the spectacle of Fasi and McClung flinging names at each
other, McClung calling the mayor a "Hitler" and a "Napoleon"
(*Star-Bull.*, Sept. 2, 1972) and the mayor hurling back similar insults
and repeating charges against the papers of an illegal monopoly,
price-fixing, and self-enrichment. This raises another point. As *Star-
Bulletin* editor Smyser put it, "Taking on the Mayor is tough work"
(Aug. 19, 1972). But Smyser has also said, "Fasi likes to fight, and
readers enjoy the fights and fusses. He's good copy—a can-do person"
(Smyser 1991). In other words, the ongoing conflict sold papers.

   In the meantime, because of public discontent and of the Islands'
dependence upon the local media for local news, another force arose
that was written up, in fact, by the weighty *Columbia* (University)
Journalism Review ("Honolulu: Trials of a Media Council," May–
June 1973). The Honolulu Community–Media Council was conceived in 1969 by the Reverend Claude F. DuTeil, an Episcopalian
rector, and formally organized on November 16, 1970. The Honolulu
organization was among the first of its kind in American cities (Rivers et al. 1972). Among the influential people promoting the council
were University of Hawai'i's President Harland Cleveland and family court's Judge Gerald R. Corbett. The grassroots council is still
very much alive. Broad based, with volunteer members drawn from
business, public service, journalism, labor, education, the profes-
sions, and everyday citizens, it is led by rotating chairpersons and
anchored by the permanent secretaryship of former journalist and
public relations professional Ah Jook Ku. The council has no official

standing but receives, studies, and mediates complaints against the media by individuals or organizations. In addition, it educates the public on issues dealing with the flow of news and provides a forum for public discussions. It has been charged by both the public and the media of lack of neutrality, as by radio station owner Lawrence Berger, in "The Media Club—uh, Council" (*Haw. Journ. Rev.*, Feb. 1972). This may be a commentary on its quiet effectiveness over the years in settling disputes. After the mayor's unsuccessful 1974 gubernatorial campaign, the council studied what was alleged to be biased coverage of that campaign. While Fasi and others remain convinced that print coverage likely contributed to his defeat in the race, the council decided otherwise: "Panel finds press fair to Fasi" (*Adv.*, June 27, 1975).

An interesting outcome of these years is that, like those in similar situations, the mayor himself has enjoyed and practiced journalism. His collection of *Advertiser* editorial cartoons by Harry Lyons with himself as the subject lined his office walls. Too, he has written articles for the dailies and *Hawaii Hochi.* During the overheated 1970s, the *Star-Bulletin* invited the mayor to write a column with the only stipulations that it had to be in good taste, observe editorial restrictions concerning laws of libel, and not be used to campaign. The mayor accepted—and continued his attack on the *Star-Bulletin* and Bud Smyser.

The mayor also has published official newspapers. The *Honolulu News* (Feb. 1971–Dec. 1971) was a monthly sponsored by "Good Guys for Fasi" and, according to the *Hawaii Journalism Review,* financed by campaign money, called a "birthday fund" by the mayor (Nov. 1971). The *Honolulu News* was edited by Jack Teehan, a professional journalist and political press aide. The mayor hired other savvy practitioners for city hall spots, like Jim Loomis, with a background in broadcast and print journalism and public relations, who was appointed director of the Office of Information and Complaints in 1971 and was periodically a consultant to the mayor.

What is the truth? Did the papers win, as Frank Fasi insists they did? "I have to read them, but I won't subscribe to them at home," the mayor has stated. "They have hurt my children and my wife. They have always tried to make me out to be something I'm not" (Fasi 1992).

Jim Loomis' viewpoint bears consideration. Loomis stated in an interview by the *Valley Isle* on Maui, "You can destroy someone in the media by only telling the truth." His cogent example is the

Kukui Plaza case (1976–1977). Kukui Plaza, a $50 million condominium development on City-owned land, bounded by Nu'uanu Avenue and Beretania Street, was built with private money. A bribery indictment was handed down against Mayor Fasi by the state administration under Governor George Ariyoshi, but a key witness refused to testify, and the case collapsed. Loomis' point is that every time the story appeared, mostly on the front pages, all the rumors and innuendos surrounding the case were carefully repeated. Fasi again lost a gubernatorial race, and the story became the "Kukui Plaza bribery case" forever after in the dailies (*Valley Isle,* Aug. 24–Sept. 6, 1977).

In the 1970s, still another force entered the fray. The alternative journal the *Hawaii Observer* (1973–1977) was among the more well known of the Islands' periodicals and admired for its independence. Created and operated as a biweekly magazine by Tuck Newport, *Hawaii Observer*'s speciality was thoughtful analysis: for example, recaps of each session of the state legislature, and investigative pieces on such topics as land use, Japanese investment in Hawai'i, Waikīkī overbuilding, and the operations of the Bishop Estate. Its circulation reached 10,000.

The young staff, mostly in their twenties, were nevertheless experienced journalists. Tuck Newport had put out an underground paper while at Punahou School, worked for the *Advertiser,* and was a press secretary to politicians Cecil Heftel and Daniel Inouye. "We asked questions that no one else was asking," states former *Observer* writer Brian Sullam, like, "'Who has the power? What makes the place tick?'" Readers who mourn its loss say that the *Observer* influenced opinions because it reached legislators, business leaders, professionals, and the mainstream papers that often picked up stories to follow up on themselves. Newport and Sullam, however, discount any long-term influence (Sullam 1990; Newport 1992).

The *Advertiser*'s Thurston Twigg-Smith and the *Observer*'s Tuck Newport believe that Fasi "manipulated" the dailies (Twigg-Smith 1992; Newport 1992). Stated another way, Norman Isaacs has said in the *Untended Gates: The Mismanaged Press* (1986), "It is clear that the smart politicians have always cast their lines among the press with the skills of master fisherman."

Opposed to this is Fasi's conviction that he has lost. When reminded of his overall success as mayor—his many election victories; his creation of highly successful satellite city halls throughout the island of O'ahu ("1st Satellite City Hall," *Star-Bull.,* Apr. 14,

1973); the public's belief that Honolulu is a very well-run city—he returns to the subject of the Honolulu dailies: "I don't feel like a success." Twigg-Smith has "laughed all the way to the bank. The biggest disappointment of my career is not being able to break their monopoly." He points out that the combined revenues of the papers and HNA have reached $100 million, giving the agency after-expense income (in 1991) of $65 million (Fasi 1992).

The upshot seems to be that Hawai'i's most famous political feud has been fought to a draw.

42. The Public Opinion Poll

The only poll that counts is on election day.
Frank F. Fasi, longtime mayor of Honolulu

Polling is a canvassing of a statistical sample of persons to analyze public opinion on a particular question. Many people view polls as detrimental to political life and are convinced that they influence others; at the same time they disclaim any influence upon themselves. Politicians scoff at them publicly but obsessively commission and consult them in private. Candidates frequently blame a poll for their defeat if they have been shown to be behind in the campaign, but they seldom credit a poll for their victory if they have been shown to be ahead. Regardless of one's opinion of polling, however, polls will continue to be conducted, and the news media will give their results, for they have become a staple of American journalism.

As experts are quick to point out, polls are certainly not all determining. Studies have shown that it is difficult in a democracy to exercise a monopoly in opinion making (Emery and Emery 1992). Professional pollsters and social scientists claim that polls are only "snapshots" of the sum of voting intentions at specified times. But there is no question, according to national expert Irving Crespi, that polls have a significant impact upon the nominating process and upon the ability of aspirants to office to attract financial support (Crespi 1988, 1989). In other words, polls enable front runners to raise money.

Those defending polling include Daniel W. Tuttle Jr., arguably Hawai'i's best pollster, considering that between 1959 and 1981 his findings were wrong exactly twice. As to whether polls have an influence, Tuttle points out that influence works both ways. "Some say, 'If this is the way it's going, I'll stay home.' But others say, 'I'll change that' and go out and vote." Tuttle adds, "I'm a great believer in polls. They are one way of ascertaining what people think, for people to have power. If you want democracy, you're for polls" (Tuttle 1993). *Advertiser* editor and pollster Gerry Keir agrees, pointing out that the public is entitled to the same information as those campaigning (Keir 1992).

Other experts disagree. Nationally, Philip Meyer in *Precision*

Journalism (1973) has warned that because such big money is involved in politics, the possibility of rigging the outcome of polls should not be overlooked. On the home front, Rick Egged, credited with John Burns' come-from-behind victory over Tom Gill in the 1970 gubernatorial race, has had a change of heart and no longer thinks the media should be doing "horse race" polls. "They have too big an impact on the process," Egged states (Egged 1993). John Simonds, *Star-Bulletin* editor, adds that the diversity and isolation of the Hawai'i electorate makes political polling all the more sensitive (Simonds 1993).

Public opinion polling is an endeavor of the social sciences and is relatively new to newspapers. With George Gallup their famous pioneer, polls came into being in the middle of the 1930s. They fell into disrepute after the 1936 presidential campaign between Franklin Delano Roosevelt and Alfred M. Landon, when the *Literary Digest,* in a glaring example of inadequate polling methods, predicted a Landon landslide on the basis of postcards sent in by the public. In Hawai'i prior to 1940, only casual and limited polling took place. Survey organizations increased in number after this (Schmitt 1987). Polling using statistical techniques became integral to political campaigning following Dan Tuttle's polling in 1959, just prior to statehood.

As a youngster, Tuttle was intrigued with polling and began predicting winners. In 1948, while he was teaching political science at the University of Wyoming, polls showed Democratic President Harry S. Truman losing to Republican challenger Thomas E. Dewey. But Tuttle felt Truman would win because Tuttle's students, who were representative of the post-war electorate—in this instance, ex-GIs from coal mining and railroad towns—were ardent Democrats and for Truman "to a man."

With rising confidence in polling methods he was developing, Tuttle arrived at the University of Hawai'i to introduce a course on "Public Opinion and Propaganda." But his reticent local students did not like to canvass door to door. This changed in 1959 with statehood in the offing. The system he put together was based on the results of precinct voting patterns. The basic process involves scheduling for ballots to be delivered to households in ten areas that are a microcosm of the voting patterns from the previous two elections. The results are then statistically balanced. "You can call it 'divine providence' or the 'law of averages,'" Tuttle wryly states, "but this system has worked over and over again" (Tuttle 1993).

The first poll in the 1959 general elections showed William F. Quinn ahead of John A. Burns for the governorship. Tuttle recalls, "No one believed us." The students repolled. Tuttle was within two percentage points, considered to be remarkably close, of the final results in which Quinn was elected the first governor of the State of Hawai'i. Tuttle said then, and he was prescient, "There may come a day when government will sponsor polls to determine the will of the people" (*Star-Bull.*, Aug. 20, 1959).

With little support from the University because his Hawai'i based efforts were considered too narrow in focus and too highly politically charged, Tuttle left the University to head up the Hawai'i Education Association. He later returned to teaching and ran his own Survey Research Company as an independent enterprise. Between 1973 and 1981, he and his partners conducted more than 200 polls, many commissioned by businesses. The polls were based on fairly large samples—800 on O'ahu, for example, and 400 each on the neighbor islands (Kaua'i, Maui, Moloka'i, and Hawai'i) for a 2,400 total. With this method he could predict county and statewide results.

In the meantime, in 1970, the *Star-Bulletin* had a very bad polling experience. This was in the Burns-Gill governor's race that attracted strong public interest. The two were incumbent Democrats: Tom Gill was John Burns' lieutenant governor. In the last published poll before the primary elections, the *Star-Bulletin* showed a "strong surge" for Gill: "Too Close to Call" (Sept. 28, 1970). But the sampling by telephone was restricted, with only 681 people interviewed. Tuttle claims he warned the *Star-Bulletin* to bury the poll but they ran it anyway. Burns won big, by 82,036 to Gill's 68,719, or 53.3 percent to 44.7 percent (*Star-Bull.*, Oct. 4, 1970). People were shocked because they had been led to believe it was a close race that Gill would win. Years later, the 1970 polls were still being discussed. The *Star-Bulletin*'s John Simonds in 1978 was still explaining "Why *Star-Bulletin* Shuns Poll Results" (Nov. 3, 1978).

The 1970 race, however, reveals another dynamic—the growing dependency on polls by politicians. The Burns campaign people polled with a vengeance. They employed two outstanding pollsters, Rick Egged, a Waipahu High School graduate who had joined Robert Kennedy's staff and returned to the Islands after Kennedy's assassination in 1968, and Joseph Napolitan, well-known Washington political consultant. Egged and Napolitan provided their candidate with up-to-the-minute voter trends. According to Egged, Burns was not "a great communicator." The internal polls helped to shape their candidate's image of warmth and integrity (Egged 1993). Their weekly poll came to be "one of the campaign's best-kept secrets," Tom Coffman, former *Star-Bulletin* politics reporter, states (Coffman 1993). The campaign won national media awards, and Coffman wrote *Catch a Wave* (1973) about the experience.

The *Advertiser*'s reaction to 1970, in contrast to the *Star-Bulletin*'s, was to jump into polling, both as a public service and to increase circulation. Gerry Keir had joined the paper after army service. As its politics writer, Keir believed that polling "was not being done well." He spent a year at the University of Michigan's Center for Political Studies and the Survey Research Center in Ann Arbor, returning to Honolulu in June 1974 to introduce public polls on a wide range of subjects, such as citizens' opinions on Honolulu's bus service, aid to Vietnam, gun control, public schools, and the seriousness of crime. Keir believes that polls tell a community about itself (Keir 1992).

But, Keir states, the political poll is "the sexiest" and draws the most interest from a wide spectrum of the people. There are the ordinary members of the newspaper reading public who participate in politics "passively" by following the news and voting. Others respond "actively," as members or contributors to organizations or movements. (A third group, Keir notes, cannot be reached, for they neither follow the news nor vote.)

The *Advertiser* adopted the position of the National Council of Public Polls that advocated "truth-in-polling." Before publishing a poll, the following questions must be answered. Who pays for the poll? When is it taken? How are the interviews obtained and who is interviewed? How are the questions worded? What is the size of the sample? The National Council recommended that the margin of error be no more than 4.5 percent. ("The Pitfalls of Polling," *Columbia Journ. Review*, May–June 1972.)

"The *Advertiser*'s Hawaii Poll" first appeared on September 3, 1974. The paper acknowledged that there was public disrespect for newspaper polling and that the Honolulu dailies "do have a credibility gap" among readers. This was, the *Advertiser* promised, "a new scientific survey" and an "in depth look" at the mood of Hawai'i politics. (*Sun. Bull. & Adv.*, Sept. 15, 1974). Rick Egged assisted with *Advertiser* polls.

Unlike many newspapers that hire outside companies to design their polls, the *Advertiser* maintained "control." A subject would be chosen through an exchange of ideas among the editors. Keir then put the questions together himself. Some topics were "tried and true," he states, like abortion. "Others you have to design from scratch," like how the public feels about a mass transit system for Honolulu or about the use of the island of Kaho'olawe as a bombing target. The three steps involved in good polling are: decide what you want to know about; decide how to construct the survey; and do the field work. The *Advertiser* turned over the third phase to market survey research firms. Sampling had to be large and polling taken as close as possible to the end (Keir 1992).

Not surprisingly, not everyone was happy with the 1974 effort. A five-way race developed for the Democratic nomination for the governorship: George Ariyoshi, Frank Fasi, Tom Gill, Dave McClung, and Henry deFries. Mayor Fasi was shown to be in the lead, with Ariyoshi and Gill in a dead heat three percentage points behind him: "A tight race for governor," the *Advertiser* predicted. McClung and deFries trailed badly, and McClung attacked the poll's "timing" (*Adv.*, Sept. 3, 4, 1974). The "undecided" vote was an unremarked-upon 14 percent that became the critical factor. It was not such a "tight race" after all. Of the three leading candidates, Ariyoshi won by more than 9,000 votes, or 71,244 to Fasi's 61,944 and Gill's 59,215 (*Adv.*, Oct. 7, 1974). The *Advertiser* was just outside its own margin of error, or 4.9 instead of 4.5 percent. In spite of this, *Advertiser* people were confident that they were close enough to continue polling. To support their conclusion, one has only to recall the myriad of polls and their effect, such as those less scientific ones in the early 1970s that overwhelmingly predicted and supported repeal of anti-abortion laws, an effect that many believe influenced not only the legislature but also a Catholic governor, John Burns, to not veto the legislation but to let it become law.

As to Dan Tuttle, one is seldom a prophet in one's own town. Labeled old-fashioned by recent pollsters—he believes, for example, that ethnicity as a voting factor is "secondary, even tertiary"—Tuttle is skeptical of the *Advertiser*'s methods that use "area sampling" based on census tracts that may be "old information" after two or three years. Tuttle believes, too, that the market research companies sometimes hire untrained people and that the *Advertiser* rationalizes its mistakes (Tuttle 1993).

As to mistakes, Keir admits, "Gaffes do happen," and readers "take great delight in beating you over the head" afterwards. "But if mistakes were the rule rather than the exception, polls would be laughed out of the newspapers and off of TV news" (*Sun. Bull. & Adv.*, Nov. 1, 1992).

They have not met that fate. In fact, polls have been adapted to the electronic age. Newspapers now link them with television, the results given in print and in the broadcast medium. The public continues to be intrigued, if not influenced. And Keir has lectured at the University of Hawai'i on public opinion polling.

43.   Anger and Wit:
The Political Cartoon

For the readers, inundated with more information than they can absorb, the editorial or political cartoon interprets and makes sense of things (Press 1981). It impacts doubly, for it combines an instantly recognizable figure or image with a sharply worded message. It is the most popular feature of the editorial page.

Political cartooning, related to the ancient art form of caricature, surfaced in American colonial newspapers soon after the papers themselves appeared. Prompted by the outbreak of the French and Indian Wars that colonialists viewed as endangering them, Ben Franklin's *Pennsylvania Gazette* in 1754 featured a snake divided into segments, each one an American colony, the caption reading, "Unite or die" (Tower 1982). What later became a national symbol of the United States—the figure of Uncle Sam—was created as a cartoon in 1812 when the fledging country was at war with its former master, England (Tower 1982).

The nineteenth century saw the development of political cartoons unrivaled for their savage power. The country's greatest cartoonist, Thomas Nast, drew fifty or so in 1871 alone on William Marcy "Boss" Tweed and the corrupt Tammany Hall ring. One depicted Tweed as a vulture with talons dug into the dead body of New York City. Another showed an obese Tweed with a money bag for a face. An angry Tweed is reported to have said that he didn't care much what the papers wrote because his constituents couldn't read, "But, damn it, they can see pictures" (Hess and Kaplan 1975). Ulysses S. Grant credited the Nast cartoons, which appeared in *Harper's Weekly,* with electing him president (Innis 1951). As Ralph Waldo Emerson noted, caricatures are often the truest history of the times.

Editorial cartooning spread through the country in the twentieth century. Larger papers employed their own cartoonists, while smaller journals bought syndicated material. Hawai'i was unusual in that although the *Advertiser* had a circulation of only about 4,000, editor Walter G. Smith in 1900 hired the Islands' first "illustrator"—

that is, cartoonist Ralph Yardly. The Advertiser was soon involved in a cause celebre. Smith printed a series of front-page Yardly drawings on a case appearing before Judge George D. Gear. One McSwillegan McCarthy (his real name) allegedly had bitten Katie Akai on the rear, both arms, one hand, and about the body. Her injuries were so severe that she had to go to the hospital. A jury of his peers found McCarthy guilty. To the great disgust of the newspaper and the public, Judge Gear sentenced McCarthy on a technicality for "mayhem" to just six months hard labor (*Hawaiian Star*, Mar. 13–15, 1902). A Yardly cartoon showed a grossly fat Judge watching frail womanhood in the clutches of a leering madman and waving a blessing over him, saying, "Bless you, McSwillegan—Bite Her Again." Gear slapped a charge of contempt of court upon Smith for intending "to be suggestive and contumellous of this honorable judge." (*Adv.*, Mar. 12, 13, 1902.) He sentenced Smith to 30 days imprisonment—in the annals of local history, an unheard of punishment for an establishment editor. Governor Dole pardoned Smith after two days. Yardly, just 23 years old and with a newsman's wanderlust, left the Islands in 1902 to work for papers in California and New York (obituary, *Adv.*, Apr. 19, 1931).

In the 1920s and 1930s, following the practice of the times, the *Advertiser* intensified the savagery of its cartoons: for example, during labor agitation, depicting plantation laborers as greedy, criminal, and the dupes of sinister outside forces.

Today, most of the 150 or so political cartoonists in the employ of American newspapers usually support the editorial opinion of the employer or, as stated pungently by former *Advertiser* executive John Griffin, "they reflect what we think" (Griffin 1985). The cartoonist sits in on editorial staff meetings, where ideas are kicked around, and may be assigned a topic or may come up with an original one (Burris 1993). The cartoonist submits three or four roughed-out drawings, and one is selected to accompany an editorial appearing the next day. But not always. A few of the best, or about 10 out of the 150, function autonomously, usually having gained leverage and prestige from being widely syndicated.

Corky Trinidad enjoys this kind of freedom. In 1969, when Corky was hired by *Star-Bulletin* editor Jim Cooey—the great cartoonists are almost always known by a single name—he had already gained an international reputation from his work on the *Philippines Herald* in Manila and *Stars and Stripes*, the Army newspaper out of Tokyo, which ran his "Nguyen Charlie" daily strip (1966–1969) during the

Vietnam War. "I came in at the right time," Corky states. The Vietnam War years provided a wealth of subjects on civil rights, the antiwar movement, and—for Corky—Philippine Islands politics (Trinidad 1993). Distributed by the Los Angeles Times-Washington Post Syndicate, the cartoons have appeared in the *Buenos Aires Herald*, the *New York Times, Paris Herald Tribune, Hong Kong Standard*, and other major newspapers worldwide.

While still living in Manila, Corky had close friends who knew of plans by President Ferdinand Marcos to impose martial law before the end of his second term because he was barred by the constitution from running again. The friends, among them Benigno Aquino Jr., whom Marcos henchmen would later assassinate, advised Corky to get out of the country. "I'd always wanted to come to America," he states. The *Star-Bulletin* hired him. His cartoon of the Marcos takeover in September 1972 depicted Marcos holding a smoking gun and standing upon the dead, prostrate figure of "Philippine Democracy" and explaining, "It was self-defense—She came at me with the constitution!" (Trinidad 1986).

The power of the cartoon is illustrated by Francisco Flores Trinidad himself, nicknamed "Corky" by his grandmother after a comic strip character in "Gasoline Alley." Both his parents were journalists, and Corky began drawing cartoons as a youth in the Philippines and sending submittals to U.S. publications while still in his teens. He was influenced by American ideals and received an invaluable formal education by Jesuit priests from America in logic and clarity of thought. By reading such novelists and poets as Ernest Hemingway and William Carlos Williams, he developed a compressed, straight-forward statement without jargon or long words. Just as those writers craft a sentence or a line, Corky crafts a drawing. A cartoon, he explains, is "a precise rhetorical and visual argument. You have to know your stand" (Trinidad 1982; Trinidad 1993). To Corky goes the credit for creating the caribou as an image for the Philippines, now a recognized symbol internationally. Among those who acknowledge his power are his subjects, like Henry Kissinger and Jimmy Carter, who have asked for inscribed originals.

Corky gets his ideas from the news. "I do a cartoon because I have a theme I'd like to get off my chest. I'm normal, but something will bug me, just like it does anyone." This is what Alan Westin, writing about successful editorial cartoonists, calls "getting angry every day" (Westin 1979). How much influence does a cartoon wield? A modest Corky is not sure his work changes things: "You've got to have a big ego to think you changed the mind of the governor." But, he adds, "You always get a lot of feedback" (Trinidad 1993). He operates on mainland time, arriving at his office by 3:00 A.M. to do the cartoon for that day. No executive or staff member knows what the subject is until Corky submits the drawing for transmittal to the syndicate (Chang 1993). While this freedom is "worth more than money" to him, he also feels its responsibility and tries to function within the boundaries of good taste. He tempers himself through variety, too. One cannot do six cartoons in succession, he says, on the contamination of island milk by heptachlor or the Honolulu Convention Center (Trinidad 1993).

Corky claims to be "apolitical": that is, uninterested in being a politician but keenly interested in politics as an "observer." He rejects labels like "conservative" and "liberal," but he is a staunch supporter of constitutional and civil rights. He explains the difference: "dealing only with the surface of topics makes the cartoon no better than the funnies or a great doodle"—loved and forgotten within seconds. By contrast, the really good editorial cartoon goes beyond specific subject matter and reacts to it in a way that illustrates a universal principle. That he touches raw nerves is attested to by the angry calls he receives, like telling him to go back to "where I came from," or labeling him "a disgrace to the Filipino people" ("A Man for All Treasons," *Haw. Journ. Review*, Aug. 1971). A Roman Catholic bishop in Hawai'i, who supported the Marcos regime, has sermonized against him from the pulpit.

Among his universal cartoons is one entitled "Evolution of man as a peacemaker." It brilliantly depicts the four stages of man but always as a Neanderthal, carrying a club, a spear, an assault rifle, and, finally, a nuclear bomb (*Star-Bull.*, Oct. 10, 1981). Another, in 1989, is on the death of a despot, with no caption but showing Marcos in an open coffin that is a safe, the unlocked door revealing his head surrounded by bags of gold (*Star-Bull.*, Sept. 28, 1989). As to Corky's further influence, it should be added that while Marcos was in power, his regime was stung enough to unsuccessfully sue Corky twice for libel. The regime also exiled him, only once allowing him to return, in 1976, for the funeral of his mother.

His colleagues like Corky personally and admire his work professionally. Tim Ryan, *Star-Bulletin* reporter who closely covered the Marcos family after they fell from power in the Philippines in 1986 and took up, in Ryan's words, a "posh but unhappy" exile in Hono-

Evolution of man as peacemaker

Hawai'i's famous political cartoonist, Corky Trinidad, is reprinted in major papers throughout the world. His rendition of man as "peacemaker," in the *Star-Bulletin* on October 10, 1981, takes up a universal theme.

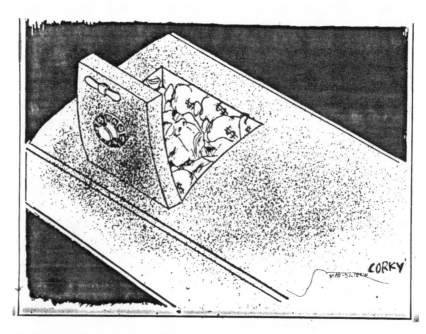

Corky's timely treatment of the death of Ferdinand Marcos in the *Star-Bulletin* on September 28, 1989, leaves no doubt as to Corky's opinion of the Philippines' former president.

lulu (obituary, *Star-Bull.*, Sept. 28, 1989), points out that no one expects the editorial cartoonist "to be fair." He contrasts this to the reporter whose work should be evenhanded (Ryan 1993).

The Islands may claim other popular editorial cartoonists who have attracted readers to the editorial page. Harry Lyons, with the *Advertiser* from 1959 until his retirement in 1979, was more of a social or humorous artist who did not go for the jugular but brought a smile to one's face. Dick Adair, Chicago-born artist who joined the *Advertiser* in 1981, like Corky developed a strong anti-Marcos bias. One cartoon is of Marcos as Rambo, heavily muscled, assault rifle in hand, and wearing a gold medallion inscribed "Swiss Bank." The succinct caption reads, "FERDINAMBO" (*Adv.*, Aug. 26, 1986).

Corky observes, "My time may pass. Then I'll do something else" (Trinidad 1993). The medium that he has mentioned for the future is comic books adapted to television. The comics, which are an American idiom that developed out of "the funnies" and are allied to editorial cartooning, have become the most widely distributed of all printed material in the world.

44. Hawaiian Sovereignty and a Satellite Universe, 1976

If we could go back to the future, to 1834 and the birth of the Islands' first newspaper, we could witness at first hand young Hawaiian men at Lahaina Luna School eagerly scanning the contents of the printed pages they have produced. This historical event at once points forward and backward. Looking forward, we see the introduction of a new technology that will come to dominate communications for almost 150 years. Looking backward, we recognize the stubborn persistence of ethnicity and the past on our lives, as in the Hawaiian language newspapers that will document and preserve the customs, genealogies, poetry, and other aspects of the culture for the benefit of future generations.

Moving instantly through two centuries, the eyewitness arrives at 1976 to find a similar pattern of the newspaper preserving the past while heralding change. The story of *Hōkūleʻa*, the sixty-foot, double-hulled canoe, takes over the front page of the Sunday morning Honolulu paper—"*Hōkūleʻa* begins her epic voyage"—accompanied by a photo of the sailing canoe that makes history by recreating an almost lost navigational art, putting Native Hawaiians "in touch once again with some of their deepest cultural roots." Captured for all time is their stunning achievement of sailing from Hawaiʻi to Tahiti, as their ancestors had done a thousand years previously (*Sun. Bull. & Adv.*, May 2, 1976).

A week later, two items announce the future. A satellite, orbiting 22,300 miles above the earth, is to transmit the evening television news instantaneously (*Sun. Bull. & Adv.*, May 9, 1976). Rather than relating what is happening in the breaking news, newspapers will henceforth occupy a secondary communications role by recounting what has already happened:

*(9) WALTER CRONKITE
CBS EVENING NEWS
VIA SATELLITE

338

IN HAWAII
IT'S
SEVEY AT SIX
(*Star-Bull.*, May 10, 1976)

And why should the ambiguity of newspapers pointing to the future even as they preserve the past seem odd? Technologies are but an extension of their inventors, who are ourselves: the pencil and Linotype extensions of our fingers, the satellite an extension of our brains (McLuhan 1964).

Ethnicity is similarly embedded in us. The "idols of the tribe," as the brilliant Harold Isaacs describes them in his study of group identity and political change, are those ancient and universal marks of identity that are linked to body, name, kinship, place, language, history or origins, religion, and nation (Isaacs 1975). In other words, we are the body we are born with, the name we carry, our family or kinship connections, the specific place we inhabit, the language we speak, the history and origins of our group, the religion we practice, and the nationality we proclaim. The helmsman of *Hōkūleʻa*, for example, recreates the lost art and skills of his ancestors as he unerringly navigates through the vast Polynesian ocean triangle with only the phenomena of the universe—sun, clouds, winds, waves, stars—to guide him.

Several significant events that newspapers actively abet in simultaneously pointing us forward and backward lead up to 1976. One is the Kalama Valley struggle, which signaled the modern Native Hawaiian fight for land rights and "sovereignty" (Trask 1987)—place, history and origins, nation. Another is the formation of the Protect Kahoʻolawe ʻOhana, the organization that took leadership in the Herculean struggle to make the U.S. government abandon its position of treating Kahoʻolawe as a military target and place the island under the watchful care of Native Hawaiians—kinship, language, religion. Both are part of the movement for a return to "sovereignty" or self-determination.

Hawaiian Sovereignty

Sovereignty is an issue that takes us back in time as well as forward while happening in the present. In the 1890s, Hawaiian journalists in opposition papers advocated the twin causes of self-determination and their country's independence. They predicted that an American takeover would further alienate Hawaiians from the core of their existence, their ancestral lands. Nationalist papers lost to the combined, concentrated power of a hostile establishment and its newspapers, but their arguments formed the foundation for the struggle of the 1970s.

Related to the rise on the mainland in the 1960s of grassroot movements in civil rights and the concomitant search for ethnic roots, opposition papers, now called the alternative press, once again took up advocacy of Native Hawaiian rights. This alternative press appeared mainly in English so as to reach a predominantly English-language audience but added columns in Hawaiian as more and more people relearned this language. These papers were an effective organizing tool for grassroots groups coming together with a renewed sense of cultural identity. A different political climate meant that the establishment press, although initially resistant, came to view the Hawaiian cause with some sympathy.

Kalama Valley in the Koko Head area provided the issue that alternative papers publicized as a problem of concentrated land ownership that was contributing to the urbanizing of O'ahu and the dispossession of Hawaiians from their land. In 1970, *Hawaii Free People's Press* (1969–1971) attracted public notice with a special edition on the disappearing rural life of Hawaiians and others in Kalama Valley who held leases on the land and had received eviction notices from the Bishop Estate (Aug. 1970).

The background to the event is that the Bishop Estate, a major landholding estate and the chief funding source for the Kamehameha Schools, the private educational institutions for Hawaiian children, had made a deal in the 1950s with industrialist Henry Kaiser. Kaiser was to develop 250 acres of "barren land" in Kalama Valley into 4,300 homesites (Trask 1987). The general plan for the east end of the island of O'ahu, adopted by the City and County of Honolulu in 1961, called for an enormous development, covering 6,000 acres, of homes, shopping centers, golf courses, and hotels and restaurants, stretching from a suburban Hawai'i Kai to a "resort complex" at Makapu'u. (*Sun. Bull. & Adv.* Sept. 13, 27, 1970).

Hawaii Free People's Press quoted Robert Wilcox, newspaper editor and revolutionist, who in 1890 stated, "these white men" are "a good for nothing lot, all they want is money, and when they get it they get up and go away" (Dec. 1970). Wilcox was wrong in one respect: white men did not go away, as evidenced by Bishop Estate trustees, who until the 1960s were all Caucasians. But he was right about money. The trustees, even with recent appointments of Asian

Americans and Native Hawaiians to their board, maintain the capitalist model of making as much money as possible for the Estate. Kalama Valley's conversion was very profitable.

Another grassroots organization and its newspaper introduced "sovereignty" as a modern topic. Kōkua Hawai'i, comprised of students, ministers, and other activists, printed *Huli* (turning or reversal) (1971–1973), as well as newsletters and leaflets, to organize opposition against the Kalama Valley evictions. *Huli*'s motto was, "*Ka 'Āina No Ka Po'e Hawai'i*," or "Land for the People of Hawaii." Photos taken at Kalama Valley showed armed police facing unarmed peaceful demonstrators (*Huli*, May 11, 1971). Kōkua Hawai'i publicized a program for land reform by taking out full-page advertisements in the Honolulu dailies (*Sun. Bull. & Adv.*, June 13, 1971). *Huli* made a connection of the issue to the Native American movement for self-determination and asked, "What About Us?" (*Huli*, July 3, 1971).

The topic had already moved from the alternative to the mainstream papers that mostly repeated the establishment line: the residents, having been served eviction notices, were "trespassers," and the Bishop Estate was "Relocating Displaced Families" (*Adv.*, July 10, 1970; *Star-Bull.*, July 29, 1970). Nonetheless, the topic garnered increased publicity and prominent placement. In 1970, the Honolulu dailies alone ran more that forty items on the impending evictions; in 1971, double the number.

It is of record that the major dailies over two centuries have employed very few Hawaiian journalists. The *Star-Bulletin* did have Pierre Bowman, from a prominent Big Island family, on its staff and assigned him to the story. Bowman's approach to Kalama Valley shows the ambiguities of being in the pay of the establishment while one's heart remains with the victims. To Bowman the resisters were "gentle rebels" attacking the roots of the social and economic structure of "the new plantation." He placed Kalama Valley—a "small skirmish"—within the larger "revolution being fought in the United States (*Star-Bull.*, May 12, 1971). Bowman's coverage contributed to public awareness and won adherents for future confrontations over land and water issues throughout the Islands. There was an obvious shift, too, in the mainstream's viewpoint; the *Advertiser*, for example, recognized "the special problems of Hawaiians" and proposed giving "serious thought to land use in the Islands" (May 12, 1971).

The Kalama Valley protest lost, but an aroused public responded to what *Huli* called, "No more Kalamas" (June 5, 1971). When heirs to another landed group, the McCandless Estate, proposed rezoning 1,337 acres from agricultural to urban use at Waiāhole–Waikāne on Oʻahu's windward side, another grassroots organization sprang into action. The mainstream press, critical of the plan, helped to defeat the proposal in 1975.

In 1976, Kahoʻolawe, the smallest of the eight major islands with just forty-five square miles, became a major subject. There had been a continuous human presence on Kahoʻolawe from settlements of Polynesians centuries ago to a small population in the nineteenth and early part of the twentieth centuries connected to fishing and ranching (MacDonald 1972). (The island never produced a newspaper.) The U.S. military used a vacated Kahoʻolawe during World War II for target practice. After the war, in 1953, the navy assumed control of the island and continued to bomb. Now the practice itself came under fire. But whenever the Territory raised the matter of reclaiming Kahoʻolawe, the navy, with intractable resistance, would declare that bombing was essential to the "national defense" of the United States.

In the late 1960s, establishment papers on Oʻahu and Maui first publicized the Kahoʻolawe situation in letters to the editors and news and feature stories. As with Kalama Valley, there was a sharp increase in the number of items on the subject in the mainstream press. Establishment papers were soon joined by alternative journals.

The perspective of the two different types of papers toward Kahoʻolawe came together as it had not over the Kalama Valley struggle and intensified newspaper influence. Why? In 1969, Maui County's first mayor, Elmer Cravalho—the county, comprised of Maui, Lānaʻi, Molokaʻi, and Kahoʻolawe, had previously been governed by a chairman—awoke one night to his home being rocked by a series of bombs. Planes from an aircraft carrier, in routine practice, had apparently dropped their hardware too close to the Valley Island, a mere 6.9 miles across the ʻAlalākeiki Channel. The *Maui News* interviewed an enraged Cravalho, as well as historian Inez Ashdown, daughter of Angus McPhee who had ranched on Kahoʻolawe prior to World War II. Both adamantly opposed the bombing (*Maui News*, Aug. 23, 1969). The Honolulu papers followed up on the story as Maui residents became more and more distressed over the dangerous, noisy intrusion of sea barrages, aerial bombing, sea-to-surface missiles, and high caliber gunfire. An unexploded aerial bomb was discovered on September 27 near the Honoapiʻilani Highway. The

Maui News reported that when detonated, it left a crater approximately thirty feet wide and fifteen feet deep: "The concussion shook residents all over Kīhei and parts of Central Maui," and the police were flooded with calls. "Immediate Permanent Bombing Stop Sought," the newspaper headlined (Oct. 1, 1969) and editorially supported. Aggressive follow-ups by staff writer Jeanne B. Johnson chronicled the mayor and the county office, joined by Hawai'i's congressional delegation in Washington, D.C., pressing for "the immediate and permanent ending of all bombing activities on Kaho'olawe" (Oct. 8, 1969). To *Maui News* management and staff, this was an issue that was no longer solely the concern of activists but one in which the entire community had a concern.

In 1976, when the Protect Kaho'olawe 'Ohana formed to halt bombing of a "sacred site" and to initiate lawsuits against federal officials, establishment and alternative papers gave serious coverage to the 'Ohana and reported its periodic occupation of the island to hold religious ceremonies and reclaim Hawaiian heritage. The counterculture paper, the *Maui Sun*, in an interview with Dr. Emmett Aluli, physician and movement leader, noted that the 'Ohana had brought back the 1890s newspaper title and phrase *aloha 'āina*— meaning if you take care of the land it takes care of you (*Sun*, Dec. 22–28, 1976). Newspaper stories thus were effective agents in underscoring the resurgent Hawaiian movement as a stubborn reiteration of a universal idol of the tribe.

After 1976 the Hawaiian language reappears in print, further illustrating newspapers as agents of ethnic persistence. A number of weeklies and monthlies have incorporated Hawaiian columns. Talented editors like Malcolm Naea Chun, as their forerunners did, articulate the Native Hawaiian position in such papers as the *Native Hawaiian* (1977–), the newsletter of Alu Like, a Hawaiian self-help organization, and *Ka Wai Ola o OHA*—(The living waters of OHA) (1981–), produced by the Office of Hawaiian Affairs.

A halt to the bombing of Kaho'olawe is finally ordered in 1990 by President George Bush. In 1991, Kaho'olawe is registered as a National Historic District, and in 1993 the island is returned to the State of Hawai'i. As to what specific form sovereignty will take, this is still pending but likely to be decided by the century's end (Dudley and Agard 1990). Newspapers across all categories and locations have editorially declared in favor of some form of self-government within the statehood structure.

The Satellite Universe

In one of those recurring ambiguities of life, an older technology will provide information about a competing newer one. After radio broadcasting began in 1922, the newspapers ran radio program logs. In 1932, newspapers carried forecasts of television: "Within Decade . . . Hawaii Will See Mainland" (*Star-Bull.*, Dec, 30, 1932). In 1952, when commercial television broadcasting began, the papers announced: "First TV Test Patterns Are Screened Here" and "First Regular Isle Telecasts Begin Tonight on KGMB-TV" (*Adv.*, Nov. 18, 1952; *Star-Bull.*, Dec. 1, 1952). "TV Programs" became a front page boxed item entitled "Where to Find It" (*Adv.*, Dec. 22, 1952). A separate TV Guide section appeared on weekends. In April 1961, the papers noted the start of cable TV—cable, which was to have such a profound effect on television itself.

Then the really big news! Instant TV programming via satellite, announced in 1966 as "Satellite Launching to Herald Hawaii into the Space Age" (*Star-Bull.*, Oct. 25, 1966). And what was the heralded event? Sports, of course, with its enormous appeal across all segments of society. The papers estimated that "more than one-half" of Hawaiʻi's population tuned in to watch the first live program, a football game between Notre Dame and Michigan State University on November 17, 1966 (*Star-Bull.*, Nov. 19, 1966). In a classic "idols of the tribe" response, the satellite beaming this event was dubbed with a Hawaiian name, *Lani Bird.*

Midway between the space age televising of football and the introduction of regular satellite service is another notable event in newspaper technology. A "new era" for the Islands' papers is the end of a Linotype, hot lead printing technology and the installation of computers and a photochemical process known as cold type (*Adv.*, July 28, 1973). Information delivery is thus radically changed on two fronts: in the skies above, as well as in the newspaper offices below.

There are other radical changes accompanying a satellite universe. "Crossover" journalists, like Bob Jones, who have worked in more than one medium, are excellent sources of information on these. If you're a print journalist, Jones states, "no one knows your face." And if you're on TV? "You're marked." Television is primarily a selling and entertainment medium that makes stars out of anchormen and women. But conversely, a column in print may receive "tons of letters," while television is so fast that "there's hardly time for the viewer to respond. There're no letters to the editor and very few phone calls" (Jones 1992). What has also been pointed out is that television, in treating the news primarily as quick "entertainment," has forced newspapers into adopting the same approach (Postman 1985).

The most pronounced change linked to the arrival of the age of satellite television is the waning influence of the newspapers themselves. By 1992, in a resident Island population of 1,108,229 (1990 census figure), there were 366,900 households. In those households, there were 359,670 television sets—or a television penetration of 97.2 percent (*Hawaii State Data Book* 1992). At a conservative figure of two viewers per household, this means that more than half of all of the Islands' residents, from infancy to the aged, watch television daily. By contrast, 1991–1992 statistics show a daily newspaper circulation on four islands (Kaua'i, O'ahu, Maui, Hawai'i) of 248,786; on Sunday mornings, 266,228 (*Hawaii State Data Book* 1992). Newspaper penetration of homes, therefore, and this is a liberal estimate, is no more than 25 percent.

How many actually read the papers? What influence do they still have? Communications analyst Herbert Altschull states that only one person in ten now reads editorials, at one time a community's primary opinion setter (Altschull 1990). If it was a truism for centuries that knowledge is power, it is now information that is power, and television, cable networks, and an international electronic superhighway are the carriers.

Yet it is premature to declare the death of the newspaper in the space age. Several media still exist side by side. Kit Smith, former financial writer for the *Advertiser*, observes that television "keeps us on our toes," pointing out that reporters and editors watch every one of the main channels (Smith 1991). Another example is that reporters have sailed on subsequent voyages of the *Hōkūle'a* which the papers always cover, as in the *Advertiser*'s thirteen-part series: Bob Krauss aboard the sailing canoe *Hōkūle'a* (Aug. 29, 1985).

To return us again to the eventful 1976 and to project us forward, in 1976 there appeared a feature on the compilation and translation of more than 100 Hawaiian language newspapers published between 1834 and 1948. Preserving the past for the future is University of Hawai'i's Associate Professor Rubellite Kawena Johnson and her students who are "Mining the Wealth of Hawaiian Newspapers" (*Adv.*, Dec. 16, 1976).

Bibliography

Shaping History: The Role of Newspapers in Hawai'i rests on a wide variety of written and oral sources. Most quotations from the newspapers and journals are referred to directly in the text. All other written sources, as well as a list of interviews and conversations, are given below to assist those who wish to pursue a particular subject about the printed press or Hawaiian history. Specific page references of written documents and dates of interviews and conversations are on deposit at the Hawaiian Historical Society in Honolulu.

Indexes to the Islands' papers are included below and are readily available in the libraries, archives, and museums throughout the state. The newspapers themselves may be read in their original form or on microfilm in a number of locations. Basic sources for finding specific locations are: for the Hawaiian language papers, Mookini, *The Hawaiian Newspapers*; and for all languages, McMillan and Morris, *Hawaii Newspapers: A Union List*. While the *Union List* is extremely useful, it is however, selective.

The author presently is compiling an annotated and complete list of the more than 1,000 separately titled newspapers that have been produced in Hawai'i in all languages from 1834 to the present and hopes to make this available by 1998.

Articles, Books, Documents, Journals, Monographs, Pamphlets, Papers

Abel, Elie, ed. *What's News: The Media in American Society*. San Francisco: Institute for Contemporary Studies, 1981.

Abler, Ronald F. "Monoculture or Miniculture? The Impact of Communications on Culture in Space." In *An Invitation to Geography*. 2nd ed. Edited by David A. Lanegran and Risa Palm. New York: McGraw Hill, 1973.

Adler, Jacob. *Claus Spreckles: The Sugar King in Hawaii*. Honolulu: University of Hawai'i Press, 1966.

Alcantara, Ruben R., and Nancy S. Alconel. *The Filipinos in Hawaii: An Annotated Bibliography*. Honolulu: Social Sciences and Linguistics Institute, University of Hawai'i, 1977.

Alexander, Mary Charlotte, and Charlotte Peabody Dodge. *Punahou, 1841–1941*. Berkeley: University of California Press, 1941.

Allen, Gwenfread. *Hawaii's War Years, 1941–1945.* Westport, Conn.: University of Hawai'i Press, 1950.

Allen, John E. *Newspaper Designing.* New York: Harper & Brothers, 1947.

Allen, Riley. "Hawaii's Pioneers in Journalism." In *Thirty-Third Annual Report of the Hawaiian Historical Society.* Honolulu, 1928.

———. "Memorandum on Newspaper Censorship in Hawaii, June 5, 1944." Hawaii War Records Depository, University of Hawai'i.

———. "Some Observations on Pamphleteering in Hawaii." Paper read before the Social Science Association, Honolulu, June 5, 1933.

Allport, Gordon W. *The Nature of Prejudice.* Garden City: Doubleday & Co., 1958.

Altschull, J. Herbert. *Agents of Power: The Role of the News Media in Human Affairs.* New York: Longman, 1984.

———. *From Milton to McLuhan: The Ideas Behind American Journalism.* New York: Longman, 1990.

America Organized to Win the War: A Handbook on the American War Effort. New York: Harcourt, Brace & Co., 1942.

Andrade, Ernest. "The Hawaiian Coinage Controversy—or, What Price a Handsome Profile?" *The Hawaiian Journal of History* 11 (1977): 91–109.

Annual Reports. Makaweli Plantation, 1892–1920. Hawaiian Sugar Planters' Association.

Anthony, J. Garner. *Hawaii Under Army Rule.* Honolulu: University Press of Hawai'i, 1975.

Armstrong, David. *A Trumpet to Arms: Alternative Media in America.* Los Angeles: J. B. Tarcher, 1981.

Armstrong, William N. *Around the World With A King.* Rutland, Vt.: Charles E. Tuttle, 1903.

Arno, Andrew, and Wimal Dissanayake, eds. *The News Media in National and International Conflict.* Boulder: Westview Press, 1984.

Arnold, Edmund C. *Ink on Paper 2: A Handbook of the Graphic Arts.* New York: Harper & Row, 1972.

———. *Modern Newspaper Design.* New York: Harper & Row, 1969.

Aronson, James. *The Press and the Cold War.* Indianapolis: Bobbs-Merrill Co., 1970.

Associated Press Stylebook and Libel Manual. Edited by Norm Goldstein. New York: Associated Press, 1992.

Atkins, Paul A. *The College Daily in the United States.* Parsons, W. Va.: McClain Printing Co., 1982.

Ayer, N. W. & Sons. *Directories of Newspapers and Periodicals.* Fort Washington, Pa.: N. W. Ayer & Sons, 1931–1984.

Bagdikian, Ben H. "Fat Newspapers and Slim Coverage." *Columbia Journalism Review,* September–October 1973, 15–20.

———. "Journalism." *Mother Jones,* May–June 1992, 48–51.

———. *The Media Monopoly.* 3rd ed. Boston: Beacon Press, 1990.

Baird, Russell N. *The Penal Press.* Evanston, Ill.: Northwestern University Press, 1967.

Baldasty, Gerald J. *The Commercialization of News in the Nineteenth Century.* Madison: University of Wisconsin Press, 1992.

———. "The Nineteenth-Century Origins of Modern American Journalism." Paper for the American Antiquarian Society, Arlington, Virginia, November 12–14, 1990.

Ballou, Howard Malcolm, and George R. Carter. "The History of the Hawaiian Mission Press." In *Fourteenth Annual Report of the Hawaiian Historical Society*, Honolulu, n.d.

Barth, Alan. "The Press as Censor of Government." *In Marquette University, Social Responsibility of the Newspapers*. Milwaukee: Marquette University, 1962.

Bartholomew, Gail. *The Index to the Maui News, 1933–1950*. Wailuku: Maui Historical Society 1991.

———, comp. and ed., assisted by Judy Lindstrom. *The Index to the Maui News, 1900–1932*. Wailuku: Maui Historical Society, 1985.

Baynes, Ken, et al. *Scoop, Scandal and Strife: A Study of Photography in Newspapers*. New York: Hastings House, 1971.

Becker, Ruth Ann. "Round Two for the *Kauai Times*." *Hawaii Business*, July 1982, 62–65.

Beckwith, Martha. *Hawaiian Mythology*. Honolulu: University of Hawai'i Press, 1970.

Beechert, Edward D. *Working in Hawaii: A Labor History*. Honolulu: University of Hawai'i Press, 1985.

Beezley, William H., and Joseph P. Hobbs. " 'Nice Girls Don't Sweat': Women in American Sport." In *The Sporting Image: Readings in American Sport History*, edited by Paul J. Zingg. Lanham, Md.: University Press of New York, 1988.

Behrens, John. *The Typewriter Guerillas: Closeups of 20 Top Investigative Reporters*. Chicago: Nelson-Hall, 1977.

Benjaminson, Peter. *Death in the Afternoon: America's Newspaper Giants Struggle for Survival*. Kansas City: Andrews, McMeel & Parker, 1984.

Bennett, W. Lance. *News: The Politics of Illusion*. New York: Longman, 1983.

Bennion, Sherilyn Cox. *Equal to the Occasion: Women Editors of the Nineteenth-Century West*. Reno: University of Nevada Press, 1990.

Bent, Silas. *Newspaper Crusaders: A Neglected Story*. Westport, Conn.: McGraw Hill, 1939.

Berelson, Bernard, and Morris Janowitz, eds. *Reader in Public Opinion and Communication*. Glencoe, Ill.: The Free Press, 1950.

Bessie, Simon Michael. *Jazz Journalism: The Story of the Tabloid Newspapers*. New York: Russell & Russell, 1938.

Bingham, Hiram. *A Residence of Twenty-one Years in the Sandwich Islands; or the Civil, Religious, and Political History*. Hartford, Conn.: Hezekiah Huntington, 1847.

Black, Cobey. "Man [William Ewing] Behind the News." *Honolulu Beacon*, September 1963.

Black, Donald. *The Behavior of Law*. New York: Academic Press, 1976.

Bowman, Donald. "The Betterment of Industrial Relations." *Hawaiian Sugar Planters' Record* 25 (1921): 227–300.

———. "General Welfare Work." *Hawaiian Sugar Planters' Record* 23 (1920): 134–138.

Boylan, Dan. "Maui's Mayor." *Aloha* 17, no. 8 (August 1992): 16–17.

Brandsberg, George. *The Free Papers*. Ames, Iowa: Wordsmith Books, 1969.

Breed, Warren. "Social Control in the Newsroom: A Functional Analysis." *Social Forces* 33, no. 4 (May 1955): 335.

Brendon, Piers. *The Life and Death of the Press Barons*. New York: Atheneum, 1983.

Brislin, Tom. "Hawaii's Japanese Press, Dual Identities: A History, Status and Outlook." Paper presented for the Association for Education in Journalism and Mass Communication, Atlanta, March 26–28, 1992.
———. "Weep into Silence/Cries of Rage: Bitter Divisions in Hawai'i's Japanese Press." Paper presented for the 88th Annual Meeting, American Historical Association, Pacific Coast Branch, Wailea, August 4–7, 1995.
Brown, Lee. *The Reluctant Reformation: On Criticizing the Press in America.* New York: David McKay Co., 1974.
Buchwach, Buck. *Hawaii, U.S.A.: Communist Beachhead or Showcase for Americanism.* Honolulu: Hawaii Statehood Commission, April 1957.
Burnett, Gerald B. Early Printing in Hawaii. In his Notes and Papers, Hawaiian Mission Children's Society.
Bushnell, O. A. *The Gifts of Civilization: Germs and Genocide in Hawai'i.* Honolulu: University of Hawai'i Press, 1993.
Byrne, Desmond. Talk on the Honolulu Community-Media Council presented to the West Honolulu Rotary Club, Honolulu, March 12, 1993.
Cabinet Council Minute Book, 1874–1891. Hawai'i State Archives.
Caraway, Nancie. "The 60 Minutes Survival Course." *Hawaii Business,* February 1984, 50–56.
Carey, James W. *Communication as Culture: Essays on Media and Society.* Boston: Unwin Hyman, 1989.
Castle Collection. No. 538. Hawaiian Mission Children's Society.
Cater, Douglas. *The Fourth Branch of Government.* Boston: Houghton Mifflin Co., 1959.
Chafee, Zechariah H., Jr. Commission on Freedom of the Press, *A Free and Responsible Press: A General Report on Mass Communication: Newspapers, Radio, Motion Pictures, Magazines, and Books.* 2 vols. Chicago: Chicago University Press, 1947.
Chambers, William, and Robert Chambers. "A Honolulu Newspaper." *Chambers' Journal of Popular Literature* 3, no. 55 (January 20, 1855): 148–157.
Chang, Thelma. "The Banzai Byline." *Hawaii Business News,* September 1984, 99–100.
Chang, Won H. "Characteristics and Self Perceptions of Women's Page Editors." *Journalism Quarterly* (spring 1975): 61–65.
Chapin, Helen Geracimos. "From Makaweli to Kohala: The Plantation Newspapers of Hawai'i." *The Hawaiian Journal of History* 23 (1989): 170–195.
———. "Newspapers of Hawaii 1834 to 1903: From *He Liona* to the Pacific Cable." *The Hawaiian Journal of History* 18 (1984): 47–86.
Chapin, Helen Geracimos, and David W. Forbes. "The Folio of 1855 — A Plea for Women's Rights." *The Hawaiian Journal of History* 19 (1985): 122–133.
Char, Tin-Yuke. "The Chinese Press." In *Communications, Encyclopedia of Hawaii.* Hawai'i State Archives. Microfilm.
Char, Tin-Yuke, and Wai Jane Char. "The First Chinese Contract Laborers." *The Hawaiian Journal of History* 9 (1975): 128–134.
"Chinn Ho's Growing Group of Newspapers," *Hawaii Business,* February 1971, 57–61.

Cirillo, Joan J. "Suit Suite: After Settling a Major Job-Discrimination Suit, AP Is Slowly Percolating Women and Minorities up Through the Ranks." *Quill,* December 1984, 14–18.

Clark, Charles E. *Three Hundred Years of the American Newspaper.* East Brunswick, N.J.: Associated University Presses, 1981.

Clurman, Richard M. *Beyond Malice: The Media's Years of Reckoning.* New Brunswick, N.J.: Transaction Publishers, 1988.

Coffman, Tom. *Catch a Wave: A Case Study of Hawaii's New Politics.* Honolulu: University Press of Hawai'i, 1973.

Cohen, Marty. "The Perils of Publishing Journalism Reviews." *Columbia Journalism Review,* November–December 1972, 25–43.

Collier, Peter, and David Horowitz. *The Rockefellers: An American Dynasty.* New York: Holt, Rinehart & Winston, 1976.

Compaine, Benjamin M., ed. *Who Owns the Media?* 2nd ed. White Plains, N.Y.: Knowledge Industry Publications, 1982.

Cooper, George, comp. *Seamen's Chaplain: Reflections on the Life of Samuel Damon.* Honolulu: Signature Publishing, 1992.

Cose, Ellis. *The Press.* New York: William Morrow & Co., 1989.

Council of State Minutes of Meetings, July 1, 1895–July 27, 1898. Hawai'i State Archives.

Crespi, Irving. *Pre-election Polling: Sources of Accuracy and Error.* New York: Russell Sage Foundation, ca. 1988.

———. *Public Opinion, Polls, and Democracy.* Boulder: Westview Press, 1989.

Criminal Cases, 1870–1900. Hawai'i State Archives.

Crocombe, Ron, ed. *Land Tenure in the Pacific.* Melbourne: Oxford University Press, 1971.

Crouse, Timothy. *The Boys on the Bus.* New York: Random House, 1972.

Culliney, John L. *Islands in a Far Sea: Nature and Man in Hawaii.* San Francisco: Sierra Club Books, 1988.

Currie, Phil R. "The Journalism of Mismanagement." *The Bulletin of the American Society of Newspaper Editors,* April 1984.

Curry, Jane Leftwish, and Joan R. Dassin, eds. *Press Control Around the World.* New York: Praeger Publishers, 1982.

Damon, Ethel M. *Sanford Ballard Dole and His Hawaii.* Palo Alto: Pacific Books, 1957.

Davies, Kath, et al. *Out of Focus: Writings on Women and the Media.* London: The Women's Press, 1987.

Davis, Eleanor. *Abraham Fornander: A Biography.* Honolulu: University Press of Hawai'i, 1979.

Davis, Joseph S. *The World Between the Wars, 1919–39: An Economist's View.* Baltimore: Johns Hopkins University Press, 1975.

Daws, Gavan. *A Dream of Islands: Voyages of Self-Discovery in the South Seas.* New York: W. W. Norton & Co., 1980.

———. *Shoal of Time: A History of the Hawaiian Islands.* Honolulu: University Press of Hawai'i, 1968.

Day, Arthur G., and Albertine Loomis. *Ka Pa'i Palapala, Early Printing in Hawaii.* Honolulu: Printing Industries of Hawaii, 1973.

Day, Nancy L. "Women Journalists: Professional/Personal Conflicts." *Nieman Reports* (summer 1979): 34–40.

Day, Richard R. "The Ultimate Inequality: Linguistic Genocide." In *Language of Inequality*, edited by Nessa Wolfson and Joan Manes. New York: Mouton Publishers, 1985.

Dennis, Everette E., and Willian L. Rivers. *Other Voices: The New Journalism in America*. San Francisco: Canfield Press, 1974.

Desmond, Robert W. *Crisis and Conflict: World News Reporting Between Two Wars, 1920–1940*. Iowa City: University of Iowa Press, 1982.

———. *Tides of War: World News Reporting, 1940–1945*. Iowa City: University of Iowa Press, 1984.

———. *Windows on the World: The Information Process in a Changing Society, 1900–1920*. Iowa City: University of Iowa Press, 1980.

Diamond, Edwin. "Multiplying Media Voices." *Columbia Journalism Review* [winter 1969–1970]: 22–27.

Dionisio, Juan C., ed. "The Filipinos in Hawaii: The First 75 Years: 1906–1981." *Fil-Am Courier*, November 1990.

Doig, Ivan, and Carol Doig. *News: A Consumer's Guide*. Englewood Cliffs, N.J.: Prentice-Hall, 1972.

"Donnybrook at the Newsstands," *Hawaii Business*, April 1977.

Dorsey, John. *On Mencken*. New York: Alfred A. Knopf, 1980.

Dudley, Michael Kioni, and Keoni Kealoha Agard. *A Call for Hawaiian Sovereignty*. 2 vols. Honolulu: Na Kane O Ka Malo Press, 1990.

Dunnet, Peter J. S. *The World Newspaper Industry*. London: Croom Helm, 1988.

Dutton, Meiric K. *Final Years of the Sandwich Islands Mission Press*. Honolulu: Loomis House Press, 1956.

———. *Henry M. Whitney: Pioneer Printer-Publisher and Hawaii's First Postmaster*. Honolulu: Loomis House Press, 1955.

Edwards, Herman S., and Noam Chomsky. *Manufacturing Consent: The Political Economy of the Mass Media*. New York: Pantheon Books, 1988.

Edwards, Julia. *Women of the World: The Great Foreign Correspondents*. Boston: Houghton Mifflin, 1988.

Emery, Edwin. *Introduction to Mass Communications*. 4th ed. New York: Dodd, Mead & Co., 1975.

———, ed. *The Story of America as Reported by Its Newspapers From 1690–1965*. New York: Simon & Schuster, 1965.

Emery, Michael C., ed. *America's Front Page News, 1690–1970*. Minneapolis: VIS-Com, 1970.

Emery, Michael C., and Edwin Emery. *The Press and America: An Interpretative History of Journalism*. Englewood Cliffs, N.J.: Prentice-Hall, 1992.

Encyclopedia of Hawaii. Edited by Robert Scott. Hawai'i State Archives, 1980. Microfilm.

Enomoto, Ernestine K. "The Hawaii Smith Act Case of 1951: An Examination of the Japanese Response." Senior thesis, Department of History, University of Hawai'i at Mānoa, May 1971.

Evans, Harold. *Editing and Design*. Vol. 5, *Newspaper Design*. New York: Holt, Rinehart & Winston, 1978.

Felix, John Henry, and Peter F. Senecal. *The Portuguese in Hawaii*. Honolulu: published by the authors, 1978.

Ferguson, James M. *The Advertising Rate Structure in the Daily Newspaper*. Englewood Cliffs, N.J.: Prentice-Hall, 1963.

Final Report of the ASUH Athletic Investigation Panel. [Honolulu], September 28, 1976. Elly Chong, chair.

Firsts in Hawaii. Edited by Ronn Ronck from materials compiled by Robert C. Schmitt. Honolulu: University of Hawai'i Press, 1995.

Fishman, Joshua. *Language Loyalty in the United States: The Maintenance and Perpetuation of Non-English Mother Tongues by American Ethnic and Religious Groups.* The Hague: Mouton & Co., 1966.

Fishman, Mark. *Manufacturing the News.* Austin: University of Texas Press, 1980.

Fixx, James F. "Journalists Behind Bars." *Saturday Review,* March 9, 1963, 54.

Forer, Lois G. *A Chilling Effect: The Growing Threat of Libel and Invasion of Privacy Actions to the First Amendment.* New York: W. W. Norton & Co., 1987.

Foster, Nelson, ed. *Punahou: The History and Promise of a School of the Islands.* Honolulu: Punahou School, 1991.

Frear, W. F. "The Development of Hawaiian Statute Law." In *Thirteenth Annual Report of the Hawaiian Historical Society.* Honolulu, 1906.

———. "The Evolution of the Hawaiian Judiciary." Papers of *the Hawaiian Historical Society,* no. 7 (June 29, 1894).

Fuchs, Laurence H. *Hawaii Pono: A Social History.* New York: Harcourt, Brace & World, 1961.

Fuhrman, Candace Jacobson. *Publicity Stunt: Great Staged Events That Made the News.* Chronicle Books, ca. 1989.

Fulton, Marianne. *Eyes of Time: Photojournalism in America.* Boston: Little Brown & Co., 1988.

Gannett News Service. *Equality: America's Unfinished Business.* Fort Myers, Fla.: News Press, 1981.

Gans, Herbert J. *What's News: A Study of CBS Evening News, NBC Nightly News, Newsweek, and Time.* New York: Pantheon Books, ca. 1979.

Garraty, John A. *The Great Depression.* New York: Harcourt Brace Jovanovich, 1956.

Gartner, Michael. "The First Rough Draft of History." *American Heritage,* October–November 1982, 33–48.

Geis, Gilbert. *Not the Law's Business? An Examination of Homosexuality, Abortion, Prostitution, Narcotics and Gambling in the United States.* Rockville, Md.: National Institute of Mental Health Center for Studies of Crime and Delinquency, 1972.

"A General Outline of Chinese Newspapers." *Liberty News,* Honolulu: August 31, 1936.

Ghiglione, Loren. *The Buying and Selling of America's Newspapers.* Indianapolis: R. J. Berg & Co., 1984.

Gibson, Walter Murray. *The Diaries of Walter Murray Gibson.* Edited by Jacob Adler and Gwynn Barrett. Honolulu: University of Hawai'i Press, 1973.

Giles, Robert H. *Newsroom Management: A Guide to Theory and Practice.* Indianapolis: R. J. Berg & Co. 1987.

Gitlin, Todd. *Sixties: Years of Hope, Days of Rage.* Toronto: Bantam Books, 1987.

———. *The Whole World is Watching: Mass Media in the Making and Unmaking of the New Left.* Berkeley: University of California Press, 1980.

Glessing, Robert J. *The Underground Press in America.* Bloomington: Indiana University Press, 1970.

Glick, Clarence E. *Sojourners and Settlers: Chinese Migrants in Hawaii.* Honolulu: Hawaii Chinese History Center and University Press of Hawai'i, 1980.

Goldblatt, Louis. *Louis Goldblatt, Working Class Leader in the ILWU, 1935–1977.* 2 vols. Berkeley: Regional Oral History Office, Bancroft Library, University of California, 1980.

Golden, Renny, and Michael McConnell. *Sanctuary: The New Underground Railroad.* Maryknoll, N.Y.: Orbis Books, 1986.

Goldstein, Richard. *Reporting the Counterculture.* Boston: Unwin Hyman, 1989.

Goldstein, Tom, ed. *Killing the Messenger: 100 Years of Media Criticism.* New York: Columbia University Press, 1989.

Good, Howard. *Acquainted with the Night: The Image of Journalism, 1890–1950.* Metuchen, N.J.: Scarecrow Press, 1986.

Gora, Joel M. *The Rights of Reporters: The Basic ACLU Guide to a Reporter's Rights.* New York: Sunrise Books / E. P. Dutton, 1974.

Graber, Doris A. *Processing the News: How People Tame the Information Tide.* New York: Longman, 1984.

Gray, Francine du Plessix. *Hawaii: The Sugar-Coated Fortress.* New York: Random House, 1972.

Greer, Richard. "Collarbone and the Social Evil." *The Hawaiian Journal of History* 7 (1973): 3–17.

———. "The Founding of Queen's Hospital." *The Hawaiian Journal of History* 3 (1969a): 110–145.

———. "In the Shadow of Death." In *Hawaii Historical Review.* Honolulu: Hawaiian Historical Society, 1969b.

———. "Oahu's Ordeal—The Smallpox Epidemic of 1853." In *Hawaii Historical Review.* Honolulu: Hawaiian Historical Society, 1969c.

Gregg, David L. *The Diaries of David Laurence Gregg: An American Diplomat in Hawaii, 1853–1858.* Edited by Pauline King. Honolulu: Hawaiian Historical Society, 1982.

Guenin, Zena Beth. "Woman's Pages in American Newspapers: Missing Out on Contemporary Content." *Journalism Quarterly* (spring 1975): 66–69.

Hackleman, Jim. "Parting Shots." Talk on sports reporting to the Honolulu Media–Community Council, June 28, 1992.

"Hagadone Expands Kauai Publishing." *Hawaii Business and Industry,* October 1968, 41–43.

Hallin, David C. *The "Uncensored" War: The Media and Vietnam.* New York: Oxford University Press, 1986.

Handbook for Newswriting Advisers. Honolulu: Office of Instructional Services, Department of Education, May 1965.

Harris, Frank. *Presentation of Crime in Newspapers: A Study of Methods in Newspaper Research.* Hanover, N.H.: The Sociological Press, 1932.

Harrison, John M., and Harry H. Stein, eds. *Muckraking Past, Present and Future.* University Park: Pennsylvania State University Press, 1973.

Harriss, Julian, et al. *The Complete Reporter: Fundamentals of News Gathering, Writing and Editing.* 4th ed. New York: Macmillan, 1981.

"Hawaii Clipping Services: Keeping Track of the News." *Hawaii Business,* April 1973, 79–82.

Hawaii Kingdom. Cabinet Council Minute Book, 1864–1891. Hawai'i State Archives.

————. Council of State Minutes of Meetings, July 1, 1895–July 27, 1898. Hawai'i State Archives.

Hawaii Media Guide. Honolulu: Aloha United Way, 1977, 1978.

Hawaii Newspaper Agency. *The News Building: Home of the "Honolulu Advertiser," "Honolulu Star-Bulletin," "Sunday Star-Bulletin & Advertiser."* Honolulu: Hawaii Newspaper Agency, 1966.

Hawaii Newspapers: A Union List. Sophie McMillen, cataloger and Nancy Morris, project manager. Honolulu: Hawaii Newspaper Project, 1987.

Hawaii Poll Survey. A Study of the Daily and Sunday Newspaper Penetration on the Island of Oahu. Honolulu: Robert S. Craig Associates, July 1961.

Hawaiian Ethnological Notes. Indexed by Elspeth Sterling and translated by Mary Kawena Pukui, n.d. Bernice Pauahi Bishop Museum.

Hawaiian Sugar Planters' Association (HSPA). Report prepared by the Social Welfare Committee on Labor Conditions in Hawaii. Miscellaneous papers, 1919. HSPA Archives.

————. Territorial Surveys: Summary and Analysis of Findings of Readership Study and a Readability Test of the *Plantation News,* Issue of February 13, 1948. HSPA Archives.

"Hawaii's Biggest Believer in Newspaper Advertising." *Hawaii Business.* November 1971, 61–64.

Hazard, William R. "Responses to News Pictures: A Study in Perceptual Unity." *Journalism Quarterly* (autumn 1960): 515–524.

Herman, Edward S., and Noam Chomsky. *Manufacturing Consent: The Political Economy of the Mass Media.* New York: Pantheon Books, 1988.

Hertzgaard, Mark. *On Bended Knee: The Press and the Reagan Presidency.* New York: Farrar Straus Giroux, 1988.

Hess, Stephen, and Milton Kaplan. *The Ungentlemanly Art: A History of American Political Cartoons.* New York: Macmillan, 1975.

Heuvel, John Vanden. *Untapped Sources: America's Newspaper Archives and Histories.* Edited by Craig LaMay and Martha FitzSimmon. New York: Gannett Foundation Media Center at Columbia University, April 1991.

Hicks, Wilson. *Words and Pictures: Photographic Communication.* New York: Hastings House, 1972.

Hills, John. "The Community's Voice." *Maui Inc.* 6, no. 6 (November–December 1941): 20–25.

Hobson, Barbara Meil. *Uneasy Virtue: The Politics of Prostitution and the American Reform Tradition.* New York: Basic Books, 1987.

Hohenberg, John. *A Crisis for the American Press.* New York: Columbia University Press, 1978.

————. *Free Press/Free People: The Best Cause.* New York: Columbia University Press, 1971.

————. *The New Front Page.* New York: Columbia University Press, 1966.

Hollingsworth, D. Jeffrey. "Farrington: Hawaii's Maine Man." *Honolulu,* November 1985, 94–99, 145–149.

Holmes, Thomas Michael. "The Reinecke Case: A Study in Administrative Injustice." *Hawaii Bar Journal* 12, no. 3 (fall 1976): 3–40.

———. *The Specter of Communism in Hawaii, 1947–1953.* Honolulu: University of Hawai'i Press, 1994.

Hooper, Paul F. *Elusive Destiny: The Internationalist Movement in Modern Hawaii.* Honolulu: University Press of Hawai'i, 1979.

Hormann, Bernhard Lothar. "The Caucasian Minority." *Social Process in Hawaii* 14 (1950): 38–50

———. "The Germans in Hawaii." Master's thesis, University of Hawai'i, 1931.

———. "Hawaii's Linguistic Situation: A Sociological Interpretation in the New Key." *Social Process in Hawaii* 24 (1960): 6–31.

———. "The Significance of the Wilder or Major-Palakiko Case, a Study in Public Opinion." *Social Process in Hawaii* 17 (1953): 1–13.

Hormann, Helmut W. "The Germans." *Social Process in Hawaii* 29 (1982): 78–82.

Horton, Brian. *The Associated Press: Photo-Journalism Style Book.* Reading, Mass.: Addison-Wesley Publishing Co., 1990.

Horvalt, William J. *Above the Pacific.* Fallbrook, Calif.: Aero Publishers, 1966.

Howell, Beatrice. *Hawaii, Pioneer of Far Western Printing.* Patterson, N.J.: John Royle, 1963.

Hoyt, Helen. "Hawaii's First English Newspaper and its Editor." In *Hawaiian Historical Society Annual Report.* Honolulu: Hawaiian Historical Society, 1954.

Hughes, Helen MacGill. *News and the Human Interest Story.* New Brunswick, N.J.: Transaction Books, 1981.

Hughes, Judith R. "The Demise of the English Standard School System in Hawai'i." *The Hawaiian Journal of History* 27 (1993): 65–90.

Hunter, Charles. Newspapers Published in Hawaii. Card index, compiled 1953. Revised by Dr. Hunter and Janet E. Bell, University of Hawai'i.

Hynds, Ernest C. *American Newspapers in the 1970s.* New York: Hastings House, 1975.

———. *American Newspapers in the 1980s.* New York: Hastings House, 1980.

Index to the "Honolulu Advertiser" and "Honolulu Star-Bulletin." Honolulu: Office of Library Services, 1929–1967, 1968– .

Innis, Harold. *The Bias of Communication.* Toronto: University of Toronto Press, 1951.

———. *Culture, Communication, and Dependency.* Norwood, N.J.: Ablex Publishers Corp., 1980.

———. *Empire and Communications.* Toronto: University of Toronto Press, 1972.

International Typographical Union 106th Annual Convention. Souvenir Album. Honolulu, 1964.

Isaacs, Harold R. *Idols of the Tribe: Group Identity and Political Change.* New York: Harper & Row, 1975.

Isaacs, Norman E. *Untended Gates: The Mismanaged Press.* New York: Columbia University Press, 1986.

Iwamoto, Lana. "The Plague and Fire of 1899–1900 in Honolulu." In *Hawaii Historical Review: Selected Readings,* 22–41. Honolulu: Hawaiian Historical Society, 1969.

Izuka, Ichiro. *The Truth About Communism in Hawaii.* Honolulu: published by the author, 1947.

Joesting, Edward. *Hawaii: An Uncommon History.* New York: W. W. Norton & Co., 1972.

Johnson, Donald D. "History of the City and County of Honolulu." Typescript. University of Hawai'i, 1977.

———. *Honolulu: The City and County of Honolulu: A Governmental Chronicle.* Honolulu: University of Hawai'i Press and City Council of the City and County of Honolulu, 1991.

———. "James Joseph Fern, Honolulu's First Mayor." *The Hawaiian Journal of History* 9 (1975): 74–100.

Johnson, Michael L. *The New Journalism: The Underground Press, the Artists of Nonfiction, and Changes in the Established Media.* Lawrence: University Press of Kansas, 1971.

Johnson, Rubellite Kawena Kinney. *Kūkini 'aha 'ilono* (Carry on the news): *Over a Century of Native Hawaiian Life and Thought From the Hawaiian Language Newspapers of 1834 to 1948.* Honolulu: Topgallant Publishing Co., 1976.

Journalism Department, University of Hawai'i at Mānoa, and The Society of Professional Journalists, UH Student Chapter. *Survey of Hawaii's Newsrooms, 1985.* [Honolulu], 1985.

Judd, Gerrit P., IV. *Hawaii: An Informal History.* New York: Macmillan, 1961.

Judd, Gerrit Parmele. *Dr. Judd, Hawaii's Friend: A Biography of Gerrit Parmele Judd.* Honolulu: University of Hawai'i Press, 1960.

Kalanianaole, Jonah Kuhio. Kamehameha IV's Reign, 1860–1861. M80, Private Collection. Hawai'i State Archives.

Kame'eleihiwa, Lilikalā. *Native Land and Foreign Desires—Pehea La E Pono Ai?* Honolulu: Bishop Museum Press, 1992.

Karp, Richard, "Newpaper Food Pages: Credibility for Sale." *Columbia Journalism Review,* November–December 1971, 36–44.

"The Kauai Times: Going on the road?" *Hawaii Business,* July 1983, 1982.

Kennedy, Bruce A. *Community Journalism: A Way of Life.* Ames: Iowa State University, 1974.

Kenny, Herbert C. *Newspaper Row: Journalism in the Pre-television Era.* Chester, Conn.: Globe Pequot Press, 1987.

Kent, Noel J. *Hawaii: Islands Under the Influence.* New York: Monthly Review Press, 1983.

Kerkvliet, Melinda Tria. "Pablo Manlapit's Fight for Justice." *Social Process in Hawaii* 33 (1991): 153–168.

Kessler, Lauren. *The Dissident Press: Alternative Journalism in American History.* Beverly Hills: Sage Hill Publications, 1984.

Kimura, Larry L. "Language." In vol. 1, *Native Hawaiian Study Commission Report: Report on the Culture, Needs, and Concerns of Native Hawaiians,* June 23, 1983. Washington, D.C.: U.S. Government Printing Office, 1985.

Kinsey, Alfred Charles. *Sexual Behavior in the Human Female.* Philadelphia: Saunders, 1953.

Kirsch, Donald. *Financial and Economic Journalism: Analysis, Interpretation, and Reporting.* New York: New York University Press, 1978.

Kishi, Arnold. "The Japanese Press." In *Communications, Encyclopedia of Hawaii.* Hawai'i State Archives. Microfilm.

Klaidman, Stephen. *Health in the Headlines: The Stories Behind the Stories.* New York: Oxford University Press, 1991.

Knowlton, Edgar. "The Portuguese Language Press of Hawaii." *Social Process in Hawaii* 24 (1960): 89–99.

Kobayashi, Victor N., ed. *Building a Rainbow: A History of the Building and Grounds of the University of Hawaii's Manoa Campus.* Honolulu: Hui o Students University of Hawai'i at Mānoa, 1983.

Kobre, Sidney. *The Yellow Press and Gilded Age Journalism.* Tallahassee: Florida State University, 1964.

Kotani, Roland. "The Makino Legacy." *Hawaii Herald,* September 3, 1982.

Kraditor, Aileen S. *Up From the Pedestal: Selected Writings in the History of American Feminism.* Chicago: Quadrangle Books, 1968.

Krieger, Susan. *Hip Capitalism.* Beverly Hills: Sage Publications, 1979.

Kuykendall, Ralph S. *Hawaii in the World War.* Honolulu: The Historical Commission, 1928.

———. *The Hawaiian Kingdom,* Vol. 1, *1778–1854, Foundation and Transformation.* Honolulu: University Press of Hawai'i, 1938.

———. *The Hawaiian Kingdom,* Vol. 2, *1854–1874, Twenty Critical Years.* Honolulu: University of Hawai'i Press, 1953.

———. *The Hawaiian Kingdom,* Vol. 3, *1874–1893, The Kalakaua Dynasty.* Honolulu: University of Hawai'i Press, 1967.

———. "Thomas George Thrum, A Sketch of His Life." *Hawaiian Annual,* 1933.

Kuykendall, Ralph S., and A. Grove Day. *Hawaii: A History From Polynesian Kingdom to American State.* Rev. ed. Englewood Cliffs, N.J.: Prentice-Hall, 1976.

Lai, H. M. "The Chinese Community Press in Hawaii." In *The Ethnic Press in the United States: An Analysis and Handbook,* edited by Sally Miller. New York: Greenwood Press, 1987.

Lang, Gladys Engel. *The Battle for Public Opinion: The President, the Press, and the Polls During Watergate.* New York: Columbia University Press, 1983.

Lee, Robert M. "First Chinese Daily Still Going Strong." In *The Chinese in Hawaii: A Historical Sketch.* Honolulu: Advertiser Publishing Co., 1961.

Lehman, Tenney K. "A Focus on Women and Journalism," *Nieman Reports* 3 (summer 1979): 3.

Leonard, Thomas C. *The Power of the Press: The Birth of American Reporting.* New York: Oxford University Press, 1986.

"Leprosy and Libel. The Suit of George L. Fitch Against the Saturday Press." In *Hawaiian Pamphlets.* Vol. 3, no. 13. Honolulu: Saturday Press, 1883.

Lerner, Daniel, and Jim Richstad. *Communication in the Pacific: A Report on the Communication in the Pacific Conference Held in Honolulu in May 1975,* East-West Center. Honolulu: June 1976.

Levy, Neil M. "Native Hawaiian Land Rights." *California Law Review* 63 (July 1975): 84–85.

Liebling, A. J. *The Press.* New York: Ballantine Books, 1961.

Liholiho: The Voyages Made to the United States, England and France in 1849–1850. Edited by Jacob Adler. Honolulu: University of Hawai'i Press for the Hawaiian Historical Society, 1967.

Liliuokalani, Queen of Hawaii. *Hawaii's Story By Hawaii's Queen.* Boston: Lathrop, Lee & Shepard, 1898.

Lim-Chong, Lily. "Opium and the Law in Hawaii: 1856–1900." Master's thesis, University of Hawai'i, spring 1978.

Limerick, Patricia Nelson. *The Legacy of Conquest: The Unbroken Past of the American West.* New York: W. W. Norton & Co., 1987.

Lingenfelter, Richard E. *Presses of the Pacific Islands 1816–1867: A History of the First Half Century of Printing in the Pacific islands.* Los Angeles: The Plantin Press, 1967.

Lippmann, Walter. *Public Opinion.* New York: Harcourt, Brace & Co., 1922.

Lister. Hal. *The Suburban Press: A Separate Journalism.* Columbia, Mo.: Lucas Brothers, 1975.

Lo, Catherine, ed. *The Garden Island Index, 1971–1980: A Subject, Author, and Photographer Index to Selected Articles in the Garden Island.* Lihue: Kauai Library Association, 1987.

Lo, Karl, and H. M. Lai, comps. *Chinese Newspapers Published in North America, 1854–1975.* Washington: Center for Chinese Research Materials Association of Research Libraries, 1977.

Loomis, Albertine. *For Whom Are the Stars?* Honolulu: University Press of Hawai'i and Friends of the Library, 1976.

———. "Summer of 1898." *The Hawaiian Journal of History* 13 (1979): 94–98.

Lotz, Ray Edward. *Crime in the American Press.* New York: Praeger, 1991.

Lueck, Vaughn. "Hierarchy and Diffusion: The Sunday Newspaper in the United States." In *An Invitation to Geography,* by David A. Lanegran and Risa Palm. 2nd ed. New York: McGraw Hill, 1973.

Luter, John. "In Newspapers and Magazines." In *The Changing Lives of Hawaii's Women,* edited by Ruth Lieban. Honolulu: Foundation for Hawaii Women's History Historians Committee, 1985.

Lydecker, Robert C., comp. *Roster Legislatures of Hawaii 1841–1918.* Honolulu: Hawaiian Gazette Co., 1918.

MacBride Commission (UNESCO). *Many Voices, One World: Towards a New More Just and More Efficient World Information and Communication Order.* London: Kogan Press, 1980.

MacDonald, Alexander. *Revolt in Paradise: The Social Revolution After Pearl Harbor.* New York: S. Daye, ca. 1944.

MacDonald, Peter. "Fixed in Time: A Brief History of Kahoolawe." *The Hawaiian Journal of History* 6 (1972): 69–90.

MacDougall, Curtis D. *Interpretative Reporting.* New York: Macmillan, 1968.

MacKintosh, Stephen D. Scrapbook, 1837–1839 at Honolulu. M168. Hawai'i State Archives.

Manlapit, Pablo. *Filipinos Fight for Justice: The Case of the Filipino Laborers in the Big Strike of 1924.* Territory of Hawaii. Honolulu: Kumalae Publishing, 1933.

Marquette University. *Social Responsibility of the Press.* Milwaukee: Marquette University, 1962.

Martindale, Carolyn. *The White Press and Black America.* New York: Greenwood Press, 1986.

Marzolf, Marion. *Up From the Footnote: A History of Women Journalists.* New York: Hastings House, 1977.

Mayo, Donald S. "Island Profile: Yasutaro Soga." *Paradise of the Pacific* 69, no. 4 (April 1957): 26, 36.

McGregor-Alegado, Davianna. "Hawaiian Resistance, 1887–1889." Master's thesis, University of Hawai'i, 1979.

McKinney, Albert J. "A Study of the Treatment of Education in the Daily Newspapers in Honolulu." Master's thesis, University of Hawai'i, June 1940.

McLean, Malcolm S., and Anne Li-an Kao. "Picture Selection: An Editorial Game." *Journalism Quarterly* (spring 1963): 230–232.

McLuhan, Marshall. *The Gutenberg Galaxy: The Making of Typographic Man.* Toronto: University of Toronto Press, 1962.

———. *Understanding Media: The Extensions of Man.* New York: New American Library, 1964.

McMillan, Michael. "The Korean Press." In Communications, Encyclopedia of Hawaii. Hawai'i State Archives. Microfilm.

McMillen, Sophia, cataloger, and Nancy Morris, project manager. *Inventory of Newspapers Published in Hawaii: Preliminary List.* Honolulu, n.d.

———. *Hawaii Newspapers: Union List.* Honolulu: Hawaii Newspaper Project, 1987.

McNamara, Robert M. "Hawaii's Smith Act Case." Master's thesis, University of Hawai'i, August 1960.

Men and Women of Hawaii: A Biographical Dictionary. Vols. 1–9. Honolulu: Honolulu Star-Bulletin Printing Co., 1917–1972.

Mencher, Melvin. "Romantics in the Newsroom." *Columbia Journalism Review,* September–October 1981, 41–43.

Mencken, H. L. *A Gang of Pecksniffs: And Other Comments on Newspaper Publishers, Editors and Reporters.* New Rochelle, N.Y.: Arlington House, 1975.

Men of Hawaii: The Story of Hawaii and Its Builders. Edited by George F. Nellist. Honolulu: Honolulu Star-Bulletin, 1925.

Merrill, John C. *The Dialectic in Journalism: Toward a Reponsible Use of Press Freedom.* Baton Rouge: Louisiana State University Press, 1989.

———. *The Elite Press: Great Newspapers of the World.* New York: Pitman Publishing Corp., 1968.

Merrill, John C., and Harold A. Fisher. *The World's Great Dailies.* New York: Hastings House, 1980.

Merrill, John C., and S. Jack Odell. *Philosophy of Journalism.* New York: Longman, 1983.

Merrill, John C., and Ralph D. Barney, eds. *Ethics and the Press: Readings in Mass Media Morality.* New York: Hastings House, 1975.

Merritt, Shayne, and Harriet Gross. "Women's Pages/Lifestyle Editors: Does Sex Make a Difference?" *Journalism Quarterly* (autumn 1978): 508–514.

Meyer, Philip. *Editors, Publishers, and Newspaper Ethics.* Washington: American Society of Newspaper Editors, 1983.

———. *Precision Journalism: A Reporter's Introduction to Social Science Methods.* Bloomington: Indiana University Press, 1973.

Miller, Susan H. "The Content of News Photos: Women's and Men's Roles." *Journalism Quarterly* (spring 1975): 70–75.

Mills, Kay. *A Place in the News: From the Women's Pages to the Front Pages.* New York: Dodd, Mead & Co., 1988.

Milz, Barbara. "Divorce *Advertiser* Style." *Hawaii Journalism Review,* April 1972, 2.

Miraldi, Robert. *Muckraking and Objectivity: Journalism's Colliding Traditions.* New York: Greenwood Press, 1990.

Missionary Album: Portraits and Biographical Sketches of the American

Protestant Missionaries to the Hawaiian Islands. Honolulu: Hawaiian Mission Children's Society, 1969.

Mitford, Jessica. *Poison Penmanship: The Gentle Art of Muckraking.* New York: Alfred A. Knopf, 1979.

Miyamoto, Kazue. *Hawaii: End of the Rainbow.* Rutland, Vt.: C. E. Tuttle, 1964.

Mookini, Esther K. *The Hawaiian Newspapers.* Honolulu: Topgallant Publishing Co., 1974.

———. *O Na Holoholona Wawae Eha o Ka Lama Hawaii: The Four-Footed Animals of Ka Lama Hawaii.* Honolulu: Bamboo Ridge Press, 1985.

Moorehead, Alan. *The Fatal Impact: An Account of the Invasion of the South Pacific 1767–1840.* New York: Harper & Row, 1966.

Mott, Frank Luther. *American Journalism: A History of Newspapers in the United States Through 260 Years: 1690 to 1950.* New York: Macmillan, 1950.

Murphy, Thomas D. *Ambassadors in Arms.* Honolulu: University of Hawai'i Press, 1955.

Nakamoto, Krisan. "Sakamaki Hall (1977)." In *Building a Rainbow: A History of the Buildings and Grounds of the University of Hawaii's Manoa Campus,* edited by Victor N. Kobayashi. Honolulu: Hui o Students University of Hawai'i at Mānoa, 1983.

Nakamura, Barry Seichi. "The Story of Waikiki and the 'Reclamation Project.'" Master's thesis, University of Hawai'i, May 1979.

Nakanaele, Thomas K. *Memoirs of Hon. Robt. William Wilcox.* Translated by Nancy Morris. Honolulu: Bishop Museum, 1981.

Nakano, Jiro. *Kona Echo: A Biography of Dr. Harvey Saburo Hayashi.* Kona: Kona Historical Society, 1990.

Nakano, Jiro, and Kay Nakano. *Poets Behind Barbed Wire.* Honolulu: Bamboo Ridge Press, 1984.

Native Hawaiian Study Commission Report: Report on the Culture, Needs, and Concerns of Native Hawaiians, June 23, 1983. Washington, D.C.: U.S. Government Printing Office, 1985.

Neier, Aryeh. "Surveillance as Censorship." In *The Campaign Against the Underground Press* by Geoffrey Ripps. San Francisco: City Lights Books, 1981.

Nelligan, Peter James. "Social Change and Rape Law in Hawaii." Ph.D. dissertation, University of Hawai'i, August 1983.

"The New Press Critics." Columbia Journalism Review, March/April 1972, 29–36.

Newspaper Clipping File, 1893–1898. Hawaiian Historical Society.

Nordyke, Eleanor C. *The Peopling of Hawaii.* 2nd ed. Honolulu: University of Hawai'i Press, 1989.

Norris, John. "Sanctuary, Church of the Crossroads, Aug. 6–Sept. 12, 1969." Honolulu, 1969. Typescript.

Norris, Stephen Sheffield. "The Pseudo-Event in the *Honolulu Advertiser* and the *Honolulu Star-Bulletin.*" Bachelor's thesis in journalism, University of Hawai'i, May 1967.

Novak, Michael. "Why the Working Man Hates the Media." In *Ethics and the Press: Readings in Mass Media Morality,* edited by John C. Merrill and Ralph D. Barney. New York: Hastings House, 1975.

Nowaki, Junko I., ed. *The Hawaii Island Newspaper Index: An Index to*

News of the Island of Hawaii as Reported in the "Hilo Tribune-Herald," the "Honolulu Advertiser," the "Honolulu Star-Bulletin." Hilo: Edwin H. Mookini Library, University of Hawai'i Hilo, 1989.

O'Hara, Jean. *My Life As a Honolulu Prostitute.* [Honolulu], 1944. University of Hawai'i. Mimeograph.

Okahata, James H. *A History of Japanese in Hawaii.* Honolulu: United Japanese Society of Hawaii, 1971.

Okimoto, Elaine, et al. *The "Hawaii Herald" Index.* Honolulu: Hawaii Herald, 1988.

Olasky, Marvin. *Central Ideas in the Development of American Journalism: A Narrative History.* Hillsdale, N.J.: L. Erlbaum Associates, 1991.

———. *Press and Abortion, 1838–1988.* Hillsdale, N.J.: L. Erlbaum Associates, 1988.

Packer, Peter, and Bob Thomas. *The Massie Case.* New York: Bantam, 1984.

Paneth, Donald. *The Encyclopedia of American Journalism.* New York: Facts on File Publications, 1983.

Park, R. E. *The Immigrant Press and Its Control.* New York: Harper & Brothers, 1922.

Peacock, Karen. "In Feminist Newsletters and Publications." In *The Changing Lives of Hawaii's Women,* edited by Ruth Lieban. Honolulu: Foundation for Women's History, 1984.

——— "In Feminist Newspapers and Publications." In *The Changing Lives of Hawaii's Women,* edited by Ruth Lieban. Rev. ed. Honolulu : Foundation of Hawaii Women's History Historians Committee, 1985.

Pease, W. Harper. Pease's catalogue of "Newspapers and Periodicals" in the order of their publication, *The Friend,* May 1, 1862.

Peck, Abe. *Uncovering the Sixties: The Life and Times of the Underground Press.* New York: Pantheon Books, 1985.

Peterson, Linda Ann. "Manifest Destiny and the Media: The Hawaiiian Revolution in 1893 as Local Occurrence and National Event." Masters thesis, University of Texas, August 1985.

———. "Power and Media Access: Using Content Analysis to Determine Power Relationships in Society." Unpublished paper, 1992.

Picard, Robert G., et al., eds. *Press Concentration and Monopoly: New Perspectives on Newspaper Ownership and Operation.* Norwood, N.J.: Ablex Publishing Corp., 1988.

Pollack, Richard, ed. *Stop the Presses, I Want to Get Off! Inside Stories of the News Business From the Pages of [More]* New York: Random House, 1975.

Postman, Neil. *Amusing Ourselves to Death: Public Discourse in the Age of Show Business.* New York: Viking Penguin, 1985.

Pratte, Paul A. "Everything Is Under Control." *Quill* 54, no. 12 (December 1966): 12–15.

———. "The Role of the *Honolulu Star-Bulletin* in the Hawaiian Statehood Movement." Ph.D. dissertation, University of Hawai'i, December 1976.

President's Statewide Athletic Committee. *Report of the Committee Appointed by the President to Investigate Allegations of Irregularities in the Intercollegiate Athletic Program, University of Hawaii at Manoa.* [Honolulu], September 28, 1976.

Press, Charles. *The Political Cartoon.* Rutherford, N.J.: Farleigh Dickinson University Press, 1981.

Press, Charles, and Kenneth Ver Burg. *American Politicians and Journalists.* Glenview, Ill.: Scott, Foresman, 1988.

"Press Control in the Hawaiian Islands." *Editor & Publisher,* June 4, 1921, 12.

Puette, William J. *The Hilo Massacre: Hawaii's Bloody Monday, August 1st, 1938.* Honolulu: University of Hawai'i College of Continuing Education and Community Service, Center for Labor Education and Research, 1988.

———. *Through Jaundiced Eyes: How the Media View Organized Labor.* Ithaca, N.Y.: ILR Press, 1992.

Pukui, Mary Kawena, and Samuel H. Elbert. *Hawaiian Dictionary.* Honolulu: University of Hawai'i Press, 1986.

Pukui, Mary Kawena, Samuel H. Elbert, and Esther T. Mookini. *Place Names of Hawaii.* Honolulu: The University Press of Hawai'i, 1974.

Quigg, Agnes. "Kalakaua's Study Abroad Program." *The Hawaiian Journal of History* 22 (1988).

Quinn, William F. "The Politics of Statehood." The Hawaiian Journal of History 18 (1984): 1–12.

Rankin, W. Parkman. *The Practice of Newspaper Management.* New York: Praegar, 1986

Rapson, Richard L. *Fairly Lucky You Live Hawaii: Cultural Pluralism in the Fiftieth State.* Lanham, Md.: University Press of America, 1980.

Reinecke, John E. "The Big Lie of 1920: How Planters and Press Used the Big Lie of 'Japanese Conspiracy' in Breaking the Oahu Sugar Strike." Honolulu, 1958. University of Hawai'i. Typescript.

———. *Feigned Necessity: Hawaii's Attempt to Obtain Chinese Contract Labor, 1921–23.* San Francisco: Chinese Materials Center, 1979.

Reynolds, Stephen. Journal, 1823–1842. Hawai'i State Archives.

Richstad, Jim A. "The Press Under Martial Law: The Hawaiian Experience." In *Journalism Monographs,* edited by Bruce H. Westley. No. 17. [Honolulu]: The Association for Education in Journalism, November 1970.

Richstad, Jim A., and Michael Macmillan, comps. *Mass Communication and Journalism in the Pacific Islands.* Honolulu: Published for the East-West Center by the University Press of Hawai'i, 1978.

Richstad, Jim A., and Michael H. Anderson, eds. *Crisis in International News: Policies and Prospects.* New York: Columbia University Press, 1981.

Rips, Geoffrey. *The Campaign Against the Underground Press.* San Francisco: City Lights Books, 1981.

Ritchie, Donald A. *Press Gallery: Congress and the Washington Correspondents.* Cambridge: Harvard University Press, 1991.

Rivers, William L. *The Other Government: Power and the Washington Media.* New York: Universe Books, 1982.

Rivers, William L., et al. *Backtalk: Press Councils in America.* San Francisco: Canfield Press, 1972.

Robertson, James. *An Accurate Version of Historical Truths. Review and Report from the "Independent."* Honolulu: Makaainana Printing House, 1897.

Russ, William Adam, Jr. *The Hawaiian Republic (1894–98) and Its Struggle to Win Annexation.* Vol. 2. Selinsgrove, Pa.: Susquehanna University Press, 1961.

———. *The Hawaiian Revolution (1893–94).* Vol. 1. Selinsgrove, Pa.: Susquehanna University Press, 1959.

Sakamaki, Shunzo. "A History of the Japanese Press in Hawaii." Master's thesis, University of Hawai'i, 1928.

Salmon, Lucy Maynard. *The Newspaper and the Historian.* New York: Oxford University Press, 1923.

Sato, Charlene. "Linguistic Inequality in Hawaii: The Post-Creole Dilemma." In *Language of Inequality,* edited by Nessa Wolfson and Joan Manes. New York: Mouton Publishers, 1985.

Satsuma, Gay. "Immigrant Patriotism: Hawaii Japanese and Imperial Victories, 1894–1905." *International Journal of Historical Studies* 1, no. 2 (March 1989): 59–83.

Schmitt, Robert C. "Catastrophic Mortality in Hawaii." *The Hawaiian Journal of History* 3 (1969): 66–86.

———. "Some Notes on Censorship in Hawai'i Before 1950." *The Hawaiian Journal of History* 28 (1994): 157–160.

———. *Demographic Statistics of Hawaii: 1778–1965.* Honolulu: University of Hawai'i Press. 1968.

———. *Historical Statistics of Hawaii.* Honolulu: University Press of Hawai'i, 1977.

———. "Notes on Hawaiian Photography Before 1890." *Hawaiian Historical Review* 2. no. 9 (October 1967): 409–416.

———. "Religious Statistics of Hawaii, 1825–1972." *The Hawaiian Journal of History* 7 (1973): 41–47.

———. "Some Construction and Housing Firsts in Hawaii." *The Hawaiian Journal of History* 15 (1981): 100–108.

———. "Some Firsts in Island Business and Government." *The Hawaiian Journal of History* 14 (1980): 80–108.

———. "Some Firsts in Island Leisure." *The Hawaiian Journal of History* 12 (1978): 99–119.

———. "Some Transportation and Communication Firsts in Hawaii." *The Hawaiian Journal of History* 13 (1979): 99–123.

———. "Survey Research in Hawaii Before 1950." *The Hawaiian Journal of History* 21 (1987): 110–125.

———. "Unemployment Rates in Hawaii During the 1930's." *The Hawaiian Journal of History* 10, (1976): 90–101.

Schmitt, Robert C., comp., and Ronn Ronck, ed. *Firsts in Hawaii.* Honolulu: University of Hawai'i Press, 1995.

Schudson, Michael. "Preparing the Minds of the People: Three Hundred Years of the American Newspaper." Paper for the American Antiquarian Society, Arlington, Virginia, November 12–14, 1990.

Seldes, George. *Lords of the Press.* New York: Julian Messner, 1938.

Shaw, David. *Press Watch: A Provocative Look at How Newspapers Report the News.* New York: Macmillan, 1984.

Shawcross, William. *Rupert Murdoch: Ringmaster of the Information Circus.* London: Chatto & Windus, 1992.

Sheehan, Ed. *Days of '41: Pearl Harbor Remembered.* Honolulu: Kapa Associates, 1976.

Sheldon, H. "Reminiscenses of Honolulu Thirty-Five Years Ago." Hawai'i State Archives. Typescript, n.d.

———. "Reminiscenses of the Press by one of the Press Gang." *Hawaiian Annual,* 1877.

Sheldon, H. L. "Historical Sketch of the Press in Honolulu." *Hawaiian Annual,* 1876.

Sheldon, J[ohn] G. M. "The Biography of Joseph K. Nawahi." Translated by
Marvin Puakea Nogelmeier. Honolulu: Hawaiian Historical Society,
1988. Typescript.
[Sheldon, John M.]. Honolulu: Kahikini Kelekona, 1906.
Shiramizu, Shigehiko. "The Ethnic Press and Its Society: A Case of the Japanese Press in Hawaii." *KEIO Communication Review*, no. 11 (1990):
49–70.
———. "The Good Old Days of the Press: Two Great Men in the Japanese
Community." Paper presented to Hawaii Newspaper Project: [The] Political Role of Newspapers in Hawaiian History, Honolulu, East-West Center, February 27, 1986.
"Should Newspapers Campaign?" *Editor & Publisher*, June 25, 1949, 10.
Shover, William R., ed. *Promoting the Total Newspaper.* Washington, D.C.:
International Newspaper Promotion Association, 1973.
Siebert, Fred S., et al. *Four Theories of the Press: The Authoritarian, Libertarian, Social Responsibility and Soviet Communist Concepts of What
the Press Should Be and Do.* Urbana: University of Illinois Press, 1974.
Sigal, Leon V. *Reporters and Officials: The Organization and Politics of
News Reporting.* Lexington, Mass.: D. C. Heath, 1973.
Sim, John Cameron. *The Grass Roots Press: America's Community Newspapers.* Ames: Iowa State University Press, 1969.
Smith, Anthony. *The Geopolitics of Information: How Western Culture
Dominates the World.* New York: Oxford University Press, 1980.
———. *Goodbye Gutenberg: The Newspaper Revolution of the 1980s.* New
York: Oxford University Press, 1980.
———. *The Newspaper: An International History.* London: Thames and
Hudson, 1979.
Smith, Wilda M., and Eleanor A. Bogart. *The Wars of Peggy Hull: The
Life and Times of a War Correspondent.* El Paso: Texas Western Press,
1991.
Sobrero, Gina. *An Italian Baroness in Hawai'i: The Travel Diary of Gina
Sobrero, Bride of Robert Wilcox, 1887.* Translated by Edgar C. Knowlton.
Honolulu: Hawaiian Historical Society, 1991.
Sontag, Susan. *On Photography.* New York: Farrar, Straus & Giroux, 1973.
Southward, Walt. *A Program to Improve News Media Relationships for the
Hawaii County Police Department.* Hilo: W. Southward, 1984.
Spaulding, Thomas Marshall. "The First Printing in Hawaii." In *Papers of
the Bibliographical Society of America* 50 (fourth quarter 1956).
Spivey, Donald, ed. *Sport in America: New Historical Perspectives.* Westport, Conn.: Greenwood Press, 1985.
Sprague, Roberta. "Measuring the Mountain: The United States Exploring
Expedition on Mauna Loa, 1840–1841." *The Hawaiian Journal of History*
25 (1991): 71–92.
Stapp, Andy. *Up Against the Brass.* New York: Simon & Schuster, 1970.
State of Hawaii Data Book: A Statistical Abstract. Honolulu: Department
of Planning and Economic Development, 1967– .
Steegmuller, Francis. *The Two Lives of James Jackson Jarves.* New Haven:
Yale University Press, 1951.
Steigleman, Walter A. *The Newspaperman and the Law.* Westport, Conn.:
Greenwood Press, 1971.
Steinhoff, Patricia G., and Milton Diamond. *Abortion Politics: The Hawaiian Experience.* Honolulu: University of Hawai'i Press, 1977.

Stephan, John J. *Hawaii Under the Rising Sun: Japan's Plans for Conquest After Pearl Harbor.* Honolulu: University of Hawai'i Press, 1984.

Stephens, Mitchell. *A History of News: From the Drum to the Satellite.* New York: Viking, 1988.

Strainchamps, Ethel, ed. *Rooms With No View: A Woman's Guide to the Man's World of the Media.* New York: Harper & Row, 1974.

Strentz, Herbert. *News Reporters and News Sources: Accomplices in Shaping and Misshaping the News.* 2nd ed. Ames: Iowa State University Press, 1989.

Summers, Robert Edward, comp. *Wartime Censorship of Press and Radio.* New York: H. W. Wilson Co., 1942.

Sutherland, Edwin H., and Donald R. Cressey. *Principles of Criminology.* 10th ed. New York: J. B. Lippincott, 1980.

Swanburg, W. A. *Citizen Hearst: A Biography of William Randolph Hearst.* New York: Charles Scribner's Sons, 1961.

———. *Pulitzer.* New York: Charles Scribner's Sons, 1967.

Taft, William H. *Newspapers as Tools for Historians.* Columbia, Mo.: Lucas Brothers Publishers, 1990.

Takaki, Ronald. *Pau Hana: Plantation Life and Labor in Hawaii.* Honolulu: University of Hawai'i Press, 1983.

Tamashiro, John Gerald. "The Japanese in Hawaii and on the Mainland During World War II as Discussed in the Editorial Pages of the *Honolulu Advertiser* and the *Honolulu Star-Bulletin.*" Master's thesis in history, University of Hawai'i, December 1972.

Tanaoye, Elyse. "Kauai, the 15 Most Influential People." *Hawaii Business News*, August 1984.

Taylor, Clarice B. "Tales About Hawaii." *Honolulu Star-Bulletin*, March 13–April 6, 1961.

Tebbel, John. *The Compact History of the American Newspaper.* New York: Hawthorn Books, 1963.

Teodore, Luis V., Jr. *Out of This Struggle: The Filipinos in Hawaii.* Honolulu: University Press of Hawai'i, 1981.

Thorn, William J., with Mary Pat Pfeil. *Newspaper Circulation: Marketing the News.* New York: Longman, 1987.

Thrum, Thomas G. "Additions to Riley H. Allen's 'Pioneers in Journalism.'" *Hawaiian Historical Society Report.* [Honolulu], 1929.

———. "Completion of the Pacific Cable." *Hawaiian Annual*, 1904.

———. "The Genesis and Evolution of Honolulu's Dailies." *Hawaiian Annual*, 1897.

Thurston, Lorrin A. *Memoirs of the Hawaiian Revolution.* Honolulu: Honolulu Advertiser Publishing Co., 1936.

Tillich, Linda Meyerson. *The Crossroads Sanctuary.* Honolulu: privately published, August 1977.

Tomsho, Robert. *The American Sanctuary Movement.* Austin: Texas Monthly Press, 1987.

Tower, Samuel A. *Cartoons and Lampoons: The Art of Political Satire.* New York: J. Messer, 1982.

Trask, Haunani Kay. "The Birth of the Modern Hawaiian Movement: Kalama Valley, O'ahu." *The Hawaiian Journal of History* 21 (1987): 126–153.

Trinidad, Corky. *A Corky Album.* [Honolulu]: American Civil Liberties Union, January 30, 1982.

————. *Marcos: The Rise and Fall of a Regime: A Cartoon Biography*. Honolulu: Arthouse Books, 1986.

Trinidad, Corky, and Dick Adair. *Two Cartoonists Look at the Philippine Revolution, February–October 1986*. Center for Philippine Studies, University of Hawai'i, 1986.

Tsutsumi, Fred. "'Hawaii Seven' Smith Act Case." *Hawaii Pono Journal* 2, no. 1 (June 1972): 1–31.

Tuchman, Gaye. *Making News: A Study in the Construction of Reality*. New York: The Free Press, 1978.

Tuchman, Gaye, et al. *Hearth and Home: Images of Women in the Press Media*. New York: Oxford University Press, 1978.

Twain, Mark. *Mark Twain's Letters From Hawaii*. Edited by A. Grove Day. Honolulu: University Press of Hawai'i, 1975.

Twombly, Wells. *200 Years of Sport in America: A Pageant of a Nation at Play*. New York: McGraw Hill, 1976.

Udell, John G. *The Economics of the American Newspaper*. New York: Hastings House, 1978.

U.S. House Committee on Un-American Activities. *Report on the "Honolulu Record."* Washington, D.C., Oct. 1, 1950.

Varigny, Charles De. *Fourteen Years in the Sandwich Islands, 1855–1868*. Honolulu: University Press of Hawai'i and the Hawaiian Historical Society, 1968.

Vought, Hans. "Division and Reunion: Woodrow Wilson, Immigration, and the Myth of American Unity." *Journal of American Ethnic History* 13, no. 3 (spring 1994).

Wagner-Seavey, Sandra E. "The Effect of World War I on the German Community in Hawaii." *The Hawaiian Journal of History* 14 (1980): 109–140.

Walker, Robert H. *Reform in America: The Continuous Frontier*. Lexington: University of Kentucky Press, 1985.

Walters, Lynne Masel, et al., eds. *Bad Tidings: Communication and Catastrophe*. Hillsdale, N.J.: Lawrence Erlbaum Associates, 1989.

Wang, James C. F. *Hawaii State and Local Politics*. Hilo: James C. F. Wang, University of Hawai'i at Hilo, 1982.

Warriner, Emily V. "Lama Hawaii." In *Ka Lama Hawaii: The Centennial Yearbook of the Lahainaluna Technical High School*. Lahaina, Maui, Territory of Hawai'i, 1931.

Wagner, Jack Russell. *"The Great Pacific Cable."* Beverly Hills: Westways, 1956.

Weinberg, Daniel E. "The Movement to 'Americanize' the Japanese Community in Hawaii: An Analysis of One Hundred Percent Americanization Activity in the Territory of Hawaii as Expressed in the Caucasian Press, 1919–1923." Master's thesis, University of Hawai'i, August 1967.

Weiner, Richard. *Syndicated Columnists*. 3rd. ed. New York: Richard Weiner, 1979.

Weir, David, and Dan Noyes. *Raising Hell: How the Center for Investigative Reporting Gets the Story*. Reading, Mass.: Addison-Wesley Publishing Co., 1983.

Wernet, Bob. "Gifted Mayor Displays Many Talents." *Hawaii Journalism Review*, October 1971, 4.

Westin, Alan F., ed. *Getting Angry Six Times a Week: A Portfolio of Political Cartoons*. Boston: Beach Press, 1979.

Whitehead, John S. "The Anti-Statehood Movement and the Legacy of Alice Kamokila Campbell," *The Hawaiian Journal of History* 27 (1993): 43–64.
Whitney, Henry. *The Hawaiian Guide Book, for Travelers.* Honolulu: H. M. Whitney, 1875.
———. *The Tourists' Guide Through the Hawaiian Islands.* Honolulu, 1890.
Wicker, Tom. *On Press.* New York: Viking Press, 1978.
Willis, William James. *The Shadow World: Life Between the News Media and Reality.* Praeger, 1991.
Winston, Brian. *Misunderstanding Media.* Cambridge: Harvard University Press, 1986.
Wist, Benjamin O. *A Century of Public Education in Hawaii: October 15, 1840–October 15, 1940.* Honolulu: Hawaii Educational Review, 1940.
Witeck, John. "The Niceties of Linguistic Genocide in Hawaii: The Attack on the Hawaiian Language in Hawaii's Schools." Unpublished paper, [Honolulu], n.d.
Wolfson, Nessa, and Joan Manes. *Language of Inequality.* New York: Mouton Publishers, 1985.
Women of Hawaii. Edited by George F. Nellist. Vol. 2. Honolulu: E. A. Langston-Boyle, 1938.
Woodburn, Bert W. "Reader Interest in Newspaper Pictures." *Journalism Quarterly,* September 1947: 197–201.
Woodiwiss, Michael. *Crime, Crusades and Corruption: Prohibitions in the United States, 1900–1987.* Totowa, N.J.: Barnes & Noble, 1988.
Wright, Theon. *The Disenchanted Isles: The Story of the Second Revolution in Hawaii.* New York: Dial Press, 1972.
———. *Rape in Paradise.* New York: Hawthorn Books, 1966.
Wynn Jones, Michael, comp. *A Newspaper History of the World.* Newton Abbott [England]: David Charles, 1974.
Yamamoto, Eric. "The Significance of Local." *Social Process in Hawaii* 27 (1979): 101–115.
Young, Douglas. "Philip Gialanella." *Honolulu,* July 1986, 27–33.
Zalburg, Sanford. *A Spark Is Struck! Jack Hall and the ILWU in Hawaii.* Honolulu: University Press of Hawai'i, 1979
Ziporyn, Terra. *Disease in the Press: The Case of Diptheria, Typhoid Fever, and Syphilis, 1870–1920.* New York: Greenwood Press, 1988.
Yzendorn, Father Reginald. "Establishment of the First English Newspaper in the Hawaiian Islands." In *Twenty-Second Annual Report of the Hawaiian Historical Society 1913.* Honolulu: Paradise of the Pacific, 1914.
———. *History of the Catholic Mission in the Hawaiian Islands.* Honolulu: Honolulu Star-Bulletin, 1927.

Interviews and Conversations

Austin, Stephanie. Interview by author. Pukalani, 29 August 1992.
Ball, Harry. Interview by author. Honolulu, 28 January 1991.
Bartholomew, Gail. Conversation with author. Wailuku, 3 October 1992.
Becker, Jim. Interview by author. Honolulu, 6 August 1991.
Benedek, Vera. Interview by author. Kāne'ohe, 1 December 1992.
Berry, Ken. Interview by author. Kāne'ohe, 18 November 1992.

Boylan, Dan. Interview by author. Honolulu, 10 July 1992.
Brislin, Tom. Interview by author. Honolulu, 13 February 1992.
Brown, Jim. Interview by author. Honolulu, 6 December 1993.
Buchwach, Buck. Interview by author. Honolulu, 24 January 1985.
Burris, Jerry. Interview by author. Honolulu, 28 April 1993.
Cahill, Emmett. Telephone conversation with author. Honolulu, 24 February 1985.
Chang, Diane. Interview by author. Honolulu, 28 April 1993.
Chaplin, George. Interview by author. Honolulu, 28 March 1985.
Coffman, Tom. Interview by author. Honolulu, 2 January 1993.
Coll, Irva. Interviews by author. Honolulu, 8 January 1991; 4 September 1991.
Conrad, Cynthia. Interview by author. Pukalani, 29 August 1992.
Cooper, Nora. Interview by author. Wailuku, 28 August 1992.
Creamer, Beverly. Interview by author. Honolulu, 13 April 1993.
Cushing, Bob. Interview by author. Honolulu, 15 December 1987.
Dooley, Jim. Interview by author. Honolulu, 15 June 1993.
Dunn, Barbara. Conversations with author. Honolulu, 1 December 1992; 19 September 1994; 15 August 1995.
Egged, Rick. Interview by author. Honolulu, 2 June 1993.
Engledow, Jill. Interview by author. Pukalani, 29 August 1992.
Fasi, Frank. Interview by author. Honolulu, 21 December 1992.
Fawcett, Denby. Interview by author. Honolulu, 24 November 1992.
Fern Stewart. Interview by author. Honolulu, 29 August 1991.
Forbes, David. Conversation with author. Honolulu, 7 January 1985.
Flanagan, John M. Conversation with author. Honolulu, 15 February 1994.
Foss, Harrison. Telephone conversation with author. Honolulu, 15 December 1987.
Frankel, Charles. Interview by author. Honolulu, 27 May 1993.
Freitas, Reyburn. Interview by author. Honolulu, 27 February 1984.
Fujikawa, Jeannie. Conversation with author. Honolulu, 21 December 1992.
Furuye, Hirao "Porky." Conversation with author. Hilo, 12 February 1993.
Gee, Harriet. Telephone interview by author. Honolulu, 7 January 1993.
Graydon, Don. Telephone interview by author. Bothell, 7 August 1992.
Graydon, Luann. Telephone interview by author. Makawao, 28 July 1992.
Griffin, John. Interview by author. Honolulu, 21 January 1985.
Harada, Wayne. Interview by author. Honolulu, 9 December 1992.
Harpham, Ann. Interview by author. Honolulu, 17 December 1992.
Henningham, John. Conversation with author. Honolulu, 26 January 1988.
Hiura, Arnold T. Interviews by author. Honolulu, 17 January 1985; 16 December 1987.
Ho, Stuart. Interview by author. Honolulu, 11 August 1992.
Holmes, Jean. Interview by author. Hilo, 17 February 1990.
Iwai, Harriet. Conversation with author. Honolulu, 14 December 1987.
Johnson, Rubellite. Conversation with author. Honolulu, 14 January 1984.
Jones, Bob. Interview by author. Honolulu, 16 December 1992.
Kato, Gerry. Interview by author. Honolulu, 11 May 1993.
Kaya, Larry. Conversation with author. Honolulu, 29 July 1994.
Keever, Beverly Ann. Telephone conversation with author. Honolulu, 4 October 1995.
Keir, Gerry. Interview by author. Honolulu, 9 December 1992.

Kelly, John. Interview by author. Honolulu, 8 December 1982.

Kennedy, Hunter. Conversation with author. Honolulu, 1 December 1992.

Knowlton, Edgar. Telephone conversation with author. Honolulu, 31 December 1993.

Kruse, Roy C. Interview by author. Honolulu, 9 September 1992.

Ku, Ah Jook. Interview by author. Honolulu, 8 February 1993.

Lai, Violet Lau. Interview by author. Honolulu, 12 April 1984.

LeDoux, Larry. Interview by author. Honolulu, 28 January 1992.

Lee, Kelly. Interview by author. Honolulu, 6 December 1993.

Liu, K. K. Interview by author. Honolulu, 8 December 1993.

Luke, Terry. Interview by author. Honolulu, 28 April 1993.

Lum, Arlene. Interview by author. Honolulu, 23 November 1993.

Luter, John. Interview by author. Honolulu, 14 November 1990.

Lycurgus, Leo. Interview by author. Hilo, 14 August 1992.

Lytle, Drue. Interview by author. Volcano, 7 November 1992.

Lytle, Hugh. Interview by author. Volcano, 7 November 1992.

Mason, George. Interview by author. Honolulu, 26 January 1985.

McElrath, Bob. Interview by author. Honolulu, 14 December 1987.

McGregor, Davianna. Conversation with author. Honolulu, 14 July 1995.

Miwa, Ralph. Conversation with author. Pearl City, 25 January 1985.

Myers, Gail. Interview by author. Honolulu, 10 September 1993.

Newport, Tuck. Telephone interviews by author. Los Angeles, 12, 13 October 1992.

Okimoto, Tadao. Interview by author. Hilo, 20 February 1985.

Olsen, Jon. Interview by author. Honolulu, 7 June 1992.

Oshiro, Ernie. Conversation with author. Pearl City, 21 December 1987.

Palmer, Beryl "Candy." Telephone conversation with author. Kāne'ohe, 14 December 1987.

Paul, Bill. Interview by author. Honolulu, 12 May 1993.

Pujalet, Lou. Interview by author. Honolulu, 29 September 1992.

Reed, Rick. Interview by author. Honolulu, 10 January 1985.

Richstad, Jim. Interview by author. Honolulu, 30 July 1992.

Ryan, Tim. Interview by author. Honolulu, 7 May 1993.

Sanford, Mary Cameron "Maizie." Interview by author. Honolulu, 15 December 1992.

Scott, Bob. Interview by author. Honolulu, 21 January 1992.

Seitz, Eric. Interview by author. Honolulu, 31 July 1992.

Shiramizu, Chiyozu "Joe." Telephone interview by author. Līhu'e, 15 December 1987.

Silverman, Jane. Conversations with author. Honolulu, 10 March 1993; 25 April 1993; 5 January 1994.

Simonds, John. Interview by author. Honolulu, 2 June 1992.

Sinnex, Ceil. Interview by author. Honolulu, 27 September 1990.

Smith, Kit. Interview by author. Honolulu, 18 November 1991.

Smyser, A. A. "Bud." Interview by author. Honolulu, 3 January 1991.

Stephan, John. Telephone conversation with author. Honolulu, 28 January 1991.

Sullam, Brian. Interview by author. Honolulu, 9 November 1990.

Taylor, Lois. Interview by author. Honolulu, 13 October 1992.

Tillman, Frank. Conversation with author. Honolulu, 25 January 1995.

Trinidad, Corky. Interview by author. Honolulu, 7 May 1993.

Tuttle, Dan. Interview by author. Honolulu, 13 May 1993.
Twigg-Smith, Thurston. Interview by author. Honolulu, 16 March 1992.
Wiley, Bonnie. Interview by author. Honolulu, 1 October 1991.
Witeck, John. Interview by author. Honolulu, 12 August 1992.
Witeck, Lucy. Interview by author. Honolulu, 9 September 1992.
Yim, Susan. Interview by author. Honolulu, 10 May 1993.
Yonemuri, Soichi "Eso." Telephone interviews by author. Pearl City, 19, 20 December 1987.
Yuen, Ray. Interview by author. Hilo, 14 August 1992.

Index